FEDERAL INCOME TAXATION

A Guide to the Leading Cases and Concepts

SEVENTH EDITION

By

MARVIN A. CHIRELSTEIN
Professor of Law, Columbia University

UNIVERSITY TEXTBOOK SERIES

Westbury, New York
THE FOUNDATION PRESS, INC.
1994

Chirelstein Fed.Inc.Tax. 7th Ed. UTS

To Boris

*

PREFACE

This book is intended as a study aid for law students taking the basic course in federal income taxation, and it is therefore largely an explanation of how the income tax affects individuals. A systematic treatment of the taxation of corporations and shareholders— usually the subject of an advanced course, and in any event requiring an entire volume to itself—is not included. Certain fundamental elements of the corporate-shareholder system are referred to at various points, but this is done only as an incident of some other discussion and never in any real detail. The focus here is on the individual income tax and on the case and statutory materials that are likely to be covered in an introductory law-school course.

My approach, I should also state, is anything but comprehensive. All sorts of topics are omitted which the student may encounter in the classroom and desire more information about, while other topics of no greater intrinsic importance are discussed at length. But I have not attempted to write a treatise, or a summary of Code sections, or a manual which can be used to answer specific questions about the tax law. Instead, my aim has been to disclose the structural characteristics of the income tax mechanism—how the plumbing works, what's at stake in the controversies that arise, what elements of internal consistency or inconsistency can be detected, and so on. Accordingly, I have used whatever legal materials seemed best to illustrate the *technical* components of the system. I have tried to sketch the outline of the house—or at least one wing of it—but have made no effort to furnish all the rooms. This concept has led to a selective coverage of the law (to put it mildly), but it has also made possible a higher level of coherence and connectedness than could have been attained if more detail had been included.

The organization of the work—Income, Deductions, Attribution, etc.—roughly mirrors that of the various casebooks now in general use in the law schools. Although they differ among themselves in many ways, the casebooks also exhibit a great many elements of similarity, and I think it safe to say that the resemblances vastly outnumber the differences. Large subject-matter headings are, of course, alike. In addition, the casebooks generally employ the same "great" landmark cases to carry the tax story from one topic to another: the sixty-or-so well-known Supreme Court decisions are always presented, and even the lesser gleanings from the lower courts and the Service are often the same. The notes that follow the cases, as well as the independent editorial materials, are very different in emphasis and style, and there any many differences in organization which are of real importance. But, again, the *lists* of leading cases and administrative rulings are remarkably uniform.

This aspect of agreement among the editors, on cases as well as subject-matter, has encouraged me to try to write a book which tracks the casebooks—follows them like a reproach, as it were—without really having to develop a closer relationship to any one than any other. I have used the landmark decisions as vehicles for explanation whenever possible because the casebooks do so, and where the casebooks diverge, I have tried to invent hypotheticals which abstract from the cases in such a way as to merge the elements that seem to be common to all. My hope is that this book can be used as a kind of universal supplement, therefore, and that the discussion it contains will have roughly equal relevance for all students taking the basic tax course, no matter what the identity of their primary course materials. So as not to seem to claim too much, however, I should state again that by no means every casebook subject is taken up in detail; and some are omitted entirely.

*   *   *   *   *   *   *   *   *

The present edition (the Seventh) reflects the tax-rate increases brought about by the Revenue Reconciliation Act of 1993, as well as other changes in the statute that have occurred since the last edition. Recent cases of importance—*Cottage Savings, Indopco, Newark Morning Ledger*, among others—are also discussed. The rise in rates and reintroduction of progression into the rate-structure particularly affect the introductory tax course, because one's interest in two major areas of study, namely, choice of taxable person and the capital asset definition, are revived as a consequence. Some will welcome that development, others regret it.

I am grateful to my colleague, Anne Alstott, for comments and advice.

MARVIN A. CHIRELSTEIN

Columbia University
June, 1994

TABLE OF CONTENTS

FEDERAL INCOME TAXATION

TABLE OF CONTENTS

*

FEDERAL
INCOME TAXATION

*

INTRODUCTION: TERMINOLOGY, TIMING AND RATES

A brief presentation of income tax terminology may be useful by way of introduction:

The computation of an individual's tax liability begins with a determination of his *gross income*. This term is defined in Code § 61 as encompassing "all income from whatever source derived" except as otherwise provided by the statute. For most individual taxpayers gross income is made up of wages and salaries, dividends, interest and rents, and gains from the sale of investments such as securities and real estate. The definition of gross income is broad enough, however, to include receipts from other, less familiar sources as well. The statutory exceptions to the reach of § 61, which are fairly numerous, are usually referred to as *exclusions* from gross income (sometimes the term *exemption* is used). A well-known example is interest on state and municipal bonds, which is specifically excluded from gross income by Code § 103(a). Excluded items simply do not enter into the computation of tax. Thus, an individual with $50,000 of salary plus $5,000 of interest on bonds issued by the State of New York has a gross income of only $50,000. Quite obviously, the effect of the exclusion is to tax the excluded item at a rate of zero. The benefit to an individual taxpayer depends on his own applicable tax bracket, which in turn depends on how much income he receives from taxable sources. If the taxpayer just mentioned would otherwise be taxed at a rate of (say) 31% on the last $5,000 of non-excludable income, the dollar value of the exclusion from his standpoint is 31% of $5,000, or $1,550. If his bracket rate were only 15%, the dollar value of the exclusion would be roughly halved as well.

Having determined his gross income under § 61, the taxpayer next subtracts all the outlays and expenditures which are allowed by the Code as *deductions*. Deductible items include the taxpayer's business expenses—wages paid to employees, depreciation on business equipment, fees paid to investment advisers, etc.—which represent the cost of earning the gross income determined above. In addition, while personal living expenses (food, apartment rent) are generally disallowed, the Code does permit certain items—for example, charitable contributions—to be deducted, even though plainly in the category of personal rather than business expense. As a matter of tax arithmetic the dollar value of a deduction from gross income is the same as that of an exclusion. If a 31% taxpayer

1

contributes $5,000 to charity, the value of the deduction from his standpoint is obviously $1,550. The effect is just the same whether the amount of the charitable gift is excluded from his gross income in the first instance, or included but then allowed as a deduction.

A major complicating factor in the federal income tax is the special treatment accorded to long-term *capital gains.* In computing gain (or loss) from the sale of property, the taxpayer subtracts his cost, or *basis,* for the property sold from the *amount realized* on the transaction. The gain, if any, is recognized and included in his gross income under § 61. If the property sold is a *capital asset*— for example, securities or real estate acquired for investment—and if the property has been held for more than 1 year, the gain may be taxed at a lower tax rate than the rate that applies to wages, salaries, business profits and other kinds of *ordinary* income. As capital gains are thus more to be desired than income that does not qualify for the lower rate, the scope of the capital asset definition becomes a matter of considerable importance.

Once gross income has been reduced by allowable deductions, including personal and dependency exemptions, the figure that remains is the taxpayer's *taxable income.*[1] Taxable income is the residual or net amount on which the taxpayer's tax liability is based. Having selected the appropriate rate schedule from § 1 (depending on whether he is married, single, or a "head of household"), the taxpayer then determines his tax by fitting his taxable income into the schedule in the manner indicated below. The tax liability that results may be reduced by statutory *credits—e.g.,* for retirement income—which are subtracted directly from the tax due. While the dollar-value of a *deduction* depends on the particular taxpayer's applicable tax rate (so that the value is greater for higher than for lower-bracket taxpayers), a credit has the same dollar-value for all taxpayers entitled to use it. This is so because a credit is a dollar-for-dollar reduction of the tax itself rather than being a subtraction from gross income.

Income tax returns are filed and taxes are paid on an *annual* basis, which for almost all individual taxpayers simply means the calendar year. Accounting rules are employed to allocate income and deduction items to one taxable year or another, with most individuals using the *cash method* of accounting and most businesses using the *accrual method.* The timing of income and deductions is important, because taxpayers strongly prefer to pay their taxes later rather than sooner. Money in the bank or invested in

---

1. An intermediate calculation between gross income and taxable income called *adjusted gross income* is necessary in computing the various personal expense allowances and for certain other purposes. See discussion at 7.06.

government bonds earns interest—until recently quite a bit—so that if given a choice between paying $1,000 of taxes today and paying $1,000 of taxes a year from now, the taxpayer will always choose the later date. Assuming interest at a rate of 8%, the present value—the value today—of $1,000 due in one year is only $926. Put differently, the sum of $926 invested at 8% today will grow to $1,000 at the end of one year. If (because of accounting or other legal rules) the $1,000 tax is not due until a year from now, the taxpayer can meet that obligation by currently setting aside the sum of $926. But if the tax is due today, the full $1,000 will have to be surrendered. It follows that a year's delay is worth $74 ($1,000 – $926) to the taxpayer in hard cold cash. The government, of course, sees the matter in opposite terms: a year's delay "costs" the Treasury exactly the same amount. As suggested in Part A and elsewhere, the question of "pay now or pay later" is at the heart of many of the legal controversies that arise in the tax field, though this fact is not always apparent to the naked eye.[2]

Coming finally to the significant subject of tax rates:

As far as individual taxpayers are concerned, the schedule of tax rates is (once again) *progressive,* or graduated, which simply means that as income increases an individual's tax liability also increases but at a greater rate. For the year 1993, the rate structure begins, in effect, with a zero-bracket—referred to as the *standard deduction*—of $6,200 for married couples, $3,700 for single persons. All taxpayers are permitted to receive income up to these levels at a tax rate of zero. In addition, a personal exemption of $2,350 is allowed for each taxpayer and each family dependent. Combining the standard deduction with personal exemptions, a family of four can receive up to $15,600 ($6,200 plus 4 × $2,350) tax-free. For a single person the tax-free amount is $6,050—the $3,700 standard deduction plus one $2,350 personal exemption.

---

2. The same point—that postponing his tax payments favors the taxpayer—can be made in another way. In the example above, if the $1,000 tax is not due for one year, the taxpayer (rather than the government) will earn the stipulated 8% return during that period. The taxpayer will then have 80 "extra" dollars of his own when the year is over. But if the $1,000 has to be paid to the Treasury immediately, the return on that money will belong to the government. Viewed as of the *end* of the year, therefore, there is $80 at stake. While the text suggests that the amount at stake is only $74, that is because the text is looking at the problem from the *beginning* of the year. Really, the $74 mentioned in the text and the $80 mentioned in this note are the same quantities. Thus, $74 is the present value (again, at 8%) of $80 due a year from now; $80 is just $74 one year later.

For convenience, an explanation of the concept of "present value," together with related Tables, is provided in the Appendix.

INTRODUCTION

Once the amount of the standard deduction plus personal exemptions is exceeded the positive rates take hold. Under the Revenue Reconciliation Act of 1993, the tax-schedule (for married couples) contains five rate-brackets, to-wit: 15% on taxable income up to $36,900, 28% on additional taxable income up to $89,150, 31% on additional income up to $140,000, 36% on additional income up to $250,000, and 39.6% on income above $250,000. As explained in Section 7, this does not quite end the matter, because the deductions for itemized personal expenses and personal exemptions are subject to certain special limitations at high levels of taxable income, of which the consequence is to raise the top marginal rate slightly above the 39.6% level for affected taxpayers. The rate table itself, however, is formally restricted to the five positive rate-brackets just mentioned.

In tax terminology the applicable rate of tax at each bracket level is called the *marginal* rate of tax, while the rate that is applicable to the taxpayer's income as a whole is called the average or effective rate. A married couple with $100,000 of taxable income, for example, is subject to a rate of 15% on the first $36,900, a rate of 28% on the next $52,250 ($89,150–$36,900), and a rate of 31% on the last $10,850 ($100,000–$89,150). Their total tax liability is $23,528. This figure represents the sum of the taxes computed at each bracket level by multiplying the dollars of income that fall within that bracket by the applicable marginal rate. Although the couple's topmost marginal rate is 31%, their effective rate of tax is less than 24% ($23,258/$100,000). Above the first bracket level, the effective rate is bound to be lower than the marginal rate on the taxpayer's last dollar of income, because the effective rate is simply a weighted average of the latter rate and all the prior marginal rates.

To illustrate the marginal-effective rate distinction still further, one occasionally hears someone say (usually of someone else): "X doesn't want to earn any more money this year because it will put him in a higher bracket." This statement may mean, simply, that the speaker thinks that X will not care to earn an additional $10,000 if that income will be taxed at a high marginal rate—say 39.6%. Since X would net only about $6,000 after tax, he may prefer to substitute more leisure for that amount of additional spendable income. This could be a valid surmise, depending on X's personal preferences and how hard he would have to work to earn the $10,000. But if the quoted comment is supposed to signify that X will sustain an after-tax loss and actually be poorer in consequence of the additional earnings, then the speaker has obviously got his marginal and effective rates mixed up. Taken in this sense

4

the comment could only be true if, by adding the $10,000 to his existing taxable income, the marginal tax rate applicable to the last $10,000 somehow became applicable to X's income overall. But it does not: the lower segments of X's income continue to be taxed at the same marginal rates as previously, *i.e.,* the first $36,900 at 15%, the next $52,250 at 28%, and so on. Hence, additional earnings will always involve *some* increase in a taxpayer's after-tax income as long as the highest marginal rate of tax is less than 100%.

As compared with prior law, the rate-structure put in place by the 1993 Act means an increase in taxes for higher income individuals, with lower and middle income people being unaffected. In addition, and of some importance philosophically, the 1993 Act represents a revival or restoration of the general idea of rate progressivity. In 1986, led by a President who was avowedly hostile to the concept of progressive taxation, Congress both reduced individual tax rates very substantially—from a top rate of 50% down to 28%—and adopted a rate-structure that was essentially proportional rather than progressive. Under the 1986 Act (omitting some details), taxable income up to about $30,000—presumably regarded as "moderate income"—was taxed at a rate of 15%, while income above the $30,000 level was taxed at a rate of 28% without any further steps or intervening brackets. Thus, an individual earning $30,001 above exemptions and the standard deduction was taxed at a marginal rate of 28% on his last dollar of income; the same was true for an individual earning ten or a hundred times more. Also, however, both the standard deduction and the personal exemption amounts were sharply increased with a view to relieving very low income people from income tax completely. The system that emerged—a flat-rate tax on income above the zero bracket and the 15% bracket—was one that is sometimes called "degressive", meaning that progression halts and the tax becomes proportional once poor and moderate-income individuals have been freed from "normal" tax burdens.[3]

Which is correct as a matter of social policy, a progressive rate-structure or a proportional rate-structure? President Reagan made his own view of this issue very clear on one occasion when, citing Biblical precedent, he asserted that "There can be no moral justification [for] the progressive tax".[4] President Clinton, on the other

---

3. Blum, *The Uneasy Case for Progressive Taxation in 1976,* in Campbell, ed., *Income Redistribution* (1977), p. 147. And see Bankman & Griffith, *Social Welfare and the Rate Structure: A New Look at Progressive Taxation,* 75 U.Cal.L.Rev. 1905 (1987).

4. "Proportionate taxation we would gladly accept on the theory that those better able to pay should remove some of the burden from those least able to

hand, though a Bible reader himself, has insisted that a flat or proportional rate-structure unduly favors upper-income taxpayers and for that reason fails to meet a standard of tax equity or "fairness". Congress overwhelmingly supported President Reagan's position in 1986, but then edged back to President Clinton's position in 1993. Hence, we have a dilemma. Since presumably nothing can be both "morally unjustified" and at the same time "fair", it appears that one of our elected leaders must have been in error. But which one? The question is left for the reader to ponder, then decide.

While not strictly a matter of terminology, the inclusion in Code § 1(f) of an "indexation" provision can appropriately be mentioned here. Thus, an individual whose dollar income increases from one year to the next might be obliged to pay tax at a higher marginal rate (say 28% instead of 15%) on the increase, this being a natural consequence of rate progression. If, however, due to inflation the benefit of the increase is wiped out by a corresponding increase in the cost of living, the effect would be a heavier tax burden with no real improvement in the taxpayer's economic position. Wage and salary-earners are especially vulnerable. Although a worker's wages generally go up each year, the raise he gets will be illusory if the prices of consumer goods rise in the same proportion. If his marginal tax rate also increased, the result would actually be a decrease in the taxpayer's real disposable income.

To prevent this, Code § 1(f) provides that the brackets used in the individual rate schedules shall be adjusted, or indexed, each year to reflect the percentage by which the Consumer Price Index, published by the Department of Labor, exceeds the CPI for the base year 1993. The same adjustment is to be made annually in the standard deduction amount and the personal exemptions.

A separate schedule of tax rates is provided for corporations under § 11. Corporations are treated by the Code as taxpaying entities and are subject to a four-step tax schedule which distinguishes, roughly speaking, between small family-owned companies and all others. Under § 11, the rate is 15% on the first $50,000 of taxable income, 25% on the next $25,000, 34% on income above $75,000 and up to $10 million, and 35% on income over $10 million.

---

pay. The Bible explains this in its instruction on tithing. We are told that we should give the Lord one tenth and if the Lord prospers us ten times as much, we should give ten times as much. But, under our progressive income tax, computing Caesar's share is a little different ..." Reagan, *Encroaching Control: Keep Government Poor and Remain Free*, 27 Vital Speeches of the Day 677 (1961).

The two low-bracket rates are phased out for taxable incomes in excess of $100,000, and the 1-point saving on the first $10 million (*i.e.,* $100,000) is phased out, or recaptured, for corporations with taxable income above $15 million. Taxable income is computed in much the same way for corporations as it is for individuals— roughly, gross income less business expenses—except, of course, that the personal expense deductions and personal exemptions allowed to individuals do not apply.

Part A: INCOME

Code § 61, which contains the definition of "gross income," is the starting point for a study of the federal income tax. The section begins with a catch-all clause—"gross income means all income from whatever source derived"—and then proceeds to enumerate more than a dozen specific classes of receipts which are regarded as within the income definition. The enumeration is extensive; it picks up most or all of the common classes of income—salaries, wages, business profits, dividends, interest, rents and royalties—and includes as well a good many special kinds of benefits, such as alimony, annuities, income from discharge of indebtedness, and income in respect of a decedent. The intent is plain: to the extent that there might be doubt about one or another of the items enumerated—alimony, say—the desire of Congress to bring that item within the definition of income is made clear and unmistakable. But the enumeration is not designed to be exhaustive. The forms that commercial dealings can take in the modern world, and the labels that can be assigned to income from different sources, are simply too various for any listing to fully comprehend. Accordingly, the catch-all clause is expected to supplement the enumeration by including any non-enumerated items which can properly be defined as "income." In that way it plays an important, if subordinate, role in determining the scope of the provision.

Unavoidably, perhaps, the language employed by § 61 is somewhat tautological—"... gross *income* means all *income* ..."—and in the old days, at least, there was considerable preoccupation with the question of how much ground the catch-all clause was actually intended to cover. Was the quoted phrase—"*all* income ..."—as sweeping, as embracing as it sounded, or were there certain inbuilt criteria which might actually operate to exclude some forms of enrichment from the tax base? In *Eisner v. Macomber*,[1] decided in 1920, the Supreme Court stated that "income may be defined as the gain derived from labor, from capital, or from both combined," a construction which could be taken to mean that *unless* the factor of labor or capital were present in a given case, the income definition would not encompass the item in question, and the income tax would not apply to it. One was therefore invited to speculate about the status under the law of such things as "give-away" prizes ($25,000 for catching the fish with the advertiser's

---

1. 252 U.S. 189 (1920).

8

identification tag on its tail[2]); awards for civic achievement (the Peace Prize—Nobel or Lenin); "subsidies" such as scholarships and fellowships for deserving students; damages for breach of promise or alienation of affection; "found" property; and so on. Since these and various other kinds of receipts were arguably unrelated either to personal services or to capital investment (or both combined), might it not be said that they fell outside the concept of "income" which the Supreme Court had approved in *Macomber?* Or could it be asserted that "labor" or "capital" somehow inheres in every human activity? The *Macomber* definition apparently possessed metaphysical properties which made it difficult to apply in an absolute fashion, and hence most commentators contented themselves with the observation that close cases would have to be resolved on an individual basis.[3]

Happily, the Supreme Court in 1955 put an end to much, perhaps all, of the uncertainty which the *Macomber* decision had generated by discarding the labor-capital formulation in favor of a broader and simpler concept of "income". In *Commissioner v. Glenshaw Glass Co.,*[4] the taxpayers had received treble damage awards under the antitrust laws. Pointing out that two-thirds of the awards represented fines or penalties imposed on the wrong-doers for violating federal laws, the taxpayers argued that only the basic one-third portion which compensated for loss of profits could be treated as derived from labor or capital or both combined. Making no real attempt to bring the punitive damages within the *Macomber* definition, the Court nevertheless held that the awards were taxable in their entirety. "Here we have instances of undeniable accessions to wealth, clearly realized, and over which the taxpayers have complete dominion. The mere fact that the payments were extracted from the wrongdoers as punishment for unlawful conduct cannot detract from their character as taxable income to the recipients." Congress, the Court stated significantly, had applied "no limitations as to the source of taxable receipts, nor restrictive labels as to their nature." *Macomber,* it said, could not be regarded as the "touchstone" to all questions of gross income.

The Court thus resolved—more or less at a stroke—much of what had seemed troublesome and tantalizing about the term "income." With "source" declared irrelevant, the "touchstone" to all income questions becomes simple enrichment; all gains are

2. *Simmons v. U. S.,* 308 F.2d 160 (4th Cir.1962).

3. Surrey and Warren, *The Income Tax Project of the American Law Institute,* 66 Harvard L.Rev. 761 (1953).

4. 348 U.S. 426 (1955).

taxable (at least if "clearly realized"), whether traceable to labor, to capital, or to mere good fortune. If punitive damages are within the scope of the income definition just because the recipient is made wealthier thereby, then so are prizes and awards (lucky or deserved); so are damages and subsidies of all sorts; and so are packets of cash found in the backs of taxicabs. Each represents an "accession to wealth," and that factor by itself, under *Glenshaw*, justifies inclusion in the tax base. The catch-all provision of § 61 is indeed as sweeping as it seems to be; the income tax is source-blind, and any measurable gain is within its reach.

The *Glenshaw* decision has survived the ensuing forty years without material qualification, and it is altogether unlikely that the Court will ever return to a narrower view of the meaning of "income." It is therefore fair to ask at this point whether there is anything still left to debate under the heading "What is income?" The answer, of course, is: just about everything. Apart from the taxability of windfalls, punitive damages and similar trivia, the *Glenshaw* case resolves none of the real difficulties in the field, though it does, perhaps, help to sharpen the issues. The problems that survive the *Glenshaw* decision are, and in the nature of things always were, the critical ones from the standpoint of the structure of the tax law, and their solutions are not greatly advanced by the assertion that all realized gains are "income." This is not to say that a contrary decision in *Glenshaw* would not have been troublesome: if punitive damages had been held non-taxable even though they plainly enriched the recipient, Congress would presumably have had to extend the enumeration in § 61 to include such receipts and then might have had to resort to further enumeration if and when other unusual items obtained exemption in the courts. Although Congress is still obliged to explicitly exempt receipts it *doesn't* wish to cover, *e.g.,* college tuition scholarships (see Code § 117), this is done as a matter of conscious legislative design rather than chance judicial action. My point, however, is that *Glenshaw* does not, and could not, reach the technical questions with which the law is chiefly concerned in taxing "income"; hence the decision, though important philosophically, has little direct effect on the learning job that lies ahead.

The structural or technical issues to be examined in this Part can very roughly be divided into three categories (implied by the *Glenshaw* opinion itself, as a matter of fact). Since income includes all "gains" that are "clearly realized" regardless of "source," the relevant questions would seem to be:

(a) What constitutes a "gain"? Has the taxpayer enjoyed the requisite "accession to wealth" by reason of some particular event, and if he has, in what amount? This question seems to have an economic ring to it rather than an abstract legal quality; it calls for a measurement of the taxpayer's personal wealth, or at least the change therein from one point in time to another—presumably the beginning and end of the calendar year. While that inquiry appears somewhat less problematic than the question of how to define "income," even so one anticipates disputes. Were the issue not resolved by the Code, for example, one could easily be uncertain about whether alimony payments represent taxable "gain" or are merely compensation for the loss of a right to support. And since income may be received in "kind" as well as in cash, there are likely to be valuation questions which will sometimes be difficult to answer.

(b) When is income "clearly realized"? Conceding the presence of gain, is the benefit sufficiently "in hand" to be properly taxable? To be sure, the question can be answered intuitively in most cases. Gain from the sale of securities for cash is obviously "realized"; mere property appreciation almost equally obviously is not. But between these extremes are a good many ambiguous situations which require further analysis. As will be seen, gain and realization questions often seem to overlap or slide together— *Eisner v. Macomber* (5.02) is an example—and part of the effort to cope with each lies in keeping the two apart for discussion purposes.

(c) Although "source" is irrelevant for purposes of § 61, this does not of course mean that Congress may not *choose* to make it relevant. In fact, the Code contains a large number of provisions which exclude particular kinds of receipts from the tax base—many more by this time than when the *Macomber* case was decided. In some instances Congress has acted simply to resolve doubts about gain or realization by excluding the item at issue or by providing fixed rules of measurement. But in many others, Congress has sought to effectuate a non-tax policy goal by affording an exemption based on source. As will be seen, the exclusion of particular kinds of receipts necessarily revives problems of definition. Suppose, for example, that "gifts" are specifically excluded from income. Since there is plainly a realized gain to the recipient of a gift, we may have to decide in close cases whether a transfer of property was indeed a "gift," *i.e.,* as that term is defined for tax purposes.

The sections that follow all entail one or another of the three limiting categories just mentioned—gain, realization, and specific exclusion. But these categories are not exhausted in this Part. Both gain and realization questions crop up at many points: indeed, it is possible to assert that these issues are the predominant

11

subject-matter of this book. Further, only a few, and not necessarily all the most important, of the Code's specific exclusions are treated here. But while the present Part is thus merely introductory, it should provide the reader with considerable perspective on a number of the detailed problems to be encountered later on.

SECTION 1.   NON–CASH BENEFITS: MEALS–AND–LODGINGS; IMPUTED RENTS

1.01   General Comment.   Many of the questions that arise about the scope of § 61 and the meaning of "income" seem to involve benefits "in kind," that is, receipts in a form other than conventional cash payments. These questions do not arise because of any basic doubt regarding the includability of non-cash receipts; it is perfectly clear that § 61 embraces cash and non-cash benefits alike. But non-cash items do often present valuation difficulties which are obviously not encountered when cash is received; moreover, there may be doubts about the application of the "realization" requirement in some instances, doubts which do not arise when property or services are exchanged for cash. Finally, the Code sometimes makes specific concessions for non-cash receipts—meals and lodgings (1.02) being one familiar example—or allows them to escape tax more or less by default—imputed rent (1.03) being a less familiar but considerably more important instance—while treating the cash equivalent as fully taxable.

In general, however, § 61 makes no distinction between cash and "kind" and it may be well to take the point in its affirmative application before going on to consider exceptions. As a first illustration, assume an employee-taxpayer receives a year-end bonus from his corporate employer consisting of 100 shares of the employer's stock. The stock has a traded value of $5 a share, or $500 in total, at the time it is issued in Year 1. Some months later, in Year 2, the employee sells the stock on the market for $6 a share, or $600. Two questions can be raised: first, how much, if anything, is includable in the employee's income in Year 1 by reason of the bonus? Second, how much gain should the employee report on the sale in Year 2?

The answer to the first question is straightforward once it is accepted that § 61 treats compensation in cash (salaries, wages, bonuses, fees) and compensation in kind alike. As there is no doubt about the market value of the employer's stock, the employee must include $500 in his Year 1 income just as if he had then received a cash bonus in the same amount.[5] To be painfully clear about the consequence, if the employee's applicable marginal rate of tax for Year 1 is 40%,* he must pay a tax of $200 cash, even though the bonus itself is obviously not in cash form.

The second question—how much gain on later sale—takes its answer from the first. Since $500 out of the total of $600 realized was already taxed in Year 1, it is plain that no more than the balance of $100 can be taxed in Year 2. In computing taxable gain (or loss) from the sale of property, the Code, as might be expected, directs that the "amount realized" on the sale—$600 in our case—be reduced by the cost, or "basis," of the property sold. A taxpayer's cost for shares of stock or other property would normally equal his cash investment. Here, however, the taxpayer actually paid nothing (except taxable services) for the stock received. But as a basis for the shares of zero would result in total taxable income of $1,100—$500 of compensation in Year 1, plus $600 of "gain" in Year 2—it is evident that a special concept of "cost" is required in order to prevent the first $500 from being counted twice. Accordingly, under a long-standing rule, property which was included in a taxpayer's income when received by him is treated as having a "cost" equal to its value at the date of receipt. Since the stock in our case was included in the employee's income at a value of $500 when received in Year 1, its basis in Year 2 for the purpose of computing gain (or loss) on sale is also $500. The additional income in Year 2 is therefore limited to $100.

This calculation, petty as it is, should nevertheless suggest that what is chiefly at stake from the standpoint of our employee-taxpayer is the *timing,* rather than the magnitude, of his taxable income. Thus, suppose the initial definitional question—whether a bonus in the form of stock is includable in "income"—were resolved in the negative, so that no portion of the stock's value was included in Year 1. In that event the taxpayer's basis for the shares would indeed be zero: the absence of a cash investment *or* a prior taxable receipt would have left the taxpayer with no basis, actual or constructive, to offset against the $600 of sale proceeds in Year 2. Hence the entire amount realized on the sale would be treated as gain. It follows that $600 is ultimately taxable under *either* view of the meaning of "income." Under the first, however, $500 is taxable in Year 1, $100 in Year 2; under the second, nothing is taxable in Year 1, but $600 is taxed in Year 2.

---

5. Regs. § 1.61–2(d). The discussion of *Comm'r v. Lo Bue, infra* at 19.01, is also relevant.

* Although 39.6% is the topmost marginal rate at present, the reader will agree that it is less awkward to round up to 40% for illustrative purposes.

So why the fuss? Does the employee care, particularly, which way the matter is resolved? In fact he does; and intuition tells us that in most cases the employee will prefer the second set of outcomes to the first—that is, will prefer to postpone, rather than anticipate, the recognition of taxable income. But again, the question is why? One reason could be the effect of the progressive rate structure. Suppose, for example, that the stock bonus represents retirement pay; the employee is put to pasture at the end of Year 1, and as a result his income in Year 2 drops substantially. If his applicable marginal tax rate were expected to be lower in Year 2, the employee would be better off if the $500 bonus could be reported in the later period. Efforts by high-paid executives, and even by much lower-paid employees, to defer income to their golden years can sometimes be explained on this ground, at least in part.

But suppose that retirement is not in view for the employee in our example, and that his marginal tax rate is expected to be the same in both periods. Or, indeed, suppose that we had a completely flat or proportional income tax; that the rate schedule contained no progression whatever. Even then the taxpayer would prefer postponement to anticipation, and would seek to define "income" so as to shift the receipt in question from Year 1 to Year 2. The reason, of course, is that taxes are scheduled and paid on an annual basis—rather than once in a lifetime—and it is always better to incur and pay one's tax obligations in later than in earlier years. An obligation to pay $200 in taxes *immediately* has a positive present value to the Treasury, and a negative present value to the taxpayer, of exactly $200. An obligation to pay $200 in taxes a year from now has a present value of $185.20 if we assume an 8% rate of interest after tax; and only $178.60 if we assume a 12% interest rate. Accordingly, as funds can always be invested at some positive rate of interest, taxpayers have a powerful incentive to defer as long as possible the surrender of their personal wealth to the Treasury. All taxpayers feel the same about this—savers and consumers alike—and it is not to any degree a function of progressive rates.

The point is an obvious one, I admit, but I choose to emphasize it here because it lies at the heart of so many of the technical and interpretative issues that arise in the tax law. Especially when the legal question is "What is taxable income?" or "What is a deductible expense?", the controversy often will involve the postponement or anticipation of tax obligations—nothing more or less. Admittedly, this generalization does not always apply, even in the areas just mentioned. As will be seen in connection with the taxability of meals-and-lodgings (1.02), for example, the income-definition question may sometimes entail the total forgiveness of tax rather than mere postponement. Nevertheless, I think the general proposition valid. At a minimum, the student should be aided in classifying the subjects of "income," "realization," etc., by noticing when, and how often, what is at stake in a controversy over legal definitions is simply the taxpayer's desire to postpone the payment of tax and the Treasury's desire to accelerate it.

The point is important enough, I think, to justify one more illustration, which abstracts from a number of decided cases.[6] Assume again that the taxpayer is a well-paid corporate executive. His age today is 50, and he looks forward to retiring in 15 years at the company's mandatory retirement age of 65. Although it has no systematic retirement program, the company is inspired to do something for this executive at least, and in order to fund his not-so-distant retirement it purchases an endowment policy[7] from an insurance company for a single lump-sum premium payment of $10,000. At a guaranteed rate of accumulation of roughly 8%, the premium payment will build up to $30,000 at the end of 15 years, at which time the executive will draw down the entire fund for use or investment during his retirement. Although the policy names the executive as beneficiary, it is issued to the company, which plans to hold the policy in its own safe until the executive reaches retirement age. The executive's rights are nonforfeitable—he gets $30,000 at age 65 even if he is fired or quits in the meanwhile—but he has no right to sell or borrow against the policy prior to age 65.

Is the $10,000 premium payment made by the company includable in the executive's gross income immediately, that is, in the year in which the policy is purchased? Or is it includable in his income only when he receives the maturity value in cash, at the end of 15 years? On the one hand, it can be argued that in view of the taxpayer's inability to realize current cash benefits through sale or pledge, the value of the policy to him in Year 1 is zero, or at least is indeterminate. To be sure, the bonus in the preceding example was taxed currently even though received in the form of stock, but there the stock could have been sold at once for cash, or pledged for a loan or traded for another security, and at all events was freely disposable by the employee from the date it was issued. Here, by contrast, the endowment policy is pretty well frozen until maturity. But, on the other hand, who doesn't feel better off, especially at age 50, when his employer buys him a sizeable retirement fund? The

6. See, *e.g., U.S. v. Drescher,* 179 F.2d 863 (2d Cir.1950).

7. An endowment policy is a contract under which the obligor agrees to pay the policy-owner a lump-sum certain at the end of a stated number of years.

executive is surely wealthier with the endowment policy than without it, and what better measure of the economic benefit received than the cost of the policy itself? One suspects, moreover, that the executive may have proposed or consented to the policy purchase in lieu of receiving the same amount in straight salary; at the very least he himself chose to accept or continue an employment which entailed that special form of compensation.

The decided cases largely hold for the government in these circumstances and require immediate inclusion of the $10,000 premium payment in the employee's gross income (see 1.02, below). For the moment, however, my particular concern is not with arguments about the meaning of "income" under § 61. What I wish to focus on instead is the overall consequence in financial terms of the two competing views presented. What is at stake? Why is the executive plainly better off if the definitional issue is resolved *against* current includability?

The answer can be given only if we settle another question first; namely, what happens when the endowment policy matures 15 years from now and the executive receives the face amount of $30,000 in cash? Plainly there is a "realization" at that point and just as plainly the "amount realized" is $30,000. The taxpayer's cost, or basis, for the claim which he then surrenders depends (as the stock-bonus case should suggest) on whether or not the earlier premium payment of $10,000 had already been included in gross income. Assuming it was included (that is, the government *won* the original litigation), the taxpayer's basis for the policy would be $10,000—the amount previously taxed to him—and the further gain recognized on maturity would be $20,000. Assuming the premium was not included in income (that is, the government *lost* the earlier case), the executive's basis would be zero, and the full amount of $30,000 would be taxable in the later period. Once again, therefore, as in the stock-bonus illustration, two sets of outcomes can be conceived of. Either $10,000 is taxed in the earlier year and $20,000 in the later year; or nothing is taxed in the earlier year and $30,000 in the later.

Now assume that the same marginal tax rate—say 40%—applies in both years so that the possible effect of progression is excluded. Assume also that the executive can invest his money at an after-tax rate of 8% throughout the relevant time period. The comparative impact of the pending legal determination—whether the $10,000 premium payment is, or is not, includable in the taxpayer's gross income in the current year—is simply the difference between a $4,000 tax payable *now* (.40 × $10,000) and the *present value* of a $4,000 tax payable in 15 years. Discounted at the same 8% rate, the present value of $4,000 due in 15 years is about $1,333, *i.e.,* $1,333 invested at 8% will grow to $4,000 by the end of a 15-year period. Hence, in terms of his current wealth status—how rich he is today—the controversy is worth $2,667 to the executive. This is the difference between the $4,000 tax which the government says is due now and the present value of the same tax—$1,333—if payment is deferred for 15 years. Although the dispute between taxpayer and Treasury *appears* to involve a tax of $4,000, in reality it is the $2,667 "difference" that they are fighting over.

As in the stock-bonus case, my point here is that the argument over income definition is essentially an argument about whether the tax should be paid sooner or be paid later, not about whether it should be paid at all. But the fact that the tax must be paid at *some* point obviously does not mean that the parties will be indifferent to *when.* Although $2,667 seems a small amount to litigate,[8] in percentage terms the executive actually will have succeeded in reducing his tax burden by 67%—from $4,000 down to $1,333—if he can establish his right to the deferral. Once again, the Treasury sees the matter in opposite terms—tax-deferral means an absolute loss of revenue—and it is therefore never content (unless compelled by law) to simply "wait."

More is said about the tax treatment of endowment and other insurance contracts at 2.03, below.

1.02 Forced Saving and Forced Consumption—"Convenience of the Employer." In the endowment policy case just given the executive was precluded from converting the endowment policy into present cash; neither sale nor pledge of the policy was permitted until retirement. If there was legal doubt about whether the $10,000 premium payment constituted "income" within the meaning of § 61, it was presumably because the taxpayer's freedom of choice had been restricted in the manner indicated. In effect, the executive was "forced" to save for his retirement, whether he wished to or not. Or so it could be argued. By contrast, most people are free—certainly one who receives a straight cash salary is free—to elect any mix of savings and consumption that appeals to him, within the limits of his own resources. This freedom may not rise to the level of a constitutional imperative, but it is certainly a common and desirable attribute of most people's economic lives. If it is constrained in some special way, then possibly he who suffers

---

8. The affluent reader should feel free, here and elsewhere in this book, to add as many zeroes as are required to make the problem seem important to him.

the constraint should be viewed as less well-off than others, both as a general proposition and for tax purposes.

The point can be illustrated with an example:

Assume an individual's life is limited to two time periods, Year 1 and Year 2. His financial resources consist of $100 cash, which he receives as income at the beginning of Year 1. He expects to earn nothing more for the rest of his "life," *i.e.*, nothing for the balance of Year 1 and nothing at all in Year 2. The individual is free to consume or save at his discretion; that is, he can consume the entire $100 in Year 1 and have nothing left for Year 2 if he chooses, or he can do just the opposite of that, or anything in-between. Finally, any amount which he does not choose to consume in Year 1 will be invested by him in a safe one-year bond at 8%.

Below is a diagram that pictures the full range of available choices. In effect, the individual can choose any pattern of current consumption-and-saving which falls on the diagonal line that connects the two axes. If he chooses to spend everything this year and save nothing for the next, he comes out at point X; if he does just the opposite, he comes out at point Y, since $100 saved and invested this year means that $108 will be available for spending next year; if he wants to spend about the same amount in both years, he should select point Z. In any event, the decision is entirely his own, given his initial resources and the prevailing interest rate.

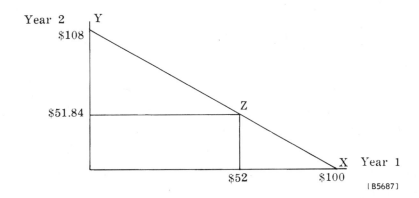

Suppose the executive in the endowment policy case actually desires to consume the entire $100 in Year 1, that is, to come out at point X without a thought for the morrow. An external power (say his employer) overrules him, however, and "compels" the executive to apportion his resources by investing $48 in an 8% bond, which is nonredeemable until the start of Year 2. However prudent this may seem to others, the result is out of accord with the executive's own preference, which is to spend everything at once. So query: should the disputed $48 be taxed in full in Year 1 even though the taxpayer has derived less than the full measure of personal satisfaction that he would otherwise enjoy? Or should his idiosyncratic nature somehow be taken into account? If so, can we really trust him to be honest about his feelings, and even if we can, what discount factor should the law apply for personal frustration?

Three possible solutions can be conceived of: (1) tax the executive on the full $48 despite the element of forced saving; (2) don't tax the $48 until the bond is cashed in because there is really no way to measure the impact of compulsion; or (3) reduce the $48 by some arbitrary figure—say 50%—in an effort to reach a plausible result.

As has been noted, the Code and the cases suggest that the full $48 would be taxed in Year 1. Presumably, all this talk of freedom and compulsion is viewed for what it is—nonsense. If the executive has taken a portion of his annual compensation in deferred retirement benefits, it is because he wants it that way; no other explanation is really credible. The Code does permit deferral of tax in the case of contributions to so-called qualified retirement plans which benefit a substantial proportion of the company's employees (not merely high-paid executives), but this is accomplished by a set of provisions designed specifically to prevent current taxability where the plan meets certain coverage requirements and related conditions.[9] Admittedly also, there is a good deal more that can be said about deferred compensation arrangements (see 11.01(b)). Nevertheless, in the very simple illustration set out above, the result is likely to be the one that I have indicated, despite the apparent element of "forced saving."

In general, then, economic benefit is measured in objective terms for tax purposes; individual preferences, real or feigned, are treated as irrelevant. Yet there are exceptions to this rule, and perhaps the meals-and-lodgings exclusion in § 119 can best be understood as one such. At all events that section—and before its adoption many of the decided cases—excludes from income the value of meals and lodgings furnished to an employee by his employer, provided that the meals and lodgings are furnished on the employer's business premises and for the employer's "convenience." The situation envisaged is one in which the employee is

---

9. Code § 401 *et seq.*

compelled, or at least encouraged, by the exigencies of his job to eat his meals and/or sleep the night on the employer's premises instead of going home (or out to a restaurant, etc.) for the purpose of satisfying those basic wants. One thinks of the hardy lumberjack felling redwoods in the Alaskan wilds, the merchant seaman rolling in his hammock, or the dedicated young interne on night call at his hospital, as probable candidates for the exclusion. Each is compelled to accept the accommodations which his employer provides, because the nature of the taxpayer's occupation excludes any feasible alternative.

But in fact the "convenience of the employer" rule has been extended well beyond hardship cases like these. In a celebrated decision,[10] the manager of a luxury hotel in Hawaii was permitted to exclude from income the value of a hotel suite which he and his wife occupied rent-free, as well as free meals furnished to them in the hotel dining room. It was established to the satisfaction of the court that the taxpayer's job required him to be present in the hotel, and "on the alert," at all times of the day and night. Since constant attention to duty was required, the taxpayer's living arrangement was found to have been dictated primarily by the employer's "convenience"; the benefit to the employee was incidental. Accordingly, the value of the meals and lodgings, his wife's along with his own, was excludable from the taxpayer's gross income.

The emphasis in *Benaglia* and similar decisions on the *employer's* convenience has been questioned by many writers. Thus, why should the employer's motive in furnishing benefits to an employee have any bearing on the status of those benefits under § 61? An employer's goal is always to produce profits for itself, after all. It pays its employees cash salaries because it wishes to exploit their services for its own purposes; yet this element of "convenience," or advantage, to the employer obviously does not prevent the salaries from being taxable to the employees. Why should non-cash benefits be treated differently, especially when, as here, the benefit takes a form that relieves the recipient of living expenses which he would otherwise have to meet out of his (taxable) cash income? In effect, "the benefit to the employee is no less real because it is a byproduct of the employer's requirements." [11]

Perhaps, however, the "convenience-of-the-employer" rule is really a short-hand way of acknowledging the factor of restricted preference mentioned in connection with the endowment policy

10. *Benaglia v. Comm'r*, 36 B.T.A. 838 (1937).

11. Bittker, *The Individual As Wage Earner*, 11 N.Y.U.Tax Inst. 1147 (1953).

case above. In *Benaglia,* as in the endowment policy case, there is an element of personal compulsion which raises doubt about the value of the benefit to the recipient. Thus the hotel-manager *must* live on the hotel premises if he is to do his job (or at least the court in *Benaglia* so found). Yet it seems not unlikely that he would prefer to live more modestly if he were allowed to choose his own accommodations, and it is quite possible that he would elect to save some portion of the equivalent cash receipt. Indeed, his freedom is still further restricted: not only is the hotel-manager forced to consume when he might prefer to save, but he is forced to consume particular goods—hotel food and accommodations—instead of having the same free choice among commodities that is afforded to the rest of us. To be sure, it is difficult to imagine the taxpayer gagging on the dining-room fare or tossing restlessly all night in his canopied bed, but it just might be the case that hotel living grows wearisome over the long term (though, of course, what doesn't?) and that one presently comes to loathe it.[12]

Whether all this solicitude for the victims of forced consumption should be taken seriously is, I concede, somewhat doubtful. Nevertheless, the meals-and-lodging exclusion does appear to reflect a willingness, on the part of Congress and the courts, to take account of the possibility that the taxpayer's rewards may be worth less to him than their market value, and to solve the measurement problem that results by valuing the benefit received at zero. That solution is the more striking because the controversy here is of the full forgiveness variety. If the value of meals and lodgings is not taxed currently, it will not be taxed at all; no subsequent opportunity to include the value of those benefits will arise. From both the taxpayer's and the government's standpoint, therefore, it is really now or never as far as includability is concerned. By contrast, as has been noted, the endowment policy case is in the sooner-or-later category: even if the premium paid by the employer were excluded from the employee's income currently, the proceeds of the policy would ultimately be taxed to the employee when the policy matured.

Quite apart from § 119 and the employer-convenience doctrine, the Treasury, in an exercise of administrative discretion, generally has not attempted to tax employee fringe benefits which are relatively small in value and which are available to higher and lower

---

12. See "Kleinwachter's conundrum" in Simons, *Personal Income Taxation* (1938) at p. 53. The Supreme Court has held that § 119 applies only to meals received "in kind," but not to cash allowances. Thus, a meal allowance paid to state troopers—which they could spend or not as they chose—was found to be "income" under § 61, and not excludable under § 119. *Comm'r v. Kowalski,* 434 U.S. 77 (1977).

paid employees alike. Free parking or free use of a company gym would be typical examples. Strictly speaking, such benefits constitute "income"; like meals and lodgings, they relieve taxpayers of expense which, if incurred directly, would usually be nondeductible. The administrative decision to exclude these items from income has been based on a sense that employees—especially lower-paid employees—would find it exceedingly burdensome to pay taxes in cash on income received in kind, as well as the burden to the Treasury of making the necessary individual assessments.

Concerned that the fringe benefit field had grown somewhat unruly, Congress in 1984 added § 132 to the Code, largely codifying what was understood to be existing Treasury practice. Under § 132, an employee's gross income does not include any fringe benefit that constitutes a "no-additional-cost service" (*e.g.,* free stand-by flights to airline employees), a "qualified employee discount" (sales of merchandise to store employees at cost), a "working condition fringe" (parking facilities, security guard protection), or a "de minimis fringe" (occasional supper-money, night-time taxi fare, company picnics, baseball tickets (but not a box for the season), etc.). While § 132 describes the excludable fringes in considerable detail and effectively insulates such items from any change or extension of Treasury policy, it is equally clear that fringe benefits which do not qualify for exclusion are now includable in gross income under § 61 unless specifically excluded by some other Code provision. § 119 would be an example of the latter. Another (of much greater importance) would be § 106, which excludes employer-paid health insurance premiums and is further mentioned at ¶ 2.04, below.

The subject of meals and lodgings is considered again at 6.01(b) in connection with the deduction of "travel expenses" incurred in business. The two topics bear an obvious relationship since, apart from special circumstances, the cost of meals and lodgings is treated by the Code as a "personal, living or family expense" and cannot be deducted from the taxpayer's gross income. Note also that from the taxpayer's standpoint "deduction" and "exclusion" have the same net effect: a dollar excluded from gross income and a dollar deducted from gross income both result in a cash saving equal to the taxpayer's applicable marginal tax rate; if the applicable rate is 40%, a dollar excluded and a dollar deducted both produce a saving of 40 cents. Should we therefore expect that the Code will *always* be symmetrical—that if a benefit is excluded when received in kind, it will also be deductible when acquired for cash? The answer—as the next subsection demonstrates—is no.

1.03 Imputed Income. Another category of benefits "in kind" which are excluded from the coverage of § 61 is "imputed income"—that is, income derived from the use of "household durables" such as a personal residence, car or television set, and income from the performance of services for one's own or one's family's benefit. This exclusion is much more important in dollar terms than, for example, the meals-and-lodgings exclusion just discussed, and it is therefore slightly astonishing to discover that it rests on no specific Code provision but simply "results" from a long-standing administrative practice of the Internal Revenue Service, which never has attempted to draw imputed income into the tax base. The Service's reasons, historically, may have included some doubt about the constitutionality of treating imputed income as "income," a concern about the valuation problems that would have to be surmounted if it were so treated, and perhaps a sense that the entire concept would be regarded by taxpayers as somewhat strange and theoretical. These reasons no longer seem compelling, it is true, but that is not to say that the Service, on its own motion, could now abruptly reverse its practice and require imputed income to be reported by individuals in their tax returns. Whatever its source or its wisdom, the exclusion is by this time of such great age and so deeply embedded in the tax system that it would take Congressional action, explicitly taxing such benefits in some form, to bring about a change. Though not instantly apparent, the imputed income exclusion hooks up in important ways with other features of the tax law—the deduction for home-mortgage interest and for child-care expenses, to name two—and needs to be understood for its role as a building block if nothing else.

The concept of imputed income—and the scope of the exclusion—can be illustrated in two settings, the first involving income from property (the "household durables" mentioned above), the second involving income from services. We may, to begin with, compare two individual taxpayers, A and B, each with $100,000 cash. A invests his money in a house to be used as a personal residence for himself and his family. B buys an identical house but chooses to rent it out to a tenant while he himself lives in a rented apartment somewhere else. The annual rental value of A's house—the sum he would have to pay to a landlord if he himself were not the owner—is $10,000. B's tenant pays *him* $10,000 annually in rent and B pays *his* landlord the same amount. While A's *money* income is thus $10,000 less than B's, their economic incomes are obviously the same and so are their housing expenditures, although both income and expenditure are "imputed" in A's case but take the form of a cash receipt and a cash outlay in B's.[13] Assuming no other relevant differences exist, it seems well arguable that both should pay the same amount in taxes. If the Code's income definition permits A (as it does) to exclude the annual imputed rental value of his residence, then a considerable measure of interpersonal discrimination develops—or, at any rate, the tax law is seen to award a bonus to persons who, like A, prefer to own their own houses, and to impose a corresponding penalty on B-types who prefer to rent.

It follows that if we now desired to treat A and B equally—to achieve "horizontal equity" in the standard phrase—we could do so in one of two ways. Since exclusions and deductions have the same effect in respect to tax-savings, we could either enlarge the definition of "income" to include imputed rent (thus requiring A to report $10,000) or else expand the list of personal deductions by permitting B to deduct the $10,000 rent on his apartment. If imputed rents were taxed, or if rental payments could be deducted, the two taxpayers would find themselves on an equal footing. To be sure, neither of these "reforms" is under serious consideration in Congress at present—the first would be fiercely resented by homeowners, while the second is too costly from the standpoint of the revenues. As a practical matter, the real question in this field is whether to limit or deny interest deductions on home mortgages, a step that would bring homeowners (at least those with mortgages) and apartment renters much closer together. To understand the precise effect of this proposal requires a detailed comparison of home-owners, renters, and mortgage-payers; such a comparison is provided at 7.04 below.

Imputed income from personal services presents pretty much the same picture and can be mentioned more briefly. The illustration usually employed is that of the housewife's uncompensated labor as nurse and homemaker. The value of those services, though in some instances a significant fraction of the family's economic income, is obviously not treated as includable "income" under § 61. By contrast, the working wife who uses some or all of her earnings to pay for equivalent domestic help gets no compensating deduction for the amounts expended. The child-care credit, mentioned at 6.01(a), below, represents an effort to modify this disparity, but its scope is limited and it does not purport to be a general solution of the problem.

Yet apart from the housework situation, and perhaps subsistence farming, it is difficult to conceive of any way in which the tax

---

13. Thuronyi, *The Concept of Income*, 46 Tax L.Rev. 45, 84 (1990).

law could reach imputed service income, or any really persuasive reason why it should. Life is full of benefit-producing activities— shaving oneself, mowing one's own lawn, jogging around the block for exercise—which might, at a stretch, be converted into market purchases for cash. But presumably no one would seriously argue that § 61 should be broadened to include such imputations, or that the range of personal allowances should be expanded to permit deduction of their cash counterparts. It is inescapably true that a progressive income tax favors leisure over work—taking "leisure" to refer to all forms of self-rendered benefits, and "work" to mean the sale of one's services to others. But nothing can be done about this bias through modification of the income definition; it is a systematic "unneutrality" that simply cannot be avoided. By contrast, imputed income from property, such as imputed rents, could fairly easily be included in the tax base if we desired to reach it. Hence, the unneutrality between owners and renters is one that we evidently prefer to tolerate and continue—to the extent, that is, that "we" are aware of it.

SECTION 2. RECOVERY OF CAPITAL INVESTMENT

2.01 General Comment. Measurement of gain or loss on the sale of property—securities, real estate, etc.—is straightforward. The cost ("basis") of the property sold is first recovered out of the sale proceeds ("amount realized"). Any excess of amount realized over basis is regarded as "gain" and is included in gross income; any shortfall is regarded as "loss" and may be deducted from other income if the property is held in business or for investment. But while these rules are easily applied in most cases, there are some situations in which refinement is required, and in which a special cost-recovery "system" needs to be invented to fit the circumstances. It is surprising, indeed, how frequently tax controversies turn on just that issue, namely, which of two (or more) competing cost-recovery systems is appropriate in a particular case. In fact, a fair part of the Code itself is explicitly devoted to the seemingly routine task of *scheduling* the recoupment of invested capital. Once again, as in our endowment policy example, what is at stake in choosing a cost-recovery system is the *timing* of income and hence the anticipation or deferral of tax payments.

Broadly speaking, cost—or basis—recovery problems can be classified as involving (1) instances of partial or periodic dispositions of property, (2) dispositions of divided interests in the same property, (3) "transactions" in human capital, and (4) special concepts of basis aimed at avoiding over- or under-counting of

25

income. This subsection and the next focus on partial or periodic dispositions; subsections 2.03 and 2.04 concentrate on human capital problems. Dispositions of divided interests are illustrated at 4.02 and elsewhere. An important special basis concept—that of adjusting the cost of property to reflect its previous inclusion in income—was mentioned at 1.01; another—the converse of the first—comes up at 3.02; yet a third—the basis of property acquired by gift—at 4.01. The problem of cost-recovery is pervasive.

What follows are two partial or periodic disposition cases, one very familiar, the other less so. Each requires the selection of an applicable basis-recovery system, and my object is to give some impression of the range of available alternatives. As will be seen (especially in the second case), the choices eventually made are sometimes pretty arbitrary. Still, one must do something, and in the end the reader may feel that the discarded alternatives are even more arbitrary than the methods chosen, if only by a narrow margin.

(a) Corporate stock. As a first and very simple case, assume that an investor buys 100 shares of stock for $5,000 with the expectation that an 8% dividend, or $400, will be paid annually. Of course, dividends may go up or down in the future and the value of the shares when he comes to sell them may be higher or lower than his cost. But let us allow ourselves a little hindsight and assume that the taxpayer actually holds the stock for 15 years, that he does receive $400 in annual dividends, and that he finally sells the stock for slightly more than he bought it, say $5,100. How should the annual dividends be treated for tax purposes, and how much gain or loss should be recognized on final sale? Three possibilities can be considered:

(i) Each annual dividend should be treated as a return of capital until the taxpayer has recovered his entire initial investment. Assuming dividends go along at the expected $400 level, nothing would be included in the taxpayer's income for the first 12½ years; thereafter all further dividends (a total of $1,000) would be included in full. When the stock was finally sold the entire sale price of $5,100 would also be includable in income because the taxpayer's cost would already have been returned to him (*i.e.,* his basis would have been reduced to zero) in the earlier years. In effect, recovery of capital would come *first* under this system and includable income would be deferred.

26

(ii) Just the opposite. Annual dividends would be included in income in full (a total of $6,000). When the shares were finally sold, the sale proceeds would be credited against the taxpayer's entire original cost of $5,000, with only the gain of $100 then being recognized as income. Recovery of capital would come *last* under this system and includable income would be anticipated.

(iii) Something in-between. For example, allocate the $5,000 original cost to the future expected dividends by discounting each expected dividend to present value at the 8% rate. Assuming that dividend payments are to be made at 12-month intervals, the first payment would then have a present value at the date the stock was purchased of $370 $\left(\dfrac{\$400}{1.08}\right)$, the second $343 $\left(\dfrac{\$400}{(1.08)^2}\right)$, the third $318 $\left(\dfrac{\$400}{(1.08)^3}\right)$, and so on. In the first year, therefore, $370

would be treated as recovery of capital and $30 as taxable income; in the second and third years, respectively, $343 and $318 would be recovery of capital while $57 and $82 would be income. This process would continue until the stock was sold, with each year's payment containing a larger income component than the one preceding it. On sale, the proceeds would be allocated to unrecovered cost—there would always be some—with the excess being recognized as gain.

Depending on one's criteria, there is perhaps something to be said for each of the above alternatives. System (i)—cost recovered first—seems to emphasize the risky character of an investment in securities. It implies that we ought to wait until it can be determined whether the taxpayer has actually made anything from the investment before imposing tax—a perfectly defensible idea from one standpoint. But on the other hand, *should* cost-recovery be a function of risk? If so, investors who buy relatively safe but low-yielding bonds will actually pay their taxes *later* than investors who buy risky but higher-yielding stocks and real estate. At a 5% yield cost-recovery will take 20 years, while at an 8% yield it will take only 12½—which is rather a curious outcome given the emphasis on risk.

System (iii), which looks kind of scientific, avoids the common fallacy of treating income and principal as if they were different things. The $5,000 initial investment, after all, is nothing more than the present value of the expected dividend stream of $400 a year. It is wrong to treat the two as if distinct, and therefore arguably right to allocate the cost of the dividend stream (*i.e.*, the

27

principal) to each successive dividend, rather than only to the earlier ones or only to the final payoff. Once again, the idea is a defensible, if not a compelling, one. Against it (among other things) is the fact that it does require a "finding" as to the investor's anticipated dividend rate, which would frequently be difficult and conjectural.

System (ii)—cost recovered last—is the method which the tax law has adopted. Each annual dividend of $400 is taxed in full, without any adjustment to basis; the original investment is recovered only when the stock is sold. To be sure, the same aggregate amount of income is taxed to the investor under system (ii) as under (i) or (iii)—the totals, both of income ($6,100) and of cost-recovery ($5,000), are identical under all procedures. Under (ii), however, income, and hence tax obligations, are reflected early; under (i) and to a lesser extent (iii), they are deferred.

But why *should* the law choose system (ii) over the others—especially as the Treasury would realize about the same revenues under any system once it got rolling? The answer, quite simply, is that cost-recovery rules in the tax law generally follow conventional accounting principles. Accounting, in turn, treats cost-recovery as a function of asset depreciation and not of risk or any other factor. As already noted, tangible assets such as buildings and equipment, and even certain intangibles such as patents, have limited useful lives and lose their value as productive instruments over a period of time. From an accounting standpoint, therefore, it is thought proper to regard each year's flow of cash receipts as consisting in part of original cost, and to treat the portion so regarded as return of capital. By contrast, financial assets, such as common stock, are viewed as having an indeterminate useful life and hence as non-depreciable. The corporate issuer—like some perpetual and self-renewing organism—is expected to replace its productive assets as they wear out and, hence, to continue in being indefinitely. As a result, its shares are assumed to retain their earning power from period to period, undiminished by the annual payment of dividends. Other things being equal, stock worth $5,000 at the beginning of Year 1 will also be worth $5,000 at the beginning of Year 2, Year 3, etc. The taxpayer's principal investment thus remains intact; the shares are a perpetuity rather than a wasting asset.

While tax law is by no means bound by the principles of accounting, it is not surprising that the tax rules should follow accounting conventions at this and at many other points. Tax returns are quasi-accounting documents, after all, and the two systems of principles have a parallel goal in view, namely, to measure the results of completed activities on an annual basis. For tax (as well as accounting) purposes, the question that is central is: how much did it *cost* the taxpayer to earn the year's gross income? In the case of dividends on corporate stock, the answer, quite obviously, is nothing (other than the opportunity to invest in something else). This follows, once again, because corporate stock is an asset of perpetual life; though it may go up or down in value, it does not "waste" or wear away. The proper cost-recovery rule is therefore pretty much self-evident: an investment in corporate shares can be recovered no earlier than the day on which the shares are sold, for it is only then that their economic value terminates as far as the taxpayer is concerned.

(b) *Easements.* The second illustrative case I have in mind is chosen for its contrasting outcome. Assume an individual owns a sizeable tract of land which he rents out to campers who value it for its quiet, scenic beauty. The land was purchased some years ago for $15,000. The State, requiring access to certain facilities which are separated from the highway by the taxpayer's property, now uses its condemnation power to carve out a perpetual easement across the property, and awards the taxpayer $10,000 as compensation. Although the land still retains value for other purposes, its attraction for campers is destroyed owing to the frequent presence of trucks and equipment in transit to the adjoining area.

How much, if any, of the taxpayer's original $15,000 cost should be allocated to the easement and offset against the $10,000 award? Once again the issue is "merely" a matter of sooner or later. If the whole award is offset by allocating $10,000 of basis to the easement, then the basis of the remaining property must be reduced thereby to $5,000; if none of the award is offset, the basis of the remaining property stays at $15,000; and if some but not all of the award is offset, the basis of the remaining property is simply reduced proportionately. The first alternative means that the cost of the land is recoverable out of the earliest proceeds of disposition, and none of the award is taxable currently; the second means the opposite—the cost is recoverable only when the entire property is finally sold, and the award is currently taxable in full; the third implies an in-between result, with partial cost-recovery early and the balance at the end. The total income ultimately taxed is the same under each alternative; it is only the timing that differs from one to the other.

Which outcome seems most appropriate? We seem to be talking, again, about property that enjoys an indeterminate or indefinite useful life—land. As in the case of corporate stock, accounting does not regard land investment as recoverable through annual depreciation allowances. Does it follow, as it did in the stock case just above, that the second solution—cost recovered last—is the right one, and that no recovery of capital should be permitted until final disposition of the entire property?

The answer to the last question might well be affirmative if the State's easement were for a term of years instead of in perpetuity. If the State had paid, say, $3,000 as compensation for a 5-year right-of-way, one senses that, like dividends on corporate shares, the payment would be viewed as "income" rather than "capital" and would be taxed in full without offsetting basis.[14] The same would certainly be true if the taxpayer had *leased* the property to the State for a 5-year term, the rent being payable annually; once again, since land, like stock, is of indefinite useful life, the rents, like the dividends, would be taxed in full. To be sure, the compensation for the right-of-way is assumed to be received in a lump sum, which may be disadvantageous to the taxpayer. But leases, too, can be negotiated on an advance-payment basis, and nothing suggests that the customary treatment would not apply. Presumably, then, condemnation of the right-of-way for a term of years would be handled in a like manner, *i.e.,* by including the $3,000 payment in the owner's income.

But our case-in-chief is somewhat different. The easement taken by the State does not expire at a fixed date like a lease. Rather, it is a right in perpetuity which represents a permanent, if forced, divestment of a portion of the taxpayers' original property. Perhaps, then, instead of a lease of the property for a term of years, the better analogy would be to an outright sale of a section of the land itself. If, for example, the State had acquired 40 acres out of an original 100-acre tract, no one would doubt that so much of the taxpayer's original cost as was allocable to the acres taken or sold would be a proper offset against the amount realized (even if the rest of the land became less attractive). Suppose the taxpayer's original cost per acre had been $150. His basis for the 40 acres would then be $6,000, and an award of $10,000 would result in $4,000 of taxable gain. The balance of his original investment, $9,000, would remain as his basis for the 60 acres retained. Taking this approach, the easement could be viewed as one unit drawn out of a larger aggregation of units—again, like 40 acres out of a 100 acre lot. In that event the condemnation award would be offset by so much of the taxpayer's original cost as was allocable to the easement-unit alone. Gain or loss would be recognized if the award exceeded or fell short of such allocable cost, and the balance

14. See *Comm'r v. Gillette Motor Transport, Inc.,* 364 U.S. 130 (1960), and *Hort v. Comm'r,* 313 U.S. 28 (1941), discussed *infra* at 17.03.

of the taxpayer's initial investment would be recovered when the remaining property-units were finally sold. In effect, the third of the alternative solutions listed above, *i.e.,* an in-between approach, would be seen as the proper one.

Curiously in view of all this, the decided cases appear to authorize the one cost-recovery system to which neither the unit-sale nor the temporary-rental analogy seems to point. In what few decisions there are on this question,[15] the courts have permitted the taxpayer to offset the condemnation award by the full cost of the property and to report no gain unless the amount received exceeds his entire initial investment. Thus, as the taxpayer's initial cost was $15,000 in our example, no gain would be reported currently on receipt of the $10,000, although it might be the case that the land had appreciated in value since the time of its acquisition. The basis of the remaining property would be reduced to $5,000, and the taxpayer's overall gain or loss on his investment would be deferred until the balance of the property had been disposed of.

The reason usually given by the courts for adopting the equivalent of our first alternative solution is that it is impossible, or perhaps just impractical, to allocate basis accurately to the easement alone. The State's right to drive trucks across the taxpayer's land cannot be isolated in the same convenient manner as a given number of acres, and hence any effort to allocate a set fraction of the taxpayer's total cost to the easement is said to be too conjectural to be accepted for tax purposes.

The result of the latter finding—which is admittedly rare in the tax law—is to convert what might otherwise be treated as a unit sale into a kind of installment sale transaction, with the condemnation award being viewed as the down payment on a larger purchase price whose amount remains uncertain until the entire property is sold. Suppose, indeed, that the State had condemned the property as a whole, agreeing first to pay $10,000 for the easement and at a later date to take the land itself at whatever value comparable property then possessed. It would not be altogether surprising, especially where the total purchase price depended on future market conditions, if the courts deferred the final reckoning of gain or loss until the last installment had been paid. The analogy is a bit rough, I admit, but perhaps it draws some support from the early treatment of annuities described in the next subsection (and indeed from the early treatment of installment sales themselves).

15. *Inaja Land Co., Ltd. v. Comm'r,*
9 T.C. 727 (1947).

To summarize, the easement case could be handled, and handled fairly satisfactorily, by any of our three familiar cost-recovery methods. Viewed as payment for a leasehold, the condemnation award would be taxed in full without offsetting basis. Viewed as a unit-sale, the award would be offset by the easement's allocable basis and some gain or loss would be recognized currently. Viewed finally as an open-ended installment-sale, the entire cost of the property would be an offset against the award, and gain or loss would be completely deferred until final disposition of the property. There is, I think, some justification for each approach: none appears wholly inapposite. The unit-sale analogy seems to fit best, perhaps, but its superiority to the other methods is hardly overwhelming. Moreover, there may be some genuine difficulty in ascertaining an allocable basis for the easement—appraisals of the property before and after the condemnation would seem to be called for—so that the installment-sale approach has the advantage of simplicity, if nothing else.

Apart from recurring references to depreciation of buildings and equipment, I have yet to offer a case that fully illustrates a prorata (that is, a year-by-year) cost-recovery system. Annuities, discussed next, do provide such an illustration. Unlike land or corporate shares, annuities are investments of limited duration. The payout period is often measured by the annuitant's life, or perhaps the joint lives of husband and wife. At the same time, however, the number of payments actually to be received by the annuitant is uncertain—he may, or he may not, outlive his statistically determined life expectancy. How should the two factors— uncertainty of duration, but certainty of termination—be combined for purposes of determining the annuitant's annual income and the appropriate rate of cost-recovery? That, briefly, is the central problem considered in the subsection immediately following.

2.02 Annuities. An annuity, generically speaking, is any sequence of equal payments made at equal time intervals, such as monthly rents, quarterly dividends, or semi-annual interest payments on a bond. In the present context, however, the term is to be taken to refer specifically to a retirement contract purchased from an insurance company which calls for equal periodic cash payments commencing at a certain date and continuing throughout the annuitant's lifetime. The annuitant pays a premium, or a series of premiums, to the company, which payment becomes the principal of the annuity very much like the principal of a loan.

That investment earns interest in the hands of the company, and in return the company guarantees to make stated payments to the annuitant for life. The cost of the annuity—the premium—depends on the annuitant's life expectancy as derived from standard mortality tables. The annuitant may or may not outlive that term, of course, but the insurance company, which issues many such contracts, expects mortality gains and losses among annuitants to balance each other out. A particular annuitant thus gambles his longevity against that of the other annuitants, while the company serves as stake-holder for the group.

It is obvious that the payments made to the annuitant over the term of the contract must, from the company's point of view, come partly from the premium paid and partly from the earnings on that amount. From a tax standpoint, therefore, the question is the (by now) familiar one: how much of each annual payment should be treated as taxable interest-income, and how much as tax-free return of capital? And again—as the reader will anticipate with a groan—there are various scheduling alternatives that can be conceived of. I need not make my own listing this time, however, because the Code itself, having varied in its treatment of annuities over the years, has pretty well rung all the changes on our customary theme of sooner-or-later.

The Code history can be summarized quickly. In the early days the law did not tax annuity payments at all until the annuitant had received an aggregate amount equal to his entire investment in the contract—rather like the easement case discussed in section 2.01. As with installment transactions generally, the theory was that capital must be returned in full before there could be any income to be taxed by way of "profit." The result, of course, was to postpone the recognition of interest until the later years of the contract, or, in cases where the annuitant died prematurely, to avoid such recognition altogether.

In 1934, Congress altered the rules on annuities to require that a taxpayer receiving annual payments under an annuity contract include in annual income a fixed percentage—3%—of the cost of the annuity. The balance of each annual payment was regarded as return of capital until the annuitant's cost had been recovered. While this approach properly recognized that every payment includes an interest component, in the end it, too, proved unsatisfactory. In particular, where the premium paid in by the annuitant represented a large proportion of the value of the annuity at the time the payments began, the 3% rule generally overstated the income component and caused the rate of cost-recovery to be too slow. Thus, in a well-known case sustaining the constitutionality of the 3% rule,[16] an annuitant aged 45, with a life expectancy of 28 years, purchased for a premium of $100,000 a right to receive approximately $5,000 a year for life.　Since under the 3% rule $3,000 a year was includable in income and only $2,000 was regarded as return of capital, the annuitant would have had to live 50 years from the date of purchase in order to recover his investment.

The 3% rule thus confronted some annuitants with well-nigh impossible longevity requirements, and it was replaced in 1954 by Code § 72, which contains the present treatment of annuities.　The general purpose of § 72 is to impute the contractual rate of interest to the annuitant, instead of fixing a statutory rate which might turn out to be excessive or inadequate.　In the case just mentioned, for example, the annual cost-recovery factor would be determined by dividing the annuitant's investment in the contract ($100,000) by the aggregate of the payments to be received during his statistically anticipated lifetime (28 × $5,000 = $140,000).　The result is an exclusion factor of 5/7ths ($100,000/$140,000), with the balance of each payment being includable in income.　The annual payment of $5,000 would thus consist of about $3,570 (5/7 × $5,000) of capital and $1,430 of taxable interest.　An annuitant who lived to exactly his life expectancy would recoup his entire $100,000 investment tax-free and pay tax only on receipts in excess of that amount.

But suppose the annuitant died too early or lived too long.　Are gains (from long life) or losses (from early demise) taken into account?　Prior to the 1986 Act they were not; mortality gains and losses were simply disregarded by the Code.　Thus long-lived annuitants continued to exclude a proportion of each annual payment from income even though their cost had already been recovered in full, while short-lived annuitants were denied a deductible loss. The Treasury, like an insurance company, came out about even on this, although individual annuitants obviously gained or lost at one another's expense.　In effect, the basic gamble among annuitants was simply extended to include the tax consequences.[17]

Feeling, apparently, that the question of mortality gains and losses should be resolved in terms of individual taxpayers rather than annuitants as a group, Congress in 1986 amended § 72 so as to recognize such gains and losses for tax purposes.　Under new § 72(b), which applies to annuities beginning in 1987, an annuitant who dies prematurely can deduct his unrecovered cost on his final tax return.　An annuitant who survives his anticipated mortality

---

16.　*Egtvedt v. U.S.,* 112 Ct.Cl. 80 (1948).

17.　See A.L.I. *Fed. Inc. Tax Stat.* (Feb. 1954) v. I., p. 252.

date—and who, therefore, will have recovered his investment in full during life—must include in income the entire amount that he receives in subsequent years, *i.e.*, without exclusion.

Does the system *now* make sense? Yes and no. While the income (interest) element is correctly determined by § 72 in overall terms, the scheduling of income and recovery of capital can still be questioned. As anyone knows who has ever paid off a home mortgage, interest always bulks very large in the early years (with repayment of principal correspondingly small), while the reverse relationship holds true of payments towards the end. Since the annuitant is in the position of a lender to the insurance company, just as the bank is a lender to the home-buyer, a more accurate view of the apportionment between income and principal would result in higher tax payments (more income) in the earlier years than in the later. Suppose, for example, that an annuitant's life expectancy is only three years (to keep the illustration brief). He purchases an annuity for $50,000 with interest at 5%, which entitles him to equal annual payments of $18,360.43 starting in Year 1. The resulting schedule of receipts—viewed apart from § 72—would look like this:

Period	(1) Outstanding principal at beginning of period.	(2) Payment	(3) Interest due at end of period. [5% of (1)]	(4) Principal repaid at end of period. [(2)–(3)]
1	$50,000.00	$18,360.43	$2,500.00	$15,860.43
2	34,139.57	18,360.43	1,706.98	16,653.45
3	17,486.12	18,360.43	874.31	17,486.12
Total		$55,081.29	$5,081.29	$50,000.00

In effect, the annuitant's income for the first year is $2,500, for the second year $1,706.98, and for the third $874.31. Under § 72, however, the annuitant's cost of $50,000 is recoverable on a level basis—$16,666.67 a year—so that his includable income is $1,693.76 in each of the three years. The result is that income of about $807 is deferred from the first year to the third (and about $13 from the second year to the third). Even though the illustration involves a time-span of just three years, the "value" of the deferral (positive to the taxpayer, negative to the Treasury) is quite considerable in percentage terms. Thus, the tax on $807 is $323 at a 40% rate. Since payment is deferred for two years, the annuitant can meet his obligation by setting aside (whether actually or mentally) only $282 at the end of Year 1 (assuming, as usual, an 8%

interest rate). The "saving"—$41—is equivalent to a 5-point re-
duction in the applicable tax-rate. This saving measures the benefit to the taxpayer (cost to the Treasury) of allowing the annuitant
to recover his investment at a level rate instead of on an ascending
basis as column (4) of the above schedule would require.

While all of this is slightly tiresome, it may help (a) to remind
the reader about the effect of income-deferral, discussed at 1.02
above, and (b) to prepare the reader for our discussion of depreciation at 6.08, where the same sort of analysis will be proposed.

2.03 Life Insurance. Everyone would agree, I suppose,
that the purpose of buying life insurance is to provide funds to
replace the earning capacity of the insured in the event that he dies
during his working life. If family savings were large enough to
maintain accustomed living standards without the insured's earnings, as they might be in the case of a very wealthy family, then
presumably insurance would be unnecessary and the amounts
otherwise expended on annual premiums could be devoted to other
uses. That, of course, is not the general case, and as a result most
people consider insurance to be an important element of family
finance. But insurance—in the pure sense of protection against
early death—is obviously not a substitute for savings. Once the
breadwinner reaches retirement age and his earnings from employment come to an end, pure insurance protection ceases to be useful.
The source of family income has then got to be some form of
savings—accumulated cash or securities, pension benefits funded
by one's employer, social security, and so on. Family financial
planning thus normally entails a two-fold obligation: insurance
protection in case death occurs prior to retirement, and a savings
plan to meet post-retirement needs and for bequests.

It happens that life insurance can (and perhaps for most
insurance buyers still does) help to accomplish both objectives. In
the case of ordinary whole-life or endowment insurance policies, the
insured's annual premium partly goes to buy pure protection
against premature death—the so-called *term* feature of the insurance contract—and partly also to build up the cash value of the
policy itself—the contract's *savings* feature. If the death of the
insured occurs very early on, the policy proceeds payable to his
beneficiary will consist almost entirely of pure insurance; if very
late, almost entirely of savings plus accumulated interest; if in the
middle, some of each. One can, of course, buy protection alone in
the form of term insurance, and a good many people do just that.
But since term insurance returns nothing if the insured survives
the expiration of the term, presumably the family will be obliged to
do its saving in some other way.

To illustrate the financial elements involved, suppose a man age 40 buys a 25-year endowment insurance policy with a face value of $100,000 at an annual premium of $3,500. The company promises to pay the face of the policy to the named beneficiary if the insured dies within 25 years, or to pay the face of the policy to the insured himself at the end of 25 years if he survives. Suppose the insured dies at the end of 15 years and his beneficiary collects the $100,000 face amount. The following is the allocation of proceeds between pure insurance and savings-plus-interest, as well as a calculation of the insured's mortality "gain":

1.	Total premiums paid ($3,500 × 15)		$52,500
2.	Actuarial cost of term insurance		18,000
3.	Cash value (terminal reserve):		
	Cash reserve fund (1–2)	34,500	
	Interest at 4%	8,000	42,500
4.	Proceeds allocable to term insurance		
	($100,000 − 42,500)		57,500
5.	Net mortality gain (4–2)		39,500

To summarize, the $100,000 of insurance proceeds consists of three elements: (1) $34,500 of paid-in-cash reserves, (2) $8,000 of accumulated interest, and (3) $57,500 of pure insurance of which $39,500 represents the excess over allocable term insurance premiums of $18,000.

Are any or all of these elements subject to income tax? The answer is no. Code § 101(a) provides a blanket exclusion for insurance proceeds payable by reason of death, so that the entire face amount of $100,000 is received tax free by the insured's designated beneficiary. Does the exclusion make sense—in tax terms, that is, and apart from considerations of personal bereavement and the like? Insofar as the cash reserve fund of $34,500 is concerned, it pretty clearly does. That fund, paid in by the insured, is the simple equivalent of a bank account which is left by will to the decedent's heir, and if one accepts that gifts and bequests are properly (or at least plausibly, see 4.01) excluded from the recipient's income, exclusion here is consistent and proper as well. But the other two components of the policy proceeds—term insurance and accumulated interest—appear to be within the reach of § 61, and their exclusion is open to question.

Thus the policy-holder in our illustration realized a mortality gain of $39,500; in effect, the insured and his family have "won" their gamble with the mortality tables, as compared with other policy-owners who survive the 25-year term. As noted, the term feature of the policy serves to replace the future earnings that are lost by reason of the insured's premature death. While the family is thus made whole financially, and there is a recovery of human capital in cash form, it should not be overlooked that the future earnings themselves would have been subject to tax as wages, salary, etc., had the decedent lived to realize them. Policy-owners who do survive are, of course, taxed on their earnings in the usual way; so that as between longer- and shorter-lived individuals, or as between earned income and mortality gains, the tax law plainly favors the latter against the former. If the law were to aim at equal treatment of all policy-owners, shorter- and longer-lived alike, it presumably would require that the proceeds of term insurance be included in the income of the beneficiary, but at the same time permit *all* term-insurance buyers to deduct their allocable premiums as costs incurred for the protection of taxable income. Decedents (or their beneficiaries) would then be taxed on their net mortality gains; survivors would be taxed on their net earnings. As matters stand, however, net mortality gains are received tax free, while term insurance premiums are treated as non-deductible personal expenses. Although, again, the Treasury comes out about even on this, individual policy-owners are better off dead than alive, everything else being equal.

The exclusion of the $8,000 of accumulated interest on the cash reserves raises still more serious questions of tax policy because its realization has nothing particularly to do with the "forced" element of premature death, family bereavement and so on. Cash value, including interest, can be realized through surrender of the policy at any time prior to maturity, and as such is fully available to the decedent throughout his lifetime. Here the most striking comparison is between insurance owners and investors in other kinds of interest-bearing debt, such as bonds or savings-accounts. The latter are taxed year-by-year as interest accrues, whether the annual accruals are withdrawn or left to compound. Taxability extends even to the purchaser of bonds issued at a discount, where no annual cash payments are made at all and "interest" is represented by the yearly increase in the value of the bond itself.[18] To be sure, most people who buy insurance do not regard the annual increase in the policy's cash value as in the category of currently available funds, though no doubt some do. But this element of "attitude" and voluntary forbearance hardly seems an adequate basis for the exclusion of very large amounts of interest income. Yet no better reason—other, of course, than a Congressional desire to shield insurance buyers from tax—can easily be proposed.

18. § 1272.

Moving to the survivors' side again, what about those policy-owners who outlive the 25-year period and who then receive the face amount of the policy as a straight refund of savings plus interest? Is there tax symmetry at this point as between longer- and shorter-lived policy-holders? § 72(e)(1) requires that the proceeds of a matured policy be included in income, but only to the extent that such proceeds exceed the *total* of the premiums paid by the insured. In our illustrative case, therefore, the $100,000 of proceeds would be offset by $87,500 of premiums ($3,500 × 25), and $12,500 would be includable in the policy-owner's income. Once again, survivors are treated less generously than decedents in the sense that interest accumulations may finally be subject to tax, though the tax is still deferred until the policy proceeds are drawn down, usually at maturity. On the other hand—adding one anomaly to another—the $12,500 figure may well fall short of the total interest that has accrued, because the premiums, which are allowed to be credited against the amount received, partly went to pay the cost of the term feature of the policy. By contrast, if the insured had purchased term insurance separately, none of the premiums paid would offset his return from other forms of savings, because insurance premiums are a nondeductible personal expense.

The exclusionary system is thus something of a tangle, though its main component (the exclusion of proceeds paid on death) is plain enough and there is a heavy flavor of condolence about the whole affair. As noted, the Code distinguishes between decedents and survivors by permitting the former to exclude all accumulated interest plus mortality gains. More generally, the law, by allowing interest on cash reserves to accumulate tax-free, substantially "prefers" insurance to most other forms of savings, and we can therefore add life-insurance to home-ownership as a source of tax-favored investment income.[19]

---

19. The term "tax preference" is often used to describe statutory (or administrative) rules that exclude certain types of income from the tax base by reference to their source. As noted, interest on municipal bonds, interest accumulations on insurance policies, imputed rents from home-ownership—these and various other kinds of benefits, though within the meaning of "income," are specifically exempted from tax (in whole or in part) for reasons of national policy.

Many have argued that tax preferences are inequitable because they favor some taxpayers over others; also, that preferences are inefficient—cost too much—in carrying out the goals that Congress has in view. See Surrey, *Pathways to Tax Reform* (1973); compare Bittker, *A "Comprehensive Tax Base" as a Goal of Income Tax Reform*, 80 Harv. L.Rev. 925 (1967); and see Graetz, *Legal Transitions: The Case of Retroactivity in Income Tax Revision*, 126 U.Pa. L.Rev. 47 (1977). While broad issues of this sort are scanted in the present volume, in a "Note" at p. 356 I do try to answer one question that students often ask about tax preferences, namely: if tax preferences are so good, why doesn't *everybody* buy tax-preferred assets? The "Note" explains why tax preferences are

2.04 Damage Awards. One way to view the exclusion of insurance proceeds under § 101(a) is to say that the exclusion serves as a proxy or substitute for a system of depreciating human capital. As will be seen (6.02(d)), the Code does not permit the costs of professional training or skills-acquisition to be deducted, either currently or over the individual's career life in the form of an annual depreciation allowance. In addition, all sorts of work-connected expenses—commuting, restaurant lunches, a new suit—are disallowed as "personal," although in many instances such costs are incurred solely because of the demands made by the taxpayer's job. As against these disallowances, however, the Code does afford certain compensating tax benefits which relate to retirement, death and disability, and which in some measure take the place of an earned-income allowance or of "personal" depreciation. Thus, income which is dedicated to the taxpayer's retirement—contributions to qualified employee pension plans, for example—is often permitted to be deferred until retirement occurs and actual payouts begin. As has been seen, death benefits—chiefly term insurance or its equivalent—which replace the decedent's future earnings, are usually excluded from income entirely. These tax concessions can hardly be described as a systematic effort to deal with the problems of retirement and death—there are anomalies in every direction—but the range of items covered is so considerable that the absence of a thoroughly articulated scheme of tax relief may not matter very much in the end.

The economic consequences of personal injury bear an obvious resemblance to those which result from premature death, and it will not surprise the reader to learn that damage awards (from individual tortfeasors or through workmen's compensation) are excluded from the recipient's gross income under Code § 104(a). Although such awards obviously serve among other things to replace lost earnings, and although such earnings would otherwise be taxable when received (indeed, *are* taxable to one who receives them in the normal course of his employment), the analogy to term insurance is easily drawn and the two exclusionary provisions, § 101(a) and § 104(a), are consistent in their premises and goals. §§ 105 and 106 carry the matter still further by generally excluding both amounts received by an employee under a health and accident plan and the employer's contributions to the plan, usually made in the form of health insurance premiums. The exclusion of employer-paid health insurance under § 106 is actually a tax concession of large proportions. From the employer's standpoint such outlays

largely taken over by upper-bracket taxpayers and considers also whether there is anything left of a preference once the market gets through with it.

are in lieu of paying additional wages to affected employees. If employees are generally taxed at a marginal rate of, say, 28%, the employer can effectively furnish a dollar's worth of compensation through the purchase of 72 cents worth of excludable health insurance. The employee is just as well off and the 28-cent tax that he would otherwise pay on the additional dollar of wages is, in effect, "remitted" to the employer.

§ 104(a)(2), which specifically excludes "any damages received . . . on account of personal injuries or sickness", was for many years interpreted by the Commissioner to refer to damages for physical injuries only. Damages for nonphysical injury—defamation, malicious prosecution and, more recently, deprivation of civil rights under federal or state statutes—were thought to fall outside the scope of the statutory exclusion, so that whether such damages were to be treated as taxable depended on whether they did or did not constitute "gross income" as defined generally by § 61. Proceeding on that theory, the Service at an early date ruled that damages for nonphysical injury would not be regarded as income or gain under § 61 where such damages represented compensation for the destruction of irreplaceable personal rights—social standing in the community, for example—for which no "market" existed and whose value could not be measured or appraised in dollars. By contrast, damages for loss of professional earnings—resulting, for example, from a libelous credit report that impaired the taxpayer's business reputation—were fully includable, because "earnings", whether actual or in the form of a damage award, plainly did entail a measurable gain to the recipient. To be sure, § 104(a)(2) expressly excludes "any damages", obviously meaning damages for loss of earnings as well as personal suffering. As stated, however, the Service insisted that the broader statutory exclusion applied only to damages for physical injury and not to recoveries for nonphysical harms.

Beyond the purported distinction between physical and nonphysical injury, the Commissioner has taken the position that *punitive* damages are includable in income no matter what the nature of the taxpayer's injury. Since punitive damages are designed to punish the offender rather than to compensate the victim, they are not "received *on account of* . . . personal injury" within the meaning of § 104(a)(2). And as punitive damages obviously enrich the victim, there can be no doubt about the element of taxable gain under § 61 and the *Glenshaw Glass* decision.

In 1989, following a series of lower court cases largely unfavorable to the Commissioner,[20] Congress amended § 104 to provide specifically that the statutory exclusion shall not apply to punitive damages for *non*physical injuries. As the amendment says nothing about (i) punitive damages for physical injury or (ii) damages for loss of earnings due to nonphysical injury, the tax status of those two disputed items might still be thought to be in doubt. Apparently, however, the legislative intent was to overrule the Service positions on both (i) and (ii) and to confirm that the § 104(a)(2) exclusion *shall* apply to each. The result, as it seems, is that physical injury and nonphysical injury are now to be treated alike under § 104 *except* with respect to punitive damages, which are excluded by § 104(a)(2) if awarded in connection with physical injury but remain taxable under § 61 if awarded in connection with nonphysical injury. But why should even the latter distinction have been retained? The answer, presumably, is that Congress regarded physical injury, which (a) hurts and (b) nearly always involves some financial loss for the injured party, as more serious and pitiful than nonphysical injury. The victim of a nonphysical injury may have suffered loss of dignity but no financial loss whatever, and the award—perhaps a very large award—might consist almost entirely of punitive damages. A TV star who has been libeled by a lurid tabloid story is no doubt justified in seeking vindication and revenge, but there is clearly an enrichment if punitive damages are paid and little reason to exclude the receipt from gross income.

Damage recoveries obviously arise out of involuntary transactions—a forced taking rather than an intended realization—and, as stated, it is not surprising that the Code should supply relief to the victim in some form. The latter observation is partly borne out even in the case of damage to tangible property, such as buildings or equipment. If the taxpayer's recovery (usually insurance proceeds) for damage done to his property just equals his basis in the property, then of course no gain results. If the recovery exceeds the property's basis, however, the excess is taxable just as it would be if realized through sale. As compared with the destruction of personal rights, both the value and the cost of the property are easily ascertained and easily compared with the damages awarded, and hence the same rationale for exclusion is lacking. Still, the occasion for realization is imposed on the taxpayer, not chosen, and it seems unfair to require him to pay tax currently on the apprecia-

20. *Rickel v. Comm'r,* 900 F.2d 655 (3d Cir.1990); *Threlkeld v. Comm'r,* 87 T.C. 1294 (1986), *affirmed* 848 F.2d 81 (6th Cir.1988); *Roemer v. Comm'r,* 716 F.2d 693 (9th Cir.1983). Compare Sol. Op. 132, 1–1 C.B. 92 (1922). And see Cochran, *Confusion Over Personal Injury Damages,* 49 Tax Notes 1565 (1990).

tion of business assets which he did not intend to dispose of, particularly if the cash received as damages or insurance is promptly put back into new assets of equivalent function. Accordingly, if a taxpayer, within a specified time period, reinvests the proceeds of an "involuntary conversion" in business property of a similar character, Code § 1033 allows him to exclude the gain that would otherwise be recognized. As the intention is merely to *postpone* such recognition—rather than, as in the case of personal injury, to forgive the tax entirely—the section requires the taxpayer to carry over the basis of the old property to the newly acquired property, regardless of the latter's actual cash cost.

Ironically in view of this concern for forced realizations, the leading case in the field of commercial damage awards—*Raytheon Production Corp. v. Commissioner* [21]—is one in which the proceeds qualified neither for the common-law recovery-of-capital exclusion (or for exclusion under § 104, since a corporate taxpayer was involved) nor, apparently, for the postponement relief afforded by § 1033. The taxpayer, a manufacturer of radio tubes, had received an award of damages in an antitrust suit which arguably represented compensation for the destruction of business "goodwill," that is, profitable relations with potential customers. Even as so viewed, however, the award was held to be fully taxable. The common-law exclusion was evidently regarded as inapplicable to business as distinguished from personal goodwill. § 1033 would also apparently have been inapplicable (actually, the section had not yet been enacted) because no similar or like property could readily be acquired—apart, perhaps, from the purchase of another company in the same field of activity.

These results, which otherwise look rather stern, may perhaps be explained on the ground that the *costs* of generating the taxpayer's goodwill had already been deducted by it in earlier years. Such costs would have consisted chiefly of the company's annual outlays for advertising, public relations and sales promotion, as well as research and development. Assuming that those outlays were treated as currently deductible expenses, Raytheon in effect would already have offset the costs incurred in building up its goodwill against ordinary taxable business income. Its basis for the goodwill said to have been damaged therefore quite properly was zero, for if the costs of acquiring the asset had previously been deducted, a *double* benefit would result if the same costs were to be included in basis when the asset was sold or "converted." By contrast, outlays by individuals to acquire professional skills through education and

---

21.   144 F.2d 110 (1st Cir.1944).

training are generally disallowed as "personal." If this disallowance of training expenses helps to explain why the Code does not tax damages for loss of an individual's earning capacity, then the earlier deductibility of the advertising and related expenses may also serve to explain why the court in *Raytheon* reached the opposite result.

Perhaps the unavailability of § 1033 relief has a related justification. To be sure, the company would be required to take the entire antitrust recovery into current income without an apparent opportunity for deferral. But if it subsequently determined to reacquire the goodwill lost—as § 1033 assumes—this would be done, again, through advertising and sales promotion. Such expenses being deductible when incurred (see 6.02), one would expect that expenditures for restoration of the company's goodwill would offset income equal to the damage award within a relatively brief period of time. The overall effect would then differ little from the pattern of relief afforded by the section itself.

A loose end: Suppose an individual taxpayer, injured in an auto accident, accepts a transfer of Blackacre from the tortfeasor in lieu of cash damages. Blackacre has a value of $20,000 at the date of transfer, and is later sold by the taxpayer for $25,000. How much gain is taxed on the sale, *i.e.,* what is the taxpayer's basis for Blackacre? The taxpayer has invested no money of his own in the property; nor, by reason of § 104(a), was the property included in his gross income. His basis, nevertheless, presumably is $20,000 and only $5,000 is recognized as gain. The reason: § 104(a) is not a postponement but a forgiveness provision, and a zero basis would mean that the damage award of $20,000 would ultimately be taxed, contrary to the Code's intention. Congress might have limited the tax-relief for personal injury awards to deferral, as it did in the case of property damage under § 1033, by requiring the recipient of cash damages to purchase an annuity or the like. But in fact it went further and forgave the tax on personal injury awards entirely.

SECTION 3.　INCREASE IN NET WORTH— CANCELLATION OF INDEBTEDNESS

3.01　General Comment. Borrowing money does not create income to the borrower or loss to the lender since each party has the same net worth before and after the loan transaction. The lender exchanges cash for the borrower's promise to pay interest and principal at fixed dates, and the borrower receives cash but issues his "bond." When repayment of principal occurs at maturity—everything else being equal—the transaction is simply reversed, cash replaces obligation, and again there is no element of taxable income or allowable loss.[22]

The pattern is thus a simple one. Nevertheless, loan transactions have generated a number of interpretative problems—largely on the borrower's side—which have seemed important enough in some instances to merit review by the Supreme Court. A few of these are briefly detailed in the paragraphs immediately following. Yet another problem—cancellation of indebtedness income—is reserved for 3.02.

(a) Effect of inflation. In *Bowers v. Kerbaugh-Empire Co.,*[23] the taxpayer had borrowed money on its subsidiary's behalf which was repayable in German marks. When the time came to repay, the mark had declined in value so that the dollar-cost of paying off the loan was less than the dollar-value of the loan at the time the funds were borrowed. The government contended that the difference was taxable income. Although the Supreme Court held for the taxpayer on the ground that the subsidiary's unsuccessful business operations had actually produced an overall loss for its parent, the Court apparently accepted that a gain resulting from foreign currency inflation will generally qualify as "income" within the meaning of § 61.

The latter conclusion is, of course, exactly what one would expect—banks and others who speculate in foreign exchange, like speculators in any other kind of "security," are plainly taxable on their gains and can deduct their losses. Such gains and losses, however, reflect changes in the purchasing power of the dollar relative to the purchasing power of other currencies, and this enables us to ask more generally how gains and losses attributable to dollar inflation (or dollar deflation) are treated under the tax law. The question is especially relevant to debtors and creditors in a period of rapid inflation. Unless fully anticipated in the interest rate, debts repaid in inflated dollars may obviously entail a gain of some sort to the debtor and a corresponding loss to the creditor. Are such gains and losses normally reflected in income under § 61, that is, apart from dealings in foreign exchange?

---

22. Interest paid on the loan is of course includable in the lender's income and (subject to a variety of limitations; see 6.05) deductible by the borrower.

23. 271 U.S. 170 (1926).

To illustrate the inflation problem, suppose that D borrows $1,000 from C to be repaid one year later. D promptly invests the $1,000 in a tangible asset, say land. Assume that an inflation of 12% occurs during the ensuing 12-month period, so that at the time the loan matures the sum of $1,120 would be required to restore to C the same real purchasing power that he parted with when the loan was made. Assume also that owing to the inflation D's land has appreciated to a value of $1,120 by the same date, though of course the value of the property in real terms is entirely unchanged.

Suppose, as one alternative, that D elects to refinance his obligation at the end of the year by borrowing $1,000 from a second lender and using that sum to pay off his debt to C. Has D made a gain? The answer is clearly affirmative: his equity in the land, which was zero at the time the property was purchased, is now $120. But does he have taxable income? The reader's intuition, I would guess, is that he does not.

As a second alternative, suppose that instead of merely refinancing, D sells the property outright for $1,120 cash, pays C $1,000 in satisfaction of the debt, and retains the balance of $120 for himself. Once again, D has made $120. This time, however, the reader's probable intuition is that the gain will be includable in D's gross income.

In both cases, as it happens, the intuition is correct. Curiously, however, it is not D's economic income that is ever taxed in either case. D's real gain is traceable solely to the loan repayment: inflation enables D to repay $1,000 with dollars that are worth only $880 on an adjusted basis, the effect being exactly the same as if there had been no inflation but the face amount of C's claim had been scaled down to the lower figure. Yet that transaction, taken by itself, is tax-free as the refinancing example shows. By contrast, the taxable gain in the second example is traceable solely to the sale of the property for cash, although in real terms the property is worth no more when sold than when D purchased it a year earlier. We must conclude, then, that only the *number* of dollars counts for tax purposes, while the presence or absence of actual gain is disregarded. The loan-repayment in our example generates real income to D but no dollar increment; the property sale produces a dollar increment but no income in real terms; yet the latter is taxed and the former is not.

I am not suggesting that anything can easily be done to resolve this dilemma. The required adjustments, though not hard to conceptualize in our simple case, would entail considerable administrative difficulty if brought to bear on all transactions and on all taxpayers.[24] Still, the problem is a serious one: a tax mechanism which measures gains and losses in nominal dollars operates poorly during periods of sharp inflation, and the effect is especially visible in the case of borrowers, lenders and property-owners generally.

At the least, the example just discussed should serve as background for the issues considered in 3.02. As will be seen, discharge of indebtedness may indeed result in taxable income where the *number* of dollars paid to the creditor is actually fewer than the number borrowed. The borrower's gain—as in *Kerbaugh-Empire*— can then be measured conveniently as a dollar increment. Yet, as suggested, the much larger instance of debt-cancellation income— which occurs when loans are repaid in full, but with inflated dollars—escapes tax entirely, owing to the inability of the tax system to adjust for changes in the general price level.

(b) Discharge by third parties. The *Old Colony Trust* case [25]— also decided by the Supreme Court in the early days—presents a very different kind of question, but happily a simpler one. In *Old Colony,* the taxpayer, president of a major corporation, received a cash salary of nearly $1 million in 1918. His employer further agreed to pay all federal income taxes incurred by the taxpayer in order to ensure that the million-dollar salary would be the taxpayer's *net* compensation after tax. As a result the corporation paid federal income tax in 1919 of about $700,000 on the taxpayer's behalf. The question before the Court was whether the latter amount should be included in the taxpayer's gross income. Reasoning that the tax was paid by the employer in consideration of the services rendered to it by the taxpayer, the Court held that the $700,000 tax-payment represented "income" within the predecessor of § 61. Hence, though paid directly to the Treasury, the amount was taxable to the employee as if first received by him in cash.

The result in *Old Colony* is not surprising, at least not today. It is obvious that a taxpayer is enriched if his obligations—whether to the government or to private creditors—are discharged by a third party, and it is not even necessary at this late date to argue that the discharge is equivalent to a cash receipt. All that is needed to attract § 61 is enrichment and "realization." Both being present in the *Old Colony* case on almost any theory, the fact that the transaction took place in an employment context and was

---

24. See Note, *Inflation and the Federal Income Tax,* 82 Yale L.J. 716 (1973).

25. *Old Colony Trust Co. v. Comm'r,* 279 U.S. 716 (1929).

intended as additional compensation to the employee plainly justifies the taxable result.

Still, there is the teasing point that under the Court's holding
the government collected more in taxes than it would have collected
if the employee had paid the first layer of tax himself. In the latter
event the total tax would have been $700,000; as it turned out the
total tax was $700,000 *plus* the additional tax on that $700,000—
perhaps another $500,000—for an aggregate tax which exceeded
the employee's basic compensation of $1 million. So isn't the
Treasury getting too much? Shouldn't the tax-collector be content
with the basic $700,000, whether paid by the taxpayer personally or
by his employer?

One way of seeing why the government's position was correct
in *Old Colony* is to consider its relationship to Code §§ 164 and
275, which authorize the deduction of State income taxes in computing taxable income but specifically disallow any deduction for
federal income taxes. The Code in effect contemplates that federal
income taxes are to be paid out of the taxpayer's *after-tax* income.
To illustrate, suppose that an individual earns $1,000 in Year 1 on
which a tax of 40%, or $400, is due and payable on April 15 of Year
2. Suppose the taxpayer's earnings in Year 2 are $1,500 out of
which he pays the prior year's tax of $400. Since federal income
tax is not a deductible expense, his taxable income for Year 2 is
unaffected by the tax payment and is equal to his full earnings of
$1,500. His tax for Year 2, at the same 40% rate, is therefore $600,
as compared with only $440 (.40 x ($1,500 − $400)) if Year 1's
income tax were allowed as a deduction.

May the taxpayer in my example avoid the higher tax result by
accepting a salary of only $1,100 in Year 2 and arranging for his
employer to pay the prior year's income tax directly to the government? If so, the deduction rule (in § 164) and the exclusion rule
(inferred from § 61) would be inconsistent with one another. To
be sure, such inconsistency can be found in other areas of the tax
law—*e.g.,* the exclusion of imputed income from personal residences
but the non-deductibility of apartment rents. Here, however, the
consequence would be to render all federal income taxes deductible
by employees through the medium of readily arranged direct-
payment schemes. This would be especially attractive for higher
bracket taxpayers, and the disallowance feature of §§ 164 and 275
would then effectively be repealed. As Congress could hardly have
intended that result, the Court's decision, reasonable in any event,
merely spared Congress the task of amending § 61 so as to expressly include in gross income federal income taxes paid on behalf of
employees.

The point just made—that the payment (or reimbursement) of non-deductible federal income taxes is taxable to an employee—can also be seen at work (backhandedly, to be sure) in *Clark v. Commissioner*,[26] a venerable Board of Tax Appeals decision. In *Clark*, the taxpayer had retained "experienced tax counsel" to prepare his and his wife's federal income tax returns for the year 1932. Apparently having misunderstood the operation of certain Code provisions, counsel prepared and filed a joint return for the spouses, whereas separate returns for husband and wife would have legitimately saved the taxpayer some $20,000 in taxes. Acknowledging his error, counsel in 1934 reimbursed the taxpayer for the taxes he needn't have paid. The Board, rejecting the Commissioner's effort to apply *Old Colony*, held that the reimbursement was not includable in the taxpayer's gross income, because "It was, in fact, compensation for a loss which impaired petitioner's capital."

The *Clark* case was rightly decided, I think, and right also in stressing the taxpayer's loss of "capital." Just because federal income taxes are *not* deductible and *do* have to be paid out of after-tax income, the recovery of taxes improperly assessed should not result in additional taxable income. Thus, an ordinary refund by the Treasury of taxes that have been over-withheld from an employee's paycheck is obviously not income to the employee. *Clark* didn't involve a refund as such—his tax liability was properly determined once the taxpayer had mistakenly been led to file a joint return—but the circumstances seem close enough to justify equivalent treatment.

Suppose the tax payment in *Old Colony* and the reimbursement in *Clark* had been of State rather than federal income taxes. Since State income taxes *are* deductible for federal income tax purposes (7.01), the results in both cases would presumably be flipped. There would be little point in insisting on inclusion in *Old Colony*, because State income taxes, being deductible, are paid out of pre-tax income anyway; in *Clark*, by contrast, assuming the taxpayer had realized a tax benefit by deducting his State taxes in 1932, the subsequent reimbursement would properly be (and of course it is) includable in income for the later period.

(c) When is a loan? Since "loans" are not currently taxable to the borrower, it may be important in a given case to decide whether a purported loan deserves that characterization or really should be treated as something else. Suppose, for example, that the sole shareholder and chief executive of a small corporation "borrows" a substantial sum of money from the company. The loan is repre-

---

26. 40 B.T.A. 333 (1939).

sented by a demand note, but as the company is entirely controlled by the borrower, any demand for repayment is obviously within his sole discretion. Is the "loan" a loan, or is it in reality a taxable dividend? At bottom, the problem arises because the law accepts the notion that stockholders and their wholly-owned corporations can actually engage in arm's length dealings with one another— sales of property, salary for services, loans, etc.—even though it is evident that the two parties are really a unit and are not at all at arm's length. Having indulged the fiction, however, it becomes necessary to take it seriously and insist that the arm's-length standard be observed. In consequence, there is a continuing and burdensome duty to scrutinize transactions between stockholders and corporations in order to determine whether the self-serving characterization adopted by the taxpayers should be respected or rejected. In many instances the Code itself takes a hand (see § 302, for example). But in others (including the loan-dividend issue) the matter is left to be thrashed out through tedious argument between taxpayer and revenue agent on the occasion of the annual audit. As a matter of practice, if the amount borrowed is large relative to the stockholder's individual resources, and if the loan remains outstanding for an extended period of time, the Service is likely to insist that it is really a dividend and includable in the recipient's income. To avoid this consequence stockholders will usually pay such loans down from time to time—perhaps through short-term bank borrowing at the year-end—or will try to keep the total "debt" within limits which they believe will be viewed as reasonable.

On another front, what about "loans" which only become loans as a consequence of subsequent events? In *U.S. v. Lewis*,[27] the taxpayer received a commission from his employer in Year 1. In Year 3 it was found that the commission had been erroneously computed and the taxpayer was obliged to repay a portion of it to the employer. Was the Year 1 receipt "income," or could the taxpayer insist that it was really a loan in view of what took place in Year 3? Finding that the commission had initially been received by the taxpayer under a "claim of right," the Supreme Court held the entire amount includable in Year 1 and refused to permit a retroactive adjustment despite the repayment. While the repayment was presumably deductible as a business expense in Year 3, it is possible that the taxpayer's marginal tax rate was lower at that time than in the earlier year, so that the deduction failed to make him entirely whole. On the other hand, one obviously cannot allow a taxpayer to exclude salary, commissions, etc., merely because his

27.　340 U.S. 590 (1951).

right to retain the item is disputed and may someday be denied. The solution, quite obviously, lies not in narrowing the income definition, but in modifying the annual accounting concept under which each year's financial events are treated as discrete. As indicated at 10.02, the Code has moved substantially in the latter direction since *Lewis* was decided, so that the potential harshness of the outcome is now considerably abated.

As a final example of the problems in this area, what about robbers? If money is embezzled, extorted, or stolen at the point of a gun, does the criminal have taxable income within the meaning of § 61? Or can it be argued that as the "taxpayer" has a legal obligation to repay his victim in the event that he is apprehended, the initial taking should be treated as a mere loan? Having considered the matter on no less than two prior occasions, the Supreme Court finally concluded in *James v. U.S.* [28] that a plausible distinction could be drawn between theft and legitimate borrowing and held that stolen money was fully taxable in the year obtained. In lieu of discussion, the reader may pursue an ample literature on this engaging if slightly idiotic topic.[29]

(d) Mortgages. Yet another range of issues affecting borrowers (on which the Court has also spoken) concerns the treatment of mortgage indebtedness. If a taxpayer purchases real estate in part with borrowed funds, issuing a mortgage as security for the loan, does his basis for the property include the borrowed money or only the cash that he draws from his own resources? If he borrows against appreciated property but without personal liability for the debt, is the borrowing merely a loan or is it a realization and hence a taxable gain? These and related questions, which truly are of wide importance, are considered in Part E, below.

3.02　Cancellation of Indebtedness. The Supreme Court has held that the retirement of outstanding indebtedness at less than its face amount results in taxable income to the debtor. Congress specifically confirmed that outcome in § 61(a)(12), which states that "gross income means ... Income from discharge of indebtedness." As shown below, however, Congress also evidently considered the general rule to be too severe in some cases and in § 108 supplied relief provisions to cushion its impact.

In *U.S. v. Kirby Lumber Co.,*[30] the taxpayer-corporation in 1923 issued more than $12 million of its own bonds in exchange for

---

28. 366 U.S. 213 (1961). The earlier cases are *Rutkin v. U.S.,* 343 U.S. 130 (1952), and *Comm'r v. Wilcox,* 327 U.S. 404 (1946).

29. See *e.g.,* Bittker, *Taxing Income from Unlawful Activities,* 25 Case W.Res.L.Rev. 130 (1974).

30. 284 U.S. 1 (1931).

property equal to their par value. Later in the same year, the bonds having obviously declined in the market, the taxpayer repurchased $1,100,000 par value of the bonds for $138,000 less than par. The Supreme Court sustained the government in treating the latter amount as taxable income. "As a result of its dealings," said Justice Holmes, "[the taxpayer] made available $138,000 [of] assets previously offset by the obligation of bonds now extinct." Accordingly, there was a realized "accession to income, if we take words in their plain popular meaning . . . ."

Although the facts in *Kirby* are not fully developed, it seems reasonable to assume that the company was able to repurchase its bonds at a discount because of a general rise in the market rate of interest. The Court stated specifically (though without supporting data) that "there was no shrinkage of assets" at the company level. Evidently, the Court (a) perceived that there had been an addition to the taxpayer's balance sheet Net Worth as a result of trading cash for bonds of greater face amount, and (b) believed that the taxpayer's "available" assets had increased in an equal measure. In the Court's view, the act of issuing bonds at one date and buying them in at a discount when the rise in interest rates had driven down their value belonged to the category of canny investment—on the "short" side of the market, so to speak. The resulting gain was taxable like any other profit derived from speculative activity.

The decision in *Kirby* is certainly correct, but the rationale— that additional assets thereby became "available" to the taxpayer— is a trifle obscure. Could the taxpayer have avoided inclusion by showing that its net worth had been reduced by losses or by a decline in the value of other property? By and large, § 61 is not subject to a "balance-sheet improvement" test: a worker's wages are includable in *gross* income even if for separate reasons his year-end net worth has shrunk. Such shrinkage may (or may not) be taken into account in determining his final "taxable income" figure, but a finding of "gross income" normally depends on the *particular* transaction at issue, not on the taxpayer's overall financial condition. Should the *Kirby* situation be regarded differently?

Perhaps a better or at least a broader way to approach the entire subject of debt-cancellation is to remind oneself that borrowed funds are not includable in the borrower's income to start with. If a taxpayer borrows $1 million and issues its bond to the lender in the same principal amount, the cash received is not regarded as income because the bond is viewed as offsetting the cash-receipt. Yet despite the exclusion of the borrowed funds from income, the expenditure of those funds by a borrower who is a business taxpayer results in a business expense deduction or an increase in the basis of the taxpayer's depreciable assets. If the funds are used to pay wages or to purchase inventory, the borrowed funds will be deductible currently because such outlays are treated as current business expenses. If the funds are used to buy machinery, the deductions will take the form of annual depreciation allowances over the life of the equipment. In either event, the expenditure of the borrowed funds will sooner or later produce a tax benefit, while the borrowing itself is tax-free.

Of course, the Treasury normally is made whole when the loan is repaid. The repayment of the bond principal is *not* deductible and therefore has to be made out of after-tax income—the prior exclusion is balanced by a later *non*-deduction, so to speak. In effect, the taxpayer is allowed both (a) to exclude the amount borrowed, and (b) to deduct the outlay of the borrowed funds. This, however, assumes that he will (c) subsequently repay the amount borrowed out of his income after tax.

If, as matters turn out, the taxpayer is *not* obliged to repay the full amount of his loan—not do (c), in effect—then, to prevent an undercounting of his taxable income, he should be asked to give up an equivalent portion of the benefit that resulted from combining the exclusion and deduction under (a) and (b). He can't have it all *three* ways. Having somehow contrived to reduce his repayment obligation, he must now either go back and include a portion of the borrowed funds in income (give up (a)), or else accept a disallowance of his prior tax benefits (give up (b)). It doesn't much matter which of these two earlier events is constructively reversed, provided that the debt-cancellation is seen to require a reversal of one or the other.

While it might, therefore, be more accurate to tax a portion of the earlier borrowing or to disallow a portion of the prior deductions, the Court in *Kirby* lacked a statutory basis for making any such refined adjustments. It did the next best thing, however, by requiring the cancelled debt to be included in current income. But in emphasizing the factor of increased net worth the Court rested its decision on a narrower ground than seems appropriate.

While there may have been no shrinkage of assets in *Kirby*, in later cases, especially those arising during the 1930's, debt-cancellation was very commonly a consequence of the debtor's financial weakness and in effect represented a kind of voluntary, or *de facto*, composition with creditors. In these cases, the fall in value of the taxpayer's outstanding indebtedness stemmed not from a general rise in interest rates, but from a decline in the taxpayer's own credit-worthiness, which led investors to attach a higher degree of risk to its securities than when those securities were originally issued. If the taxpayer then took steps to reduce the danger of default by repurchasing its debt at a discount, should the "saving" be treated as a taxable gain? The Supreme Court supplied an affirmative answer in *Commissioner v. Jacobson*.[31] By repurchasing his bonds at a discount, said the Court, the taxpayer, though in straitened financial condition, improved his net worth by the difference between the face amount of the bonds and the price he paid for them. The taxpayer's gains were comparable (the Court thought) to those he would have realized had he bought a third party's bonds at a discount and later resold them at face value.

Technically defensible, the outcome in *Jacobson* is nevertheless somewhat unappetizing, and it is understandable that Congress should have responded to the plight of debtors in these circumstances by enacting § 108, which, as amended, provides that debt-cancellation income shall be excluded from a taxpayer's gross income if the taxpayer is insolvent or the debt discharge occurs in a formal bankruptcy proceeding. As a corollary, the taxpayer must reduce certain "favorable" tax attributes—chiefly net-operating loss carryforwards (see 10.01)—in the same amount so as to prevent a double benefit.[32]

It may be worthwhile, finally, to note that prior to the 1986 Act relief under § 108 was made available not only to debtors in distress (like the taxpayer in *Jacobson*), but also to *Kirby*-type taxpayers who might be in perfectly healthy condition and simply benefiting from a general rise in market rates of interest. While perhaps not very significant in earlier times, the latter phenomenon took on large proportions in the early 1980's, a period in which interest rates went sharply up and, as a corollary, bond prices went sharply down. Offered an opportunity to improve their balance sheets, many publicly-held companies reacted by repurchasing their own outstanding debt at market prices well below face value, in that way generating debt-cancellation income in large amounts. Such income was reported as such to shareholders and for accounting purposes, but for tax purposes it would usually be excluded under § 108.

---

31. 336 U.S. 28 (1949).

32. Reacting to the current slump in real estate values, the 1993 Act added § 108(c), which extends the exclusion to the cancellation of mortgage debt on business real estate, provided that an election is made under § 1017 to reduce the basis of such (or similar depreciable) property in the same amount. Since deductible depreciation will be lower, taxable income in future years will be increased. The effect, therefore, is to postpone or defer the excluded income to later periods.

Presumably feeling that statutory relief was inappropriate in these circumstances, Congress in 1986 amended § 108 so as to confine exclusion to debtors that are insolvent or in formal bankruptcy. As a result, solvent debtors—again, typically, public companies that repurchase their outstanding bonds at a discount—are now required to recognize debt-cancellation income currently, that is, in the year the cancelling transaction takes place.

A loose end: The discussion above is in terms of a business taxpayer—a corporation, say—which in most cases would have acquired depreciable property with the funds it had borrowed and, as stated, would be entitled to an annual deduction for depreciation. At the risk of some confusion, I should add that precisely the same rationale supports the inclusion of debt-cancellation income where the borrowing is personal and the borrowed funds are expended on non-deductible consumption. Unlike business expenses, consumption expenditures are supposed to be made out of *after*-tax income. Since the borrowing itself is not taxed, however, the related consumption is actually being purchased out of *pre*-tax resources. Once again, the apparent tax benefit disappears when the consumer's loan is repaid, provided that the repayment is in full. But if a portion of the debt is cancelled for some reason, then to that extent, in retrospect at least, the earlier borrowing should be included in income.

The relationship between personal consumption and debt cancellation was fairly dramatically tested in the *Zarin* case,[33] which involved the settlement of a very large gambling debt between the taxpayer, a compulsive craps-shooter, and an all too accommodating Atlantic City casino. Using chips supplied to him on credit by the casino, and playing day and night, the taxpayer rolled up a debt of nearly $3.5 million (having previously lost and paid $2.5 million out of his own pocket). The casino finally demanded payment and, when the taxpayer failed to pay (actually, he issued checks that bounced), brought suit in State court. The taxpayer's defense was that the debt was legally unenforceable because the casino had been found by the New Jersey Casino Control Commission to have violated State law limitations on the permissible extension of credit to any single patron. Ultimately, the parties settled the matter for a payment by the taxpayer of $500,000. Ever alert, the Commissioner (of Internal Revenue) thereupon asserted that the taxpayer

33. *Zarin v. Comm'r,* 916 F.2d 110 (3d Cir.1990).

had realized, and must include, cancellation of indebtedness income in the amount of $3 million.

A closely divided Tax Court held for the Commissioner chiefly on the ground that the chips supplied on credit represented a true loan, one that the taxpayer expected to repay and would have had to repay if he had won at the crap-table instead of losing. Settling the debt for less than face amount produced taxable income, therefore, under § 61(a)(12). Symmetry or consistency required such a result, the court thought, even though the casino's claim might in fact be unenforceable. If it were otherwise—that is, if unenforceability meant that there had really been no debt at all—then the receipt of the chips should have been treated as income in the first instance, since plainly the casino did not intend to make the taxpayer a gift. The taxpayer obviously regarded himself as a borrower throughout, however, so that his failure to repay the debt in full must have a taxable consequence.

The dissenters (in one way or another) simply would not or could not accept the proposition that a man who has lost $3.5 million gambling somehow winds up with $3 million of taxable income because the "house" agrees to settle for $500,000. In the words of one dissenter, "the concept that the petitioner received his money's worth from the enjoyment of using the chips (thus equating the pleasure of gambling with increase in wealth) produces the incongruous result that the more a gambler loses, the greater his pleasure and the larger the increase in his wealth." Yet another dissenter indignantly observed that the majority decision was "tantamount to taxing the petitioner on his losses."

On appeal, the Third Circuit reversed (2–1), holding, among other things, that the element of unenforceability created doubt about the *amount* of the taxpayer's liability to the casino as well as the fact of liability itself. In effect, the dispute about liability necessarily subsumed a dispute about just how much the taxpayer owed, the casino claiming $3.5 million and the taxpayer holding out for $0. The $500,000 settlement meant that the parties had resolved their disagreement through the customary process of give-and-take, but it did not mean that the taxpayer had *acknowledged* a debt of $3.5 million and then obtained the cancellation of a part. Until the parties settled their dispute by accepting the $500,000 figure, there was no agreed-upon indebtedness to be cancelled.

Only a grouch would object to the outcome in *Zarin,* and perhaps one way to rationalize the decision would be to make the convenient surmise that the taxpayer never really expected the casino to demand the full face amount of the borrowed chips unless he came out winners. The settlement could be taken as an indication that the casino itself anticipated that there would be some renegotiation of losses beyond a certain point, with the lawsuit merely being a way of opposing the taxpayer's effort to get away scot-free. What is affecting about the taxpayer's position, of course, is the fact that his debt was the product of a rather pitiable mental state, which the casino did not hesitate to exploit. On the other hand, the law obviously cannot assess consumption benefits on an individual basis or depart from the general rule that benefit is measured by market price. Thus, while most unaddicted people would agree that the consumption benefits realized by an addict are negative if viewed objectively, presumably a "sick gambler" exception to the *Kirby Lumber* rule would be unworkable as an administrative matter. In the end, therefore, it might be simplest if the Service read the *Zarin* decision to mean that the settlement of *any* sizeable gambling debt implies or presumes a prior informal understanding between the parties. As evidenced by the settlement itself, the implied understanding is that large players who are also heavy losers may ultimately be entitled to a volume discount.

SECTION 4. GIFTS AND BEQUESTS

Code § 102(a) excludes gifts and bequests from the gross income of the donee or heir. Presumably such benefits could be reached under the broad approach to "income" taken by the Supreme Court in the *Glenshaw Glass* case, and one could even imagine a *de minimis* exemption for birthday gifts and the like that would help to make sense of the matter administratively. But as things now stand it is only the capital transfer levies—the federal gift and estate taxes—that are applicable to "donated estates." In effect, gross income does not include intra-family divisions of wealth, whether during the donor's life or at his death.

Three kinds of structural or interpretative issues remain. First: what should be done about a gift of property which has appreciated or declined in value relative to the donor's cost? Who bears the tax on the appreciation, and who deducts the loss? Second: how should we handle gifts of divided interests in the same property, that is, gifts in trust with income to A and remainder to B? Third: what about "gifts" that take place in a commercial setting? What class of recipients is the exclusion really designed to protect?

4.01 Gains and Losses—Realization by Whom? Gifts or bequests of *cash* present a single straightforward issue, to-wit, shall the gift or bequest be included in the income of the donee or heir?

As indicated, § 102(a) excludes the receipt and in effect permits family wealth to be transferred from older to younger, or richer to poorer, or dead to living, without the imposition of an income tax on the grateful recipient. But suppose the gift or bequest is "in kind"—say shares of stock. And suppose the property has appreciated in the transferor's hands so that its value at the time of the transfer is above the transferor's original cost. Should the transferor (donor or decedent) be taxed on the transfer as if it were a sale? Or should the previously unrealized appreciation remain unrealized until the shares are actually sold for cash, and then be taxed to the transferee (the donee or heir)? Not one but *two* candidates for taxability emerge on the scene. Since presumably it would be improper to tax both transferor and transferee on the same element of property appreciation, and perhaps equally improper to tax neither, the obvious task is to choose between them. Although the stock appreciation "accrued" while the shares were held by the transferor, the sale-for-cash, when made, will be effected by the transferee. Which of these events should be regarded as the vital link to taxability?

The pattern of gift and bequest—older-to-younger, richer-to-poorer—plainly suggests that transferors on the whole may be subject to higher marginal tax rates than transferees. In making the choice referred to above, therefore, the impact of the progressive rate structure is fully implicated. If gifts and bequests can be used to shift unrealized gains from higher to lower bracket individuals within the family, then taxpayers who own appreciated property can minimize the effect of the progressive rates at their own discretion. *Inter vivos* gifts, in particular, would become a major element in family tax-planning. If gifts and bequests are treated as "realizations," on the other hand, their value is obviously reduced from the standpoint of personal tax-saving. To be sure, owners of appreciated property can still decide for themselves whether to retain their property or to sell it for cash and incur a tax, but the further discretion to determine *who* should be taxed on the appreciation would be denied.

For reasons that will become apparent, the Code treatment of capital transfers in kind can best be understood if gifts are discussed separately from bequests. And as respects gifts, it will also help to talk separately about transfers of appreciated, and transfers of depreciated, property. As usual, my explanation is by example. I should add that the theme briefly sounded in this subsection— that of income-shifting among family members—attains symphonic proportions in Part C, below.

(a) *Lifetime gifts.* Code § 1015(a) provides that for the purpose of determining *gain* on the sale of property acquired by gift, the donee's basis is the same as the basis of the property in the hands of the donor. For the purpose of determining *loss* (other than in the case of a donee-spouse), the donee's basis is the donor's basis or the market value of the property at the date of the gift, whichever is lower. The reason for establishing different basis rules to measure gains and losses will appear when we consider gifts of property whose value has *declined* in the donor's hands. But for the moment, confining ourselves to gifts of *appreciated* property, it is apparent that the main effect of § 1015(a) is to carry over the donor's basis to the donee. § 1015(a) thus makes the donee responsible for any appreciation in value that took place while the property was held by the donor, as well as any further change in value between the date of gift and the date of final sale.

Adapting the illustration used by the Supreme Court in *Taft v. Bowers,*[34] assume that the donor's original cost for certain shares of stock was $1,000. Assume further that the shares were worth $2,000 at the date of gift; and that the donee finally sells the shares for (i) $5,000, or (ii) $1,750, or (iii) $600. As the donee's basis under § 1015(a) is the same as the donor's—$1,000—the respective outcomes are: (i) gain of $4,000, (ii) gain of $750, and (iii) loss of $400 [35]—the gain or loss in each case being taxable or allowable to the donee. The donee steps into the donor's shoes for the purpose of computing gains and losses, and all the results are the same in dollar amount as if the donor had retained the shares and sold them for his own account.

In *Taft v. Bowers,* the taxpayer, a donee of appreciated property, argued that § 1015(a) should be struck down as unconstitutional on the ground that it ultimately required donees to treat gifts as taxable income by limiting their basis to the donor's cost. While the Court sustained the provision as "appropriate to a general scheme of lawful taxation," the taxpayer's description of the *consequence* of § 1015(a) was nevertheless perfectly correct. The section does in fact restrict the scope of the gift exclusion by denying the donee a basis for the property equal to its value at the date the gift is received. § 102(a) thus *permanently* excludes from the donee's income no more than the original cost of the property. The pre-gift appreciation factor—from $1,000 to $2,000 in the above example—

---

34. 278 U.S. 470 (1929).

35. In case (iii), the entire decline in value occurred after the date of gift. Since the value of the shares at the date

of gift exceeded the donor's basis, that basis ($1,000) is still carried over to the donee.

is merely deferred, and is ultimately taxed to the donee if the property retains its value.

But despite this analysis, the decision in *Taft v. Bowers* must be regarded as favorable to taxpayers of wealth. Had the case gone the other way—had the donee succeeded in establishing her constitutional right to a basis of $2,000—the government would obviously have had to press the courts or the Congress to adopt a concept of "realization by gift." The Treasury could not have tolerated for long a system in which property appreciation was periodically obliterated for tax purposes through back-and-forth transfers among family members. Its response to an adverse decision in the *Taft* case, therefore, would have had to be an insistence that the donor himself be regarded as the "taxable person," and that gifts of appreciated property be treated as equivalent to sales for cash. In effect, the issue in *Taft v. Bowers* was not whether to tax pre-gift appreciation at all, but whether to tax it to donors or donees—Congress, with the Court's approval, opting for the latter.

As suggested, the choice of the donee as the "taxable person" particularly benefits families with substantial property, if we assume that donors (parents) are generally in higher tax brackets than donees (children, trusts, etc.). In addition, of course, no tax is payable until the property is finally sold. Put another way, the effect of § 1015(a) and the *Taft* decision is really to permit taxpayers to decide for themselves just *who* shall be the recipient of taxable income in the light of their own tax situations. If the donee's tax rate is lower than the donor's, the property can be transferred in kind and then sold by the donee at a lower tax cost than the donor would incur. If the donor's tax rate is lower than the donee's, the property can be sold in advance of the gift and the cash proceeds transferred net of tax. Taxpayers are free to adopt whichever procedure will minimize the impact of the rate structure on family income, and in that sense can decree their own tax obligations.

Can a donor also give away his *losses* if that seems advantageous? Suppose the donor owns property with a basis higher than its current value and the donee is a well-paid executive whose tax bracket exceeds the donor's or who happens to have realized exceptionally large gains in a particular year. At this point the Code becomes exceedingly moralistic, not to say draconic, in its effort to prevent taxes from being minimized. As indicated, § 1015(a) provides that for purposes of calculating loss on the sale of property acquired by gift, the donee's basis is the *lower* of cost or market at the date the gift is made. Suppose that the donor's original cost for certain stock was $2,000 but the stock was worth only $1,000 at the date of gift. For purposes of computing *loss* on subsequent sale, the donee would have to use the lower market value of $1,000. Assuming the donee finally sells the stock for (i) $750, (ii) $1,500, or (iii) $2,250, his recognized gain or loss is as follows:

Sale Price	Basis under § 1015	Recognized Gain or (Loss)
$750	$1,000	($250)
$1,500	$1,000/$2,000	–0–
$2,250	$2,000	$250

In case (i) the donee's allowable loss is limited to $250 because his basis is the market value of the stock at date of gift, $1,000. In case (ii) the basis for determining loss is irrelevant because the stock went up after the gift, while the basis for determining gain, $2,000, still exceeds the sale price of $1,500. In case (iii) the basis for determining loss is again irrelevant, but the sale price of $2,250 exceeds the gain basis by $250.

Cases (i) and (ii) show that built-in losses (in contrast to built-in gains) *cannot* be shifted from donor to donee. The donee simply cannot take advantage, by way of loss recognition, of any decline in value which occurred prior to the gift. Just *why* the Code should be tougher on losses than on gains is not completely obvious, however, since the tax-saving on a dollar of gain which is shifted from a high- to a low-bracket taxpayer is precisely the same as that to be had on a dollar of loss shifted in the opposite direction.

What happens to the unrecognized losses in cases (i) and (ii), *i.e.*, $1,000 and $500 respectively? Answer: they are never allowed to *anyone*—a curious result, to be sure, but one which few taxpayers are likely to experience in view of the ready salability of most kinds of property. Where the property consists of marketable securities, for example, the donor obviously is free to sell it and give away the cash proceeds, thus realizing his loss in advance of the gift and avoiding the penalty of a permanent disallowance.

As indicated at 5.04, the lower-of-cost-or-market rule was eliminated by the 1984 Act where the donee is (or was) the donor's spouse. In the latter case, the donee's basis is now the same as the donor's for purposes of calculating gain and loss alike.

(b) Bequests. The treatment of bequests differs from the treatment of gifts in one major (some would say horrendous) respect. Although there is no realization of gain or loss by a decedent, under § 1014 the basis of all property acquired by inheritance becomes its fair market value at the date of the decedent's death. Thus, appreciation and depreciation in value are both wiped out by death,

and the decedent's heirs are obliged to recognize only those changes in property value that take place subsequently. If an investor buys property for $1,000 for example, and the property is worth $1,500 at his death, the investor's heirs will take it over at a stepped-up basis of $1,500 and the $500 of appreciation will be eliminated for tax purposes. By obvious contrast, under § 1015 a lifetime gift of the same property would leave the donees with a basis of $1,000 and hence with $500 of potentially taxable gain. While property that has declined in value takes a stepped-*down* basis at death, it may be assumed that older people will often act to realize their potential losses at least to the extent of currently realized gains, so that the penalty feature of § 1014 is no doubt far less painful in aggregate than the bonus feature is pleasuresome.

Apart from the obvious benefit conferred by § 1014 on families of wealth, it can also be observed that § 1014 extends and magnifies an existing inequality between taxpayers who are otherwise similarly situated. If taxpayer A earns, say, $100,000 a year in cash salary, while taxpayer B "earns" $100,000 in unrealized stock appreciation, A will pay a current tax of some $26,000 while B will pay nothing. The advantage to B of tax-postponement is very considerable, as has been shown, but one tends to accept it as an unavoidable consequence of the realization requirement (see 5.01). If, however, tax-postponement is turned into absolute forgiveness—which is the effect of a step-up in basis under § 1014—the discrimination between A and B becomes too great to be justified solely on grounds of administrative convenience. Nor does the imposition of an estate tax on B's estate explain the disparity in treatment. A's estate is also subject to the estate tax, and A has paid an income tax as well.

No convincing rationale for the death-basis rule has ever been offered, I believe, and in 1976, after decades of intermittent urging by the Treasury, Congress actually abolished § 1014 (prospectively) and substituted for it a version of the carry-over-basis rule that applies to lifetime gifts. Such legislative boldness astonished cynics who had thought the death-basis rule immutable, but in the end the new provision proved to be short-lived—indeed, unborn. Criticized for technical defects, the effective date of the carryover-basis rule was postponed for three years almost immediately after its enactment. In 1980 it was withdrawn entirely and old § 1014 put back in force.

4.02 Divided Interests—Gifts in Trust. Assume that an individual dies owning corporate securities with a basis and value of $100,000. Under the decedent's will, the securities are to be held by a bank as trustee for the benefit of the decedent's wife and son.

The wife is to get the "income" from the securities, estimated to be $8,000 a year, for life. At her death the trust is to terminate and the corpus—the securities or whatever other property the trustee then holds—is to be transferred to the son absolutely. The wife's age is 60 at the date of the decedent's death and she has a life-expectancy of 15 years; the son's age doesn't matter for our purposes.

How does § 102(a) apply in these circumstances? If the decedent had left his securities outright to a single individual—say the son—the legatee would obviously be entitled to exclude no more than the value of the securities—$100,000—as a "bequest or inheritance." Income *from* the property in the form of dividends or interest would of course be taxable to the son as owner of the securities, just as it was taxable to the decedent during his lifetime. The exclusion for gifts and bequests applies to the value of the securities at the time of their receipt, but not to the income which they subsequently generate.

Is the outcome any different if the beneficial interest in the property is divided between two individuals, as in the example above? In *Irwin v. Gavit* [36], the Supreme Court held, in effect, that § 102(a) applies to the corpus of a trust only. The taxpayer had been left an income interest in a testamentary trust for a period of 15 years, with remainder to his daughter. Arguing that the income which he received annually from the trust was "property" acquired by bequest, the taxpayer sought to exclude such amounts from his gross income under the literal language of § 102(a). The Supreme Court held for the government. Stressing what Justice Holmes regarded as the commonly understood distinction between principal and income, the Court held that the annual payments were fully includable in the taxpayer's income. The Code provision excluding gifts and bequests, said Holmes, "assumes the gift of a corpus and contrasts it with the income arising from it, but was not intended to exempt income properly so-called . . . ." Two dissenting Justices, evidently out of touch with common understanding, argued that since the taxpayer's interest in the trust was in fact a "gift by will—a bequest," the payments received by him literally qualified for the exclusion.

Although somewhat oracular, the *Gavit* opinion is plainly correct in its main conclusion. If both corpus *and* income were exempt from tax under § 102(a), the exclusion for gifts and bequests would be greater when divided interests were created than when the entire property was given to one person. Using our

36.　268 U.S. 161 (1925).

example again, a victory for the taxpayer in *Gavit* might have meant that not only the $100,000 of securities ultimately received by the son, but also the $8,000 of annual income paid to the wife, would qualify for exclusion. Assuming the wife lived out her 15-year expectancy, the total amount excluded would then be $220,-000—$100,000 principal plus $120,000 (15 × $8,000) of income—a result which Congress could not possibly have intended unless it meant to encourage all testators and donors to create split interests in their property. The holding in *Gavit,* now codified in § 102(b)(2), makes it clear that only the principal of a gift or bequest is excludable from the income of the donee or heir.

There is, however, another feature to the *Gavit* decision—one that deserves the reader's careful attention. In holding that trust income cannot be excluded by a life-tenant or other income beneficiary, the Court in effect decided not merely how much should be taxed, but *to whom.* The dissenting Justices, after all, were literally correct when they pointed out that the income-beneficiary, as well the remainderman, had received an "inheritance" from the decedent; that there were two heirs under the decedent's will, not merely one. Conceding, as the majority in *Gavit* held, that the income of the trust was not exempt under § 102(a), why should it necessarily follow that all such income must be taxed to one of the decedent's heirs and none to the other? Why not treat the income as divided in some way between the life tenant and the remainderman? And correspondingly, why not allow each to get some benefit from the § 102 exclusion? *Gavit* implies that the exclusion goes to the remainderman alone (perhaps because in common understanding it is he who owns the corpus), while the life-tenant gets all the taxable income. This conclusion, however, is at least debatable and, as will be seen, the "system" thus approved is not the only one that can be conceived of.

The point can be made clear, I hope, by returning to our example. Again, assume two beneficial interests in the trust property, life-estate and remainder. The life-tenant's interest is a "wasting asset"; it terminates at the wife's death, which is expected as a statistical matter to occur in 15 years—though, of course, it may occur sooner than that or later. We can place a present value on the life tenancy by discounting the expected 15 annual payments of $8,000 at, say, 8%. The amount so determined—about $68,-000—represents the wife's "share" of the total bequest at the time the trust is created. As there is no more than $100,000 of property in total, the present value of the remainder interest is necessarily worth the balance of $32,000. With each year that passes the present value of the life estate decreases, because one less payment can be expected before the widow's statistical life expectancy is reached. For the same reason the present worth of the remainder goes up; the remainderman is one year closer to obtaining full possession of the entire property.

These actuarial verities suggest that instead of taxing all the trust income to the life-tenant, as required by *Gavit,* we could, in the alternative, treat the life-tenant as if she owned an *annuity.* Her "investment" would be equal to the present value of the life-estate at the decedent's death—that is, $68,000—and this amount would be recovered ratably over the period of her life-expectancy. Indeed, had the decedent simply left his wife the $68,000 in cash, she could presumably have purchased an $8,000 life annuity for that very sum. With a 15-year life-expectancy, she would then anticipate payments totalling $120,000 (15 × $8,000). Under the formula applicable to annuities (see 2.02), she would treat 68/120ths of each annual payment—$4,533—as recovery of capital, and the balance, $3,467, as taxable income. The total cost-recovery over the period of her life expectancy would, of course, equal $68,000, the present value of the life estate at the commencement of the trust.

What about the remainderman under this approach? As noted, the decline in the value of the life estate which results from the passage of time is necessarily mirrored by a growth in the value of the remainder interest. In fact, assuming that the value of the trust principal remains constant, the value of the remainder will increase from $32,000 to $100,000 over the 15-year period. Using the same straight-line method as was allowed to the life tenant, the remainderman would therefore be required to report annual income of $4,533, the yearly increase in the value of the remainder. Since he would receive no actual cash distribution, however, the remainderman would be entitled to add the amount taxed to the basis of his remainder interest, so that if the life tenant were to die at the end of 15 years, the remainderman's basis for the corpus received on termination of the trust would be $100,000.

In effect, under the above approach, the remainderman is treated as if he had purchased a 15-year endowment policy for $32,000 cash. It might, indeed, be argued that as the interest-accumulation on an endowment contract issued by an insurance company is not taxed until the policy matures (see 2.03, above), the same element of deferral should be allowed when the policy is "issued" by a private individual, that is, the decedent. If this view were accepted, the average remainderman would still be taxed on an aggregate income of $68,000, but not until the termination of the trust.

The "system" just described divides the exclusion afforded by § 102(a) *between* the life-tenant ($68,000) and the remainderman ($32,000). By contrast, the *Gavit* decision (as the Treasury Regs. indicate [37]) allocates the entire exclusion to the remainderman as if he alone were the recipient of the "bequest." Thus, the life tenant is annually taxed on the full $8,000 of trust "income"—no portion of her annual distribution is excludable as recovery of basis.[38] The remainderman, on the other hand, is taxed on *nothing* during the term of the trust. Although the remainder interest grows in value from year to year, that growth is excluded from the remainderman's income under § 102(a). When the trust terminates, the remainderman's basis for the trust property, which he then receives from the trustee, will be the same as the trustee's basis for the property—$100,000 in our example. In effect, the son's basis for his remainder interest goes up from $32,000 to $100,000 over the term of the trust, until, on termination, that basis equals the basis of the property in the hands of the trustee. This adjustment assures that the remainderman will get the full benefit of the gift exclusion just as if the property had been left to him outright instead of being placed in trust. Thus, if the son sells the property for cash after the trust has terminated, he will recognize no gain on such sale unless the property has appreciated in value since the date of the decedent's death. Once again, the effect of all this is to tax the trust income to the life-tenant alone, and to allocate the entire exclusion to the remainderman.

In summary, if the trust lasts exactly 15 years, the overall taxable income, overall excludable gift, and basis on termination under each of the two "systems" would be as follows:

	Gavit System		"Annuity" System	
	Income beneficiary	Remainderman	Income beneficiary	Remainderman
Total taxable income	$120,000	–0–	$52,000	$ 68,000
Total excludable gift	–0–	$100,000	68,000	32,000
Basis on termination		100,000		100,000

The choice between these two approaches to the taxation of divided interests thus essentially is a question of who shall bear the tax on current trust income. The annuity system (rather like the dissent in *Gavit* itself) stresses the fact that there are two bequests involved, and in effect allocates the exclusion, and hence the income, between them. The *Gavit* approach in a sense disregards the two-bequest factor, allocating the entire exclusion to the remainderman and all the income to the life tenant.

37. Regs. § 1.1014–5.   **38.** Code § 273.

On the side of the *Gavit* approach—which otherwise seems slightly inferior on theoretical grounds—is a considerable element of practicality and convenience. The life tenant does, after all, receive the annual cash flows of the trust, and everything else being equal, one can argue that tax-payment obligations ought to be associated with cash inflows if no serious distortion results. It is true that the imposition of tax does not generally depend upon the receipt of cash by taxpayers; but where two candidates for taxation appear, one of whom receives cash while the other receives implicit income only, the choice problem is probably best resolved by taxing the former and excusing the latter. The so-called annuity system, moreover, requires the imputation of a suitable discount rate. This can be done fairly confidently in the case of a fixed-income security like a bond, but where the trust property consists of stock, real estate or other assets whose expected yield is uncertain, the selection of a discount rate often would be difficult and controversial.

At all events, the taxing system adopted in *Gavit* is the foundation for a much more elaborate superstructure of rules governing the taxation of trusts and trust beneficiaries.[39] Apart from a very brief mention in Section 9, below, those rules, which are exceedingly technical, are omitted from this volume. At bottom, however, their purpose, like the Court's in *Gavit,* is chiefly to determine who gets the gift (or bequest) exclusion, and who is stuck with the taxable income, when more than one or even two plausible candidates are in the running and available for either role.

Problems relating to divided interests in the same property are a recurring nuisance in the tax law, as will be seen at many points. The *Gavit* discussion, as well as some of the remarks made at 2.01 in connection with the taxation of dividends, should help to introduce certain mechanical elements—chiefly discounting and compounding—which are common to all.

4.03 Commercial Gifts. The term "gift" is not defined in § 102(a). While the context—"gift, bequest, devise or inheritance"—strongly suggests that the exclusion is aimed at intrafamily transfers of wealth, I suppose one must concede that generosity is not solely a function of family relationship, and that one may have friends, household servants, employees, even business associates, towards whom one feels a generous impulse now and then. In any event, motives are sometimes mixed. An employer may feel both a business and a personal obligation to a retiring employee, and a gift of the traditional gold watch, along with the employer's check for $10,000, may partly be explained in business

---

39. Code § 641 *et seq.*

terms but partly also as an expression of personal affection. Must the employee treat the check (putting to one side the miserable watch) as a taxable bonus, or can it be excluded from income under § 102(a)? What standards or guidelines should the law apply in distinguishing "gifts" from compensation?

The Supreme Court has indicated that the term "gift" in § 102(a) is largely to be defined by reference to the motives of the payor.[40] If the payment, though voluntary, is "in return for services rendered," or proceeds from "the constraining force of any moral or legal duty," or anticipates a "benefit" to the payor, then it is taxable to the payee even if characterized as a "gift" by the payor. On the other hand, if the payment proceeds from a "detached and disinterested generosity," if it is made "out of affection, respect ... or like impulses," then it is an excludable gift even though the relationship between payor and payee has previously been in a business context. Apparently feeling that further efforts at formal definition would be useless, the Court in the *Duberstein* case [41] stated that "primary weight in this area must be given to the conclusions of the trier of fact," that is, the trial judge or the jury, whose task is evidently to determine in each case, mainly on the basis of the parties' self-serving testimony, whether the payor acted out of affection and respect or constraint and obligation. The government's effort to promote specific rules aimed at distinguishing transfers of property made for "personal" reasons from those made for "business" reasons was rejected as overly mechanical. Instead, the Court held that each case must be approached individually and that in ascertaining the payor's motives resort should be had to the "fact-finding tribunal's experience with the mainsprings of human conduct."

Presumably, the Court realized that it was inviting a wide variety of results among the decided cases in the field of commercial gifts; in any event, the cases generally show a lack of coherence. Thus, although the "retiring employee" cases have usually been found to involve taxable income, triers of fact have sometimes been led to regard what surely looks like severance pay as an excludable gift. In the *Stanton* case [42] for example, the taxpayer, president of the real-estate investment subsidiary of Trinity Church in New York, was awarded a "gratuity" of $20,000 on his resignation after many years of service. It was explained by a church official that

40. See, *e.g., Robertson v. U.S.,* 343 U.S. 711 (1952); *Bogardus v. Comm'r,* 302 U.S. 34 (1937).

41. *Comm'r v. Duberstein,* 363 U.S. 278 (1960).

42. *Stanton v. U.S.,* 186 F.Supp. 393 (E.D.N.Y.1960).

the taxpayer "had a pleasing personality ... did a splendid piece of work ... was liked by all the members of the Vestry personally." Finding nothing but "good will, esteem and kindliness" in the minds of the Vestrymen, the trial court held the payment to be excludable from income under the Supreme Court's motivation test.

The "gifts-to-widows" cases show even greater diversity. A corporation, typically closely-held, makes payments to the widow of a deceased executive, usually by continuing the decedent's salary for a year or two.[43] In some instances the decedent, and through him his widow or estate, is actually the company's controlling stockholder. Emphasizing the absence of legal obligation to the widow or economic benefit to the corporation, some courts have held the payments to be exempt; others, stressing the value of the decedent's prior services to the company, have found the payments to be taxable income. No systematic basis can be suggested for distinguishing the tax winners in these cases from the tax losers. In the end, it is simply a matter of divergent perceptions about "the mainsprings of human conduct" on the part of the triers of fact.

Must there be such diversity of result? Or could a standard be proposed which would lead to a larger measure of uniformity among the cases? If no such standard exists, because motivation (even under the government's personal-or-business test) inevitably depends on the fact-finder's subjective impression of the parties' sincerity, could we at least find ways of limiting the occasions for controversy and dispute? To be sure, the Supreme Court's emphasis on the fact-finder's role pretty well assures that the Court itself will never again review the question of how "gift" should be defined for income tax purposes. But is there also some means of reducing the burden on the trial courts and administrators who meet the problem on a day-to-day basis?

Code § 274(b), added in 1962, has undoubtedly accomplished a good deal in this direction by imposing tax symmetry on the payee and the payor (other than employees and employers; see below). The section prohibits the deduction of gifts to individuals (in excess of $25), and thus makes clear—as the decided cases had not previously done—that payments treated as exempt gifts to payees cannot also be deducted as business expenses by payors.[44] If the payor wishes to support the payee's "gift" characterization, he (or

43. *E.g., Poyner v. Comm'r,* 301 F.2d 287 (4th Cir.1962).

44. Compare *Carter's Estate v. Comm'r,* 453 F.2d 61 (2d Cir.1971), holding a payment to an employee's widow excludable under § 102(a), with *Bank of Palm Beach & Trust Co. v. U.S.,* 476 F.2d 1343 (Ct.Cl.1973), allowing the employer to deduct the same payment as a "business" gift. The cases arose prior to § 274(b).

it) will have to forgo a deduction for the amount paid, and in effect make the payment out of after-tax income. Thus, Congress is content if at least one party pays the tax, whether it is the payee (through inclusion) or the payor (through disallowance). Although payor and payee still can adopt contrary characterizations of the same item, the contradiction between the payor's stated motive in making the payment and the payee's attempt to label it a gift should render the payee's position untenable in most (and perhaps all) such instances.

In the 1986 Act Congress decided to go beyond tax symmetry and to deny the "gift" characterization entirely in the case of employee-payees. Accordingly, § 102(c) now provides that no exclusion shall be allowed for amounts paid by an employer to an employee (other than gifts regarded as *de minimis* under § 132, *e.g.*, the retiree's gold watch, and certain limited safety and length-of-service awards). Of the cases mentioned above, *Stanton* would appear to be most clearly affected by the newer provision. The taxpayer having been an employee of the payor, the $20,000 cash "gratuity" paid to him on his resignation would no longer qualify for exclusion even though the employer's motives were found to be wholly generous and disinterested. Payments to employees are simply placed outside the "gift" category as far as the payee is concerned, nondeductibility by the payor being irrelevant.

In a sense, § 102(c) confirms or supports the result reached by the Supreme Court in the *Old Colony* case, discussed at 3.01. There the employer's effort (unsuccessful) was to compensate a valued executive *net* of the executive's income tax by paying that tax directly. A similar effort was made in *Stanton* (successfully as it turned out) by characterizing the retirement bonus as a "gift." In ruling out the latter characterization, § 102(c) in effect bars employers from assuming their employees' tax burdens by forgoing otherwise allowable deductions. In *Stanton,* of course, the employer, a church, was presumably exempt from tax, so that a forgone deduction would have cost it nothing in any case.

SECTION 5. THE REALIZATION REQUIREMENT— MACOMBER, BRUUN, AND THE DIVORCE CASES

5.01 General Comment. The realization requirement has such a varied application in the income tax field that it cannot be summarized or canvassed in a single section and is best taught on the pervasive method. Still, some sort of general introduction should be attempted, and this is done here, as it is in many of the casebooks, by briefly examining certain of the acknowledged classics in the field, namely, *Eisner v. Macomber, Helvering v. Bruun,* and the *Davis* and *Farid-Es-Sultaneh* cases. Another group of realization problems, largely associated with real estate transactions, appears in Part E.

It is important to remind oneself at the outset that realization is strictly an administrative rule and not a constitutional, much less an economic, requirement of "income." Early cases, like *Macomber,* do give support to the idea that the Constitution limits "income" to realized gains, but at present most tax commentators would be likely to feel that the Congressional taxing power is not seriously restricted by such an implied requirement, and that Congress is free to treat gains and losses as "realized" pretty much whenever it chooses. As was suggested at 4.01(b), Congress could surely tax property appreciation at gift or at death if it desired to do so, and while a gift or bequest can be regarded as a realization event through semantic manipulation, it is difficult to suppose at this late date that the constitutionality of taxing such appreciation would depend on whether gifts and bequests could be forced into the mold of "realization."

Assuming, moreover, that "income" refers to the annual increase in one's disposable wealth, then, from an economic standpoint, a stockowner whose unsold shares have appreciated in value by $1,000 over the course of a year has just as much "income" as a stockowner who receives $1,000 in dividends or a speculator who sells his shares and realizes $1,000 of trading profits. The latter two, of course, are taxed currently, while the former, owing to the realization requirement, is permitted to treat his gain as exempt from tax until he disposes of his appreciated shares. Yet the increase in disposable wealth is identical for each, though reflected in cash in the latter cases and in kind in the former. To be sure, stock that has gone up one year may go down the next and finally be sold for no more than the original purchase price. But the same is true for the trader who sells his stock at year-end and reinvests the gain in other shares which subsequently decline, or of the dividend-recipient whose company sustains an operating loss in the period following. We may indeed wish to do something about fluctuating income through the adoption of an averaging device of some sort (see 10.01); but the possibility that income will fluctuate from year to year, or that gains *may* be succeeded by losses, can hardly be taken to show that the taxpayer has not been enriched when the value of his property appreciates. "If all business ventures were initiated and completed within the fiscal period, the realization criterion would lead to no serious confusion. But, in a world where ventures often have neither beginning nor end within the lives of interested parties, it is hard to argue that one may grow richer indefinitely without increasing one's income." [45]

Yet all this argumentation should not be taken to mean that an overall change in the realization requirement is contemplated or even desirable. Our tax system does not reach mere changes in property value, and apart from recurring proposals to treat gifts and bequests as realization events, few commentators would suggest that the realization requirement should be materially altered. The difficulty of making annual property appraisals may be the chief reason for this attitude of acceptance; the absence of ready cash to pay the tax on property appreciation and the consequent "forced liquidation" of assets to meet tax obligations is another. To be sure, neither reason is especially compelling where readily marketable property (*e.g.*, listed securities) is concerned; nor, as has been seen, does the law shrink from taxing compensation even when received in kind. Still, the justifications for a realization requirement seem reasonably strong to most observers, and as stated, no overall change is imminent. My main purpose here, in any case, is not to question realization as a policy matter; rather, my object is to stress that because the realization requirement exists, the income tax is a tax on *transactions* instead of being a tax on income in the economic sense. Dividends, interest and rents, gains on sales of property, salaries, wages and fees—all these are taxable because they occur through the medium of an "exchange." Property appreciation, though undoubtedly an enrichment to the property owner, is exempt from tax precisely because the transactional aspect is thought to be lacking.

The materials that follow should help to illustrate the scope of the realization requirement. They should also confirm (as the reader perhaps already suspects) that its application in close cases is fairly arbitrary. In that respect, as in others, realization bears a resemblance to the problem of cost-recovery considered in Section 2. Once again, what is chiefly at stake from the taxpayer's standpoint is the anticipation or deferral of tax payments—that is, the timing of taxable income. An investor who sells appreciated property for cash pays a tax on the appreciation currently and can reinvest only the after-tax proceeds. An investor who retains his

---

45. Simons, *op. cit.* note 12, p. 82. For discussion (extensive), see Shaviro, *An Efficiency Analysis of Realization and Recognition Rules under the Federal Income Tax*, 48 Tax L.Rev. 1 (1992); Strnad, *Periodicity and Accretion Taxation: Norms and Implementation*, 99 Yale L.J. 1817 (1990); Fellows, *A Comprehensive Attack on Tax Deferral*, 88 Mich.L.Rev. 722 (1990); Shakow, *Taxation Without Realization: A Proposal for Accrual Taxation*, 134 U.Pa.L.Rev. 1111 (1986).

appreciated property—or who can somehow dispose of it without triggering off a "realization"—pays no tax and therefore has more available for reinvestment. Although unrealized appreciation may be taxed in the future if the property is sold, the postponement can be of considerable value to the property-owner, as has been seen, and it is often worth his while to litigate when the application of the realization rule is in doubt.

5.02 Stock Dividends. In *Eisner v. Macomber*,[46] the Supreme Court was required to decide whether a common stock dividend could constitutionally be taxed as "income" to the shareholder-recipients. The taxpayer owned 2,200 shares of Standard Oil common stock. Standard Oil declared a 50% stock dividend and the taxpayer received 1,100 additional shares of which about $20,-000 in par value represented earnings accumulated by the company since the effective date of the original income tax law. The statute then applicable expressly included stock dividends in income, in effect taxing such dividends in much the same way as dividends in cash. In a lengthy opinion by Justice Pitney—matched by an interminable dissent from Justice Brandeis—the Supreme Court held that stock dividends could not be treated as income within the meaning of the 16th Amendment:

> "We are clear that not only does a stock dividend really take nothing from the property of the corporation and add nothing to that of the shareholder, but that the antecedent accumulation of profits evidenced thereby, while indicating that the shareholder is the richer because of an increase of his capital, at the same time shows he has not realized or received any income in the transaction."

The Brandeis dissent—based more on concepts of corporate finance than taxation—argued in effect that a stock dividend is really a two-step affair consisting of (i) a cash distribution, followed by (ii) a purchase of additional shares through the exercise of stock subscription rights. Looked at in that way, stock dividends are actually the equivalent of cash dividends and are therefore properly taxable.

Congress responded to the *Macomber* decision by amending the statute to exempt stock dividends from tax, and the same exemption (with exceptions not relevant for us) appears in § 305(a) of the present Code.

The constitutional and definitional issues raised by *Eisner v. Macomber* have been discussed in many places and need not be

---

46. 252 U.S. 189 (1920).

rehearsed again here.[47] From our standpoint it may be more useful to focus instead on the relationship between the holding in *Macomber* and the overall treatment of corporations and shareholders under the Internal Revenue Code. In effect, *Macomber* held that the tax law applies differently depending on whether a dividend is received in stock or in cash. Is this distinction a sound one, given the structural design of the Code in this area, or does it create an inconsistency which ought to be regretted? Viewed apart from the Constitution, and viewed also as if Congress had never legislated on the subject of stock dividends but had left the matter entirely to common law development, which of the two positions taken in *Macomber*, Pitney's or Brandeis', seems best to accord with the acknowledged elements of the taxing scheme? In short, is the outcome good or bad, wise or foolish?

A description of the tax treatment of corporations and shareholders should begin with Code § 11, which imposes a separate tax on corporate earnings at what amounts to a 35% rate for larger companies. Taxable income is determined for corporations in pretty much the same way as it is for individuals, but the separate 35% corporate income tax applies without regard to whether the individual shareholders who "own" the company would pay tax at higher or lower rates if the corporate income were charged to them directly. The corporate tax is imposed on corporations as entities; it does not purport to be a proxy or substitute for the tax that would otherwise be payable by the individual security-owners.

This distinction between a corporation and its owners is reflected in the fact that a second-level tax is imposed on the corporation's shareholders when corporate earnings are distributed as dividends. The dividend (if in cash) is includable in the shareholder's gross income in full—it is "ordinary" income in the customary phrase—and is taxable at whatever marginal rate happens to apply to the individual recipient. But although taxable to the shareholder, the dividend distribution is *not* deductible by the corporation. Dividends are not regarded as business expenses and cannot be deducted in computing corporate taxable income. As a result, corporate income is taxed *once* at the entity level when received by the company itself; when (or if) the company's after-tax earnings are distributed to the shareholders as dividends, a *second* tax is imposed on the individual recipients at their personal marginal rates.

Of course most corporations do not distribute all of their after-tax earnings as dividends—indeed, closely-held corporations usually

47. See, *e.g.*, Magill, *Taxable Income* (1945) p. 31.

distribute none. Typically, a corporation will retain some (often the greater part) of its annual earnings to finance the replacement or expansion of its plant and equipment, to pay for research and development, or to make new investments. Everything else being equal, the amount retained by the company and reinvested in productive assets will be reflected directly in the value of the company's shares. Undistributed earnings are obviously not lost to the shareholders; rather, they show up as unrealized stock appreciation which in some measure reflects the increase in tangible and other assets held by the firm. From a tax standpoint, however, the important point is that retained earnings are not taxed to the shareholders *until* they are actually distributed as dividends. No "constructive" dividend is imputed to the shareholders; the only tax imposed is at the corporate level as long as earnings are kept back by the corporation for use in its business. To be sure, unrealized stock appreciation will ultimately be converted into taxable gain when the stock is sold for cash. But, as noted, that event may be deferred for many years—perhaps for a lifetime—and in the meanwhile a shareholder whose stock appreciates from year to year enjoys an increase in his personal wealth without increasing his income subject to tax.

Prior to the Tax Reform Act of 1986, gain realized on the sale of appreciated stock—whenever that should occur—qualified for a further tax preference of major importance. If the stock sold had been held for more than 6 months and thus represented "long-term capital gain," 60% of such gain was deducted from the shareholder's gross income and only 40% was taxable. Accordingly, while dividends, like other "ordinary" income items, were taxed at regular rates, the tax on retained corporate earnings realized by the shareholder, indirectly, through a sale of his stock was pegged at a bargain level. In 1986, Congress acted to sharply reduce the tax rates applicable to ordinary income. As a corollary, it repealed the 60% long-term capital gain deduction. Dividend income and gains from the sale of securities were thus (and for the first time in many decades) placed on a parity as far as rates were concerned, both being fully includable in the shareholder's gross income and both taxed at a maximum marginal rate of 28%. In 1993, however, concerned about the federal budget deficit, Congress increased the marginal rates on higher levels of ordinary income (to nearly 40% at the very top), yet at the same time insisted on maintaining the capital gain rate at the same level (28%) that had been established in 1986. The effect of the latter move was to recreate a significant rate differential that once again favors capital gains over ordinary income.

At this point we need not concern ourselves with the rationale for the capital gain preference, with the reasons for its repeal and reinstatement, or with the current debate about its future role in our tax system. All that needs to be emphasized here is the contrast—with us in any event because of the realization requirement—between the tax treatment of corporate earnings distributed as dividends and undistributed corporate earnings reflected in increased share value.

The difference in the tax treatment of distributed and undistributed corporate earnings creates an urgent need to draw a clear dividing line between dividends and retentions. Investors, as well as the Treasury, have an interest in clarity at this point since individual investment choices will be guided in part by the tax consequences of the distribution policies which particular corporations adopt and make known to the public. Many investors prefer large annual dividends and a regular flow of cash despite the tax disadvantage; others prefer the opposite pattern. What is important, obviously, is that the investor have some idea in advance of just what sort of tax-and-distribution package he is buying.

Unfortunately, the dividing line between dividends and non-dividends cannot be drawn in the same way as the line between income and non-income: that is, one cannot say that dividends entail gain or enrichment while non-dividends do not. A shareholder who owns stock worth $110 *prior* to the payment of a $10 dividend is no richer *after* the dividend is paid when the stock (ex-dividend) drops to $100. The investor's personal net worth remains $110, whether represented by stock alone or stock plus cash. In *Macomber,* Justice Pitney stressed that the stock dividend added nothing to the interests of the shareholders, that the shareholders were no richer after the additional shares had been received than they were before. He was, of course, correct. The trouble is that exactly the same observation can be made about cash dividends—they, too, leave the shareholder no richer after than before. Essentially, therefore, the question in *Macomber* was not whether the shareholder had gain in an economic sense, but whether in legal or accounting terms the stock dividend was to be regarded as a taxable event.

Stripped of its Constitutional element, the issue in *Eisner v. Macomber* in the end comes down to a "battle of similarities." Is a stock dividend (as the majority held) "more like" a situation in which a corporation simply accumulates its earnings and makes no distribution at all? Or is it (as Brandeis thought) "more like" the receipt of a cash dividend which is followed by a reinvestment of the cash received in additional shares? So limited, it seems apparent that Pitney had the better of the debate. Overall, the aim of the tax law is to impose a tax on "dividends" when assets representing corporate earnings are transferred to the shareholders. Stock dividends, however, merely give the shareholders additional pieces of paper to represent the same equitable interest; they do not transfer assets or create new priorities among the security-holders. The total value of the common shares, though now spread out over a larger number of units, is left unchanged from its previous level. In effect, nothing of substance has occurred. Justice Brandeis' effort to construct, or read in, a cash distribution was strained and unconvincing. The plain fact is that Mrs. Macomber did not receive, and could not have obtained, a cash payment from Standard Oil. Had she wished to substitute cash in an amount equivalent to the value of the stock dividend, she would have had to sell the dividend shares to other investors. No other cash source was made available. The Brandeis analysis would have had more force if Standard Oil had announced itself willing to pay a dividend in stock *or* cash at the shareholder's election, or if shareholders had been given an option to redeem their dividend shares (that is, to cash them in) immediately after the distribution. But no such option or election was afforded. In purely mechanical terms, therefore, the Brandeis view was unpersuasive. The majority was right: a stock dividend more closely resembles a simple accumulation of earnings than it does a cash dividend or even an optional dividend of cash-or-stock.

Having thus awarded the palm to Justice Pitney, one may still confess to some slight uneasiness about the outcome. Logically or not, many shareholders do tend to regard small-scale stock dividends—in the range of 5% to 10%—as the equivalent of periodic income, especially if the company follows a practice of declaring such dividends annually. Often, the dividend shares are sold off (or given away to grandchildren) with a feeling that the shareholder's basic "round-lot" investment still remains intact. If this is done on an annual basis, the shareholder in effect secures a relatively steady cash flow which is not so very different from a regular cash dividend. To be sure, the similarity is partly an illusion: the sale of the dividend shares reduces the shareholder's percentage interest in the corporation in exactly the same way as would the sale of a small amount of his original stockholding. But the annual sale of a little stock from a larger holding is regarded as an expenditure of capital, and it involves complications. The sale of dividend shares which are described as representing the current year's earnings is likely to be viewed quite differently.

Considerations of the latter sort notwithstanding, Code § 305 adopts the *Macomber* decision by excluding common stock dividends from the shareholder's gross income. § 307 provides as a corollary that the shareholder's basis for the dividend shares is a proportionate part of the cost of the original lot. To illustrate, suppose A owns 100 shares of General Motors at a cost of $49.50 a share, or $4,950. GM now declares a 10% stock dividend and distributes 10 additional shares to A, which he promptly sells on the market for $50 a share, or $500. Under § 307, A's basis for his GM stock becomes $45 a share ($4,950/110). The 10 dividend shares thus take a basis of $450, and when sold for $500, a capital gain of $50 results. By contrast, if the Brandeis view of stock dividends had prevailed, the shareholder would presumably have $500 of ordinary income on receipt of the dividend shares. The dividend would be taxed in full rather than being offset by a portion of the shareholder's original cost; it would be taxed on receipt rather than when sold; and it would be taxed at ordinary rather than capital gain rates. Given this set of consequences, stock dividends, like smallpox, would by now have become a thing of the past.

A loose end: In *Macomber,* Justice Pitney observed that common stock dividends "take nothing from the property of the corporation ..." His point, presumably, was that the absence of significant effect at the shareholder level is mirrored by a like absence of effect at the corporate level. To illustrate this element, assume that X Corporation has the following balance sheet *prior* to the declaration of any dividend:

Assets		Liabilities and Net Worth	
Cash	$ 3,000,000	Common stock (1,000,000 shares at $10 par)	$10,000,000
Other current assets	7,000,000		
Fixed assets	10,000,000	Retained earnings	10,000,000
	$20,000,000		$20,000,000

Assume that at the year-end X Corporation declares, and promptly pays, (i) a dividend of $1,000,000 in *cash;* or (ii) a dividend of $1,000,000 face amount of its own newly issued *bonds;* or (iii) a 5% common *stock* dividend with a value of $1,000,000. Its balance sheet after each alternative form of distribution would look like this:

(i) Cash Dividend

Assets		Liabilities and Net Worth	
Cash	$ 2,000,000	Common stock (1,000,000 shares at $10 par)	$10,000,000
Other current assets	7,000,000		
Fixed assets	10,000,000	Retained earnings	9,000,000
	$19,000,000		$19,000,000

(ii) Bond Dividend

Assets		Liabilities and Net Worth	
Cash	$ 3,000,000	Bonds	$ 1,000,000
Other current assets	7,000,000	Common stock (1,000,000 shares at $10 par)	10,000,000
Fixed assets	10,000,000	Retained earnings	9,000,000
	$20,000,000		$20,000,000

(iii) Stock Dividend

Assets		Liabilities and Net Worth	
Cash	$ 3,000,000	Common stock (1,050,000 shares at $10 par)	$10,500,000
Other current assets	7,000,000	Capital surplus	500,000
Fixed assets	10,000,000	Retained earnings	9,000,000
	$20,000,000		$20,000,000

The cash dividend produces a contraction *both* in total assets and in Net Worth—and in any case is known to be taxable. The bond dividend is more difficult to categorize; indeed it, rather than the stock dividend, is really the hard case. Total assets are unchanged, but Net Worth is reduced through a shift of $1,000,000 of Retained Earnings to the Bond account. The shareholders still hold nothing more than "pieces of paper," however, and it seems well arguable that without a severance or disinvestment of corporate assets the distribution should be viewed as non-taxable. On the other hand, the shareholders are now elevated to a creditor status to the extent of $1,000,000. The bond-capital is insulated, to a degree, from the ups and downs of the operating business; the bonds represent a right to withdraw corporate assets on maturity; and interest payments are deductible by the corporation (dividends are not). While the correct treatment is by no means self-evident as an original matter and *Macomber* could certainly be cited in support of a tax-free outcome, the Supreme Court in *Bazley v. Commissioner* [48] held that bond distributions are taxable to the stockholders in the amount of their fair market value at the distribution date. Hence bonds and cash are treated alike for this purpose, with the result that bond dividends are now extremely rare.

48. 331 U.S. 737 (1947).

Coming finally to the stock dividend alternative, it appears that the only balance sheet changes are an increase in the number of shares outstanding and an obligatory transfer from the Retained Earnings account to the Capital Surplus and Common Stock accounts to reflect the value of the newly issued shares. No reduction in the corporation's total assets occurs, because no assets have been distributed. Even more important in view of *Bazley,* there is no contraction of corporate Net Worth, which includes the Common Stock as well as the Capital and Retained Earnings accounts. Whereas the cash or the bond dividend reduces the overall value of the common stock by $1,000,000, the stock dividend leaves the total value of the common shares unchanged and, as stated, merely spreads that value over a larger number of shares. To be sure, the increase in number of shares outstanding is a change of some sort, yet the alteration is of a nominal character when regarded in objective, economic terms.

5.03 Leasehold Termination—Helvering v. Bruun. *Helvering v. Bruun,*[49] another old-timer in the realization field, furnishes a brisk little exercise in tax mechanics. Reducing the main elements to a hypothetical, suppose a taxpayer purchases a tract of land for $800,000 and promptly leases it to a manufacturing concern for 20 years. The lease calls for annual rental payments which are relatively low by market standards, but it also requires that the lessee promptly construct a factory-building on the land at a cost of not less than $1,000,000. The building is to become the property of the lessor on termination of the lease and thus apparently constitutes a form of rent-in-kind. Assume that the new building (which is immediately put up by the lessee and costs exactly $1 million) has a useful life of 30 years—10 years longer than the lease itself—and is expected to have a depreciated value of $200,000 at the time the lease expires.

Conceding that the annual cash rentals are income to the lessor, what about the value of the leasehold improvement, which is to vest in the lessor absolutely at the end of 20 years? Does the factory-building represent an "accession" to the taxpayer's wealth? If it does, is it "clearly realized?" And if it is, just when does such realization occur?

An inspection of the *Bruun* opinion indicates that no less than *four* possible answers can be given to these questions. The first three all assume that the factory building is taxable as additional "rent" to the lessor at some point, but they diverge as to the proper *time* of inclusion. In effect, these three alternatives reflect the

---

49. 309 U.S. 461 (1940).

various positions which the Treasury took prior to the *Bruun* decision in an effort to develop a "rule" that would satisfy the courts. The fourth alternative—that argued unsuccessfully by the taxpayer in *Bruun*—apparently assumes that the factory building is not to be viewed as rent (or at least as *realized* rent) at *any* point during the term of the leasehold. In summary, the alternatives are:

#1. *Prepaid rent.* Treat the anticipated value of the factory as includable rent in the year in which the building is erected—Year 1—but discount that anticipated value for the 20-year duration of the lease. If the building is expected to be worth $200,000 at the end of 20 years, the present discounted value of that figure, using an 8% discount rate, is about $50,000. Since this $50,000 of additional rent would be treated as realized in Year 1, perhaps the "transaction" would be regarded as closed at that point and nothing further would be realized when the lease came to an end. The lessor's basis for the building on termination of the lease would then be $50,000—equal to the amount previously included—and his depreciation allowance for the remaining 10 years of the building's useful life would be $5,000 a year, computed on the straight-line method.

#2. *Prorated rent.* Treat the anticipated value of the factory as rent, but instead of including the discounted value in Year 1, spread the full $200,000 over the term of the lease. Thus the lessor would realize and be taxed on $10,000 a year throughout the 20-year term. On expiration of the lease the taxpayer's basis for the building would be $200,000, and his deductible depreciation for the next 10 years would be $20,000 annually.

#3. *Postpaid rent.* Treat the factory as taxable rent, but include nothing until Year 20 when the lease expires and the building becomes the property of the lessor. Assuming actual value equals anticipated value at that date, the effect would be to tax $200,000 on termination of the lease. As with alternative #2, the lessor's basis for the building then would become $200,000, and his subsequent depreciation allowance would be $20,000 a year.

#4. *No rent at all.* Treat the building as unrealized property appreciation and do not tax its value as "rent" at any time. With nothing included in income, the lessor's basis for the building on termination of the lease would obviously be zero, and he would get no depreciation allowance during the 10-year period that followed.

Alternatives #1 and #2—the prepaid and prorated rent alternatives—both require a prediction as to what the value of the factory-building will be 20 years into the future. But prediction is inherently difficult. Being a tangible asset, the building may or may not be worth $200,000 when the lease expires, and any current estimates of future value are likely to vary over a fairly wide range. While this does not mean that an appraisal is impossible (long-lived assets are bought and sold every day), it does suggest that the risks of making an incorrect prediction are considerable. As already observed (see, *e.g.,* the easement example at 2.01), where uncertainty about valuation exists, the tax law often finds *deferral* to be a convenient and expedient way of coping with the problem. It is not surprising, therefore, that the Treasury's earliest Regulations in this area supported alternative #3, the postpaid rent alternative. Those Regulations held that the value of leasehold improvements was income to the lessor, but only on termination of the lease, that is, in Year 20 in the above illustration. Since termination was the event that caused the realization, "value" for this purpose meant the actual, rather than the expected, value of the improvements at the end of the lease. If, for example, the factory-building were worth as much as $300,000 when the lease expired, the taxpayer's includable rent would be that larger figure. His basis for the purpose of computing depreciation thereafter would also be $300,-000.

Eminently practical, and ultimately approved by *Bruun* itself, alternative #3 was initially rejected by the courts. Indeed, the pre-*Bruun* cases held that no taxable realization occurred *either* when the leasehold improvements were installed *or* when the improvements vested in the lessee on expiration of the lease. The factory-building, it was reasoned, could not be severed and disposed of separately from the land, was not "portable and detachable" unless torn down and scrapped. While there might be gain to the lessor in economic terms, since the land and building were physically "merged" such gain must be treated as unrealized until the entire property was sold for cash. *Macomber* was said to support this approach—essentially alternative #4—because it, too, stressed the need for a severance of "profit" from underlying "capital" as a condition of taxability.

In the *Bruun* case, the taxpayer-lessor acquired title to certain leasehold improvements through forfeiture of the lease for nonpayment of rent. Impliedly rejecting these earlier court decisions, the Supreme Court held that the value of the improvements was realized by the taxpayer in the year in which the forfeiture occurred.[50] The improvements, the Court observed, were received by

---

50. Under the actual facts of *Bruun,* the term of the lease exceeded the useful life of the improvements. Accordingly, the Court's choice was apparently limit-the taxpayer "as a result of a business transaction," namely, the leasing of the taxpayer's land. It was not necessary to the recognition of gain that the improvements be severable from the land; all that had to be shown was that the taxpayer had acquired valuable assets from his lessee in exchange for the use of his property. The medium of exchange—whether cash or kind, and whether separately disposable or "affixed"—was immaterial as far as the realization criterion was concerned. In effect, the improvements represented rent, or rather a payment in lieu of rent, which was taxable to the landlord regardless of the form in which it was received.

Although acceptable as an interpretation of the realization requirement, the outcome in *Bruun* in some respects is rather harsh. It seems likely, for example, that the taxpayer's underlying land—which, of course, also reverted to his possession on forfeiture of the lease—had declined in value over the term of the lease for the very same reason (the Depression of the 'thirties) that had caused the lessee to default on his rental obligation. If the lessor had shown that the fall in land-value relative to his original cost was equal to, or greater than, the value of the leasehold improvements, could he have offset his economic loss against that rental income? The answer, most probably, is no. A mere decline in the value of the land, resulting from a drop in the real estate market, would be treated as unrealized property depreciation (*Macomber* would indeed be applicable as to that element), and hence that decline could not be used to offset the realized value of the leasehold improvements. This interplay between the realization rules is unfortunate from the lessor's standpoint, even unfair. But, in a sense, it can't be helped. As already noted, the realization requirement turns the income tax into a tax on transactions rather than a tax on economic gains and losses, with consequences that can sometimes be distressing to the taxpayer as well as beneficial.

In the end, Congress disapproved the result in *Bruun* and eliminated the "realization" by adding § 109 and § 1019 to the Code. § 109 excludes from a lessor's income the value of leasehold improvements realized on termination of a lease.[51] As a corollary, § 1019 denies the lessor a basis for the property so excluded. In effect, nothing is required to be taken into income when the lease terminates, but no depreciation is allowed thereafter. Under *Bru-*

---

ed to inclusion at the time of the forfeiture or no inclusion at all.

51. Under Regs. § 1.109–1(a) the exclusion does not apply to improvements whose value is intended to be in lieu of current rents. Taken literally, this exception would seem to undermine the deferral treatment apparently authorized by §§ 109 and 1019 and to revive something like the prepaid rent alternative described above. However, it has rarely been applied.

un, as stated, if the factory building is worth $200,000 on the termination date, then that amount is included by the lessor in his income and becomes the "tax-paid" basis for the property. With a remaining useful life of 10 years, the lessor would deduct $20,000 a year as depreciation. Under §§ 109 and 1019, nothing would be includable at termination, but there would be no tax-paid basis for depreciation during the ensuing 10-year period. §§ 109 and 1019 precisely embody the result sought unsuccessfully by the taxpayer in *Bruun*—my alternative # 4 in effect—which goes to show that there is more than one forum in which taxpayers can dispute their tax obligations.

The choice between the *Bruun* "solution" and that of §§ 109 and 1019 involves nothing more than the *timing* of the lessor's tax payments. Under either, the deductible depreciation allowance precisely offsets the amount (if any) previously included in the lessor's income. But timing choices are important. From the taxpayer's standpoint, the present statutory treatment offers maximum deferral of income, and it is therefore preferable to any of the alternatives.

5.04 Marital Property Settlements—Davis and Farid-Es-Sultaneh. A taxpayer who transfers appreciated property in satisfaction of a debt obviously realizes a taxable gain just as if the property had been sold for cash. To illustrate, suppose an individual agrees to buy a car from a dealer for $10,000, but instead of paying cash he somehow persuades the dealer to accept 100 shares of X stock, a listed security. The stock has a market value exactly equal to the purchase price of the car—$10,000—but has a basis in the car-buyer's hands of $3,000. It is clear that the swap results in a realization to both parties; the buyer realizes $10,000 and has a $7,000 gain; the dealer also realizes $10,000 and has a profit represented by his mark-up on the car. Gain and profit having thus been recognized on both sides of the transaction, each party thereafter holds the property acquired from the other at a basis equal to its fair market value on the date of the exchange—again, $10,000.

But suppose the car-buyer's dollar obligation to the dealer is disputed. The car actually lists for $10,200 but the buyer asserts that one of the dealer's salesmen told him he could have it for only $9,800. After much wrangling the buyer agrees to transfer and the dealer agrees to accept the X stock worth $10,000 in full satisfaction of the claim. Should the tax outcome be any different merely because the parties contested the amount of the buyer's debt, neither conceding that the other's calculation was correct? Obviously not: the fact that the buyer's obligation was unliquidated, in the sense that it was open to dispute, has no bearing either on the existence of a realization event or on the "amount realized" by the parties pursuant to their settlement. Again the buyer recognizes a gain of $7,000, the dealer is taxed on his profit, and each party holds the property received at a basis of $10,000.

The question raised by the *Davis* and *Farid-Es-Sultaneh* cases was whether these simple conclusions should apply in a family setting in the same way as in a commercial context—the gift problem turned upside-down, so to speak. If a husband transfers appreciated property to his wife in consideration for her release of marital property rights (*e.g.,* dower or statutory right of intestate succession), should that "transaction" be regarded as a taxable exchange? By painful analogy, the wife's status *could* be equated with that of the dealer in the illustration above, the husband's with that of the buyer. The marital property settlement would, of course, be viewed as equivalent to the settlement of the unliquidated claim. But *should* the marital relationship be viewed in these cold-hearted terms?

In *Farid-Es-Sultaneh v. Commissioner,*[52] the taxpayer-wife sold certain shares of stock which she had previously received from her husband pursuant to an antenuptial agreement. Under that agreement the taxpayer, in consideration for the shares, had surrendered all marital property rights in the husband's estate. The stock had a basis in the husband's hands of 15 cents a share, but a fair market value of $10 a share when transferred to the taxpayer. The Commissioner contended that the taxpayer's basis in the shares was the same as her husband's—15 cents—because the shares had been received by her as a gift. The court held, however, that the transfer from husband to wife was not a gift for income tax purposes but an exchange of valuable property interests—stock for marital property rights. As a result, it found the taxpayer's basis for the shares to be $10—their fair market value at the date transferred—and reduced her taxable gain accordingly. In effect, the wife's status was treated as identical with that of the auto-dealer in the illustration above, whose basis for the stock received from the buyer in exchange for the car was also equal to its fair market value.

In *U.S. v. Davis,*[53] which involved a property settlement incident to divorce rather than marriage, the husband's side of the transaction was at issue. Pursuant to an agreement reached by the parties after a lengthy dispute, the taxpayer transferred appreciat-

---

52.   160 F.2d 812 (2d Cir.1947).   **53.**   370 U.S. 65 (1962).

ed securities to his wife in consideration for the surrender of her marital property claims. Consistent with the *Farid* approach, the Supreme Court found that the transfer was not a gift (nor a mere division of property belonging to the marital partnership as might be true in a community property state), and held that the taxpayer had realized a taxable gain on the exchange. The husband and the car-*buyer* in the illustration were thus also put on a par, each realizing a taxable gain by reason of the transfer.

The *Davis* and *Farid* decisions are undoubtedly defensible in terms of the realization criterion: in general, transfers of property in satisfaction of contract obligations, fixed or disputed, are taxable events, with the amount realized being measured by the value of the property transferred. But as against the larger Code policy embodied in the gift exclusion—§ 102 and its corollary, § 1015— the cases seem misguided, or at least doubtful, in result. If property transfers between spouses are "gifts" when they take place during marriage (with the result that the basis of the proper- ty in the transferor's hands carries over to the transferee), it is difficult to see why transfers which are prompted by the formation of the marital unit should be treated differently. And if transfers from deceased husbands to surviving widows are viewed as *non*- realization events (see 4.01) even though the marital relationship thus comes to an end, it is hard to see why a realization should be deemed to occur when the marriage is terminated through divorce. The presence of a contract obligation, though it otherwise justifies a finding of taxable event, seems insufficient on the whole to remove pre-marital and (much more important) post-marital property ar- rangements from the ambit of the gift provisions. Quite obviously, family wealth is being divided between husband and wife in both instances, and it is this circumstance—rather than the presence of "consideration" in *Farid* or of arm's length dealing in *Davis*—that ought to govern the tax outcome.

Having heard criticism of the *Davis/Farid* rule for many years, Congress in the 1984 Act finally overcame those decisions by adding § 1041 to the Code. The new provision states that a transfer of property between spouses, or between former spouses where the transfer is incident to divorce, shall be treated as a "gift" for income tax purposes. Overruling *Davis,* § 1041(a) provides that no gain or loss shall be recognized by the transferor-spouse; as a corollary, § 1041(b) provides that the basis of the transferred property in the hands of the transferee-spouse shall be the same as it was for the transferor. The lower-of-cost-or-market exception— which, under § 1015, limits the basis of a donee for the purpose of determining *loss* on subsequent sale—is made inapplicable; in effect, the basis of gifts between spouses is now governed by § 1041 exclusively.   In the *Farid* case itself, somewhat oddly, the stock transfer actually took place before the marriage—indeed, while the taxpayer's husband was married to somebody else.   Hence, the taxpayer would not have qualified as a "spouse" under § 1041 at the time of the transfer.   More commonly, I suppose, a property transfer pursuant to an antenuptial agreement would be contingent on and would follow the marriage ceremony, so that the transferee would in fact be a "spouse" as defined.

The legislative changes just described were regarded by most tax specialists as overdue and welcome.   Larger issues to one side, the *Davis/Farid* rule had been a complicating factor in divorce settlements and resulted also in better treatment for residents of community property states (the Service having held that *Davis* does not apply to an equal division of community property) than for residents of common law jurisdictions.   From the standpoint of the Treasury itself, moreover, the *Davis/Farid* rule added considerably to the burdens of enforcement in this area.   Thus, transferor-spouses sometimes seemed not to know about *Davis,* or to find it counter-intuitive, and hence often omitted to report their taxable gains when appreciated property was transferred.   By contrast, transferee-spouses, well aware of *Farid,* almost invariably computed gain or loss on the subsequent sale of such property by using a basis equal to the fair market value of the property at the time it was received.   The Treasury thus ran the risk that gain would be reported by neither spouse, unless it was prepared to audit every substantial property settlement.

5.05   Cottage Savings and the Realization Threshold. As the cases discussed in this Section might suggest, the Code contains no general rule or explicit set of criteria that enables us, with confidence, to determine just when a realization has taken place for tax purposes.   We would ordinarily say that there is a "realization" when one property is exchanged for another.   In a sense, however, that statement begs the question, because we may still be obliged, in a close case, to decide whether what has happened does in fact constitute an "exchange".   In the *Cottage Savings* [54] case, the taxpayer, a savings bank, held a portfolio of residential mortgage loans with a face value of $6.9 million.   Mortgage interest rates having risen sharply (the year was 1980), the market value of the taxpayer's mortgage portfolio had dropped to $4.5 million.   Eager to realize a deductible loss of $2.4 million, the taxpayer swapped its beneficial interest in the portfolio for an

---

54. *Cottage   Savings   Assoc.   v. Comm'r,* 499 U.S. 554 (1991).

equivalent interest in a residential mortgage portfolio held by another savings bank (actually several others) in the same locale. To avoid disturbing or confusing individual mortgagors, each bank continued to receive monthly payments from its own original borrowers and would then remit the amounts received to the other. The Federal Home Loan Bank Board, which then had supervisory authority over savings banks, ruled that the parties to the swap were not required to record their losses for regulatory purposes, presumably because the substitution of equivalent mortgage portfolios had no impact on the banks' financial status and net worth.

The taxpayer's loss having been disregarded for regulatory purposes, the Commissioner insisted that it should similarly, and for analogous reasons, be disallowed for tax purposes. Losses are recognized only when realized, and a realization occurs only when the properties exchanged are "materially different" from one another. Here, far from being "different", the underlying mortgage portfolios were virtually identical in economic substance, from which it followed (in the Commissioner's view) that the purported exchange should be viewed as a non-event.

Reversing the court of appeals, the Supreme Court held for the taxpayer and allowed the loss as claimed. The Court agreed that "material difference" is the applicable test of realization under Code § 1001(a), but it did not agree that that test had been flunked merely because the properties exchanged were economic substitutes or equivalents. While the test for regulatory purposes might indeed be one of economic substance, for tax purposes the question was one of administrative convenience only. As the mortgages exchanged were secured by different homes and involved different mortgage-borrowers, the banks on either side emerged with "legally distinct entitlements". More important, the swap itself sufficed to meet the administrative aims that underlie the realization requirement. The transaction was an arms-length deal between unrelated parties. As such, it "put both Cottage Savings and the Commissioner in a position to determine the change in the value of Cottage Savings' mortgages relative to their tax bases" and thus to reckon up gain or loss under § 1001(a).

The *Cottage Savings* decision, and in particular the Court's emphasis on realization as an administrative requirement, seems quite correct on the whole, but of course it does—yet again—make evident the capricious role that realization plays in the tax field. Thus, if the realization requirement can be met at a very low threshold, as the decision implies, then "realization" virtually becomes elective with the taxpayer, which presumably accounts for the Commissioner's determined opposition in the *Cottage Savings* case itself. If mortgage interest rates had gone down in 1980 and the value of its mortgage portfolio had risen, the bank would simply have retained the portfolio and avoided any current gain recognition. With a loss on hand, it chose to swap and trigger a realization. The result is to expose the Treasury to something of a whipsaw and, conversely, to award the savings-bank industry a tax benefit that Congress probably did not intend.

The problem of elective or voluntary realization is not confined to savings banks, of course, but arises in connection with investment activity of all sorts. A stock-market investor is likely to find at the end of the year that some of his stocks have appreciated (relative to his cost) while others have declined. Since gain or loss is realized and recognized only if a security is actually sold, the investor would be prompted to sell the losers and retain the winners if, as in *Cottage Savings,* the realized losses could be deducted from gross income without restriction. To prevent this, the Code permits the investor to offset so-called capital losses *only* against his realized capital gains (with any unused losses allowed to be carried forward to subsequent years.) Except in very limited amount, capital losses cannot be offset against salary or business profits or, indeed, against income from any source other than realized capital gains. Investment losses are thus confined by the Code to a separate schedule and in that way kept isolated from other kinds of taxable income.

While the whipsaw danger illustrated by the *Cottage Savings* case is by this means eliminated in most instances, the statutory machinery that has had to be fabricated in order to deal with the problem is fairly awesome, as will be seen at 16.03. Once again, the realization requirement deserves the credit, or the blame, for much Code detail and complexity.

Part B: DEDUCTIONS

Are deductions necessary? Couldn't we simply have a tax on *gross* income and in that way dispense with the niggling subject of deductions altogether? The answer, unfortunately, is no. Reducing gross income to a net figure by subtracting the taxpayer's expenses is an unavoidable step unless the income tax is to be turned into a kind of sales or excise tax on transactions by volume. Our income tax system is premised on the idea that enrichment is the best measure of the taxpayer's ability to bear the costs of government. While gross income may give some indication of the taxpayer's income status, it would obviously be arbitrary and in many instances highly unfair to accept that figure as final. A lawyer who receives $100,000 in fees this year may, or may not, derive an economic benefit from his professional activities: it all depends on how much he had to spend in the process. Office rent, library costs, employees' wages, outlays for travel and entertainment of clients—these and many other expenses will have been incurred in generating the fees received. Whether the lawyer made or lost money, and in either event how much, cannot be known until his costs are counted and subtracted from his receipts. Without quibbling about whether Congress *could* tax the gross figure if it wished to do so, there can certainly be no doubt that the *net* figure is the only suitable measure of the taxpayer's "income" properly so-called.

The importance of taxing net, rather than gross, income might lead one to expect that the definition of "deductible expense" would be as broad and sweeping as the definition of includable income. If § 61(a) defines gross income to mean "all income", then perhaps the corollary should be to define taxable income as gross income less "all expenses." But plainly this approach would go too far. The income tax is aimed at the taxpayer's net accession to wealth, and it is obvious that unless the latter figure is automatically to be reduced to zero in every case—that is, receipts less all expenditures—a distinction must be drawn between business outlays, on the one hand, and expenditures that represent personal consumption on the other. Business expenses—the costs incurred by the taxpayer in earning gross income—are nondiscretionary in the sense that the income is conditioned on the outlay. Personal expenditures reflect the disposition which the taxpayer elects to make of the wealth that he has earned. Business expenses must necessarily be deductible if the income tax is to be imposed on

90

"income"; for the same reason, personal expenditures should be disallowed.

In contrast to the all-embracing definition of gross income in § 61, therefore, the Code's definition of deductible expense, though broad, is limited to those costs which are associated with the taxpayer's business or investment activities. §§ 162(a) and 212 allow deduction for *all* the ordinary expenses incurred in business or other profit-seeking pursuits, thereby achieving that generality of application which is required if the income tax is to be a tax on *net* income. On the other hand, the connection with business or profit-seeking is equally stressed: nothing is deductible unless it represents a cost incurred in earning gross income. § 262 makes the same point doubly clear by expressly disallowing all "personal, living, or family expenses."

While the line between business and personal expense is of the essence in all this, the fact is that Congress itself has chosen to cross that line fairly freely by allowing deductions for a variety of items which are plainly personal in nature. Doctor's bills, gifts to charity, interest on home-mortgages, residential property taxes—these and certain other expenses, concededly personal, are expressly permitted to be deducted by the taxpayer in computing his taxable income. Quite obviously, the question raised thereby is why there should be *any* allowance for personal expense. What special reasons can be given for excepting the enumerated items from the general rule?

The discussion in this Part is divided into two sections. Section 6 takes up business expenses in general, with emphasis on the limitations which the Code and the courts have imposed on the scope of § 162(a). Section 7 reviews the personal expense deductions and their apparent, or at least asserted, justification.

SECTION 6. BUSINESS EXPENSES

As indicated above, Code § 162(a) authorizes the deduction of "all the ordinary and necessary expenses incurred during the taxable year in carrying on any trade or business." § 212 extends the same treatment to costs associated with investment activities. Together with a few other provisions of a more specific nature—chiefly, § 163 relating to interest and §§ 167 and 168 relating to depreciation—the quoted language constitutes virtually the entire statutory framework for the deduction of business expenses.

Given the breadth and generality of § 162(a), it is customary to analyze the provision by reference to its limitations and boundaries, by showing what is outside its scope, rather than by attempting to enumerate all the various expense items that do qualify for deduction. Taking this approach, the principal limitations on the scope of the section are usually said to involve the following issues:

(1) Whether or not the particular expense was "ordinary and necessary;"

(2) Whether the expenditure was a current expense or a capital investment; and

(3) Whether the expense was incurred in business or for personal reasons.

Apart from certain specific items which entail special criteria, almost all of the cases that students are asked to consider can be assigned to one or another of these three categories.

Although they emerge from a different perspective, the questions presented by the deduction cases often have a good deal in common with the gross income problems that were discussed in Part A. Exclusions and deductions from gross income would generally be expected to run together when the same items are involved, because the question in either event is essentially as to the composition of taxable income. While this expectation is sometimes disappointed, the theoretical issues will at least be similar and familiar. In addition, the concern about timing which received such emphasis in Part A is equally important in the present context. Quite frequently—especially when the question is one of current expense versus capital expenditure—the controversy between taxpayer and Treasury ultimately concerns the acceleration or postponement of tax payments. Just as the taxpayers in Part A preferred to include an item in income later rather than sooner, so the taxpayers in this Part prefer the immediate deduction of an expense to the deferral of that deduction. The reason for this preference has already been explained; my purpose here is merely to point out that even though the focus now is on deductions from, rather than inclusions in, gross income, the stakes are often much the same.

6.01 Personal or Business. The distinction between personal expenses and business expenses presents what may be the hardest classification problem in the entire tax field. One is almost compelled to proceed by rote rather than by attempting to articulate general principles. The reason for the difficulty, I suppose, is that the notion of a sharp division between pleasure-seeking and profit-seeking is alien to human psychology and essentially unrealistic. Everybody combines work with pleasure to some degree; no one is able to separate and quantify the two elements at every point, nor even always to state which objective is predominant. But the tax law cannot embrace this comfortable commonplace; it *must* proceed as if individual behavior were divisible into two parts, because the concept of net (taxable) income depends directly on the idea that one's business and one's personal life can be distinguished. The problem, then, is how to draw a dividing line that is equitable and meaningful—one, moreover, that can be administered without resort to truth serum. If X, a corporate executive who pays tax at a rate of 40%, spends $5,000 on a trip to Europe, and if the cost can be reduced to $3,000 by asserting that the purpose of the trip was to investigate prospective markets for his employer, the temptation for X not merely to claim but to believe that he had a business goal in view is well-nigh irresistable. And of course he really may have. The dilemma, at all events, is evident.

What follows is a partial listing of items whose status as a personal or business expense has been disputed by taxpayers and the government. I have already admitted that classification is difficult in this field, but perhaps—and very tentatively—one might suggest that the *potentially* allowable expenses can be divided into two groups. The first includes those outlays which represent the special cost of being an employed person. Child-care and commuting costs presumably belong to this category; perhaps there are other members, such as higher clothing expense. In general, though with exceptions, expenses of this sort are treated as personal and are disallowed under § 262. The second and more troublesome class includes expenditures which reflect a departure from the taxpayer's everyday pattern of employment, but which also appear to afford a considerable measure of strictly personal gratification. Travel and entertainment are the prime examples here; "necessary" attendance at business conventions might be another. In this area the law follows a winding course, allowing some items, disallowing others (wholly or partly), and occasionally attempting to make an allocation between "business" and "personal" elements based on what appear to be objective factors.

Educational expenses—investment in professional skills—might also be discussed under the "personal or business" heading, but, for various reasons, that subject is taken up at 6.02 in connection with "capital expenditures."

(a) Everyday expenses of employment—child-care and commuting. In *Smith v. Commissioner,*[1] the Board of Tax Appeals denied a deduction for babysitting expenses. The taxpayers, a working couple, argued that since Mrs. Smith would have been unable to

---

1.   40 B.T.A. 1038 (1939).

leave her child and take a job "but for" the services of a nursemaid, the latter's fee should be regarded as a necessary business expense. Observing that child-care was one of the basic functions of family living, the Board reasoned that if the nursemaid's fee were allowed because essential to the taxpayer's employment, then by extension all consumption expenditures—food, shelter, clothing, recreation—which enable taxpayers to carry on the day's activities must become deductible as well. "Yet these," said the Board, "are the very essence of those 'personal' expenses the deductibility of which is expressly denied."

Male chauvinism? Perhaps not—but still not wholly satisfying as to rationale. While it is true that one must have food and shelter in order to work, it is also true that one must eat and live somewhere even if one doesn't work. Expenses which are common to everyone, employed and non-employed, are clearly not deductible. But what has that "rule" got to do with Mrs. Smith's babysitting fees? We can assume, I think, that the taxpayers were honest in asserting that those fees would not have been incurred had Mrs. Smith remained a housewife; the Smiths were apparently not in a position to hire a maid merely to provide Mrs. Smith with more leisure. Accordingly, nursemaid service was simply *not* among the family's basic consumption expenditures if we take an *unemployed* Mrs. Smith as our starting point. The disputed child-care expense was plainly an additional cash outlay that would have been avoided had Mrs. Smith remained a non-worker, and in this sense it was clearly an expense of her employment. Why, then, should it not have been allowed?

The issue in *Smith* can be made more general. If we compare A, who has $10,000 of income from employment, with B, who has $10,000 of dividends, it is easy to predict that A's cost of living will be higher than B's (everything else being equal) and that the difference will be traceable directly to A's status as an employed person. Quite obviously, it is costlier to go to work than to stay at home. Commuting to and from the job, for example, entails substantial expense. If you live in New York City and travel round-trip on the subway every day, the annual cost now runs to more than $500; if you come in from Scarsdale, the figure is very much higher. People who are not employed are free of regular commuting expense; if they ride the subway, it must be because they want to. Other kinds of expenses which fall more heavily on working people would include restaurant lunches (more costly than eating at home), business clothing (more costly than informal dress), and housekeeping services (more costly than keeping house yourself). In brief, there is a cost-of-living differential which results from carrying on an employment, and the amount is certainly not insignificant in most cases.

The question presented by the *Smith* case, broadly speaking, was whether this differential (or any part of it) should be allowed as a business expense. The answer—that it should not—was undoubtedly correct, although not (as the Board maintained) because all the personal expenses of every employed person would otherwise become deductible. The *additional* expenses of earning a living—as compared with the basic expense of just living—can presumably be identified in many instances and, as stated, the nursemaid's fee in *Smith* was pretty clearly of that class. The real justification for the disallowance of these additional expenses is simply Congressional intent, which was surely clear by the time the *Smith* case was decided. In effect, the tax law *never* has been interpreted to contemplate a deduction for the everyday expenses of being employed. Since almost every family includes at least one working person, expenses of the kind described are almost universal. To allow those expenses would be similar in effect to an across-the-board reduction of tax rates, but with the greater benefit going to higher-income families for whom deductions have the largest value. The effect, moreover, would be to complicate individual tax returns enormously by requiring every employee to keep a detailed day-to-day account of his business-related expenses. Presumably for these reasons, employment income is, and always has been, taxed on what virtually amounts to a gross basis. The *Smith* decision really demonstrates that it is the basic terms of existence of a person *already at work* which marks the boundary between business and personal expense.[2]

Some of what has been said about the *Smith* case may also help to explain the Supreme Court's approach to "travel" costs in *Commissioner v. Flowers*.[3] Although it has long been established that daily commuting expense is personal and not deductible, § 162(a)(2) specifically allows the deduction of "traveling expenses (including amounts expended for meals and lodging . . .) while away from home in the pursuit of a trade or business." The term "traveling expense" is a term of art in the income tax; it refers both to transportation costs and to the ordinary living expenses—"meals and lodging"—which are incurred by a taxpayer in connec-

2. Although the tax law still contains no general allowance for the additional costs incurred by a family when both spouses are employed (see "loose end", below), since 1954 the Code has permitted working couples with children (and single parents) to take a partial credit against tax for childcare and housekeeping expenses. Under § 21, the maximum yearly credit is $1,440 and declines to a minimum of $960 as family income increases.

3. 326 U.S. 465 (1945).

tion with a business trip. But since transportation and restaurant meals (less commonly special lodging) are part of almost every employed person's daily expense, there is an obvious need to define the status of business travel rather narrowly. Somewhat surprisingly given its inherent ambiguity, the statutory phrase "away from home" has been made to carry the entire burden of definition.

In *Flowers,* the taxpayer, a lawyer, lived and practiced law in Jackson, Mississippi. He presently was offered a full-time job with a railroad whose main office was in Mobile, more than 200 miles from Jackson. As he was unwilling to move to Mobile, the railroad allowed the taxpayer to do most of his work in Jackson, but required him, at fairly frequent intervals, to perform services in Mobile as well. The taxpayer sought to deduct the cost of meals and lodgings during his visits to Mobile on the ground that these costs were travel expenses incurred while away from home. The Internal Revenue Service, opposing the deduction, contended that the word "home" in § 162(a)(2) must be understood to refer to the taxpayer's place of business rather than the location of his family residence. In this view, the taxpayer's "home" was Mobile, not Jackson, so that in effect the cost of traveling to and living in Mobile was not a business expense within the meaning of the statute.

The Supreme Court, although refusing to decide upon the meaning of "home" in this context, sustained the disallowance on the ground that the expense in question had been incurred by the taxpayer for his own convenience rather than for business reasons. The Court stated that the appropriate test of deductibility was whether the travel had been motivated by the "exigencies of business" or by considerations of personal preference. Because Flowers could have chosen to live in Mobile, thereby avoiding the need for travel, the expenses were found to be self-imposed and "personal".

Like the *Smith* decision, the opinion in *Flowers* makes more out of the confusing element of causation than may really be necessary.[4] It would have been enough, I think, to have identified the taxpayer's expenses as commuting costs and to have disallowed them on the straightforward basis that commuting expenses, while certainly a matter of business exigency, have never been deductible. Again, such costs are part (perhaps the main part) of the living-cost differential mentioned above. The fact that Flowers had a long

---

4. See Klein, *Income Taxation and Commuting Expenses: Tax Policy and the Need for Nonsimplistic Analysis of* *"Simple" Problems,* 54 Cornell L.Rev. 871 (1969).

commute was indeed a matter of personal choice—commuting costs obviously vary depending on whether an individual prefers to live in the city or in the suburbs. Yet it was not the absence of a business nexus that justified the outcome in *Flowers,* since even the minimum cost of commuting is disallowed by § 262. Although the bus or subway fares which the city-dweller pays each day to go to work are an unavoidable expense of his employment, the implied statutory purpose is to deny them. The *Flowers* decision is quite properly a finding that the same disallowance applies to long-distance commuting, even when that entails additional living costs. Though awkward semantically, the Service's interpretation of "home" as synonymous with principal place of business is really a way of asserting that the ordinary expenses of the working day are to be treated as personal. One's "day" begins at work as far as the tax law is concerned.

§ 162(a)(2) has occasioned a sizeable quantity of litigation over the years as taxpayers and the Treasury have struggled to identify the dividing line between commuting and business travel. Two recurring issues can be mentioned by way of illustration. First, what constitutes being "*away* from home" for the purposes of the statute? Suppose a salesman who lives and works in New York City spends a day visiting customers in Connecticut. He gets an early start, and eats breakfast in Bridgeport, lunch in New Haven and dinner in Hartford. He then drives all the way home to New York, briefly greets his wife and stumbles into bed. Can the salesman deduct the cost of his restaurant meals as a "travel expense"? In *U.S. v. Correll,*[5] the Supreme Court upheld the Commissioner in denying a deduction in these circumstances and approved the Commissioner's interpretation of "away" as meaning away *overnight.* In effect, had the salesman elected to spend the night in Hartford, the preceding day's meals and the night's lodging would have been deductible. Any sense in this? Perhaps not, although the reader is hereby challenged to come up with something better. Essentially, the question raised by *Correll* is whether taxpayers who sometimes put in long hours and cover many miles during the working day should be treated more favorably than those who punch a clock and are wholly sedentary. The general answer is no,[6] and the overnight rule is simply a device for making

---

5. 389 U.S. 299 (1967).

6. Fortunately for law firm associates working late, the Service has never attempted to tax reimbursed "supper money," O.D. 514, 2 C.B. 90 (1920), and the Committee Reports accompanying § 132—see 1.02, above—expressly state that "occasional" supper money is to be excluded from income as a *de minimis* fringe.

the necessary distinction between everyday living expenses on the one hand, and on the other, "travel."

The overnight rule ties into a second important interpretative issue. If the salesman is not regarded as away from home unless he spends the night in Hartford, what should be his status if his employer sends him to Hartford for a 6-month period to open a new branch office? At this point we need to look at the question of away-ness from the opposite end. Could it now be argued that the taxpayer has actually shifted his home from City A to City B, that he is not so much a traveller from New York as a resident of Hartford? Another rule-of-thumb is called for, it appears, but this time one that distinguishes between permanent removals and temporary absences from the original place of employment. The Service has conceded that the cost of meals and lodgings incurred during a period of temporary reassignment are deductible, and has ruled that "temporary" may be taken to mean a stay whose termination is foreseeable within a reasonably brief period not to exceed one year. Once again, the one-year time limit—now codified in § 162(a)—is necessarily arbitrary, and one's intuition is that it tends to err on the generous side. At all events, the rule is especially beneficial to an otherwise neglected group of taxpayers, namely, college professors. In effect, a professor who spends a year as a visiting instructor at another institution can deduct as travel expense all of his/her reasonable living expenses for that period. What about the professor's spouse, who assists (or at least encourages) the professor in his/her research during the visiting year? Prior to 1993, it might have been asserted that the spouse's "travel expenses" should be deductible as well. Under amended § 274(m), however, such deductions are disallowed unless the spouse is the taxpayer's employee and performs services that are more than incidental.

Perhaps the final twist in all this relates to the status of *real* traveling salesmen, those luckless individuals who spend all of their working time on the road, living in hotels and eating in restaurants, strangers wherever they go. May such a person deduct his travel expenses? While pure transportation costs must certainly be allowed—airfares from city to city, for example—the cost of meals and lodgings has been denied in these circumstances on the simple basis that the traveling salesman (at least if unmarried) has no home to be "away" from.[7] Quite obviously, any other holding would convert all the salesman's normal living expenditures into deductible business expense.

7. *Rosenspan v. U.S.*, 438 F.2d 905 (2d Cir.1971).

U.S. v. Gilmore[8]—which arose under § 212 rather than § 162—also raises a problem of "causation" which bears some resemblance to that presented in *Flowers* and *Smith*. In *Gilmore* the taxpayer had incurred substantial legal fees in litigating a hotly contested divorce. A major portion of the fees was attributable to defending against his wife's claim to ownership of a controlling interest in the family business. Had the wife succeeded, the taxpayer's principal source of livelihood—his salary as chief executive—might have been threatened or lost. Accordingly, the taxpayer sought to deduct a part of his legal fees as an expense incurred for the "conservation . . . of property held for the production of income." Following its earlier decision in *Lykes v. U.S.*[9], the Supreme Court sustained the Commissioner in disallowing the deduction as a "family" expense under § 262. The Court reasoned that the deductibility of legal fees depends upon the origin of the litigated claim rather than upon the potential consequence of success or failure to the taxpayer's income status. Since the origin of the present litigation was to be found in the taxpayer's marital difficulties, no deduction was allowable.

While the outcome in *Gilmore* is generally viewed as satisfactory, the argument from cause-and-effect is, as usual, slightly circular. To be sure, there would have been no litigation without the divorce; but without the property ownership the taxpayer's legal fees would have been appreciably smaller. Just why the divorce rather than the property interest must logically be viewed as the "source" of the added legal expense is not completely obvious. But perhaps the result in *Gilmore* can be explained more simply by pointing out that the costs of rearranging titles within a family group—costs which fall at random on the large class of persons owning valuable assets—have always been regarded as a personal expense of property ownership. Legal fees incurred in preparing a will are viewed as personal from the standpoint of a testator; likewise, the costs of collecting a legacy—for example, fees incurred in a will contest—are treated by the Regulations as nondeductible from the standpoint of the legatee.[10] Of course a property settlement that is incident to a contested divorce is likely to be much more expensive than a simple will, and Congress might have chosen, as it has for extraordinary medical expenses, to allow such costs as a deductible personal expense. But since it has not done so, the Court in *Gilmore* correctly perceived that it had no warrant

---

8. 372 U.S. 39 (1963).

9. 343 U.S. 118 (1952).

10. Regs. § 1.212. § 212(3), however, does permit a deduction for fees incurred in connection with taxes of all sorts, so that the cost of "estate planning" may in some circumstances be allowed.

to differentiate between divorce settlements and other kinds of intrafamily property dispositions.

A loose end: While the working wife and mother may have been (in the Board's phrase) a "new phenomenon" when the *Smith* case was decided, she is obviously anything but unusual today. What *is* new, or at least newer, is the phenomenon of working spouses who also *live* separately—actually occupy separate residences—because their jobs are centered in different localities. The customary economies of a combined household have to be sacrificed under these circumstances and the cost-of-living differential noticed in connection with the *Smith* case is increased substantially. Does the Code, and in particular the travel expense deduction as interpreted in *Flowers,* provide relief?

In *Hantzis,*[11] the taxpayer, a second-year student at Harvard Law School, took a ten-week summer job with a firm in New York City. The taxpayer's husband held a full-time teaching position in Boston, where the couple maintained their regular family residence. To carry out her summer clerkship, the taxpayer rented a small apartment in New York and for the most part, apparently, ate her meals in restaurants. Asserting that she had been "away from home [*i.e.,* Boston] in the pursuit of a trade or business" for the summer months, she sought to deduct the apartment rent, meals, and cost of transportation between Boston and New York (roughly equal in total to all her summer earnings) as travel expense under § 162(a)(2). The Court of Appeals, reversing the Tax Court, upheld the Commissioner's disallowance on the ground (in effect) that Ms. Hantzis had no business-home in Boston to be "away" from. Ms. Hantzis' summer work in New York might be regarded as a trade or business, but if so that was the only one she had, because being a student, even a student in professional school, does not constitute a trade or business for tax purposes. Hence, while Ms. Hantzis plainly occupied two homes during the summer months, the home in Boston was maintained as a matter of personal choice rather than business necessity. It followed that her transportation and added living costs in New York were not deductible as "travel expense". Mr. Hantzis, to be sure, had a full-time professional commitment that made it necessary for *him* to maintain a residence in Boston; but, though taxed as a couple, each of the spouses (in the court's view) "must independently satisfy the requirement that

---

11. *Hantzis v. Comm'r,* 638 F.2d 248 (1st Cir.1981).

deductions taken for travel expenses incurred in the pursuit of a trade or business arise while he or she is away from home."

Apart from the not very surprising conclusion that going to law school is not a "trade or business" (see 6.02, below), the *Hantzis* case merely confirms the holding in *Flowers* that long-distance commuting—even when combined with meals and lodging expense—does not qualify as "travel". Like *Smith* in an earlier era, the decision also makes clear that two-career families create no special exception to the general disallowance of employee business expenses. It is true, after all, that the Hantzises were *obliged* to maintain two separate residences in order to generate a given level of household income, and for that reason they obviously had less discretionary income after meeting essential housing costs than either a single-earner household or a two-earner household with a single residence. The taxpayer hoped to mitigate the resulting disadvantage by converting § 162(a) into a limited two-career family allowance. As in *Smith,* however, the court was presumably correct in regarding the larger purpose of the Code as contrary.

(b) Business or pleasure—travel and entertainment. If it isn't pressed too hard, I think a distinction can usefully be made between the issues raised in *Smith* and *Flowers* and those presented in this subsection. The question in the two cases named was whether the business-related expenses of the working day can be deducted under § 162 (they cannot); the question here, by contrast, is whether an expense which is concededly deductible *if* it is a business expense is in fact what it is claimed to be. The trip to Europe mentioned earlier represents a deductible expense if the executive's purpose is to drum up export business for his company, but it is not deductible if his purpose is vacationing. Quite obviously, there is a danger that taxpayers whose jobs may sometimes justify travel and entertainment will be tempted to classify as business-expense what is actually pure consumption, while those of us who lack such opportunities are compelled to buy our pleasures out of after-tax income. Code amendments over the past few years have imposed new limitations on travel and entertainment expenses which are summarized below. These limitations chiefly serve to reduce the amount that can be deducted in certain cases, but the central problem of classification—whether a particular outlay qualifies as a business expense to begin with—for the most part is left at large.

The character of that problem—trivial but difficult—is illustrated by the Supreme Court's decision in the *Rudolph* case.[12] In

12. *Rudolph v. U.S.,* 370 U.S. 269 (1962).

Rudolph, a Dallas insurance company sponsored a "convention" in New York City for insurance agents who had achieved sales above a certain level. Wives were included and all expenses were reimbursed by the company. The Court sustained the Commissioner both in refusing to permit the taxpayer to exclude the reimbursement and in denying him a deduction for the expense. Although the taxpayer argued that he was constrained to attend the convention out of loyalty to his employer, the Court noted that only one morning of the 3-day convention period was taken up with business meetings and concluded that the entire arrangement was a bonus in the form of a paid vacation. Dissenting, Justice Douglas pointed out that the Commissioner had previously consented to the deduction of convention expenses for many other categories of professionals—clergymen, lawyers, teachers, etc.—and demanded to know why insurance agents should be singled out for disallowance. Confused at some points and absurdly gullible at others, the dissent nevertheless reflects a certain basic truth about conventions generally: they are often just an opportunity for frolic. If clergymen may frolic deductibly, then why not insurance salesmen? The presence of wives (it was said) was to keep the frolic within proper bounds. Taken seriously,[13] Douglas' dissent is really an objection— not altogether without reason—to the *ad hoc* quality of administration in this area.

As has been noted, § 162(a)(2) permits deduction of the cost of meals and lodging as well as transportation, so that if a taxpayer makes a business trip (overnight, yet temporary), not only his air or railroad fare but his hotel and restaurant expenses are allowable. The deductibility of transportation is perhaps self-explanatory—the business traveller must get to his destination and then return to his regular place of employment—but the deduction of meals and lodging, which are clearly personal expenses in any other context, requires brief explanation. As to lodging, a twofold justification for the deduction can be offered. First, the purely personal satisfaction which a taxpayer derives from living in a hotel room is likely to be less than its cost when the travel is occasioned by business rather than pleasure. One must have shelter, of course, but where his travel is solely a function of business need, it is not unreasonable to assume that the taxpayer would not incur the same expense for personal enjoyment. Second, and relatedly, the hotel expense usually duplicates the cost of maintaining the taxpayer's regular household at home and in that respect can be viewed as an added

---

13. Not easy to do, I admit. The dissenting opinion is characterized as "utterly reckless" in Wolfman *et al., The* *Behavior of Justice Douglas in Federal Tax Cases,* 122 U.Pa.L.Rev. 235, 272 (1973).

financial burden. As to food, the element of duplication is obviously lacking—the traveller can't eat one meal in two places at the same time—and hence the justification for the deduction is somewhat weaker. The explanation must reside, therefore, in the notion that a restaurant meal is a "constrained" expenditure, that it involves more expense than the taxpayer would otherwise incur, and so on. Once again, the concept is that the taxpayer's personal satisfaction in being "forced" to eat out may be less than the cost of the meal itself. At an early point the Service took the position that the deduction for restaurant meals should be limited to the excess over what the taxpayer would have spent on food at home. But while logical, this approach proved difficult to administer and was ultimately abandoned. Expenditures which are "lavish and extravagant" may still be disallowed under a 1962 amendment, but lacking a specific dollar limitation it is unlikely that this restriction has had significant effect in practice.

Entertainment expenses—the alleged cost of currying favor with customers and business associates—present related problems. Suppose A, a Wall Street lawyer, takes B, a valued client, to lunch. No travel is involved—both live in New York City. Over lunch the two men discuss a range of topics, including business, politics and religion. They eat well—the bill is $100—and part from each other with a feeling that their relationship has been cemented. Is the cost of the lunch deductible by A as "business entertainment?" If so, then especially under the higher tax rates that applied before the 1986 Act, the martinis, quiche and paupiettes de boeuf were a bargain. Assuming that A was in the 50% tax bracket, the after-tax cost of *both* lunches would be only $50. By contrast, if A had eaten alone (which in any case he dislikes), his own non-deductible meal would have cost him the same amount. Hence from one standpoint B's companionship actually produced a free lunch. The same banal scenario could be extended to attendance at nightclubs, theatres, sporting events and so on, as well as the use of luxury facilities such as yachts and country clubs.

Prior to 1962 (when § 274 was added to the Code) the feasting just described was probably fully deductible provided that A's expenditure could be shown to have *some* element of business purpose. While some cases required that the business purpose outweigh any other purpose for the activity in question, other cases seem to have settled for a good deal less. In the famous African safari case,[14] for example, the owner of a local dairy company sought to deduct the expenses which he and his wife had incurred

14. *Sanitary Farms Dairy, Inc. v. Comm'r,* 25 T.C. 463 (1955).

on a big game hunt. Although hunting was a life-long family hobby, the taxpayer contended (with loyal support from his advertising manager) that he had obtained valuable goodwill for the dairy business by showing films of the safari to local groups, displaying his trophies—heads and things—in a "museum" at the plant, and inviting customers to dine on the remains. The Tax Court actually bought this argument and allowed the safari costs to be deducted in full as an advertising expense. The taxpayers "admittedly enjoyed hunting, but enjoyment of one's work does not make that work a mere personal hobby .... There is evidence that this trip represented hard work on the part of the taxpayers, undertaken for the benefit of the Dairy, rather than a frolic of their own ...." Thus "evidence" of a business *connection,* though not proof of a predominant business *purpose,* appears to have sufficed.

Two other features of the pre-1962 treatment should be noted, the first reflected in the *Sutter* case,[15] the second in the much-abused *Cohan* decision.[16] In *Sutter,* the question for decision was whether an individual should be permitted to deduct the expenses of his *own* entertainment if incurred in the company of customers or clients. The taxpayer, a physician engaged in industrial medicine, claimed deduction for the cost of attending business luncheons and entertaining clients aboard his cabin cruiser. The Tax Court held that the cost of self-entertainment, even though incurred in a business setting, was not deductible unless the expense could be shown to be "different from or in excess of" that which the taxpayer would have incurred for his own gratification. The qualification established by the Court resembles the one which formerly applied to the excess cost of restaurant meals purchased while on travel status, and as with the earlier limitation the difficulty of segregating "excess" entertainment costs made the *Sutter* rule virtually impossible for the Service to administer. As a result, with the exception of "abuse" cases—an effort by lawyer A to deduct *all* his lunches on the theory that every luncheon companion is a prospective client or business associate [17]—the Service in practice disregarded *Sutter* and allowed the expenses of self-entertainment to be deducted in full.

The *Cohan* decision furnished the administrative framework for the policing of "T & E" expenditures prior to 1962. In *Cohan* the Board of Tax Appeals, having found that the famous showman had spent substantial sums on travel and entertainment, some

15. *Sutter v. Comm'r,* 21 T.C. 170   **17.** *Moss v. Comm'r,* 758 F.2d 211
(1953).   (7th Cir.1985).
16. *Cohan v. Comm'r,* 39 F.2d 540
(2d Cir.1930).

portion of which was admittedly business-related, nevertheless disallowed his claimed deduction in full on the ground that the amount claimed was unsupported by vouchers or bookkeeping entries. On appeal, the Board's decision was remanded by the Circuit Court, which held (in an opinion by Learned Hand) that "absolute certainty in such matters is usually impossible and is not necessary." T & E expenses can be estimated if documentary proof is lacking, and hence "the Board should make as close an approximation as it can, bearing heavily if it chooses upon the taxpayer whose inexactitude is of his own making." The *Cohan* case was decided in 1930: tax rates were low and the practice of business entertaining probably not widespread. Both conditions reversed themselves in the ensuing decades, and by 1962, when Congress finally took a hand, the *Cohan* rule reportedly had become a leading source of controversy between taxpayers and internal revenue agents on field audits. In effect, the *Cohan* rule had degenerated into a form of gamesmanship, with a good many taxpayers deliberately overstating their unsubstantiated T & E expenditures in the expectation that a given percentage would in any event be disallowed on audit. From a national perspective, the problem with this practice was that most returns necessarily escaped audit altogether, so that the overstated amount was usually allowed in full by default. *Cohan* thus represented an invitation to tax cheating through the exaggeration of entertainment expenses, a practice which could be rationalized on the ground that all taxpayers of a certain class engaged in it. What is puzzling, at least in hindsight, is how Hand could have failed to foresee this consequence when he led the Second Circuit in authorizing a rule of "approximation."

"The slogan—'It's deductible'—should pass from our scene," sloganized President Kennedy in his Tax Message of 1961, and later Presidents—notably Carter, Reagan and Clinton—have also stressed the need to eliminate or restrict the deduction for expense-account spending. Congress responded rather weakly to Kennedy's plea for legislative change in this area, but in 1962 it did add § 274, which overruled the *Cohan* case among other things. Thus, § 274(d) requires that the taxpayer maintain "adequate records" of time, place, amount and business purpose in order to support a claim for entertainment expense deductions; the right to approximate (and to do so after the fact) has been withdrawn. More generally, § 274(a) allows deduction of entertainment expenses only if the outlay is "directly related" to the taxpayer's business or precedes or follows a "bona fide business discussion." While the latter requirements have presumably strengthened the Service's hand in challenging doubtful items, the relevant evidence is obviously within the taxpayer's control and one generally assumes that the *kinds* of expenditures—restaurant meals, tickets to sports events—that were deductible prior to the addition of § 274 continue to be deductible today.

President Reagan launched a new attack on the entertainment expense deduction in his "Tax Proposals" of 1985, and this time Congress reacted by imposing a flat percentage disallowance on all outlays falling into the entertainment category, business meals included. Under § 274(n), added in 1986 and amended in 1993, only 50% of amounts expended on business meals and business entertainment may be taken as an expense deduction, the remaining 50% being disallowed. In addition, the Code now singles out and either limits or disallows certain alleged business expenses that are pretty plainly personal—club dues, the cost of traveling to a business meeting on a luxury cruise ship, the cost of much "educational" travel—but that were, or might have been, allowable under prior law.

In a rough-and-ready way, the 50% disallowance rule purports to approximate and filter out the personal consumption benefit that inheres in any entertainment activity; the allowable 50% is taken to reflect the business component. Quite obviously, a 50/50 rule is no more or less defensible as a matter of theory than any other ratio, though one's (or at least my) intuition is that the personal element in a fancy restaurant meal stands higher than 50%. Still, as compared with the prior (*i.e.*, pre-1986) treatment of entertainment expenses, the present treatment is fairly stringent in effect. Thus, Lawyer A and Client B, referred to above, spent $100 on their business lunch. As noted, the after-tax cost to A was only $50 when the outlay was fully deductible *and* the top marginal tax-rate was 50%. Reducing the top rate to 40% by itself raises the after-tax cost of the lunch expense, so that now, taking both lower rate and disallowance into account, A's after-tax cost becomes $50 (disallowed) plus 60% of $50 (allowed), or $80. A higher disallowance level (...100%?) would of course reduce the tax advantage still further, but at this point the benefit to A is getting pretty small, even if it is not quite negligible.

Business meals and entertainment expenses that are reimbursed by an individual's employer are fully deductible (really, excludable) by the employee, but the employer itself is then made subject to the 50/50 restriction. An independent contractor is treated as an employee for this purpose, a rule which the House Committee illustrates by citing a lawyer representing (and presumably charging business meals to) a client. In these circumstances it is the client that will suffer (and no doubt be irritated by) the 50%

disallowance—assuming that "meals" are set out as a separate "disbursement" category on the final bill.

The 50% rule does not apply to the value of *de minimis* fringes excludable from an employee's income under § 132 (see 1.02). Firm parties and picnics, and likewise an occasional lunch or dinner aimed at improving employee morale, are presumably within the *de minimis* category and hence free of the disallowance rule.

I might add, finally, that the general idea of disallowing business entertainment expenses effectively puts that class of outlays in the same category as the "commercial gifts" discussed at 4.03. If (as in the *Duberstein* case) Lawyer A had made a gift of some sort to Client B—say a case of the best champagne—the cost would *not* be deductible by A unless B were willing (which is unlikely) to include the item in income. The restaurant lunch gets the same treatment, at least to the extent of the disallowed 50%. B includes nothing, but A's expense is partly disallowed. In that respect, as with commercial gifts, there is tax symmetry: A bears the tax on B's benefit. The same, in a sense, is true of the lunch A buys for himself. Theoretically, A (the lawyer) *should* be allowed to deduct the lunch if the outlay really has a business purpose; but it is also well arguable that A (the diner) should be required to include the same amount in income as a consumption benefit. Putting the expense and the benefit together obviously produces a wash: in effect, the "correct" outcome is reached by including nothing but allowing no deduction.[18] Precisely this—limited, again, to 50%—is what § 274(n) accomplishes.

6.02 Capital Expenditures. § 263 (with help from § 263A) disallows deductions for the cost of acquiring property whose useful life extends substantially beyond the close of the taxable year. Land and buildings, machinery and equipment, patents and trademarks, are major types of assets that continue in use for more or less extended periods of time. Since the cost of such properties represents a present payment by the taxpayer for economic benefits that will accrue to him in the future, the tax law requires that the expenditures be "capitalized" rather than deducted as a current expense. This of course does not mean that the taxpayer will never be allowed to recover such expenditures. § 167 (discussed at 6.08 below) authorizes an annual allowance for the exhaustion or wear and tear of capital assets, so that in the case of plant, equipment or other productive assets with limited useful lives the construction or acquisition cost will be recovered on a

---

18. Halperin, *Business Deductions for Personal Living Expenses: A Uniform Approach to an Unsolved Problem,* 122 U.Pa.L.Rev. 859 (1974).

year-by-year basis through the medium of depreciation or amortization deductions. The cost of non-depreciable assets—land is an example—is also recoverable, but as such property is assumed to be of perpetual or at least indefinite useful life the recovery is postponed until the property is sold.

Whether a given outlay should be treated as an "expense" under section 162 or a capital expenditure under § 263 thus usually boils down to a question of timing. If the outlay in question is an expense, it is deductible at once and reduces the taxable income of the current year. If the outlay is a capital expenditure, it is deductible over a period of years that relates to the asset's useful life. If the outlay is a capital expenditure but the property acquired is of indefinite useful life, then the outlay is recoverable only as an offset against the proceeds of final sale.

While the classification of an outlay as an expense or a capital expenditure is normally clear, there are, inevitably, instances in which the proper treatment is in doubt. Four such problem areas are discussed below: (a) the distinction between "repairs" and "alterations"; (b) the treatment of business intangibles; (c) the distinction between "lease" and "purchase"; and (d) the treatment of education expenses. At stake in categories (a)–(c) is simply the acceleration or postponement of tax payments—deduction now or deduction later. In category (d) the issue is a sharper one in a sense, because a finding of "capital expenditure" is equivalent to a permanent disallowance. In all four situations, of course, it is in the taxpayer's interest to treat doubtful items as deductible expenses and in the Treasury's "interest" to treat such items as capital expenditures.

(a) Repairs or alterations. In addition to the original acquisition cost of plant, machinery and the like, which always has to be capitalized, the Regulations require that subsequent expenditures that alter the property's capacity or function, or that extend its useful life, be capitalized as well. Thus, the addition of three storeys to an existing office building would obviously be a capital expenditure. Similarly, amounts spent to restore wornout equipment to its original condition—rebuilding an old building, for example—would be treated as "making good the depreciation previously allowed" and would also have to be capitalized.

By contrast, amounts spent for "incidental repairs" are permitted to be deducted as a current expense under § 162(a). This is true even though the repair itself would usually have an economic value to the taxpayer that extends beyond the current taxable year. Suppose a machine part breaks for some reason and has to be replaced. Although the new part (if it doesn't break) is expected to last as long as the machine itself, it presumably qualifies as a "repair" and is therefore deductible under § 162. But why should that be so? If the general rule is that an expenditure for property having an extended useful life must be capitalized, why should the cost of the new machine part be treated as a current expense merely because it has the status of a repair? Why not simply add the outlay to the basis of the machine and then recover the taxpayer's total investment through depreciation over the balance of the machine's useful life?

The somewhat long-winded answer is that there is (or ought to be) a certain parallelism between the deduction for repairs under § 162(a) and the deduction for business casualties under § 165(a). A machine that breaks down because a vital part malfunctions can be said to have sustained a kind of accidental impairment that *resembles* a casualty in the sense that it results in a sudden loss in the value of the machine itself and is more or less unexpected. If the taxpayer's equipment were damaged by a true casualty—fire, let's say—the resulting loss (unless covered by insurance) would be deductible *as* a casualty, while subsequent outlays for repair would be capitalized and added back to basis. Thus, if a machine with a value and adjusted basis of $10,000 sustains $2,000 of fire damage, the casualty loss is fully deductible and the basis of the machine is reduced to $8,000. If the taxpayer then spends $2,000 to repair the machine, the outlay is nondeductible (the casualty loss having been deducted already) but is added back to basis, which is restored to $10,000. An equivalent loss attributable to a malfunction results in no deductible loss and no reduction of basis. If, however, the taxpayer repairs the machine at the same $2,000 cost, a current deduction *is* permitted for the repair expenditure and the overall tax effects are just the same. The taxpayer's $2,000 economic loss is recognized in both cases—in the former, by treating the casualty itself as the realization of a deductible loss, in the latter, by accepting the repair expenditure as a proxy measure of the loss caused by the malfunction.[19]

In larger terms, the point to be made is that the casualty or the malfunction simply serves to precipitate the loss in value that will in any case take place over time as the taxpayer's equipment is used up in production. Thus, the taxpayer in the above example is entitled to recover his adjusted basis of $10,000 in future taxable years through annual allowances for depreciation. Casualty or

19. Johnson, *Soft Money Investing*   1019, 1089 (1989).
Under the Income Tax, 1989 U.Ill.L.Rev.

malfunction causes an instant loss in value; depreciation is anticipated, in effect, and to the extent thereof is allowed to be deducted
all at once.

A "repair"—as distinguished from a use-expanding or life-
prolonging alteration—is described by the Regulations as an outlay
whose limited purpose is to continue the property's operation for
the duration of its expected life or to maintain its normal output
and existing capacity. Adding the word "incidental" further suggests that current expense treatment is contemplated only if the
repair is of a small-scale and recurring nature—patching a flat tire,
replacing minor parts—so that a requirement to capitalize would
simply be a bookkeeping nuisance for most taxpayers. The Regulations do not attempt to specify a limitation based on dollar amount
or percentage of original cost, however, and, inevitably, taxpayers
have sought to expand the category of deductible repair to include
outlays that are neither small-scale nor recurring and that go well
beyond what might ordinarily be regarded as incidental. The latter
effort has sometimes been successful, sometimes not, and it is
commonplace to observe that the decided cases are difficult or
impossible to line up in a consistent fashion.

The question that has proved most troublesome in this field is
how to classify relatively large-scale outlays of which the aim is not
merely to correct a malfunction or replace a worn-out part, but to
adapt the equipment in the light of changed or newly discovered
conditions that otherwise compromise its usefulness. The equipment has operated satisfactorily to date within its own mechanical
limits. Now, however, owing to a change in surrounding circumstances, the taxpayer finds that it simply won't do its accustomed
job unless it is modified or augmented in some respect. The
taxpayer accordingly makes a sizeable expenditure that alters or
adds to the equipment in a material way. Yet the taxpayer's only
aim is to maintain existing operations; he expects no increase in
future revenues. Should the outlay be treated as a capital investment or as a mere repair?

In the well-known *Mt. Morris Drive–In* case,[20] the taxpayer
acquired a tract of farm land for the purpose of building an outdoor
movie theater. Covering vegetation was cleared from the property
in order to build ramps for automobiles, and as a result of this
removal of ground-cover the drainage of rain-water onto a neighboring farm increased substantially. Threatened with suit by the
adjoining landowner, the taxpayer at a cost of $8,000 installed a
drainage system which carried the excess rainfall to a public drain.

---

20. *Mt. Morris Drive–In Theatre Co.
v. Comm'r*, 25 T.C. 272 (1955).

The original acquisition of the farm land took place in 1947; the drainage system was added in 1950, although the lawsuit was threatened some two years earlier. The drainage system itself, quite obviously, had a useful life that extended well beyond the current taxable year.

On these facts, a majority of the Tax Court held that the outlay was a capital expenditure and rejected the taxpayer's effort to deduct it as a current expense. The majority found that the need for a drainage system had been obvious and foreseeable at the time the original construction work was undertaken. Accordingly, the taxpayer's initial capital investment was "incomplete" until the drainage system was added to the property: the outlay was part of the basic cost of the drive-in theatre, just as gutters and drains would be part of the basic cost of a house. In a brief concurring opinion, Judge Raum asserted that capital expenditure treatment was proper *whether or not* the need for a drainage system could have been foreseen in 1947, and whether the outlay was contemporaneous with the original construction or took place at a subsequent time. Finally, a dissent argued that since the drainage facility "did not improve, better, extend, increase, or prolong the useful life of the property," the outlay ought to be allowed as an ordinary and necessary business expense. Though somewhat cryptic on this point, the dissenting judges apparently thought that the need for a drainage system arose *after* completion of the original theatre construction and was attributable to events that could not have been anticipated.

The *Mt. Morris* decision can be contrasted with that in *Midland Empire Packing Co. v. Commissioner,*[21] in which the question was whether the cost of lining basement walls with concrete to prevent oil seepage created by a neighboring refinery should be treated as a deductible repair or as a capital expenditure—*Mt. Morris* from the perspective of the drainee, as it were. The walls of the basement, which had been used for 25 years for the storage of meat and hides, had proved entirely effective to keep out moisture until the refinery went up, at which point the said seepage began and the taxpayer was told by federal inspectors that it had to line the walls or shut down its plant altogether. The Tax Court held, this time unanimously, that the expenditure for wall-lining, nearly $5,000, was "essentially a repair" and hence deductible as a current business expense.

Can the two decisions, *Midland Empire* and *Mt. Morris,* be reconciled? One senses that the installation of drainage equipment

21. 14 T.C. 635 (1950).

in *Mt. Morris* represented an addition to the taxpayer's plant rather than a mere replacement, while the concrete lining in *Midland Empire* could be viewed as responsive to an unexpected event that somewhat resembled a natural disaster—seepage if not flooding. Hence, perhaps current expense treatment was more plausible in the latter case than in the former. On the other hand, as noted, the basement walls in *Midland Empire* were already 25 years old, which may mean that the storage facility had been fully depreciated at the time the outlay in question was made. If so, the facility would have had an adjusted basis in the taxpayer's hands of zero and its useful life would be over, *i.e.,* for tax purposes. Any further expenditure would therefore have to be viewed as life-prolonging within the sense of the Regulations mentioned above. As suggested earlier, the repair deduction is apparently to be explained on the ground that it takes the place of depreciation otherwise allowable to the taxpayer in future periods. Accepting that proposition, it would seem to follow that one cannot "repair" a fully depreciated asset.

(b) Business intangibles and advertising. The general requirement that the cost of long-lived assets be capitalized applies not only to tangible property such as plant and equipment, but also to intangible assets from which the taxpayer expects to realize economic benefits in future years.[22] Here, however, there may be some difficulty in identifying the "asset" to which the expenditure relates. Suppose, for example, that a business taxpayer spends money training employees to handle certain complex office machinery. The outlay obviously improves work performance, and it is also true, no doubt, that trained employees are expected to continue their employment beyond the current year. On the other hand, the training costs create no identifiable asset as such—no separate "property" to which the expenditure can be allocated—and perhaps for that reason such costs might be treated as a current business expense.

In the recent *INDOPCO* case, the taxpayer, a publicly held company, incurred investment banker's fees and related costs in connection with a friendly merger offer by another firm. Pointing out that no separate and identifiable asset had been created to which such outlays could be allocated, the taxpayer sought to deduct the banking fees (which ran into the millions) as a current expense. The Supreme Court held for the Commissioner. "Although the mere presence of an incidental future benefit . . . may

---

22. *See* Mundstock, *Taxation of Business Intangible Capital,* 135 U.Pa. L.Rev. 1179 (1987); Cunningham and Schenk, *How To Tax the House that Jack Built,* 43 Tax L.Rev. 447 (1988).

not warrant capitalization, a taxpayer's realization of benefits beyond the year in which the expenditure is incurred is undeniably important ..." Here, quite obviously, the transaction—that is, the merger—produced "significant benefits" that would be realized by the taxpayer, or by the merged entity, in future years. It followed that the fees could not be deducted currently but had to be capitalized under § 263.

The "future benefits" rationale adopted in *INDOPCO* is quite broad and would seem to give the Commissioner considerable latitude in determining whether intangible assets outlays are or are not to be classified as capital expenditures. Environmental cleanup costs of all sorts could readily be brought within the *Indopco* rationale, one would think; other examples, as suggested, might be employee recruitment and training expenses, plant-closing costs, perhaps even bonuses paid to encourage early retirement. The Service to date has issued no comprehensive ruling or regulation on how it intends to apply the *Indopco* decision, and one suspects that it may ultimately decide to handle questions that arise on a case-by-case basis.

It should be noted that the Court's decision left the taxpayer in *Indopco* with a capitalized item that apparently has no determinable or finite useful life. The economic benefits of the merger transaction presumably continue in being as long as the merged entity itself continues in being. Accordingly, no annual depreciation or amortization deduction would be allowed and the capitalized expenditure would be recovered by the taxpayer only when (if ever) the corporation was sold or dissolved. In other instances—environmental cleanup costs, for example—the Service can be expected to insist on capitalization under the *Indopco* rationale, but then might also choose to allocate the expenditure to a tangible asset (other than land) having a finite useful life. The result, a sort of compromise, would be to permit the taxpayer to recover its outlay over time through annual depreciation.[23]

But whatever its scope, the *Indopco* decision is unlikely to alter the long-standing treatment of one major category of intangible expenditure that may exceed all others in size and importance, namely, advertising. From a very early date, and presumably now with implied congressional sanction, amounts spent by business taxpayers for the purpose of stimulating sales of their products or

---

23. Certain expenditures—business start-up expenses, corporate organization costs—that would otherwise appear to be of indefinite duration and hence non-amortizable are "given" a limited life by specific Code provisions and thus permitted to be recovered over a stated period prescribed by statute. Code §§ 195, 248.

services through advertising and sales promotion have been treated as trade or business expenses under § 162(a) and allowed to be deducted currently. As a purely theoretical matter, it might be argued that the annual cost of promoting brand-X should somehow be divided between current sales, a deductible expense, and future sales activity, a capital expenditure. In practical terms, however, such an allocation would be difficult and perhaps impossible to carry out in other than an arbitrary fashion. As a result, the Service, with rare exceptions, permits advertising and related outlays to be deducted currently and makes no effort to identify a separate capital expenditure component. For the usual reason— namely, that deduction now is preferable to deduction later—the effect is generally favorable from the taxpayer's standpoint.

The discussion above concerns self-developed or self-generated intangibles, that is, intangibles created by the taxpayer through its own direct expenditures. As stated, such outlays may be deductible currently, as in the case of advertising expenses, or capitalized and then recovered through annual amortization allowances, or else, as in *INDOPCO*, capitalized but recovered only when the taxpayer itself is sold or liquidated.

A somewhat different set of considerations applies where intangible assets, including goodwill, are acquired by the taxpayer on the purchase of an entire business—that is, where the taxpayer buys intangible assets as part of the acquisition of another firm. This topic, which has been the subject of important recent legislation, is taken up at 6.10, below.

(c) Lease or purchase. In *Starr's Estate*,[24] the taxpayer acquired an automatic sprinkling system under a 5-year lease for an annual rental of $1,240. The lease was renewable for another five years at virtually no cost, and while no further provision was made for additional rental periods, the court found that because of the individualized nature of the equipment the lessor-manufacturer would not reclaim it once the first 5-year term had been completed. The taxpayer sought to deduct the annual rental payments as ordinary business expenses, but the Commissioner disallowed the deductions on the ground that the purported lease was really an installment purchase which must be capitalized. The Court of Appeals sustained the Commissioner. Stressing that the manufacturer had retained no significant residual interest in the property, the court held that the arrangement amounted to a conditional "sale" for federal tax purposes, even though formal title had not

24. *Starr's Estate v. Comm'r,* 274 F.2d 294 (9th Cir.1959).

114

passed to the "buyer," and even though the contract was a "lease" under local law.

Although the Commissioner had sought to capitalize the entire amount paid by the taxpayer—a total of $6,200—the court in *Starr's Estate* quite properly observed that as the payments were made in installments over a 5-year term, some portion of each payment must be regarded as implicit interest. Since the lump-sum purchase price of the same equipment was known to be $4,960, the court suggested that the difference—$1,240—be allowed as a deduction over 5 years at the rate of $248 a year. The sprinkler system itself was found to have a useful life of 23 years, so that the taxpayer presumably would be entitled to a yearly depreciation allowance of about $216 as well. His total annual deduction would thus be $464 during the 5-year payment period, and $216 thereafter, as opposed to $1,240 for each of the first 5 years if the "lease" had been recognized as such. The court also intimated that the entire matter was rather piddling. Once depreciation and interest had been allowed, it said, "the attack on many of the 'leases' may not be worth while in terms of revenue."

In a sense the latter observation is the most interesting feature of the court's opinion. *Was* the litigation "worth while" from the Treasury's standpoint? If we assume a 50% tax rate in all relevant periods, the "tax value" in a given year of deducting $1,240 as rent was obviously $620. The present value of $620 a year for 5 years discounted at a rate of (say) 5% is about $2,700. By contrast, the tax benefit of deducting $464 as depreciation and interest was $232, and of deducting $216 as depreciation alone, $108. The present value of $232 for 5 years and $108 for 18 years thereafter turns out to be about $2,000. Hence the controversy was worth roughly $700 ($2,700 minus $2,000) on a present basis. While that amount seems rather small in absolute terms, it would have reduced the after-tax cost of the sprinkler system by some 14%. Moreover, the transaction in *Starr's Estate* was not an isolated phenomenon: if the arrangement had gone unchallenged, then presumably many other installment sales of long-lived and higher-priced equipment would have been converted into "leases" for tax purposes.

Yet even when this is said, what *real* difference does it make to the government whether equipment transactions are treated as sales or leases? It is true that Starr's deductions as a "lessee" exceeded the depreciation which he would have been allowed as an "owner" during the years in question. But on the other side of the transaction, the manufacturer—who is also a taxpayer, of course—would (or should) have been required to report the payments as rental income. Instead of deducting its manufacturing costs over

115

the same 5-year period (as was permitted in the case of an installment seller), the manufacturer as "lessor" and legal owner of the equipment would have had to depreciate the sprinkler system over its much longer useful life. What the "lessee" gained by anticipating deductions, the "lessor" would lose by delay. Hence the Treasury would appear to be a mere stakeholder; the lessee's tax saving would be offset by the lessor's sacrifice, and the reduction in purchase price referred to in the preceding paragraph would really be borne by the manufacturer of the equipment.

So shouldn't the Treasury be content in all such cases? Why contest the parties' effort to characterize the transaction as a "lease" when the advantage to one taxpayer is compensated for by a disadvantage to the other? The answer is that *if* the benefit and sacrifice were *always* mutually offsetting, the Treasury might well be inclined to leave the matter to the parties and accept whatever characterization they adopted. Indeed, in that event the parties themselves might just as well bargain directly about the purchase price of the equipment instead of fooling around with tax arrangements. If, for example, Starr and the sprinkler manufacturer were *both* 50% taxpayers, then they achieved nothing by labelling the transaction as a "lease" that could not have been accomplished as well by knocking 14% off the price of the sprinkler system.[25]

The difficulty with adopting this view, of course, is that in many cases either there is a difference in applicable marginal tax rates between the parties to a transaction or one party has positive taxable income while the other does not. As a result, the accelerated deductions may be of greater tax value to one taxpayer than to the other. Where such differences in individual tax circumstances exist, the taxpayers, if free to characterize the transaction as a "sale" or "lease" entirely at will, would choose whichever label minimized their *combined* tax burden, and then on some basis would divide the tax saving between them. In all such cases the government would be the loser—indeed, the only loser—and would bear the entire burden of the adjustment. The Treasury's authority to insist that leases or sales shall be recognized as such only if *federally* established criteria are satisfied operates as a check on this process and limits the freedom of taxpayers to allocate and schedule deductions for their own benefit. In a sense, then, the

---

25. Unless they reported the transaction inconsistently, which is precisely what they did. According to 30 T.C. 863–4, the sprinkler manufacturer devised the "lease" as a means of stimulating sales to deduction-hungry customers. The manufacturer itself, however, reported its profit from the transaction in the same manner as the profit from an installment sale. The cost-saving "offered" by the manufacturer was thus entirely at the Treasury's expense, or would have been apart from the litigation.

real issue in *Starr's Estate* was whether the Treasury possessed such authority. The determination that it did is the chief significance of the decision.

There is more to be said about the lease-purchase distinction, especially in connection with the larger subject of depreciation. Accordingly, the topic is raised again, and discussed in a more contemporary setting, at 6.09(b), below.

(d) Education. Roughly stated, the cost of education or training is deductible as a current expense if the aim of the expenditure is to maintain or improve skills used by the taxpayer in an existing trade or business, or if the education is required by the taxpayer's employer as a condition of continued employment. The expense of a refresher course or a keeping-up-with-current-developments course is thus deductible as a sort of intellectual repair. A practicing lawyer, for example, was allowed to deduct as an expense the cost of attending the annual N.Y.U. Federal Tax Institute—a week-long presentation of entirely forgettable papers on current tax questions—because the "education" there received enabled him "to keep sharp the tools" that he used in his practice. The Service had argued that the outlay should be disallowed as a personal expense, thereby threatening the Institute with virtual extinction.[26]

The cost of acquiring *new* skills—by rough analogy to the status of alterations as distinguished from repairs—is usually denied unless the taxpayer can show that his intent is merely to enhance the skills that he already possesses. A teacher who goes to summer school in order to qualify for a higher civil service classification may deduct his costs on a showing that he is seeking to advance within his existing profession. But an accountant who goes to law school, allegedly to improve his performance as an accountant, is denied deduction by the present Regulations on the ground that the educational expense qualifies him for a new trade or business, whether he intends to enter that business or not. In most cases, therefore, the cost of acquiring an education which leads to a degree—J.D., M.D., Ph.D.—is not deductible; presumably the same is true of other vocational training expenses—learning to be a computer operator, auto mechanic, and so on.

The cost of a professional education is said by the Regulations to represent an "inseparable aggregate of personal and capital expenditures." Actually, of course, the "personal" component in attending law or medical school is pretty small for most people;

---

26. *Coughlin v. Comm'r*, 203 F.2d 307 (2d Cir.1953). And see Regs. § 1.162–5(b).

nonexistent for some. While the cost of going to college can perhaps be viewed differently, professional and vocational training is almost entirely business-related and unquestionably represents a capital expenditure. Nevertheless, the tax law does not recognize a right to recover the investment in professional training through annual depreciation or amortization deductions. The reason usually given for the denial is that capital investments may be depreciated or amortized only if they have an ascertainable useful life, and since one cannot be sure just how long the individual's training will serve as a productive resource—he may never practice law or he may still be wobbling into court at ninety—the cost cannot be amortized. On the other hand, it has been argued that human life being the finite thing it is, the individual's statistical life-expectancy, perhaps even his career-expectancy, is just as reliable and accurate a measure of the useful life of a professional education as an appraiser's estimate of the life of a building. Indeed, buildings seem to go on forever; lawyers plainly don't. "It is true that an asset with an indefinite life may not be amortized, but it does not follow that the life of an asset must be definitely predictable in order that it be definite or finite." [27]

The argument for permitting professional education costs to be amortized has undeniable force. Its defect—if it can be called that—is that it contains no intrinsic means of distinguishing between professional or vocational school expenses and the costs of general education. Apparently, it remains true that a college degree promises a higher income for the recipient than he would otherwise attain, and perhaps the same can be said of prep school or even private grade school. While Congress could no doubt draw a defensible line between general and specialized or between lower and higher education,[28] the same task would be exceedingly difficult if attempted through administrative rule-making or a process of case-by-case judicial development. In effect, the denial of training expenses is of such long standing that a reversal of policy—rather like taxing imputed rents or permitting a deduction for commuting costs—would now require Congressional action to establish the relevant criteria.

A loose end: In economic terms, the largest investment that a law student makes in his professional education is probably not the

27. Wolfman, *The Cost of Education and the Federal Income Tax,* 42 F.R.D. 535 (1966).

28. McNulty, *Tax Policy and Tuition Credit Legislation: Federal Income Tax Allowances for Personal Costs of Higher Education,* 61 Cal.L.Rev. 1 (1973).

cost of books and tuition, but the sacrifice of the salary-income that he would otherwise have earned during the three-year period. Assuming the student could have averaged $16,000 to $17,000 a year from other work, going to law school must be viewed as involving an "investment" of some $50,000 in forgone wages. Hopefully, this $50,000 investment will generate a higher level of earnings in the future than could have been attained without the legal training, and sufficiently so to make the sacrifice worthwhile.

For tax purposes, we can compare the law student with another individual who chooses to work during the same three-year period and who will in fact earn a total salary of $50,000, all of which he intends to invest in an annuity. The difficulty, of course, is that the working youth's $50,000 of salary is subject to an income tax. Hence, he will obviously have less in cash at the end of three years than the law student will have "in kind." Whereas the formation of human capital is tax-free by analogy to imputed income, the accumulation of tangible capital through wage-producing labor is fully taxable.[29] On balance, then, the tax treatment of professional training costs turns out to be comparatively favorable. In many instances (law school among them), the non-taxation of the imputed income should more than compensate for the disallowance of deductions for out-of-pocket costs.

6.03 "Ordinary and Necessary." To be deductible under § 162(a) an expenditure must not only be incurred in "carrying on a trade or business," but also qualify as "ordinary and necessary." Just what this further limitation means has never been entirely clear, although the quoted phrase has appeared in the statute virtually from its inception. The leading case on the subject is *Welch v. Helvering*,[30] decided by the Supreme Court in 1933. Unfortunately, Justice Cardozo's opinion contains so much soggy philosophy that its main thesis is difficult to locate. As a result, the case itself has been a source of some confusion. Most commentators today, I think, would view the decision as chiefly involving the distinction between current expense and capital expenditure, and in fairness it is that issue which the opinion seems to emphasize.

The taxpayer in *Welch* had been an executive of a corporation that went bankrupt in the grain business. Having decided to establish a similar business on his own, the taxpayer paid off the bankrupt company's debts in an effort to establish his own finan-

---

29. See Klein, *Timing in Personal Taxation*, 6 J. of Legal Studies 461 (1977).

30. 290 U.S. 111 (1933).

cial credit and regain his status and reputation with customers of his former firm. The Supreme Court sustained the Commissioner in denying deduction for the payments on the ground that the expenditures were not "ordinary" within the meaning of § 162(a), even though they might have been "necessary" for the buildup of the new business. Perhaps without really intending to, the Court used the word "ordinary" to express two quite different limitations on the scope of § 162(a), of which the first seems largely unwarranted. Initially taking the term to mean customary or typical, the Court found that the taxpayer's action in repaying the bankrupt's debts was "in a high degree extraordinary." "Men do at times pay the debts of others without legal obligation ... but they do not do so ordinarily ...." Until such conduct should become the business norm, therefore, it must be viewed as falling outside the statute. No evidence was cited to support a finding that the voluntary repayment of debts discharged in bankruptcy was altogether novel, and indeed one reads the fact-recital with a feeling that the taxpayer's action was entirely sensible from a business standpoint. Even if it *were* unprecedented, it is difficult to think of any reason why the tax law should bar deduction on that ground alone. Once satisfied that the expenditure was in fact designed to generate business income—a point conceded in *Welch*—the object of the statute would appear to have been met. § 162(a) aims at reducing the gross income derived from business by related expenses. If the expenditure was dictated by the taxpayer's business judgment, it ought to be deductible even if also found to be unusual "in a high degree."

In any event, this aspect of the *Welch* opinion has had no more than a limited application in later cases, and the Treasury has not regarded itself as authorized thereby to create normative classifications for business outlays. A few courts have followed *Welch* in disallowing voluntary debt repayments on a finding of "unusualness", but in most such instances the disallowance can also be explained on the ground that the taxpayer's action lacked a clear relationship to business goals, *i.e.,* that the repayment was personal, and hence not "necessary." [31]

Justice Cardozo applied the term "ordinary" in another sense in *Welch,* and by and large it is this second meaning which has received the greater emphasis in subsequent decisions. In effect, the Court found that in paying off the old creditors of his former firm the taxpayer really was engaged in making an outlay that

---

31. *Friedman v. Delaney,* 171 F.2d   ring opinion.
269 (1st Cir.1948), especially the concur-

belonged to the category of capital expenditure. The debt repayments were designed to restore the taxpayer's credit and to reestablish his reputation with other firms. Hence they could reasonably be regarded as the purchase price of customer goodwill, a capital asset. "Ordinary" business expenses, by contrast, were those which belonged to the category of deductible current expense. Used in the sense of "everyday" or "recurring", the term merely served as a short-hand way of distinguishing between capital expenditures and current items. To be sure, § 263 accomplishes the very same end, just as § 262 expressly disallows expenditures that are personal; hence, as has often been observed, the "ordinary and necessary" restriction seems at best to be excess statutory baggage.

Actually, the question whether the debt repayments in *Welch* qualified as current expenses may have been closer than the Cardozo opinion makes it appear. The taxpayer's "new" business activity was largely a continuation of the old business enterprise, of which he and his father had been the sole owners. From the standpoint of the taxpayer's individual business career it seems plausible that the challenged payments were made for the purpose of protecting something he already possessed, to-wit, a reputation in the grain trade. Under this view, the taxpayer was not entering a new field but reentering an old one; the debt-repayments merely helped to refurbish and shore up his "goodwill" among business associates he already knew well. Taking this approach, the outlays were more in the nature of deductible repairs to an existing capital asset than payments for the creation of a new resource.

Caught up in its own phrase-making, however, the Court gave little attention to the business context before it. From the taxpayer's standpoint the result was particularly painful. Self-created "goodwill" is regarded by the tax law as a capital asset of indeterminate useful life, one that lacks a predictable or ascertainable expiration date. As a consequence, its cost cannot be recovered through annual deductions for depreciation or amortization. Instead such cost would be recoverable only when the business was finally sold or liquidated. In *Welch*, however, even this distant expectation of a tax benefit was placed in doubt. Although the debt repayments seem to have related exclusively to the taxpayer's professional interest, the Court also saw a personal element in the matter, as if the money had been spent to meet a moral as much as a business obligation. Viewed in this way—that is, as involving an "inseparable aggregate" of personal and professional expenditures—it is by no means clear that any form of cost recovery would ever be allowed.

A loose end: Business expenses have sometimes been disallowed under a so-called "public policy" exception where deductibility of the expenses would frustrate a well-defined state or national policy. Thus, fines paid by a trucking company for deliberately overloading its trucks were disallowed by the Supreme Court in *Tank Truck Rentals, Inc. v. Commissioner.*[32] The Court reasoned that the state law would be frustrated if the fines were allowed as business expense, because the deduction would take the sting out of the penalty.

Illegal or "improper" payments are also occasionally held to be non-deductible under the public policy exception (or on the ground that they aren't "necessary"), although the Supreme Court has permitted deduction for wages and rents paid by an illegal bookmaking business. *Commissioner v. Sullivan,* 356 U.S. 27 (1958). The state law defined the wage and rental payments themselves as illegal, but the Court apparently thought it more important to avoid imposing tax on the gross receipts of the business. Code § 162(c) now specifically denies deduction for certain illegal bribes and kickbacks. The section does not stop at the water's edge, because it disallows payments made to foreign government officials which "would be unlawful under the laws of the United States if such laws were applicable to such payment and to such official".

6.04 Reasonable Compensation. § 162(a)(1) provides that the taxpayer's business expenses shall include a "reasonable allowance" for salaries and other compensation. Since payments to employees for services rendered would plainly qualify as business expenses without specific mention, it is generally assumed that the quoted phrase is intended as a limitation on the amount allowable: in effect, no deduction is permitted for salaries which *exceed* a "reasonable" amount. Even so, the purpose of the subsection is not intuitively obvious. Why isn't every salary reasonable by definition? Apart from possible imprudence (for which he oughtn't to be penalized anyway), why would an employer ever pay more to obtain his employees' services than market conditions "reasonably" require?

The answer can be seen in two contexts. In both, the issue of reasonable compensation arises only because payor and payee are related parties—either as corporation and shareholder or as members of the same family—so that the "overpayment" actually entails no economic loss to the employer. With infrequent exceptions—the *Patton* case, discussed below, is one—the reasonable-salary rule has been used by the Service not as general authority to

32. 356 U.S. 30 (1958).

impose wage-ceilings, but as a means of preventing income-shifting between related taxpayers whose economic interests are essentially identical.

As has been noted (5.02), under the present tax system corporate income is exposed to an extra measure of taxation. Corporate earnings are taxed first to the corporation itself at the rates set forth in Code § 11. When, or if, the corporation distributes the amount that is left as a dividend, the shareholders are taxed again at their individual rates. To be sure, the corporation is not *compelled* to distribute its after-tax earnings. It may elect to retain such earnings for use in the business, and in that event only the corporate-level tax is applicable. If it does make a dividend distribution, however, or is found to have done so, then a tax is imposed at both the corporate and the shareholder levels.

The somewhat volatile role of "salary" in this system—particularly in the case of smaller, closely-held corporations—can easily be surmised. If the corporation's shares are largely owned by its chief executive, then, apart from the reasonableness limitation, it would be a simple matter to reduce the corporate-level tax by substituting deductible salary payments for non-deductible dividends. All that is needed is to increase the shareholder-executive's compensation to the dollar-amount desired. To illustrate, suppose Smith owns all of the shares of X corporation and also serves as its president. The corporation usually "earns" about $100,000 a year *before* Smith's salary, but since Smith normally takes a "reasonable" salary of precisely the same amount, the corporation's annual taxable income is customarily zero and it pays no tax whatever. Smith, of course, pays an individual tax on the salary he receives. Suppose, however, that in the current year the corporation's pre-salary earnings balloon to $250,000. Smith is eager to withdraw the entire amount for his personal use. If Smith's salary for the year is limited to the customary $100,000, the corporation will have taxable income of $150,000 and will pay a corporate-level tax of $39,250. If the corporation then distributes its after-tax income of $110,750 ($150,000 − $39,250) to Smith as a dividend, Smith himself would have total taxable income of $210,750, on which he would pay an individual tax of about $61,400. The sum of corporate and individual taxes on the $250,000 of business income would thus be about $100,650—a corporate tax of $39,250 plus an individual tax of $61,400—leaving "only" $149,350 for Smith to add to his personal resources.

Apart from the hurdle raised by § 162(a)(1), Smith could obviously reduce this overall tax burden by causing the corporation to pay him a "bonus" equal to its abnormal earnings of $150,000.

A single, individual-level tax is *always* less than the two-level tax on distributed corporate earnings. If Smith has $250,000 of salary income, his personal tax will be about $75,500 and the addition to his private resources will be $174,500, which is $25,150 better than the net of the salary-plus-dividend arrangement. The beauty of it all, of course, is that the choice between "salary" and "dividend" lies entirely with Smith—the corporation is obviously his creature and does his bidding. From a business standpoint, moreover, it makes no difference whether corporate assets are conveyed to Smith as salary or as a dividend except, of course, as the choice of form may succeed in minimizing taxes.

It is at this point that the Commissioner is likely to assert that the purported bonus violates the reasonable salary limitation. Citing external evidence of salary levels in similar firms as well as the past practice of Smith's own company, the Commissioner would argue that $100,000 represents a "reasonable" wage for Smith's services and that the additional $150,000 must be disallowed as excessive. This disallowance, of course, does not mean that the $150,000 receipt is any the less a "distribution" as far as Smith is concerned. In effect, the bonus would be recharacterized as a *dividend,* includable as income by Smith in his capacity as shareholder, but not deductible by the corporation. Assuming that the corporation has no previously accumulated earned surplus (all earnings have heretofore been paid out as salary), the dividend amount would presumably be limited to $110,750, *i.e.,* the corporation's taxable income of $150,000 less its tax of $39,250, so that the result would be the same as if the "bonus" arrangement had not been attempted.

Smith's effort to convert dividends into compensation—and the Commissioner's response—has a good deal in common with the shareholder-loan device described at 3.01. There the shareholder's aim was to withdraw funds from the corporation for his personal use, but at the same time to avoid the *individual*-level tax by characterizing the withdrawal as a borrowing. Since borrowed funds are not included in the borrower's income, a "loan" of $150,000, though not deductible by the corporate lender, results in no additional tax at the individual level. Here, by contrast, the effort is to avoid the *corporate*-level tax by withdrawing funds in the form of "salary." In both situations, the Treasury's aim is to defend the two-level tax system by insisting that the withdrawal, objectively viewed, is neither a loan nor a salary payment but a dividend.

The second of the two related-party contexts in which § 162(a)(1) may be applicable can be mentioned more briefly. If

Smith has a dependent—say an aged parent—for whose support he is, or feels, responsible, there may be a considerable tax saving in putting that individual on the company payroll. Support payments, or gifts, to family members would normally have to be made out of after-tax income, just like any other personal expenditure. But if Smith's aged parent can be made to serve as an employee—at least for payroll purposes—then the effect is to allow Smith to meet his personal obligation out of pre-tax income and to substitute the payee's (lower) marginal tax rate for his own. Once again, the reasonable salary limitation empowers the Commissioner to disallow the deduction (in a proper case, of course) by recharacterizing the purported salary payment as family support or as a gift.

§ 162(a)(1) has occasionally (though infrequently) been applied to disallow salary payments to *unrelated* individuals on the ground that the amount paid was simply too large to be regarded as "reasonable." In *Patton v. Commissioner,*[33] for example, the taxpayers, father and son, operated a small machine shop in the form of a partnership. For a number of years they employed a bookkeeper—one Kirk, the possessor of a grammar school education and two years of commercial training in high-school—at an annual salary of less than $2,000. In 1941 General Motors began sending the partnership very sizeable quantities of work; and immediately thereafter the taxpayers contracted with Kirk to pay the latter an annual salary equal to 10% of the partnership's net sales. Under this agreement Kirk received, and the partnership deducted, $46,000 for the year 1943. The Commissioner determined that $13,000 represented reasonable compensation for Kirk's services as bookkeeper and disallowed the balance as excessive. Kirk was not related to the Pattons, and it was not suggested that the payment had been intended as a gift.

A majority of the Court of Appeals sustained the Commissioner's action on the ground that persons of similar training doing similar work for other firms were paid far less than $46,000 a year. Kirk's responsibilities obviously did not justify a salary of that size, and the mere fact that the parties themselves may have regarded the arrangement as reasonable was not binding on the government. In effect, the Commissioner was free to apply his own salary standard, presumably on the basis of objective market data. A dissent argued that the contract between Kirk and the partnership was "bona fide" even if improvident from the company's standpoint. Although the salary turned out to be "too high", that was "no business or concern of the Government." The decisive ques-

33.   168 F.2d 28 (6th Cir.1948).

tion was whether the parties had intended the payment as salary, and since no contrary showing was made, the amount paid should have been allowed in full.

The dissenting opinion is, of course, perfectly correct as a matter of tax policy. No reason whatever can be advanced for disallowing salary payments to employees, provided they really are salary payments and not dividends or gifts in disguise. Further, the disallowance in *Patton* can be objected to on the ground that it actually led to a double tax on the company's earnings, though without the customary justification of a corporate-shareholder relationship. Thus the salary disallowance increased the partnership's net income and hence the taxable income of the two partners. At the same time Kirk himself remained taxable on the full amount received. The Commissioner did not assert that the $46,000 was anything *other* than salary—the disallowance was based solely on reasonableness of amount—and Kirk had no apparent obligation to repay the alleged excess to the partnership. Accordingly, the disallowed portion—some $33,000—was taxed both to the payors *and* to the payee at the high wartime rates which then prevailed, a result that can only be characterized as punitive.[34]

Could there be more to the *Patton* saga than meets the eye? It is striking that the Patton Company entered into the contingent pay arrangement with Kirk *after* it had been assured of the GM business, and at a time when a very large increase in company income could easily be foreseen. But why would the partners ever have done *that?* The reported record of the trial in the Tax Court shows that Kirk received his salary in cash but that he neither deposited it in a bank account nor used it to purchase investments or other property. Queried as to where the money had actually gone, Kirk testified that he had simply "kept it at home,"[35] presumably in a cookie jar. While the latter assertion was never disproved, one senses that the government may have suspected, or perhaps even have been convinced, that the cash in question (net of Kirk's personal tax) had ultimately found its way back into the hands of the Pattons themselves. The excess compensation claim may thus have been a way of taxing the company profits to the persons whom the government regarded as the real payees.

---

34. As noted, the Commissioner has rarely used the reasonableness limitation as authority to review arm's-length salary arrangements, and indeed the Regulations confirm that contingent payment contracts made "pursuant to a free bargain" will generally not be challenged even though the amounts paid thereunder turn out to be unusually large. Regs. § 1.162–7(a)(2).

35. 6 T.C.M. 486.

As will be seen below, there is another side to the reasonable compensation problem. If the payment of excessive compensation presents dangers from the standpoint of the Treasury, especially as between related parties, what about arrangements involving the contrary pattern? In our initial illustration, suppose that Smith elects to take *no* salary from the corporation in a given year. He has substantial income from other sources and his own marginal tax rate is higher than the corporation's, so that overall taxes can be minimized if the customary salary payment is simply omitted. In effect, there is income-shifting in the opposite direction, *i.e.*, from an individual to his controlled corporation. Although § 162(a)(1) could be read to *require* the payment of a reasonable salary, the fact is that it has not been so construed. On the whole, income-shifting between shareholders and corporation by means of *under*-compensation for services is tolerated by the tax law. The explanation (to the extent there is one) for what thus appears to be an asymmetrical application of the reasonable salary standard is given at 9.03, along with a description of the special and contrasting rules that govern family partnerships.

* * *

A loose end: Reacting to a steady stream of adverse publicity about the astronomic salaries paid to American corporate executives (especially as compared with the relatively modest compensation levels of their German and Japanese counterparts), Congress in 1993 added § 162(m), which denies deduction for salaries in excess of $1 million where the employer-payor is a publicly-held corporation and the payee is one of the corporation's 5 highest paid executives. An exception is made, and deduction is allowed, if the excess salary is based "on the attainment of one or more performance goals". Such "performance goals" are required to be formulated in advance (not in hindsight) by so-called outside directors and to be approved by a majority vote of the corporation's shareholders.

Focusing first on the exception, we might wonder how the term "performance-based compensation" should be defined as a conceptual matter. A preliminary question would be whether "performance" is to be measured on an absolute or a comparative basis. If X Corporation shows a 50% increase in earnings per share this year, that would appear to be good enough (absolutely) to support deductible performance bonuses for management. Yet, if the earnings of Y Corporation jumped 100%, then X would not appear to have done well at all (comparatively) and it is hard to see why X's managers should get extra pay for falling behind the competition.

But are X and Y really comparable? Both are toy manufacturers, let's say, but X makes educational toys for pre-school children while Y makes cap-guns and rubber daggers. And is it appropriate to judge performance by a single year's profit-and-loss statement? Suppose X has invested in research and development that won't pay off for a decade, while Y has done everything it can to increase current sales. And so on.

Comparability issues of this sort are familiar in the field of corporate litigation but usually require a lot of time and effort to resolve. Probably, therefore, administrative practicality makes it necessary to take a simpler approach under § 162(m). The accompanying Committee Report states that the relevant performance criteria might include the company's sales, earnings or share price, but the Report says nothing about intercompany comparisons and apparently regards "performance" as an absolute rather than a comparative measure of executive success.

Since deductions for fixed or non-performance based salaries in excess of $1 million are now disallowed, such excess payments (if made at all) will have to be made out of the payor's after-tax income. The effect from a tax standpoint would then be equivalent to the distribution of a dividend. Dividends, though taxable to the recipient, are not deductible by the distributing corporation. In a closely-held setting, as noted above, the "reasonable salary" limitation of § 162(a)(1) is intended to achieve precisely the same effect: salary payments found to be unreasonable in amount remain taxable to the payee, but deduction is denied to the payor-corporation and the purported salary is added back to corporate taxable income. There is of course a major difference between the closely-held and the publicly-held situation. In a closely-held case, the excess salary recipient is invariably the corporation's principal shareholder. As such, he is obviously indifferent to whether the cash he receives is paid to him as a deductible salary payment or as a nondeductible dividend—he gets it all in any event. What he does care about, and all he cares about, is how the legal characterization—salary or dividend—affects the corporation's tax bill. By contrast, the executive of a publicly-held corporation is a "mere" employee (certainly not a controlling shareholder) and would therefore get no benefit if the excess salary amount were simply added to the corporation's annual dividend and distributed to shareholders generally. Put otherwise, the executives and the shareholders of a publicly-held corporation are two different sets of people—executives don't get dividends and shareholders don't get salaries—so that the customary rationale for disallowance is lacking.

Many, of course, have argued that the formal structure of the modern public corporation hides a deeper reality. Although its shareholders have legal power over corporate management, the publicly-held corporation is said by some to be an entity that is essentially within the domination and control of self-perpetuating managers—managers who are practically, if not legally, independent of the company's shareholders and therefore free to put their personal income goals ahead of the interests of the ostensible owners. In effect, the salaries received by inside managers (not just annual pay, but also bonuses, stock options and pensions) are said to include a kind of "rent" or status-income that reflects the entrenched power of incumbent office-holders who cannot easily be dislodged. If one accepts this analysis (some do, some don't), then, as a matter of tax policy, I suppose it can be argued that inside managers hold a kind of super-equity and that excess salary payments (defined as payments over $1 million) may be characterized as quasi-dividends. It would follow, again as a matter of tax policy, that such payments ought not to reduce the corporate tax base any more than conventional dividends do, and that disallowance is for that reason justified.[36]

6.05 Interest. Speaking generally, § 163(a) allows a deduction for interest paid or accrued during the taxable year. Thus, interest expense incurred by a corporation, say, on funds borrowed to finance current operating expenses (a short-term bank loan, typically) or to build a manufacturing facility (perhaps a long-term loan from an insurance company or even a public bond issue) qualifies for deduction on the same basis as any other recurring outlay. The same is true (special limitations aside) for an individual investor who pays interest to his broker on funds borrowed to buy securities on margin or to a bank on a real estate mortgage loan. In either case, the borrower hopes and expects to generate gross income by putting the borrowed funds to work in its (or his) business or investment activities. Interest paid to the lender obviously subtracts from the borrower's profits—may even reduce such profits to a negative figure—so that deductibility fully accords with the goal of the system, which is to impose a tax on net income.

To be sure, there can be problems even in this context. Although § 163(a) states that interest is deductible when "paid," *prepaid* interest—interest paid in advance—presumably has to be capitalized. Thus, under § 263A, interest incurred by a builder on a short-term construction loan—even though payable currently— must be added to the cost of the completed structure and recovered

---

36. Zelinsky, *The Tax Policy Case for Denying Deductibility to Excessive Exec-* utive Compensation, 58 Tax Notes 1123 (1993).

over the structure's entire useful life. This, however, merely shows that interest, like any other business outlay, is subject to the capital expenditure limitation described at 6.02, of which the object is to match gross income from a particular source with its associated costs.

In certain situations, nevertheless, the Code disallows the interest deduction by specific provision. The courts, on occasion, have done the same even *without* specific statutory authority. Although the transactions so affected are relatively narrow, the *reason* for such disallowances is both general and important and needs to be understood as background for the major changes made by the 1986 Act in the tax-shelter area, the latter being described at 13.02. The discussion that follows attempts to clarify this moderately complex feature.

Though by no means unrelated to the material in this section, the subject of *personal* interest—interest on home loans, auto loans, credit cards, etc.—is taken up separately at 7.04.

(a) "Tax arbitrage" and special disallowances. Despite its apparent similarity to other kinds of expenditures, interest—the cost of "hiring" capital funds for business, investment or personal use—turns out to be one of the most volatile elements in the entire Code structure, an observation that is attested to by the sheer number of Code provisions addressed to the question of when or in what amount interest must be included in income, excluded, deducted, capitalized, disallowed, and so on. Some of these topics are discussed elsewhere in this volume—bond discount, a species of "hidden" interest, is considered at 17.04, for example—but it may be useful here to emphasize one particular problem that makes the interest deduction an especially sensitive Code topic. Actually, it is not so much the deduction itself that causes the problem alluded to as it is the presence in our law of so many categories of exempt or partially exempt income which may be *combined* with deductible interest in the hands of a single taxpayer. This, in turn, creates a dangerous and unstable condition for which the Code—at its own peril, so to speak—simply must provide a remedy.

The point can be made very easily by asking how high-income taxpayers would behave if the Code *lacked* present § 265(a)(2), which disallows the deduction of interest on indebtedness incurred to purchase tax-exempt municipal bonds. Absent § 265(a)(2), a 40% taxpayer would be well-advised to borrow money in order to buy tax-exempt municipals even if the interest he had to pay on his loan was greater than the interest he expected to receive on his bond investment. Thus, suppose the taxpayer buys $100,000 of municipal bonds yielding 8%, or $8,000 a year, tax-free. To finance the investment he borrows $100,000 from a lender (pledging the bonds) at an interest cost of 10%, or $10,000 a year. Is he crazy? Not if the loan interest is deductible. Apart from taxes, the investment results in a loss of $2,000 a year; but when we observe that the $8,000 inflow is tax-exempt while the $10,000 outflow is deductible (§ 265(a)(2) aside), the result is a *positive* annual return of $2,000, *i.e.*, the $4,000 tax saving (40% of $10,000) less the net interest cost of $2,000. This, moreover, although the taxpayer hasn't put a penny of his own money into the deal.

All of this looks pretty much like tax-avoidance—sophisticated tax-avoidance, if you like—which, if unimpeded, could have serious consequences for the income tax. Especially during recent periods when tax-rates were higher and the rate-structure was more sharply progressive, but even under the rate structure we have today, one would expect upper-income taxpayers to resort very freely to arrangements of the sort described. The taxpayer's *taxable* income would be reduced to a minimum thereby, though his *after-tax* income would actually be increased. Nothing, perhaps, could have so damaging an impact on the morale of *other* taxpayers (once they came to understand what was happening) than the realization that higher-bracket people had been provided with an easy means of subverting the system in their own interest.

As indicated, Code § 265(a)(2), which goes back many years, largely blocks my illustrative device by denying deduction of interest on funds borrowed to buy municipal bonds, although the practical difficulty of tracing borrowings to bond purchases may limit the effectiveness of the disallowance in some cases. Even if wholly effective, however, the important fact remains that municipal bonds are not the only source of exempt or partially exempt income. Others, equally prominent, have already been mentioned. Insurance (see 2.03) is one: although interest on ordinary savings accounts is taxable whether or not withdrawn by the depositor, the "inside" interest build-up under a life-insurance policy or annuity contract is generally exempt. Depreciation on plant and equipment is another: while business income is of course generally taxable, the effect of rapid depreciation allowances—ACRS (6.09)—is to create a partial exemption through the medium of income-deferral. A third example, here based on the common-law realization requirement, is investment in appreciating securities (5.01): an increase in the value of a stock investment is taxed to the investor only if he happens to sell the stock during the taxable year; no tax is imposed if he doesn't sell, even though the year's unrealized appreciation plainly represents an "accession to wealth" in economic terms. Finally, as observed (1.03), the purchase of household durables—homes, cars, washing machines—generates imputed income equal to the annual rental value of the property, though of course no effort is made to include such amounts under § 61.

In each of these (and other) situations, the asset yielding exempt income can be, and often is, purchased by borrowing the purchase price. In each, therefore, the opportunity exists for achieving a "tax arbitrage" effect—taking in exempt income with one hand and paying out deductible interest with the other—of the sort illustrated by my municipal bond example. As already emphasized, the consequences, from the standpoint of both revenues and taxpayer morale, may be serious. Hence, the question of how to cope and what to do becomes a critical issue in tax policy.[37] Two obvious legislative alternatives arise. The simplest (simplest to conceive of, I mean) would be to eliminate the income exemptions that represent the first leg of the arbitrage device. If municipal bond interest, insurance policy build-up, unrealized stock appreciation and imputed income were made taxable, and if rapid depreciation were converted into economic depreciation, all by Code amendment, the risk of structural damage in these areas would disappear. No objection could be raised against an investment program or a course of dealing that combined *taxable* income with deductible interest, the latter then simply being an appropriately recognized cost of earning the former. But if such legislative action is unfeasible, whether for practical or political reasons, the danger of tax-avoidance has presumably got to be met by dealing with the other leg of the device—that is, by denying or restricting the deductibility of interest on amounts borrowed to finance the purchase of the exempt-source asset. What is needed, in the end, is tax-symmetry: if income is exempt, then the related financing cost should be non-deductible; equating the deduction side with the income side—treating *both* as "non-existent" for tax purposes—effectively removes the arbitrage effect referred to above, at least as far as loan-financed investors are concerned.

Congress has slowly—very slowly—reacted to the exemption-deduction problem just described by imposing restrictions in specific areas of known abuse. Code § 265(a)(2), mentioned above, is one such. Another, as will be seen in the subsection immediately following, is § 264(a)(2)—added to the Code in 1954—which disallows interest on debt incurred to purchase a single-premium insurance or annuity contract. Still another (a 1969 enactment) can be

---

37. See Warren, *Accelerated Capital Recovery, Debt, and Tax Arbitrage,* 38 The Tax Lawyer 549 (1985). And see Shakow, *Confronting the Problem of Tax Arbitrage,* 43 Tax L.Rev. (1987).

found in § 163(d), which limits the deduction of "investment interest" in any taxable year to an amount not in excess of the taxpayer's investment income (*e.g.*, dividends and interest), with disallowed amounts being carried forward to subsequent periods. The aim of the latter provision, obviously, is to prevent taxpayers from combining a *present* interest deduction with *deferred* property appreciation by borrowing to purchase growth stocks or other investments that produce little current income and may ultimately generate capital gains taxable at a lower rate.

In the 1986 Act, Congress further undertook to limit tax arbitrage by restricting the deductibility of interest and other expenses attributable to real estate tax shelters. The new provisions—chiefly § 469—are important, even vital, to the integrity of the income tax, but they do add detail and complexity to a statute already famous for those attributes. Such complexity could have been avoided, perhaps, if the first leg of the arbitrage device— exempt-source income, here in the form of over-rapid depreciation—had been the focus of reform, but that is a lot to ask of a legislative process exposed to pressure from many quarters. As might be expected, therefore, it is the second element—the deduction leg—on which the 1986 changes concentrate. These changes and related matters are taken up at 13.01 and 13.02, my hope being that the comments made here will have helped to set the stage for later discussion.

(b) Sham transactions. The seductive appeal of tax arbitrage has led, on occasion, to the framing of transactions that have virtually no investment substance but apparently fall within the literal terms of § 163(a). On the whole, though not invariably, the courts have been able to block the sought-for arbitrage effect by resorting to "general legal principles." The Supreme Court's decision in *Knetsch v. U.S.*[38]—a case which arose in a year prior to, but which was decided after the enactment of § 264(a)(2)—is an example.

Simplifying somewhat, in *Knetsch* the taxpayer bought a 2½% annuity contract from an insurance company for $4,004,000, of which only $4,000 was paid in cash while $4,000,000 was "borrowed" from the company on a 3½% non-recourse note. Under the terms of the contract, the annuity would return $90,000 a month (*if* all indebtedness was paid up) commencing when Knetsch reached the age of 90. The interest due on the $4,000,000 note—$140,000—was paid by Knetsch in advance. Under the "Table of Cash

---

38. 364 U.S. 361 (1960). See Blum, *Knetsch v. United States: A Pronounce-* *ment on Tax Avoidance,* 1961 Sup.Ct. Rev. 135.

and Loan Values" which was attached to the annuity contract, the cash value of the annuity would increase to $4,100,000 at the end of the first year, with a similar increase in each succeeding year. Knetsch was permitted to "borrow" this increase of $100,000 as well—again on a non-recourse note—to meet the interest charge on the $4,000,000 premium loan, so that his actual out-of-pocket interest payment was only about $40,000. Knetsch also prepaid $3,500 of interest on the second note.

As a result of all this paper work, Knetsch actually parted with some $47,500 in cash. Total "interest payments," however, if recognized as such, were $143,500. Assuming Knetsch was in the 50% bracket, the interest deduction, if allowed, would have resulted in a tax saving of $71,750 (.50 × $143,500). The net benefit to Knetsch for a single year (he repeated this procedure the following year) would have been the difference between the tax saved ($71,-750) and the cash laid out ($47,500), or $24,250, which was not a bad day's work. As noted, the annual interest build-up in the cash value of an annuity is not currently taxable, and Knetsch (or his advisor) apparently expected that such build-up would be treated as a low-taxed capital gain when the annuity finally matured.

Finding that the transaction lacked a business purpose, the Supreme Court disallowed the interest deduction in full. Since the interest payable on the notes—3½%—exceeded that receivable under the annuity—2½%—the arrangement was plainly pointless apart from the expected tax saving. The taxpayer took no real risk because his debt was in the form of a non-recourse note which could not be enforced against his personal assets, and the insurance company took only the very remote risk that interest rates might someday fall below 2½%, thereby making it profitable for Knetsch to repay the amounts that he had "borrowed." The statute, said the Court in effect, was not set up to cover make-believe transactions. It was evident that no one would have done the deal that Knetsch did other than for tax reasons; hence § 163 did not apply. The Court was disturbed neither by the fact that § 264(a)(2) was inapplicable to the year in question, nor by any negative implication arising from its subsequent enactment.

While the outcome in *Knetsch* seems correct, it must be conceded (as the dissenting opinion stressed) that there is something troublesome about adding a "business purpose" requirement to the Code at this particular point. There are, after all, a great many transactions which are undertaken solely with a view to minimizing taxes—buying tax-free municipal bonds instead of higher-yielding corporate securities, selling property at the close of one year rather than the start of another in order to accelerate the recognition of a loss, and so on. These actions might not be taken without the expectation of a tax benefit, and yet no one would argue that they should be disregarded solely for that reason. Nor does it suffice to say, for example, that the exclusion of municipal bond interest is specifically authorized by the Code. So is the deduction of interest on indebtedness; yet the Court in *Knetsch* held that the absence of an independent business purpose was disqualifying under § 163. The difficulty, then, is to state just *why* business purpose is a condition which taxpayers must satisfy in some instances but not in others. The Court majority attempted no general answer to this question, and thus made it possible for the dissenters to urge that the loophole (if that's what it was) which Knetsch sought to exploit should have been left for Congress to close.

Perhaps the majority could have avoided the slippery problem of motivation and business purpose by simply affirming the trial court's finding that "no indebtedness . . . was created by any of the . . . transactions." Whether or not a legal debt had been created presumably depended on the intent of the parties. Did they, or did they not, expect and intend that Knetsch would eventually repay the amounts allegedly borrowed? If not, then quite apart from Knetsch's motive to escape tax, the notes themselves would lack the status of "indebtedness" under federal and perhaps even local law standards. The question of intent to repay is one of fact, and on a fact-question the trial court's finding normally is conclusive unless clearly erroneous. Had the Supreme Court done no more than accept that finding (perhaps with the observation that any other finding *would* be clearly erroneous), it could have affirmed the disallowance on a narrower, and more comfortable, rationale.

6.06 Losses. § 165(a) authorizes a deduction for any loss "sustained" (*i.e.,* realized) during a taxable year which is not compensated for by insurance or otherwise. In the case of individual taxpayers (taxpayers other than corporations), § 165(c) limits the deduction to losses incurred in a trade or business or in connection with "any transaction entered into for profit," and to losses resulting from "casualty" or theft. Apart from casualty losses (discussed at 7.02 below), the aim of § 165(c) is to carry out the customary distinction between costs (here, losses) which relate to a taxpayer's business or investment activities and are therefore properly deductible in determining his taxable income for the year, and costs which are personal and hence properly disallowed. The distinction is essentially the same as that discussed at 6.01 in connection with business or personal expenses. Here, however, the problems of classification are somewhat easier to cope with. "Losses" typically result from dispositions of *property,* and as compared with ambiguous expense items like travel and entertainment the status of property is normally clear.　A hundred shares of General Motors stock is plainly an investment asset; the family automobile is just as clearly personal.　As shown below, interpretative problems of a recurring nature do exist—chiefly in connection with sales of personal residences—but it is fair to say that these are minor on the whole.

The disallowance of losses from sales of personal property deserves a brief explanatory comment.　With the exception of losses from casualty or theft, the tax law has always treated any realized decline in the value of "household durables" as personal.　If a taxpayer buys a car for $8,000, devotes it to family use for a year and then sells it to a used-car dealer for $6,000, the $2,000 "loss" is assumed to represent a personal consumption expenditure of the same character as food, clothing or recreation.　Once again, unless taxable income is to be reduced to zero, the taxpayer's expenditures for personal living must be disallowed.　This is true whether the expenditure is for current items—food, recreation—or reflects the annual decline in the value of capital goods, such as a home or car. To be sure, the used-car market may have fluctuated (upward or downward) between the time of purchase and the time of resale, so that the $2,000 "loss" may actually be greater or smaller than the amount of depreciation originally anticipated.　But while the tax law could (and perhaps should; see 15.02) take separate account of market changes by distinguishing between expected and actual depreciation, the plain fact is that it does not.　Logically or otherwise, the law regards the decline in value as wholly attributable to personal use and allows no portion of the loss.

Questions of "motive" or "intent" are common in the controversies that do rise under § 165(c).　In *Gevirtz v. Commissioner*,[39] the taxpayer purchased a tract of land for the purpose of constructing an apartment building, but then, finding that other apartment houses were going up in the same area, changed her mind and built a large personal residence which she herself occupied for a period of some five years.　At the end of that period the taxpayer vacated the residence, and having made unsuccessful efforts to sell or rent it, finally surrendered the property to the mortgagees who had financed its acquisition.　Contending that her original profit motive in buying the land had continued throughout her occupancy (the residence, she said, could have been broken up into separate apartments), the taxpayer sought to deduct her investment in the property as a loss.　The Court of Appeals found that the taxpayer

39.　123 F.2d 707 (2d Cir.1941).

had abandoned her original commercial purpose when she built and occupied the residence, and sustained the Commissioner in treating the loss as personal. An individual's motives may sometimes be mixed, the court observed, but here it was apparent that profit-seeking had ceased to be the taxpayer's dominant interest once the residence was built, and that business goals were "only on the edge" of her mind thereafter.

Actually, of course, Judge Frank hadn't the faintest idea of what was on Mrs. Gevirtz' mind at any given moment. For all he knew she never thought of anything *but* profit during the years in question. Yet even if the "motive" evidence had been more favorable to the taxpayer, the court's decision in all likelihood would have been the same. Suppose, for example, that Mrs. Gevirtz had been able to demonstrate—by reference to correspondence with real estate brokers or even prospective tenants—that she had continued throughout the years in question to make active plans to exploit the property commercially. If such evidence were strong and believable, would the loss have been allowed? One suspects a negative answer: in effect, evidence of business purpose *never* could have been strong enough to overcome the factor of *personal occupancy* unless the latter had been extremely brief in duration. The decline in value for which a deductible loss was claimed occurred while the taxpayer was living in the residence. As a result, it simply had to be treated as a personal consumption cost. To allow a "loss" on the ground that the taxpayer's profit motive had continued to be central would be to invite all taxpayers to attempt to treat personal assets as investment property by claiming that their personal use was only incidental or subordinate. The burden on the Treasury of sorting out the true from the false in every case would then become considerable. It is obviously simpler, and presumably also consistent with Congressional intent, to view personal occupancy or personal use as *absolutely* inconsistent with the presence of a profit motive. Hence, even if Mrs. Gevirtz's original business purpose had remained active and visible throughout, the factor of personal occupancy would almost certainly have "convinced" the court that profit-seeking had become a secondary goal.

Weir v. Commissioner,[40] which can be contrasted with *Gevirtz,* may help to support the point just made. In *Weir* the taxpayer bought shares in a corporation which owned an apartment building in which he himself was a tenant. His aim in becoming a stockholder—as shown by the fact that he sold the stock when he decided to move from the building—was to have a voice in the

---

40. 109 F.2d 996 (3d Cir.1940).

building's management, presumably to help assure that the accommodations remained to his liking. The Court of Appeals held that the loss incurred on the stock sale was deductible under § 165(c)(2). Since dividends on the stock would constitute "profit," the statutory requirement was met despite the taxpayer's obvious personal motive in acquiring the shares. The taxpayer's capital was being "used to produce taxable income," and that being so he was entitled to his deduction without "a hectic and ridiculous search for non-profit motives." In effect, although § 165(c)(2) appears to refer to the taxpayer's state of mind ("transaction entered into *for* profit"), both *Weir* and *Gevirtz* reflect a judicial interest in avoiding the use of subjective factors in distinguishing between personal property and business or investment assets. If the property in question generates receipts which are includable in the taxpayer's gross income, as in *Weir,* then any loss incurred will almost certainly be deductible; if the property is devoted to personal consumption, as in *Gevirtz,* the loss will almost certainly be denied.

Somewhat more typical than situations in which the taxpayer's "motives" are mixed are cases in which property—usually residential—is alleged to have been converted by the taxpayer from an admittedly personal to an arguably commercial use. Suppose a home-owner decides to sell his residence and move to an apartment. The residence was purchased for $50,000, but the best offer the taxpayer can get today is $40,000. Convinced that the market will improve if he waits, the taxpayer decides to rent the house on a month-to-month basis until a better price can be had. Two years later he regretfully sells the residence for only $35,000. Is the owner's "loss" deductible under § 165(c)(2)? The answer depends upon whether a "conversion" from personal to commercial property has taken place, with the cases generally holding that an actual renting, at least if moderately continuous and prolonged, will be accepted as proof of the requisite change in character. Unsuccessful efforts to rent apparently will not suffice—the property does not shed its "personal" character until it actually produces includable gross income.

While the distinction between an actual and an attempted renting seems artificial (no such distinction would be made had the property never been devoted to personal use), the *amount* of deductible loss that is at stake will often be small. The Regulations prescribe that the basis for computing loss on the sale of a converted residence cannot exceed the property's original cost, or its value at the time of conversion, whichever is *lower*.[41] In the example above, therefore, assuming an actual renting occurred immediately, the home-owner's basis for computing loss on sale would be only $40,000, reduced by depreciation allowable during the two-year rental period. The $10,000 difference between his original cost ($50,000) and the value of the house at the conversion date ($40,-000) would still be disallowed as "personal."

A loose end: § 165(b) provides that the basis for determining loss under § 165(a) shall be the adjusted basis provided by § 1011 for determining loss from the sale or other disposition of property. To get a deduction, therefore, the taxpayer must establish that he *has* a basis for the property disposed of. Suppose a lawyer is entitled to a fee of $1,000 for work performed for a client. The client doesn't pay, goes bankrupt. Can the lawyer deduct the $1,000 that he has lost? Assuming he uses the cash method of accounting and has not yet taken the fee into gross income, the answer is: no. Generally, "basis" requires either a cash investment or a prior inclusion in income. A claim to *untaxed* wages, salaries or fees has a basis of zero, and hence there is nothing to deduct under § 165(b) even though the claim proves uncollectible. (For the same reason—absence of "basis"—the claim could not be deducted as a "bad debt" under § 166, discussed next.)

6.07 Bad Debts. In the case of both corporations and individuals, debts which become worthless during the taxable year are deductible from gross income under § 166. If the debt is a "business" debt—as it would always be in the case of a corporation—it may be deducted when it becomes wholly worthless, or it may be deducted when partially worthless. In the case of an individual taxpayer, deduction is also permitted for "nonbusiness" debts— whether incurred in connection with a profit-seeking activity or in a personal setting such as a loan to a relative—but such debts must have become wholly worthless, because a deduction for partial worthlessness is not allowed. In addition, under § 166(d) the loss sustained on the worthlessness of a nonbusiness debt is treated as a short-term capital loss, and is therefore available only as an offset against capital gains plus $3,000 of ordinary income per year (see 16.03).

The distinction in § 166 between business and nonbusiness debts requires that a line be drawn between those activities of the

---

41. Regs. § 1.165–9(b)(2).

individual taxpayer which constitute a "trade or business" and those of his pursuits which, although clearly of a profit-seeking nature, solely involve the management or conservation of investment capital. The necessity for making this often difficult distinction is avoided elsewhere in the deduction sections of the Code, with an apparent gain in simplicity of administration, by permitting similar treatment for "trade or business" activity and for profit-seeking activity of a nonbusiness character (*e.g.,* the management of investments). Thus, as respects losses, § 165(c) allows deduction both of losses incurred in a trade or business and of losses incurred in any profit-seeking transaction, though not connected with a trade or business. In either case, the characterization of the loss as ordinary or capital depends on the nature of the asset disposed of. Similarly, §§ 162 and 212 permit the deduction of ordinary and necessary expenses whether incurred by the taxpayer in his trade or business or in the management of investments, though here the business-investment distinction is relevant for purposes of the adjusted gross income computation (see 7.06).

The distinction between business and nonbusiness bad debts is most clearly felt where the taxpayer is the sole or principal stockholder of a corporation, is active in its affairs, and has made loans to the corporation in the form of advances on open account.[42] In *Whipple v. Commissioner,*[43] for example, the taxpayer, an active businessman who had promoted a number of corporate ventures, made sizeable loans to a particular corporation of which he was the major stockholder and chief executive. The corporation was unsuccessful, and on liquidation its assets proved insufficient to repay the taxpayer's loans in full. Contending that his work as corporate manager and promoter constituted an independent "trade or business", the taxpayer sought to deduct the unpaid balance of the loans as a business bad debt. Disapproving a number of lower court decisions which had been favorable to taxpayer-promoters, the Supreme Court held that the loans were nonbusiness debts and hence could only be utilized as capital losses offsettable against capital gains. The Court found, in effect, that entrepreneurial activity—devoting one's energies to the promotion and management of corporate enterprises—was not of itself a "trade or business." The taxpayer's aim was to generate dividends and capital gains for himself by producing business income for his corporations. While the corporations were obviously in "business," the individual

---

42. Debt represented by a "security"—a bond or debenture—specifically is given capital loss treatment when worthlessness occurs. Code § 165(g). Mere "advances" do not create a "security," however.

43. 373 U.S. 193 (1963).

was not. Dividends and capital gains, said the Court, are "distinctive to the process of investing," and "investing is not a trade or business."

By placing loans to controlled corporations in the nonbusiness category, the *Whipple* decision in effect produces symmetrical tax treatment of promoters' gains and losses. To see why this is so, suppose an individual finances a new corporate venture by investing $50,100 cash, of which $50,000 is in the form of a loan to the company and $100 is for the company's common shares. Assume the business succeeds and the company is finally sold for $80,000. Since debt is "senior" to equity, the proceeds of sale would first be allocated $50,000 to repayment of the loan, and then the balance of $30,000 to the promoter's stock. The promoter realizes no gain on the debt repayment because the debt is simply paid off at face amount. The entire promotional gain—$29,900—would therefore be attributable to the shares, and as corporate stock is a capital asset, the gain would be taxed as capital gain. Now suppose that the enterprise is unsuccessful and is sold for only $20,000. Once again, the proceeds of sale would first be allocated to the debt of $50,000, so that a bad debt loss of $30,000 would result (together with a stock loss of $100). If the bad debt were treated as a "business" bad debt, then virtually the entire promotional loss would become a deduction from ordinary income. Promoter's gains would thus always be treated as capital gains, while promoter's losses would be treated as ordinary.

But presumably such unbalanced treatment of gains and losses from the same activity would be improper. Whipple himself, as the Court's opinion relates, had had a number of "winners" to go along with the "loser" for which the business bad debt deduction was claimed, and it could well be said of him, as of any promoter, that his losing promotions were a "cost" of his successful ventures. Since § 166 distinguishes between "business" and "nonbusiness" debts, rather than between capital and noncapital assets, a symmetrical result could be achieved only if promoters' loans were placed in the nonbusiness category. Although "nonbusiness" classification seems somewhat strained in this context, the *Whipple* decision ultimately reflects a finding that Congress did not intend to afford a special benefit to entrepreneurial activity by permitting the "profits" thereof to be treated as capital gain while allowing the "costs" to be deducted from ordinary income.

6.08 Depreciation—General Background. Though not the sort of topic that lawyers love, the depreciation allowance has grown so important over the past dozen years or so that a somewhat lengthy discussion of it appears unavoidable. The Economic

Recovery Tax Act of 1981 made significant changes in this field which obviously need to be summarized, but I do not think that the 1981 rules will mean very much to readers unless some general accounting and economic background is provided first. Accordingly, the subject of depreciation is here dealt with in two jumps: background and historical elements are discussed in this Section, while the current rules and related matters are left to 6.09 and 6.10.

(a) Eligible property. Code § 167—which still supplies the basic authorization—takes account of the progressive exhaustion of plant, equipment and other long-lived business and investment property by allowing an annual deduction for depreciation. Generally (and apart from the special procedures introduced by the 1981 Act), the cost of the property, less salvage value, is recovered on a year-by-year basis over the period during which the property is expected to be economically useful to the taxpayer. To illustrate, suppose a businessman buys a machine for $4,500. He expects to use the machine in his business for 5 years and then sell it as "scrap" for $500. Using the straight-line method of depreciation (other methods can also be devised, as shown at (d), below), the taxpayer would deduct $800 a year over the 5-year term, a total of $4,000. Since a portion of the cost of the machine is thus converted into a deductible expense each year, the taxpayer's basis for the machine, initially $4,500, also must be reduced by $800 a year. At the end of the first year, therefore, his basis would be $3,700, at the end of the second year $2,900, and at the end of the fifth year, $500. If the machine is finally sold to a junk-dealer for its anticipated salvage value of $500, no gain or loss results from the sale; if for more or less than $500, a gain or loss is recognized accordingly. In effect, the taxpayer's original expenditure of $4,500 is "returned" to him through a combination of (a) depreciation deductions during the property's useful life, (b) the amount realized as salvage, and (c) taxable gain or deductible loss on the final disposition of the asset.

The depreciation allowance is available both for business property—plant and equipment—and for investment property such as an apartment house or an office building. It extends to intangible assets—patents, copyrights, leases—as well as tangibles, though as respects intangibles the deduction is usually referred to as "amortization" rather than "depreciation." Property is depreciable (or amortizable) for purposes of § 167 if its useful life is definite and predictable, as it would be in the case of buildings and machines which wear out over a determinable period of time; it is not depreciable if the property's useful life is perpetual or indefinite, land being the chief example.[44]

(b) *Limitation to cost.* The depreciation allowance is limited in total to the taxpayer's basis, or cost, for his property.[45] Cost is generally equal to cash investment, though as has been seen the concept of basis is subject to a good many special rules and formulations. Since depreciable property is often acquired in part with borrowed money—a mortgage loan to buy a building, for example—it is obviously important to decide whether basis for depreciation purposes includes the borrowing or is restricted to the amount drawn from the taxpayer's own resources. This question is considered in some detail at 13.01, below, but for the present the short answer is that "cost" includes borrowed funds as well as equity investment.

"Cost" in the present context refers to *historical* cost, not the cost of replacing the property in the future when it wears out. The depreciation allowance, both for tax and for accounting purposes, is designed to offset the taxpayer's *original* investment against the gross income received in subsequent years, and in that way to limit the taxpayer's net taxable income to the excess of revenues over related expenses. It does *not* purport to measure the amount that would have to be set aside each year in order to fund the cost of replacement; nor, of course, being a mere bookkeeping entry, is it designed actually to generate such a fund. One consequence of this distinction is that taxpayers who own depreciable assets during a period of inflation are likely to suffer what amounts to an increase in their tax burdens without enjoying an equivalent increase in their "real" incomes. Thus, a company which before an inflationary price increase has annual income of $1,200 and depreciation deductions of $800 has taxable income of $400. At a 35% tax rate, its tax liability is $140, which represents 11⅔% of its gross income. If prices suddenly double because of inflation, the company's gross income becomes $2,400 but its depreciation allowance remains $800. It then has taxable income of $1,600 (*four* times the pre-inflation amount) and pays a tax of $560, which is 23⅓% of gross income. Since the doubling of prices means that there is no *real* increase in the company's gross income, it can be argued that the depreciation allowance should also be doubled so that the company's taxable income and its resulting tax may continue to be the

---

44. Prior to the 1993 Act, acquired intangibles such as "goodwill" would have been another example. As shown at 6.10, however, Code § 197 now affords such assets a fixed period of amortization.

45. Except in the case of certain mineral properties, to which special rules—beyond the scope of this discussion—may be applicable.

same percentage of gross income as previously. But while the argument has undeniable force, the effect of inflation is not limited to owners of depreciable property, and any effort to adjust for inflation—presumably through basis indexation—should properly be extended to all property-owners, certainly including lenders and other recipients of fixed incomes. As suggested at 3.01, however, no such general reform is now in view (though often discussed), and there appears to be no good reason why owners of depreciable assets should be singled out for special consideration. The point must simply be conceded that the tax law works poorly during periods of sharp inflation.

    (c) Useful lives. Estimating an asset's useful life—how long it is likely to be in service in the taxpayer's business—is obviously of considerable importance. Too brief an estimate of useful life will result in tax deferral, too long an estimate in tax anticipation. If, for example, a machine costing $4,000 net of salvage has an *actual* service life of 10 years, the proper straight-line deduction is $400 a year. If the estimate of useful service life is only half that term, however, the deduction taken in the first 5 years of use will be $800 and in the last 5 years zero, with the result that the tax on $2,000 of taxable income will be deferred from the earlier 5-year period to the later. While the taxes postponed are ultimately recouped by the Treasury, the taxpayer (for reasons already amply noted) gains a tangible benefit from the deferral of his tax obligations. To be sure, the opposite consequence arises if the estimate of useful life is longer than the period of actual use. If a machine has an actual service life of only 5 years and the estimate is 10, then depreciation which should have been allowed during the earlier period will be postponed until the asset is retired; taxable income will have been anticipated and taxes paid "too soon."

    As will be seen, the Code in 1981 pretty well abandoned the notion that depreciation should be spread out over an asset's *true* useful life and instead permits business taxpayers to depreciate their property over periods that are (and are expected to be) much shorter than the periods of actual service. In enacting the Accelerated Cost Recovery System (ACRS) described at 6.09, Congress' stated aim was to stimulate investment in plant and equipment, and with this overriding goal in view it simply discarded accuracy of measurement as an objective for the tax law to pursue. Actually, as the next few paragraphs show, the idea of manipulating the depreciation allowance in order to influence private investment decisions was not a new one in 1981. While the 1981 enactment went much further than any of its predecessors, the same concept has been promoted by economic policy-makers, and in one form or another accepted by Congress, for nearly forty years. This has been so, moreover, whether control of Congress and the Treasury was in the hands of liberals or of conservatives during any particular era.

(d) Permissible methods. As just implied, there are really two different approaches that can be taken to the question of what constitutes a "proper" depreciation allowance. One approach is concerned with the effect of the allowance on the measurement of taxable income. From this standpoint, the adequacy of the allowance is tested by the accuracy of the income measurement that results. The question is: what system of depreciation generates a "true" picture of the taxpayer's income experience for the taxable year? The second approach involves the use of the depreciation allowance as a method of encouraging (or, perhaps, retarding) investment in depreciable assets. Here the adequacy of the allowance depends on whether it influences businessmen to expand (or contract) the level of their outlays for such property in accordance with the aims of government economic policy. Accurate income measurement, surely the aim of "pure" tax policy, is more or less consciously subordinated to fiscal objectives, employment goals, and so on.

Most would agree, I think, that at least since the enactment of the 1954 Code, the depreciation allowance has largely been shaped by the second approach and has reflected a Congressional policy of encouraging growth and expansion. Prior to 1954 taxpayers were generally required to use the relatively conservative straight-line method of depreciation in apportioning the cost of depreciable property over its useful life. The 1954 Code, however, liberalized the rules relating to apportionment by authorizing taxpayers to elect an "accelerated" method of depreciation—*e.g.*, the declining balance method at twice the straight-line rate—for new tangible property having an extended useful life. These accelerated methods, like the straight-line method, spread recovery of the taxpayer's investment over the entire service life of the asset. But unlike the straight-line method, which results in equal annual deductions throughout an asset's useful life, the newer methods concentrated larger deductions in the earlier years of the asset's life and thus effected a speedier return of the greater part of the taxpayer's cost.

It is easy to see why the availability of accelerated depreciation methods would be expected to spur investment in depreciable property. Consider again a machine that costs $4,000, has a useful life of 5 years, and can be expected to generate gross income of $1,200 a year (net of maintenance expenses). Should a businessman, whose income is taxed, say, at a rate of 50%, buy the thing or not? The answer depends on whether the present value of the expected after-tax revenues generated by the machine exceeds, or falls short of, the required investment of $4,000. If the present value of expected after-tax revenues exceeds the required investment, then of course he *should* acquire the machine because the effect is to replace cash with tangible property of greater worth. If the contrary is true, the investment should be rejected.

Assume that the businessman is able to raise money from banks or other investors at an after-tax cost of 8%. Since that is what he has to pay for investment capital, it is logical to use the same 8% rate of discount in determining the present value of the income-stream which he expects to receive. The following are the relevant calculations, comparing (a) the straight-line method with (b) the double declining-balance method of depreciation:

(a) Straight–Line

	(1)	(2)	(3)	(4)	(5)	(6)
					Net	Present
	Gross	Deprecia-	Taxable	Tax	Cash Flow	Value of
Year	Income	tion	Income	Payable	(1)–(4)	(5) at 8%
1	$1,200	$ 800	$ 400	$ 200	$1,000	$ 926
2	1,200	800	400	200	1,000	857
3	1,200	800	400	200	1,000	794
4	1,200	800	400	200	1,000	735
5	1,200	800	400	200	1,000	681
Totals	$6,000	$4,000	$2,000	$1,000	$5,000	$3,993

(b) Declining–Balance

	(1)	(2)	(3)	(4)	(5)	(6)
					Net	Present
	Gross	Deprecia-	Taxable	Tax	Cash Flow	Value of
Year	Income	tion	Income	Payable	(1)–(4)	(5) at 8%
1	$1,200	$1,600	($400) *	($200) **	$1,400	$1,296
2	1,200	960	240	120	1,080	926
3	1,200	576	624	312	888	705
4	1,200	346	854	427	773	568
5	1,200	518	682	341	859	585
Totals	$6,000	$4,000	$2,000	$1,000	$5,000	$4,080

* Loss offsettable against other income
** Amount refunded

With one exception, the column *totals* are the same under both depreciation methods. The critical exception is column (6)—"present value of net cash flows"—which totals $4,080 under the declining-balance method, but only $3,993 under the straight-line method. The reason for the difference is that under the declining-balance method net cash flows are larger in the early years and smaller in the later years (yearly tax-payments necessarily follow a converse pattern), while under the straight-line method net cash flows (and tax-payments) are level throughout the five-year period.

Because the discounted value of near-term receipts is greater than that of distant ones, the present value of the sum of the net cash flows is greater under the declining-balance method than under the straight-line method, even though the total dollar amount received over the five-year period is the same for both.

The important point, at all events, is that the investment in the machine has a *positive* net present value of $80 ($4,080–$4,000) if the declining balance method of depreciation is used, but a *negative* net present value of $7 ($4,000–$3,993) if the taxpayer is restricted to the straight-line method. Quite obviously, therefore, the businessman should buy the machine if, but only if, the declining-balance method of depreciation is available. Hence Congress can directly influence businessmen's investment decisions by permitting (or denying) the use of the accelerated cost-recovery procedure.

But now suppose we alter our approach to the depreciation allowance and emphasize income measurement instead of investment incentives. Suppose that the "economic policy" approach is abandoned or renounced at this point and that Congress decides to require all taxpayers to use the depreciation method which results in a "true" measure of annual taxable income. Which of the methods just discussed (if either) would be appropriate? Since the declining-balance method has been described as "accelerated," does this imply that the straight-line method is "correct" in the sense that it produces a more accurate measure of the change in the taxpayer's wealth-status between the beginning and the end of the taxable year?

Presumably the purpose of tax or accounting depreciation (putting fiscal policy aims aside) is to reflect the *annual loss in value* of the taxpayer's depreciable assets that results from their use in the taxpayer's business. The question which the depreciation allowance *ought* to answer is: how much less are such assets worth at the end of the year than they were at the beginning? The taxpayer's "true" annual income, then, is his gross income less the sum of (a) his current expenses plus (b) the decline for the year in the economic value of his capital equipment.

In our illustration above, the $4,000 machine is expected to generate gross income (after current maintenance expenses) of $1,200 a year for 5 years. The implied before-tax rate of return on the taxpayer's investment is about 15%; that is, $1,200 a year for 5 years discounted at a rate of 15% equals $4,000. If we apply this discount rate to each expected payment in turn, the schedule of present values looks roughly like this:

147

Year:	1	2	3	4	5	Totals
Expected receipt	$1,200	$1,200	$1,200	$1,200	$1,200	$6,000
Present value	$1,045	$ 905	$ 790	$ 687	$ 573	$4,000

The present value of all five payments must of course add up to $4,000, the original cost of the equipment.

How does this schedule look after the first year of use has passed? The second, the third, etc.? As each year of useful life expires the expected stream of payments becomes shorter and the present value of the sum of all remaining payments necessarily declines. There is just that much less to anticipate in the way of future returns. The taxpayer's economic loss from the year's operations—his annual cost—is measured by the decline in the present value of anticipated receipts which takes place between the beginning and the end of the taxable year. In effect, the difference between the value of the future income stream on January 1 and its value on January 1 of the following year represents the cost of using the machine for the year in question. If the object of the depreciation allowance is to reduce gross income by the true cost of operations, then the annual allowance should be no more or less than that amount.

Here is a schedule of the yearly decline in the present value of the taxpayer's investment:

	Present Value of Investment	Present Value of Remaining Payments					Annual Loss in Present Value
		1	2	3	4	5	
Start of Year 1	$4,000	$1,045	905	790	687	573	
End of Year 1	3,427		1,045	905	790	687	$ 573
End of Year 2	2,740			1,045	905	790	687
End of Year 3	1,950				1,045	905	790
End of Year 4	1,045					1,045	905
End of Year 5	–0–						1,045
						Total:	$4,000

The last column shows the true measure of economic cost from year to year and indicates that the correct apportionment method is one which *starts low and rises:* $573 in Year 1, then $687, $790, $905, and finally $1,045 in Year 5. The resulting schedule of taxable income, of course, is the inverse: $627 of taxable income in Year 1, $513 in Year 2, $410 in Year 3, $295 in Year 4 and finally $155 in Year 5. Income is thus *higher* in the earlier years than in the later.

This corrected depreciation method—sometimes called "sinking-fund" depreciation—looks peculiar and unfamiliar at first glance. Really, however, it is nothing more than the ordinary and conventional method by which a bank amortizes the principal amount of a mortgage loan. As stated elsewhere (2.02), anyone who has ever paid off a home mortgage knows that principal payments are small in the early years and large in the later ones, with interest (income) being correspondingly greater in the beginning and smaller at the end. The machine-owner above occupies essentially the same status as a mortgage-lender: both invest their capital in the expectation of a future periodic return. Hence if the depreciation allowance were designed to produce an accurate measure of taxable income, the same cost-recovery procedure would seem to be appropriate for each.

It must be admitted, on the other hand, that the sinking-fund depreciation method is a great deal easier to apply in the case of mortgages, leases and other property whose future yield is fixed by contract than it is for tangible assets like machines. The income from a mortgage or a lease can be determined without engaging in predictions and projections that depend entirely on future events. By contrast, the cash-flow to be derived from the operation of a tangible asset is not a fixed quantity and would have to be estimated. Since such estimates are very hard to make, it is understandable why the sinking-fund method has never been used for machinery, equipment and other tangibles. The larger point, however, as stated, is that economic depreciation is simply a function of expected cash flows.[46] Once again, "true" depreciation is the difference between the present value of expected cash flows at the start of the taxable period and the present value of expected cash flows at the end of such taxable period. Where, as in my example, expected cash flows are level from period to period, the sinking-fund method is the *only* proper method of apportioning the taxpayer's capital investment in accordance with the economic cost of use. By contrast, even the straight-line method of depreciation turns out to be accelerated.

6.09 ACRS, ITC and Leveraged Leases

(a) ACRS and ITC. As indicated at 6.08, the permission to use accelerated depreciation methods—declining-balance, for example, in place of the slower straight-line method—has the effect of increasing after-tax returns to the owners of depreciable property. Investments that might otherwise have been unprofitable are transformed into profitable ones, and businesses are thus encouraged to replace and expand their existing stock of capital goods. It

---

46. Samuelson, *Tax Deductibility of Economic Depreciation to Insure Invari-* ant *Valuations,* 72 J. of Pol. Econ. 604 (1964).

should be stressed (and of course I already have) that the increase in after-tax returns is here accomplished not through an outright tax-exemption (as in the case of municipal bond interest, for example), but by the slightly subtler device of allowing business taxpayers to defer their *current* income tax liabilities to later periods. But though it goes by another name, tax-deferral is really no different from tax reduction or exemption—the effect would be the same if the income from depreciable property were taxed at lower rates than those that normally apply, or if all or a portion of such income were exempted from tax entirely.

This can be seen in a fairly dramatic way if we carry the accelerated cost-recovery idea to its extreme and allow expenditures for machinery and equipment to be deducted all at once, as if they were current expenses. Thus, suppose we ditched the "capital expenditure-depreciation allowance" concept altogether and simply permitted taxpayers to "expense" their outlays for long-lived property under § 162(a). What would be the impact on the investor's tax liability, at least as it relates to income from the property in question?

The answer, as has been shown,[47] is that the income from the property would effectively become exempt from tax—exactly as if an explicit exemption, rather than a "mere" accelerated deduction procedure, had been enacted. To illustrate, suppose a taxpayer is prepared to invest $4,000 in a machine that will generate revenues of $6,000 (150% of cash investment) in one or more future years. The investor's *pre-tax* profit, $2,000, thus represents a 50% return on his investment. Assume the investor is a 40%-bracket taxpayer. If the $4,000 outlay is not deductible until the $6,000 of revenues are received, the investor's *after-tax* return will be 30%. Thus, the pre-tax profit of $2,000 is reduced by a tax of 40%, or $800. After-tax profit is then $1,200, which represents a 30% return on the taxpayer's investment of $4,000. Since the pre-tax rate of return is 50%, and since tax is imposed at a rate of 40%, the 30% after-tax return (60% of 50%) is exactly what one would expect.

But now suppose the Code is amended to provide that outlays for machinery shall be fully deductible when made. Since the taxpayer was willing to invest $4,000 with no immediate deduction, he will be willing to invest $6,667 once a full deduction is allowed.

47. Brown, *Business-Income Taxation and Investment Incentives,* in Income, Employment and Public Policy 300 (1948). And *see,* Andrews, *A Consumption-Type or Cash Flow Personal Income Tax,* 87 Harv.L.Rev. 1113, 1123 (1974); Warren, *Fairness and a Consumption-Type or Cash Flow Personal Income Tax,* 88 Harv.L.Rev. 931 (1975); Graetz, *Implementing a Progressive Consumption Tax,* 92 Harv.L.Rev. 1575, 1598 (1979).

The $6,667 deduction will offset other income taxable at a 40% rate, and hence the machine will cost the taxpayer only 60% of $6,667, or $4,000 net of the tax saving. The future revenues to be expected will now be $10,000 (150% of cash investment, as before), but this sum will be taxed in full when received because the taxpayer's original investment would already have been deducted and his basis for the asset will be zero. The taxpayer will therefore have taxable income of $10,000 on which he will pay a tax of $4,000—40% of $10,000—and his net realization will be $6,000. Since he originally invested $4,000 in the machine ($6,667 before tax but only $4,000 after the benefit of full deduction), his after-tax profit will be $6,000 – $4,000, or $2,000. This, of course, represents a 50% return—rather than merely 30%—and, hence, it is as if the income on the originally contemplated investment had been exempted from tax entirely. Stated axiomatically, immediate deduction equals full exemption if the applicable tax rate is assumed to be constant for all affected periods.

The 1981 Tax Act, which added § 168 to the Code, did not go all the way to full and immediate deduction for capital expenditures. It did, however, move quite substantially in that direction by substituting sharply abbreviated depreciation schedules for the "useful life" limitation that had governed the depreciation allowance in the past. Under earlier practice, the depreciation allowance was spread out over the period during which the property was expected to have continuing economic value in the taxpayer's business. Since estimates rather than certainties were involved, determination of the useful life of physical assets was for many years a major source of controversy in individual cases. In the 1960's, and again in the early 70's, the Treasury and Congress adopted standardized useful-life tables for broad classes of property in an effort to minimize such disputes. The result of this was to shorten applicable depreciation schedules in many instances, but at least in theory the service life of the asset and the period over which depreciation was allowable were still intended to bear a proximate relationship.

Code § 168—which contains the so-called Accelerated Cost Recovery System—largely discards the concept of actual service life and instead frankly treats the depreciation allowance as a means of subsidizing capital investments. Under ACRS, the cost of an asset is recoverable over a predetermined period that is, and is intended to be, significantly shorter than the useful life of the asset or the period during which the asset is expected to be used in the taxpayer's business. Thus, most tangible personal property (machinery and equipment) is now depreciable over periods of 3 to 10 years, even though actual service lives are typically a good deal longer. Real property—previously depreciable over periods ranging up to 60 years—is now assigned a recovery period of 27.5 years in the case of residential buildings and 39 years for other business structures. Generally, the double declining balance method is to be used in computing the annual depreciation allowance for personal property and the straight-line method for real property. Finally, the salvage value limitation is eliminated and the full cost of the property is allowed to be recovered over the relevant term.

As stated, the cost-recovery periods established under § 168 are substantially shorter than the true useful lives of most kinds of business equipment—automobiles, for example, are placed in the 3-year class, although the anticipated service life of a car is said to be 7 or 8 years. The result (as usual) is that the effective rate of tax on income from investment in plant and machinery is much lower than the statutory rate; put differently, it is as if a portion of such income were tax-exempt. Actually, the status of business investment was even more favorable prior to the 1986 Act. Under 1954 Code § 38—now repealed—taxpayers were permitted to take a credit against tax equal to 10% of the cost of new depreciable property (other than real property) having at least a 5-year recovery life (6% for 3-year property). Combining the 10% investment tax credit (ITC) and ACRS reduced the effective tax rate on capital income to zero for many business taxpayers; for some, indeed, the effective rate was negative, meaning that such taxpayers—for the most part larger corporations—were better off under a 46% corporate income tax (as it then was) *plus* ITC and ACRS than they would have been if their property-generated income had been exempted from tax entirely.[48]

Eager to reduce individual (and corporate) tax rates without loss to the Treasury of net revenues, and perhaps doubting that the high level of tax subsidies had really succeeded in increasing business investment, Congress, with the President's agreement, repealed ITC in 1986. The revenue gain from ITC repeal over the five years following was estimated to be more than $140 billion, substantially exceeding the revenue loss from corporate rate reduction. ACRS was only slightly modified, however. While the House version of the 1986 Act would have restored the depreciation system that prevailed prior to 1981, a system that can be described, loosely, as "intermediate acceleration," the Senate considered that

48. See Steines, *Income Tax Allowances for Cost Recovery*, 40 Tax L.Rev. 483 (1985); Gann, *Neutral Taxation of Capital Income: An Achievable Goal?*, 48 Law & Contemp. Prob's 77 (1985); Johnson, *Tax Shelter Gain: The Mismatch of Debt and Supply Side Depreciation*, 61 Texas L.Rev. 1013 (1983).

it would be unwise to go beyond ITC repeal in limiting existing investment subsidies, and in the end it was the Senate view that carried the day.

(b) *Leveraged leases and the transfer of tax benefits.* As suggested, quick-depreciation rules generate very substantial benefits for corporations and other taxpayers whose businesses call for large-scale capital investment. On the other hand, since ACRS is a tax-*reduction* mechanism, it is obviously only those taxpayers that actually *have* taxable income, and hence do owe taxes, that will welcome the relief. Unprofitable companies (certain steel manufacturers, airlines, etc.) may have equally urgent capital investment requirements, but as they currently operate at a loss, accelerated cost-recovery affords them no benefit, at least for the time being.

To cope with this "problem," tax lawyers long ago invented a legal device by which, in effect, unprofitable companies may simply *transfer* their excess depreciation deductions to profitable companies that can use them. The device in question—generally known as a "leveraged lease"—is nothing more or less than an up-dated version of the arrangement that was at issue in *Starr's Estate* (see 6.02(c)). To see how it works, suppose L, a loss company, decides to purchase certain heavy equipment for $10 million. Assuming the equipment is 5-year property, allowable depreciation under ACRS would be $2 million in the year of purchase (even if purchase is at the year-end), $3.2 million in the first full year of service, $1.92 million in the second full year, $1.152 in the third and fourth years, and $.576 in the last.[49] L, however, does not expect to be able to use these deductions—it has no taxable income this year and probably will have none for a few years to come. Accordingly, matters are arranged so that P, a profitable company, will formally purchase and own the equipment but will then at once lease it to L for a period that represents a substantial proportion of the equipment's economic life, which is always well in excess of the 5-year ACRS period. P will have borrowed (hence the term "leveraged") the greater part of its purchase price, say $8 million, from a bank or other lender on the security of the equipment itself. The balance of the purchase price—$2 million—will be drawn by P from its own resources, and it is this $2 million of "equity" that represents P's actual investment in the deal.

In order to repay its $8 million indebtedness, P will turn over L's annual rental payments to the lender, which will apply them to interest and principal. The amount of such rentals will suffice—but usually just suffice—to amortize P's $8 million indebtedness

---

49.   Code § 168(b)(1) and (d).

(plus interest) over the term of the lease. Sometimes there will be a little left over for P to put in its own pocket after annual debt service is accounted for, but such excess is likely to be small. In effect, L's rental obligation is pegged at or near a level that will just satisfy the debt requirements; P itself can expect little or nothing in the way of an annual return on its $2 million investment.

So what does P get by laying out $2 million in cash for equipment that it has never seen? Obvious answer: chiefly the ACRS deductions described above—plus any net rents, plus whatever residual value the equipment may possess at the end of the lease. On the minus side, P will have to include in income the $8 million of rents allocable to the repayment of debt principal; while the annual interest paid by P to the lender is deductible, payments on principal are not. Since, however, much the greater part of such rents will be "received" by P and taxed in later years than those in which the ACRS deductions are taken, P will enjoy the usual benefit of income-deferral. The net present value of all of these factors (but most especially the deferral benefit) will exceed P's initial cash outlay and will afford P a better return on its $2 million than P could get by investing the same funds in its own business or in other projects of equivalent risk. This will be true even though, as noted, P is likely to receive little or no cash or other property of value until the lease expires (if then).

As to L, the benefit of the arrangement is also clear. Without P's participation, L would presumably have had to borrow (or otherwise obtain), and repay with interest, the full equipment purchase price of $10 million. Now, however, L needs to "borrow" only $8 million. The remaining $2 million will have been supplied by P virtually interest-free—that is, largely in exchange for L's ACRS deductions, which L could not have used anyway.

As usual, the Treasury will be the only loser in all this; in effect, the leveraged lease is just a roundabout way of cashing in L's unused tax benefits. Indeed, it might be simpler (certainly cheaper: no legal fees or brokerage commissions) if the Code permitted L to obtain the tax value of its unused deductions *directly* from the Treasury as a cash refund (*i.e.*, of the taxes L *would* have saved if it *had* had any taxable income to apply the deductions against). At the other extreme, the Code could conceivably (at least in the case of long-term leases) restrict the availability of ACRS to the actual *user* of the equipment—here L—and thus deny those benefits to P, a mere lessor. But in fact the Code follows neither course. As matters stand, L can effectively sell its tax entitlements to P, provided only that the legal arrangement between them constitutes a "lease" rather than a loan or (as in *Starr's Estate*) a conditional sales contract. Federal standards—among others, that the expected residual value and remaining useful life of the equipment be more than minimal, so that P will really "own" something when the lease is over—are determinative in this regard. The fact that P and L *call* their arrangement a "lease" does not make it one for tax purposes [50]. Aided by skilled counsel and an accommodating appraiser, however, the parties usually find the applicable requirements not difficult to meet.

6.10. Purchased Intangibles; Code § 197. Suppose X Corporation buys the entire business of Y Corporation for a purchase price of $5 million, of which $3 million represents the value of tangible property—plant and equipment—and $2 million represents the value of Y's "goodwill", that is, the excess of the value of the business as a going concern over the separate value of its tangible assets. The $2 million goodwill value reflects a number of special elements, including Y's well-established customer base and its reputation for reliability and prompt customer service. Having paid $5 million for the business as a whole, X wants to know what its basis will be in the several Y assets for the purpose of calculating annual depreciation under Code § 167.

Prior to the 1993 Act the answer would be $3 million, the cost of the acquired tangibles. Plant and equipment are of course depreciable, and X is plainly entitled to recover its basis in those assets through annual depreciation allowances in the usual manner. To be sure, X also has a basis of $2 million for the goodwill. But goodwill, like land or corporate stock, has traditionally been regarded as an asset of indefinite useful life and, as such, deemed non-amortizable. Cost-recovery would therefore be postponed until the goodwill itself was disposed of, presumably through a sale of the acquired business to yet another purchaser. In the latter event—but only then—X would be entitled to offset its unrecovered investment against the sale proceeds.

Faced with this painful limitation (again, prior to the 1993 Act), taxpayers in X's position have very often attempted to separate out and identify some particular intangible—customer-lists and supply contracts are the usual candidates—for which a finite or determinable useful life could be established. The Commissioner has generally opposed that effort, and disputes have been frequent.

---

50. But see *Frank Lyon Co. v. U.S.*, 435 U.S. 561 (1978), in which the Supreme Court approved a leasing transaction that entailed a transfer of tax benefits and little else. The decision is criticized in Wolfman, *The Supreme Court in the Lyon's Den: A Failure of Judicial Process*, 66 Cornell L.Rev. 1075 (1981).

In the *Newark Morning Ledger* [51] case, a notable taxpayer victory, the Supreme Court permitted a corporation that purchased a chain of newspapers to amortize that portion—some $68 million—of the total purchase price that was allocable to "paid subscribers". Using expert testimony, the taxpayer was able to show the approximate rate—14 years for one paper, 23 for another—at which existing subscriptions could be expected to lapse, whether because the subscriber died, moved away or simply failed to renew. Dissenting, Justice Souter argued in effect that customer patronage was within the "settled meaning" of "goodwill"; hence, under rules of long standing, annual amortization was impermissible even if the taxpayer's self-serving statistical projections were accepted as valid.

§ 197, added by the 1993 Act, supersedes the *Newark Ledger* decision and presumably puts an end to controversies between taxpayer and government over the treatment of purchased intangibles. Under the new provision, the cost of most intangibles acquired in connection with the purchase of a business—but most particularly goodwill or going-concern value—are permitted to be amortized on a straight-line basis over a 15–year period. The list of intangible assets to which the new provision applies is a long one and includes (besides goodwill) franchises, trademarks, know-how, customer lists, covenants not to compete, and more. The 15–year term is admittedly arbitrary. In some instances—non-compete agreements would be one—§ 197 actually lengthens the period of amortization for which the intangible would otherwise qualify. The statutory approach is generally known as "rough justice", with accuracy being sacrificed for convenience and simplicity.

As stated, § 197 puts to rest an issue that has been the source of frequent dispute and for that reason alone is welcome. From the standpoint of "tax theory," on the other hand, the idea of permitting purchased goodwill to be amortized can be questioned. Put very simply, while the tangible assets purchased by X (in the hypothetical above) will in fact wear out and be used up over a period of years, the goodwill acquired by X from Y should not. Thus, X will certainly take steps to maintain the value of the acquired goodwill by spending money on advertising, sales promotion, customer relations, etc., just as Y did when the business belonged to it. Under settled practice (see 6.02b), those outlays, although made for the purpose of maintaining or enhancing the value of a capital asset, are themselves treated as currently deductible business expenses. In combination, then, the taxpayer is

51. *Newark Morning Ledger v. U.S.,*
___ U.S. ___ (1993).

permitted both (i) to amortize a capital asset that is presumed (by § 197) to have a limited useful life, but then also (ii) to deduct as a current expense the annual cost of "rebuilding" that asset in order to prevent its useful life from ever coming to an end. As our earlier discussion of "repairs" should suggest, (i) and (ii) are essentially in conflict. If goodwill is permitted to be amortized, then advertising should be treated as a capital expenditure. If advertising is treated as a current expense, then goodwill should be regarded as a non-amortizable perpetuity. Allowing both annual amortization *and* current expense deductions amounts to doubling-up.

The latter point can be illustrated by the *Newark Ledger* case itself.[52] We may grant that existing subscribers will disappear for one reason or another over a period of time. But we can also assume that over the same time-period new subscribers will be added to the subscription lists and take the place of old ones. Whether by spending money on subscription drives or by simply putting out a good newspaper, the taxpayer will do whatever is necessary, or whatever it can, to attract new subscribers and keep its subscription lists from declining. The expenses incurred in that effort will be treated as ordinary business expenses. In effect, the value of the subscription lists at time of purchase will be continuously maintained (or, as suggested, "rebuilt") with pre-tax dollars. That being so, it seems inconsistent as a matter of principle to allow the capital cost of such subscription lists to be amortized as well.

SECTION 7. PERSONAL EXPENSE DEDUCTIONS

7.01 General Comment. Much of the discussion in Section 6 was directed at the distinction between business and personal expenditures. Though sometimes difficult to formulate, that distinction is vital to the concept of a tax on "income." Personal consumption expenses must obviously be treated as non-deductible on the whole; if they were allowed, the individual tax base could be eliminated through expenditures on personal living items and the notion of a tax on economic gain would have been abandoned. Yet despite this general approach, the Code does permit deductions for a variety of expenses which are clearly personal in character. Medical expenses, casualty losses, contributions to charity, interest on home-mortgage loans, and state and local income taxes are the

52. Johnson, *Newark Ledger: Kicking the Mass Asset Bucket,* 56 Tax Notes 629 (1992).

most important examples of personal expenses which are allowable in computing individual taxable income. Since these allowances represent a significant departure from the concept of economic gain as the relevant tax base, it is reasonable to ask what justifies or explains their presence in the tax law. That question is the more urgent because deductions of any kind necessarily generate larger tax benefits for high than for low-bracket taxpayers, and in that respect detract from the progressivity of the income tax.

From the standpoint of their purpose or effect, the personal expense deductions allowed to individuals can be divided into three categories. The first includes involuntary and unexpected outlays which are large enough to exhaust a significant proportion of a taxpayer's annual income. Extraordinary medical expenses are an obvious example: a taxpayer who is hit with large medical bills for himself or for a member of his family is plainly less well off than a taxpayer with equal income whose family is healthy, and a tax law which failed to recognize his loss in tax-paying capacity would appear harsh. The same can be said of casualty losses involving personal property, such as a car or a home. A taxpayer whose house had been damaged by fire suffers a reduction in personal wealth (unless he is reimbursed by insurance) which most would agree should entitle him to be differentiated from taxpayers who have escaped disaster.

The second category of personal expense deductions includes outlays which Congress wishes to encourage and subsidize. A clear example is the deduction for contributions to charity. Unlike medical expenses, charitable contributions are entirely voluntary and represent the donor's personal and unforced choice among all of his various consumption alternatives. By permitting this "good," but not others, to be paid for in pre-tax dollars, the Code obviously intends to make charitable giving less expensive from the standpoint of donors. From the standpoint of donees, moreover, it might be expected that, unless deductible, charitable gifts would shrink to offset a portion of the donor's tax liabilities, and the scope of philanthropic activities would necessarily contract. While some critics have argued that private philanthropy should not be supported indirectly out of public funds, it seems probable that most people regard the activities of charities as socially desirable and would oppose withdrawal of the deduction.

Yet another, and a very important, example of a "subsidy" is the deduction permitted to homeowners for mortgage interest and local property taxes. Homeowners are favored by the tax law relative to apartment renters, both because the imputed income from home-ownership is excluded from gross income (see 1.03) and because a portion of the owner's expenses are allowable as deductions (see 7.04). Apartment rents, of course, are non-deductible. The effect, quite obviously, is to encourage home-ownership over tenancy by extending a substantial tax preference to those who choose to buy instead of rent.

The third category of personal expense deductions includes state and local taxes—now limited to income and personal and real property taxes. This deduction, probably, is to be explained as an intergovernmental coordination device. Regarding income taxes in particular, it would seem that unless deductible the combined state and federal rates might appear excessive; high income tax jurisdictions would then be obliged to reduce their rates or perhaps even to abandon the income tax as a revenue source. In effect, the deduction moderates existing interstate differentials. The same justification cannot be offered as readily for the deduction of state and local sales and property taxes, and in 1986 Congress took a major step by repealing the deduction for sales taxes (property taxes continue to be deductible). Personal deductions for state and local gasoline and for various minor state and local taxes, as well as federal excise taxes, were once permitted, but have also been eliminated unless they qualify as business expenses. Federal income taxes, of course, are not allowable in any event.[53]

Critics of the personal expense deductions have argued over the years that the existing allowances are too generous, particularly in subsidizing voluntary outlays like charitable gifts and home-mortgage interest. Also, as stated, it has been objected that their impact is anti-progressive: the value of a deduction depends on the taxpayer's marginal tax rate; hence, high-bracket taxpayers enjoy the largest benefit per dollar of outlay for any allowable personal expense.[54] Partly in response to criticism of this sort, Congress in 1990 adopted an overall (yet selective) limitation on personal expense deductions, of which the purpose and effect is to cut back on the deductible amount for upper-income individuals. Under § 68, the itemized deductions otherwise allowable to a taxpayer are reduced by 3% of the excess of the taxpayer's adjusted gross income over $108,450 for 1993 (in the case of married couples). If, for example, the taxpayer has adjusted gross income for the year of $308,450, allowable expenses are reduced (and taxable income is

---

53. § 275.

54. Pechman, *Federal Tax Policy* (1983) p. 91. Compare Andrews, *Personal Deductions in an Ideal Income Tax,* 86 Harv.L.Rev. 309 (1972), and Turnier, *Personal Deductions and Tax*

Reform: The High Road and the Low Road, 31 Villanova L.Rev. 1703 (1986). And see Griffith, *Theories of Personal Deductions in the Income Tax,* 40 Hastings L.J. 343 (1989).

increased) by 3% of $200,000, or $6,000. Medical expenses and casualty losses, both being subject to independent percentage limitations (see 7.02) and both being in the category of non-voluntary outlays, are exempt from reduction under § 68; also exempt is "investment interest", which really represents a cost of earning taxable income.

Some of the allowable personal expenses have already been mentioned or are mentioned later on. Thus, the credit for child-care expenses was briefly described at 6.01, the allowance for personal bad debts at 6.07; the treatment of alimony payments is referred to at 9.05, below. The present section is limited to medical expenses and disaster losses, charitable contributions, home-mortgage interest and local property taxes. A few further remarks are made about the "standard deduction" device (which has taken the place of the old zero bracket), as well as personal exemptions and the concept of "adjusted gross income." The section concludes with a comment on the "earned income tax credit", which has been expanded under the 1993 Act.

7.02 Medical Expenses and Casualty Losses. As noted above, the medical expense and casualty loss deductions serve similar purposes: the refinement of a taxpayer's net income base by excluding from it large and unanticipated outlays or losses that impair the individual's ability to meet his tax obligations. While the general intent is reasonably clear, there are, as usual, problems of classification and definition which test the scope or coverage of the provisions.

(a) Medical expense. Code § 213(a) allows a deduction for all medical and dental expenses paid by the taxpayer (and not reimbursed by insurance) for himself, his spouse and dependents. Included are payments made during the year for diagnosis and treatment, prescription drugs (but not medicine-cabinet items like aspirins and band-aids), and medical equipment, hospital care, and health and accident insurance. Under a 1990 amendment, the cost of elective cosmetic surgery—*e.g.*, face-lifts—is no longer deductible.

§ 213(a) limits the medical expense deduction to the amount which exceeds 7½% of the taxpayer's "adjusted gross income" (roughly, gross income less trade or business expenses) for the year. An individual with $40,000 of adjusted gross income is thus denied deduction for the first $3,000 of the year's medical costs. The purpose of the limitation is, of course, to distinguish between recurring expenses which can be planned for in the family budget— annual check-ups, periodic visits to the dentist—and extraordinary outlays which impose a large and unexpected burden on the family's resources.

In reality, these days many families budget for extraordinary outlays, especially hospital bills, by carrying medical insurance, whether personally or through their employers. To encourage this practice, § 213(d) includes insurance within the definition of "medical care," so that the premiums are deductible in the same way as direct medical expenses. More important, perhaps, in view of the 7½% floor, § 106 generally excludes medical insurance premiums paid by an employer from the employee's *gross* income.

Since expenditures "prescribed" for sick people—a vacation in Florida; an air-conditioning unit—also frequently are made by healthy people as well, there are, inevitably, controversies over whether a particular outlay really constitutes an expenditure for medical care. In *Ochs v. Commissioner,*[55] for example, the taxpayer's wife, having had a serious throat operation, was advised by a doctor that her recovery would be impaired unless she was separated from her two young children, who caused her "nervousness and irritation." Accordingly, the children were sent off to boarding school. The taxpayer sought to deduct the school expense as an expenditure for medical care made necessary by his wife's condition.

Over a heart-rending dissent by Judge Frank, the Second Circuit denied the deduction on the ground that the outlay in question was a personal family expense within § 262 rather than a medical expense under § 213. In effect, the court distinguished between the direct costs of medical treatment, obviously deductible, and the increase in family living expenses which inevitably results from the illness of a parent, especially a housewife. As noted previously (1.03), while the imputed value of self-rendered household services is traditionally excluded from gross income, no equivalent deduction is allowed to those who prefer to pay for such services in cash and spend their free time doing other things. The question in *Ochs,* ultimately, was whether a deduction should be permitted when the family is *compelled* to purchase housekeeping services because of the housewife's illness and inability to do housework, rather than from mere personal preference. It seems evident, even then, that Congress did not intend § 213 to have so large and indefinite a reach. The section speaks primarily of "medical care" and does not refer to other increased costs of illness. Hence the court was undoubtedly right, or at least consistent with

55. 195 F.2d 692 (2d Cir.1952).

161

Congressional intent, in disallowing the children's boarding school expense.

While the dissenting judge in *Ochs* plainly thought the majority approach too strict, he himself would have disallowed that part of the boarding school expense which was attributable to the children's education and to periods during the day when either the wife or the children would have been away from home anyway. The distinction, apparently, would be between increased living expenses which served exclusively to relieve the mother of child-care duties, and those expenses which also conveyed some further benefit to the children or the family. Only the former would be allowable. One suspects that in the end no more than a small portion of the total outlay would have qualified for deduction under this approach, while the administrative task of making the requisite allocation would have been burdensome indeed.

(b) Casualty losses. § 165(c)(3) allows a deduction for unreimbursed casualty losses resulting from casualty or theft, even though the property lost or damaged is of a personal character. Since no deduction is permitted for depreciation or ordinary wear and tear in the case of personal assets, a distinction needs to be drawn between losses which arise through processes of slow erosion and losses which are swift and unexpected. The Service has held that termite damage is in the former category, for example, though the courts have sometimes held the contrary. Under § 165(h), added to the Code in 1982, personal casualty losses are allowed only to the extent that they exceed, in aggregate, 10% of adjusted gross income. In addition, in order to avoid the itemization of small routine casualties—broken dishes, dented fenders—deduction is denied for the first $100 of each casualty or theft. No deduction is allowed for casualty insurance premiums, presumably because such premiums represent a cost of earning tax-free imputed income through personal use of the insured property.

The measure of the allowable casualty loss is simply the difference between the value of the property before and after the casualty, but not in excess of the taxpayer's original cost. If a residence which was purchased for $50,000 and has a value of only $40,000 is totally destroyed by fire, the deductible loss is limited to $40,000. If the residence was worth $60,000 before the fire, the deduction is limited to the original purchase price of $50,000. In the first case the decline in value from $50,000 to $40,000 is treated as a personal expense resulting from "use" (see 15.02). In the second case, the rise in value from $50,000 to $60,000 represents unrealized and untaxed property appreciation, and hence is not included in the taxpayer's cost.

7.03 Charitable Contributions. With exceptions to be noted, § 170(a) allows a deduction for contributions to charity up to a limit of 50% of a taxpayer's adjusted gross income. Contributions are deductible only if made to an organization—educational, religious, scientific, etc.—which the statute describes as an eligible donee. Gifts to designated individuals are not deductible even if funnelled through a charitable organization; and no deduction is allowed to the extent that the donor receives something of value, such as a raffle ticket or admission to an entertainment event, in return for his contribution. The 50% limitation (raised from 30% in 1969) appears generous from one standpoint and is obviously designed to encourage charitable giving by higher-income taxpayers. From another standpoint, the presence of an upper limit shows that Congress was unwilling to permit the very rich to reduce their taxes to zero by turning over their entire incomes to charity and living out of savings.

Deduction is allowed under § 170(a) whether the taxpayer makes his contribution in money or in "property." Where the property has appreciated in the taxpayer's hands, a double benefit is allowed in most cases because the full value of the property (not merely its cost) is deductible, while the appreciation is *not* regarded as realized by virtue of the gift. The result is that donors are generally better off by donating appreciated property than by making equivalent gifts in cash. To illustrate, suppose a taxpayer purchased certain shares of stock some years ago for $5,000. The stock is now worth $25,000 and the taxpayer, as it happens, is eager to donate $25,000 to his favorite charity. Assuming a 28% capital gain tax, the cost of a $25,000 gift to the donor will obviously be $5,600 less (.28 × $20,000 of appreciation) if the stock is donated in kind than if it is sold first and the donor is left with the after-tax proceeds. Hence all donors would follow the former course.

Some critics have argued that the combined benefit to property donors of a deduction plus the non-realization of appreciation is excessive. Those who confine their gifts to cash—presumably lower-income donors—get the deduction benefit only. While gifts of property are not generally treated as realization events (see 4.01), the fact that the property donor is given a deduction for the untaxed appreciation could, and perhaps should, be taken as the equivalent of a realization. The overall benefit, then, would be limited to the deduction feature alone. One difficulty with this approach (if it is a difficulty) is that some donors might be led to retrieve at least a portion of their increased tax cost by simply reducing the size of their donations to charity. Thus, the stockowner above might elect to sell the appreciated shares, hold back the $5,600 capital gain tax, and contribute only the net after-tax proceeds of $19,400. Since charities would get less thereby, they have opposed the realization idea with unimaginable fervor.

In 1969 Congress did modify the treatment of appreciated property under § 170, but as far as conventional gifts of appreciated securities are concerned the modification consists only of applying a 30% limitation on the amount which can be deducted instead of the higher 50% limit. The effect of the restriction is not likely to be serious for most donors—especially as a 5-year carryover of excess contributions is permitted—and it remains a standard item of promotion for charities to stress the tax benefits that result from making appreciated gifts in kind. On the other hand, in the case of property-gifts which entail even more serious tax avoidance potential—where a sale of the property would result in ordinary income (inventory, for example) or short-term capital gain—Congress acted more firmly by restricting the donor's deduction to the property's cost and disallowing the appreciation.

No deduction is allowed under § 170 for uncompensated services to charity, *i.e.,* for volunteer work. As suggested at 8.01 below, such services generate a kind of imputed income to the volunteer himself, rather like the value of a leisure-time activity. The volunteer is not taxed on the value of such services, of course, but he cannot take a deduction for the taxable income forgone. The same is true of the rent-free use of property: a taxpayer who allows a charity to use his property rent-free may exclude the rental value of the property from income; but he cannot also deduct such rental value as a contribution. These limitations can easily be viewed as inconsistent with the permission to combine the exclusion and deduction of property appreciation described in the preceding paragraphs; but as will be seen in Parts C and F, the same element of conflict appears at other points in the income tax.

7.04 Home Mortgage Interest Before the 1986 Code revision, interest on personal borrowings of every kind was fully deductible by taxpayers who chose to itemize their personal expenses. Thus, interest on residential mortgages, on installment purchases of cars and home appliances, on vacation loans, credit cards and charge accounts—all such payments were allowable (to itemizers) under § 163(a), a section that makes no distinction between borrowing for business and for personal reasons. Just *why* that distinction is lacking—it is of course central to the aim of § 162 and other deductible expense provisions—has never been very clear. As noted at 6.05, an interest deduction is plainly justified when the amounts borrowed are used to generate taxable income, but when the property acquired is personal and (as with a car or a home) produces only nontaxable income, the allowance of interest expense is arguably anomalous.

Largely for the latter reason, apparently, though with one major exception, the 1986 Act added § 163(h), which disallows *all* deductions for "personal interest." Consumers' financing costs—even including interest on federal tax deficiencies—are now, like other consumer outlays, required to be paid out of after-tax income.

The exception (without which passage of the Act presumably would have been doubtful) is for interest on home mortgages. Generally, under § 163(h) home mortgage interest continues to be allowable as an itemized expense deduction. There are, however, certain restrictions that apply to mortgages taken out after October, 1987. First, the amount treated as "qualified" home mortgage debt is limited to the taxpayer's basis for his residence—his original purchase price plus the cost of improvements—so that borrowing against unrealized appreciation after the value of the property has gone up will not generate additional deductible interest. Second, while a homeowner is free to refinance his old mortgage if a decline in interest rates makes that step desirable, the new debt will "qualify" only up to the amount of the balance of the old mortgage principal just before the refinancing. In effect, a homeowner who has paid off part or all of his original mortgage (and, as a consequence, has lost part or all of his original interest deduction) cannot "re-qualify" by borrowing back the amount repaid. At all events, the total amount of qualified home mortgage debt may not exceed $1 million.

The restrictions just described are plainly intended to confine the taxpayer's interest deduction to his original acquisition indebtedness—the amount he borrowed to buy his home in the first instance. They are not, however, nearly as stern as they appear, because § 163(h)(3) specifically allows deduction of interest on up to $100,000 of so-called "home equity indebtedness"—typically, indebtedness placed on the property long after its acquisition and secured by the "equity" which the homeowner has built up through repayment of the original mortgage principal, or which builds up because the property appreciates, or both. The proceeds of a home equity loan would presumably be used by the borrower to meet personal obligations entirely unrelated to home purchase—children's college tuition, for example—although such obligations, if financed by loans not secured by his residence, would otherwise generate nonallowable "personal interest". Further, none of the new restrictions applies to "grandfathered" mortgages, meaning mortgages taken out before the October, 1987 date. Finally, deduction for home mortgage interest is allowable not only with respect to the taxpayer's principal residence, but also with respect to one (1) so-called second residence. In effect, Congress was induced to give vacation homes preferred status, a decision that instantly (and successfully) raised a claim from boatowners that nothing in the term "residence" excludes a home at sea.

Even when the new restrictions are taken into account, home mortgage interest, when added to residential property taxes, bulks largest among all the itemized deductions. As noted at 7.06, personal expenses are worth itemizing only to the extent that the total of such expenses exceeds $6,200 on joint returns ($3,700 for single persons). Presumably, however, most middle-income taxpayers do not regularly incur deductible expenses in excess of the $6,200 figure apart from expenses that are residence-related. Hence, if home mortgage interest and property taxes were not allowed, relatively few would find it worthwhile to itemize at all. Homeowners as a group (a very large group, to be sure) are thus the principal beneficiaries of the whole expense-itemization scheme.

Is it "equitable" and consistent with the net income concept to permit homeowner-mortgagors to deduct their mortgage interest? The answer (unfortunately) is yes-and-no; it all depends on whom the mortgagor is being compared with. If the comparison is with a homeowner who owns his residence free and clear, the interest deduction allowed to the mortgagor is equitable. The free-and-clear owner earns imputed income on his investment which is regarded, by fixed tradition (1.03), as exempt from tax. The mortgagor's interest deduction simply puts him on an equal footing. But if the comparison is with an apartment-dweller or other tenant who rents his home, then the interest deduction gives the mortgagor a clear advantage. The reason, obviously, is that the tenant gets no deduction for his cash rental payments, because these are treated as a nonallowable personal expense. As noted previously, the basic inconsistency in the law arises from the fact that the imputed rental value of owner-occupancy is not taxable, while cash rental payments are not deductible. Mortgage interest is in a sort of swing position between the two: allowing the interest as a deduction creates equity in one direction but not the other; disallowing it would have the same effect, but the directions would be reversed.

To illustrate all this, assume that O (for outright owner) and M (for mortgagor) each purchases a home for $50,000 which yields gross imputed rent of $4,000 a year. Annual depreciation (not deductible) is $1,000, so the net imputed rent is $3,000. M's annual mortgage amortization is $4,000, of which $3,000 is deductible interest and $1,000 is non-deductible principal. Finally, T (for tenant) rents an apartment for $4,000 a year, the rent, of course, being non-deductible.

Both M and T own securities which yield $3,000 a year in taxable dividends (so did O but he sold his securities to buy his house). O, M and T are all in the 40% bracket. Here is how the three taxpayers compare:

		O	M	T
1.	Gross imputed rent from occupancy	$4,000	$4,000	$4,000
2.	Less:			
	a. Depreciation/principal	1,000	1,000	–0–
	b. Cash rental payment	–0–	–0–	4,000
3.	Net imputed rent (1 minus 2)	3,000	3,000	–0–
4.	Taxable income:			
	Dividends	–0–	3,000	3,000
	Less: Mortgage interest	–0–	3,000	–0–
		–0–	–0–	3,000
5.	Tax at 40% of line 4	–0–	–0–	1,200
6.	Net yield on $50,000 investment (3 plus 4 minus 5)	3,000	3,000	1,800

The effect of § 163 in these circumstances is to place M in the same favorable position as O, while leaving T to absorb a 40% reduction in the net yield from his equivalent investment. It is easy enough to argue that T is treated inequitably as compared with the other two, and that the "solution" is to require both O and M to include their "net imputed rent" in income. But if this step is ruled out, whether for administrative or political reasons, the proper treatment of M becomes uncertain. Obviously, M could argue that to disallow his interest deduction would place him at a disadvantage relative to O, and that this would be unfair. But it is equally true that allowing the interest deduction gives M an advantage over T, which is unfair to the latter. In any case, if the Code *were* amended to disallow the deduction of mortgage interest, M would presumably sell his securities and pay his mortgage down to zero so as to obtain the same benefit from the imputed income exclusion as is now received by O. Those M's who are unfortunate enough to be paying off their mortgages out of salary income would be unable to make this switch, though, and would find themselves unhappily grouped with T to the extent of their annual interest payments. In reality, then, it is the imputed rent exclusion, rather than the interest deduction, that is responsible for the lack of tax equity in this area.

Somewhat ironically, when it is applied to other "consumer durables"—automobiles, I suppose, would be the largest item for most people—the same sort of analysis might lead us to conclude that a borrower's interest expense *should* be allowable in computing his taxable income. As noted above, a taxpayer who buys a car on time can no longer deduct his interest payments, such payments being treated as "personal interest" under § 163(h). And that, to be sure, is what they are. But it is also true that if interest on auto loans cannot be deducted, then installment buyers are penalized relative to those who buy their cars outright, since the latter earn imputed income that is exempt from tax. Here, as compared with home buyers, the element of interpersonal discrimination is less ambiguous. In the case of home-mortgages, denial of interest deductions would disadvantage mortgagors relative to outright owners but, on the other hand, would place mortgagors on a parity with tenant-lessees and thus eliminate a tax bias against the latter. Where family automobiles are concerned, however, the status of "lessee" is still, I think, less common than that of owner. If so, there are really only two major classes of consumers to compare: installment buyers, whose interest expense is disallowed under § 163(h), and outright owners, whose imputed income exclusion is, of course, untouched. One hesitates to complain about the disallowance of *any* personal deduction, but in this instance tax-equity may point in the opposite direction.

* * *

Having scattered my discussion of this topic, it may help to note that "interest"—at least those interest expenses most likely to be encountered by taxpayers generally—is now subject to a *fourfold* classification under the Code:

(1) Interest incurred in the conduct of a trade or business. For example, a company (proprietorship or partnership) borrows money from a bank to finance its operating expenses. Interest costs of this kind are, of course, deductible from gross income like any other business expense.

(2) Investment interest. For example, an individual maintains a margin account with his broker and borrows money to finance his securities investments. As indicated at 6.05, § 163(d) limits the deduction of investment interest in any taxable year to an amount not in excess of the taxpayer's investment income (including gains from the sale of investment property), with disallowed amounts being carried forward to later years. Also as indicated, interest on debt incurred to finance certain tax-exempt investments—*e.g.*, municipal bonds—remains nondeductible.

(3) Interest taken into account in determining a taxpayer's income or loss from a so-called passive activity. For example, a limited partnership borrows funds to finance the purchase of depreciable real estate. For the reasons given at 13.02, new § 469 restricts the deduction of interest attributable to passive activities to the income *from* such passive activities, and thus bars the taxpayer from reducing taxable income derived from other sources.

(4) Consumer interest: disallowed by § 163(h) except for interest on home mortgage loans.

From the standpoint of deductibility, therefore, the "best" kind of interest is obviously business interest, allowable without restriction. Second, perhaps, is home mortgage interest, also allowable without restriction (other than the cost and dollar limitations) provided that the taxpayer itemizes his personal expenses. Third in line would be investment interest, and behind that, passive activity interest: both are allowable, but both are restricted to offsetting income from related sources only. Dead last is nonresidential consumer interest, which is not allowable at all.

7.05 Miscellaneous Deductions. For historical reasons of no great importance, the Code distinguishes (in the case of individual taxpayers) between "trade or business" expenses, allowable under § 162(a), and expenses incurred in managing investment property such as a securities portfolio. The latter are deductible under § 212 provided they meet the usual criteria of "ordinary and necessary," current rather than capital expenditure, and so on. As these are the same criteria that apply to trade or business expenses, one might suppose that investment-related outlays would simply be netted off against investment income—in effect, be deducted from gross income to reach *adjusted* gross income—in the same way that business expenses are netted off against business income. Not so. Presumably in order to minimize record-keeping and simplify returns for taxpayers electing the standard deduction, § 62(a) requires that investment-related expenses [56] (as well as unreimbursed employee business expenses) be deducted from adjusted gross income in the same manner as allowable *personal* expenses. The result is that "miscellaneous deductions" of the sort described are of benefit only to those taxpayers who find it worthwhile to itemize their personal deductions.

For taxpayers who do itemize, however, the "miscellaneous deduction" category serves as a handy repository for all kinds of expenditures, some of them only doubtfully qualifying for deduction in the first place. One familiar example would be subscriptions to

---

56. Other than expenses relating to rents and mineral royalties; § 562(a)(4).

newspapers and periodicals. Is a subscription to the New York Times or Time Magazine deductible under § 212 because it helps keep the subscriber abreast of political and economic news that affects his investment planning? Presumably not, but the subscriber is likely in many cases to resolve the doubt (or rather *his* doubt) in favor of deduction anyway. Examples in the fields of education and travel could also be given. In effect, the "miscellaneous deduction" category may stimulate the itemizing taxpayer to find *something* that belongs there—"errors of law" in this connection are perhaps not uncommon—with the consequence that the Service's auditing burdens are multiplied.

To reduce those burdens, the 1986 Act added § 67, which provides that "miscellaneous itemized deductions" shall be allowed only to the extent that they exceed 2% of the taxpayer's adjusted gross income. Deduction of small-scale outlays—subscriptions, union dues, safe-deposit rentals, tax-return preparers' fees—is thus effectively eliminated for most individuals. In addition, certain employee business expenses—chiefly unreimbursed travel and transportation expenses—which had previously been allowed as deductions *from* gross income (*i.e.*, without having to be itemized) are demoted to "below-the-line" status (*i.e.*, now have to be itemized) and hence become subject to the 2% floor limitation. The 5-year revenue gain expected to result from these seemingly modest changes was estimated to be nearly $20 billion.

7.06 Standard Deduction; Adjusted Gross Income; Personal Exemptions. Roughly two-thirds of all individual taxpayers elect to take the standard deduction in lieu of itemizing their allowable personal expenses. Introduced in 1944 as a means of reducing the need for individual record-keeping, the standard deduction has slowly increased in amount over the years and now (as adjusted for inflation) stands at $6,200 for married couples, $3,700 for single persons. Thus, all married taxpayers who elect the standard deduction are taxed at a rate of zero on the first $6,200 of taxable income. Taxpayers who incur allowable personal expenses in excess of the standard deduction amount will still want and be entitled to itemize such expenses and deduct them from adjusted gross income, but, of course, as a practical matter it is only the excess over the standard deduction that generates a tax benefit.

The term "adjusted gross income," as defined in § 62, means the taxpayer's gross income less his trade or business expenses. This intermediate figure represents the base-point for determining certain of the personal expense deductions, in particular those that are limited to, or are allowable only to the extent they exceed, a certain percentage of income. If these percentage restrictions were calculated by reference to *gross* income, the results would frequently be illogical or unfair. For example, a businessman with $400,000 of gross income and $300,000 of business expenses would be allowed to deduct his medical expenses only to the extent that they exceeded $30,000 (7½% of $400,000), whereas a taxpayer with a salary of $100,000 could deduct all medical expenses in excess of $7,500. But as each taxpayer has the same $100,000 of net income after business expenses, it is plain that the 7½% floor on medical expenses should also be the same for both.

In effect, then, adjusted gross income represents the taxpayer's gross income from all sources, reduced by the business expenses described in Section 6 (and by certain special items such as alimony payments). The standard deduction or, alternatively, the itemized deductions described in this Section, plus the taxpayer's personal exemptions, are then subtracted from adjusted gross income in order to reach "taxable income" under § 63. The latter, of course, is the figure to which the rate schedule is finally applied in arriving at the individual's tax liability for the year.

Every taxpayer is entitled to deduct a $2,350 personal exemption for himself, his spouse and each of his dependents, as provided in §§ 151 and 152. The $2,350 exemption level, which represents a near doubling of the amount previously allowed, was a major feature of the 1986 Act, designed especially to benefit lower and middle-income taxpayers.

Commencing in 1991, the personal exemptions and exemptions for dependents are slowly phased out for higher-income taxpayers. Under § 151(d), total exemptions are reduced by 2% for each $2,500 by which the taxpayer's adjusted gross income exceeds the so-called "threshold amount", which is $162,700 for a married couple. To illustrate: A couple with two children is entitled to exemptions of $9,400 (4 × $2,350). If the couple has $212,700 of income in 1993 (*i.e.*, $50,000 above the threshold amount), their exemptions will be reduced by 40% ($50,000/$2,500 × 2%), and taxable income will be increased by $3,760 (40% of $9,400). Assuming the couple pays tax at a marginal rate of 36%, increasing their taxable income by $3,760 means that they owe additional taxes for the year of $1,354. In effect, the marginal rate on the last $50,000 of income actually becomes 36% plus ×% = $1,354/$50,-000, or 38.7%. If the same couple had, say, 7 exemptions (five children instead of two), the addition to their taxable income would be $6,580 (40% of 7 × $2,350), they would owe $2,369 more in tax, and their applicable marginal rate would be nearly 41%. Thus, the larger a couple's family the higher its marginal rate (assuming family income is high enough to invoke the exemption phaseout). Just what "policy" this reflects is difficult to say.

Older taxpayers—individuals age 65 or over—are entitled to an additional standard deduction of $1,200 if married (and both spouses qualify) or $750 if unmarried, as well as a tax-credit equal to 15% of the first $5,000 of retirement income in the case of single persons, $7,500 for married couples. The credit is phased out as the taxpayer's income increases and thus is limited, in effect, to low and lower-middle income taxpayers. Before 1983, under a long-standing administrative practice (which reflected Congressional intent), Social Security benefits were wholly excluded from the recipient's gross income no matter how much income (dividends, rents, etc.) he received from other sources. This was true even though only half of the contributions paid in during the recipient's working life had come out of his own after-tax income—the other half having been paid in by his employer but never taxed to the individual himself. Concluding that this arrangement was too generous to higher income retirees, Congress adopted § 86, which, as amended in 1993, now can include in gross income as much as 85% of the benefits received annually if the recipient's income exceeds $44,000 in the case of married couples or $34,000 for single persons.

7.07 EITC. Heretofore relatively modest in its aims and revenue cost, the Earned Income Tax Credit was greatly expanded by the 1993 Act and now assumes a major role in our national welfare system. Simply put, EITC is an earnings-subsidy for working families. Other more traditional family welfare programs—of which Aid to Families with Dependent Children is much the largest—provide benefits to people who qualify for assistance on the basis of "need" and who may be unemployed and have no earnings whatever. By contrast, EITC ("pro-work, pro-family") is a program that benefits low-wage working people only. In effect, the subsidy is directed and largely confined to people who do hold jobs and do earn taxable income, and who also have parental responsibilities.

The subsidy provided for by Code § 32 is in the maximum amount of $3,370, and it is "paid" in the form of a credit against income taxes otherwise due. If the credit exceeds the taxpayer's positive tax liability, the excess becomes a tax "refund" for the year. For a worker with two children, for example, the subsidy rises with the taxpayer's wages up to an earnings level of $8,425, then remains constant for earnings up to $11,000, and then is phased out as earnings go higher, finally falling to zero at an earnings-level of $27,000. Thus, if the worker had wages of $10,-

000 in the current year, his positive tax liability (after personal exemptions and the standard deduction) would be zero and his refund would be the full amount of $3,370. If the same worker had wages of $20,000, his positive tax liability might be about $750. At this higher wage-level the credit would be phased down to about $1,475, and the taxpayer's net refund—really, his net subsidy— would be reduced to $725.

Experts apparently disagree about whether, as a matter of social policy, it is or is not a good idea to tie work and welfare together. That issue we must necessarily leave to them. From our narrower standpoint what is notable is the particular use to which Congress now has put the federal tax system.[57] The income tax is a mechanism that is aimed at collecting revenues. EITC is a device that is designed to do just the opposite, that is, to push out subsidies. Joining the two together (other considerations to one side) is therefore slightly ingenious. In effect, we have a large-scale public assistance program that relies upon the same legal rules and calculations that apply generally to the tax-paying middle class—a program, moreover, that is to be administered by the Internal Revenue Service rather than by a government welfare agency. Because it is part of the tax system, EITC enables low-income taxpayers to make their benefit claims not by showing "need" but by the simple act of filing annual income tax returns. Benefits, as shown, then take the form of tax "refunds" rather than ordinary welfare checks. The expectation, or the hope, is that EITC will be cheaper to administer than a traditional welfare program and also less demeaning to its beneficiaries. In time, EITC is expected to become an even larger program than AFDC itself: for 1997, EITC's projected cost is $26.6 billion, that of AFDC (federal and state together) $25.4 billion.

7.08 The Alternative Minimum Tax. Although legislation has moved in the direction of broadening the regular tax base in recent years, there remain and continue to be a good many preferences and exceptions of importance. As stated much earlier, some preference features—the non-inclusion of unrealized property appreciation, say—simply represent inbuilt limitations of the system itself about which relatively little could be done even by the most reform-minded legislator. Others, however, such as accelerated depreciation (so labored over at 6.08 and 6.09), the municipal bond interest exemption or the deduction for residential mortgage interest, plainly reflect a Congressional decision to subsidize particular categories of business, investment and even personal activity. As amply explained, quick depreciation rules are intended to encourage the purchase of plant and equipment, exemption for municipal

---

57. Alstott, *EITC and the Oversimplified Case For Tax-Based Welfare Reform*, 108 Harv.L.Rev. ___ (1994).

bond interest is intended to reduce state and local borrowing costs, mortgage interest deductions are intended to encourage home-ownership, and so on and on. Whether it is wise or foolish to use the federal tax system as a subsidy device has been debated for decades, but on the whole Congress appears to accept the idea that the tax system may properly be used to foster non-tax objectives. Indeed, on some occasions—the adoption of ACRS in 1981 is a famous instance—it has shown itself willing to narrow the tax base in ruthless and dramatic fashion in order to promote other national goals.

One much-publicized consequence of treating certain categories of income preferentially, however, is that some taxpayers—inevitably [58] those at the highest-bracket level—will, through ownership of exempt-source assets, wind up paying tax at very low effective rates or, perhaps, not paying tax at all. A Treasury study of 1983 tax returns, for example, showed that 11% of taxpayers reporting income over $250,000 paid taxes at a rate of 5% or less and 20% at a rate of 10% or less. Roughly the same was true for returns reporting income in excess of $1 million. The corporate picture has been even more striking. Due, no doubt, to the combined effect of ACRS and the investment tax credit, many large corporations paid zero taxes during the years 1981–86 or paid at an effective rate much lower than the nominal statutory rate, then 46%. Although statistics of this sort have been around for a long time, in recent years they seem to have become better known to the general public and to be greatly resented. Presumably as a consequence, the notion that no one should be allowed to escape tax entirely or substantially has come to play an important, even an integral part in legislative thinking about the tax system. "[I]nequities of this magnitude," intoned the House Committee recently, referring to profitable businesses reporting zero taxable income, "should not continue as a regular function of the tax system, whose orderly function rests squarely on popular opinion that it is operating fairly."

There is thus, to put it mildly, a fundamental conflict in the minds of our law-makers. Plainly, Congress wishes to continue to favor certain categories of *income* through the customary medium of exemption or deferral. Plainly also, however, the circumstance that certain categories of *taxpayers* are thus enabled to avoid their apparent tax obligations is, or has become, unacceptable. President Reagan himself, while in office, acted to put a sharper edge on *both* horns of the dilemma. A strong supporter of reduced taxes on

---

58. See Note, "What is the True Value of a Tax Preference?" *infra*, p. 356.

business and investment income—ACRS was a major element in the Reagan tax legislation of 1981—the President was also a popular and effective critic of those egregious "loopholes" which allow the "powerful or privileged ... to keep from paying taxes when the middle class with no protection from clever accountants bear more than their share of the load. [Applause.]" [59] ACRS, evidently, was not among the "loopholes" which the President had in mind.

The alternative minimum tax, considerably strengthened by recent amendments, represents a compromise or *modus vivendi* between these two irreconcilable aims. Applicable in different ways to both individuals and corporations, the minimum tax is intended to ensure that the "powerful or privileged" pay *some* significant tax on their economic incomes despite the continued availability of tax-exempt income sources. To accomplish this, the Code establishes what amounts to a second tax system [60]—one that defines the income base more broadly than the regular tax system, but then applies a lower rate of tax to that broadened income-base. Taxpayers otherwise benefiting from certain preferences are required to compute their regular tax liability (on the narrower base) and their minimum tax liability (on the broader base), compare the two, and finally pay whichever is the greater (in practical effect). Thus, both aims are served (or defeated). Taxpayers can still benefit from the use of such preferences for regular tax purposes, but the benefit is limited because the minimum tax establishes a floor below which the taxpayer's actual liability may not fall.

Under Code § 55(b), as amended by the 1993 Act, the tax rate for individuals is 26% on the first $175,000 of alternative minimum taxable income above a so-called exemption amount and 28% on AMTI over $175,000. The exemption amount is $45,000 for married couple, $33,750 for single taxpayers, both being phased out at higher AMTI levels. High-income taxpayers may still, as in the past, seek to arrange their affairs so as to pay no more than the minimum rate of 26% or 28%, but with minimum and regular rates only about twelve points apart at most, the inducement and the benefit are obviously somewhat reduced.

Roughly speaking, the minimum tax base equals the regular tax base increased by the add-back of certain designated preference items. Where individuals are concerned, the latter include: the excess of depreciation on real property under normal ACRS rules

---

59. Remarks of President Reagan to Citizens of Bloomfield, New Jersey, released by The White House, Office of the Press Secretary, June 13, 1985.

60. See Shaviro, *Perception, Reality, and Strategy: The New Alternative Minimum Tax,* 66 Taxes 91 (1988).

over the amount that would result using a 40-year life for such property; the excess of ACRS depreciation on business equipment, which entails use of the double declining balance method, over the allowance determined under 150% declining balance and longer useful lives; the benefit of the installment and certain other long-term methods of accounting; and incentive stock option gains (see 19.01, below). Unrealized appreciation on property contributed to charity was a preference item under prior law but, as a benefit chiefly to museums and universities, it has been eliminated from the preference list by the 1993 Act. Finally, certain itemized expenses, including miscellaneous expenses and state and local taxes, are reduced or disallowed for minimum tax purposes. Various additional items are treated as taxable preferences for corporations, which are subject now to a minimum tax rate of 20% (as compared to a regular rate of 35%).

I should add, finally, that although broader than the regular tax base, the minimum tax is by no means all-inclusive or "ideal." Thus, interest on municipal bonds (with certain exceptions) still enjoys exemption, and the same is true for the interest build-up on life insurance policies. Likewise, the so-called "middle class" preferences—home mortgage interest, pension plan contributions, employee fringe benefits—are unaffected by the minimum tax. The reason for these omissions is that the minimum tax is intended not so much to raise revenues as to reassure popular opinion about the fairness of the system. Preferences that are widely, even if not universally, enjoyed obviously do not especially trouble "popular opinion".

Part C: ATTRIBUTION OF INCOME

Although a taxpayer generally regards his immediate family—his wife and minor children, say—as an economic unit from the standpoint of resources and expenditures, the federal income tax treats each member of the family as a separate taxable person. This means, for example (and except as explained at 9.02, below), that if a child owns property in his own right, the income which the property produces is taxed to the child himself. The tax law does not lump the child's income together with his parents', even though parents and children are obviously members of a single household. The same is true of other family "entities", such as family trusts and family corporations. All such beings, natural or otherwise, are viewed as separate taxpayers, each with its own independent status under the tax law.

At the same time, of course, the federal income tax structure is (once again) progressive: as an individual receives additional income, his tax also goes up but at a greater rate of increase. This is so because additional segments of income may be taxed at higher marginal rates than their predecessors. It follows that a family whose income is taxed to one member only—say the father—would usually pay a higher overall tax than a family whose income is divided evenly among all the members of the group. For example, if a taxpayer with two children has taxable income this year of $150,000, the tax (on a joint return filed by himself and his wife) is nearly $40,000. But if the same income can somehow be reported on three returns (the joint return plus one each for the two children) at the rate of $50,000 for each return, the overall tax on the family will be about $30,000, and a tax-saving of $10,000 will have been achieved.

Potential savings of this size operate as an inducement to the taxpayer to find some means of shifting taxable income to the lower-bracket children. If part of the taxpayer's income derives from property, a simple and obvious step is to transfer that property to the children by outright gift. Thus, if a father gives a hundred shares of stock to his daughter, the periodic dividends which the daughter receives thereafter will be taxed to her as owner of the property (subject, again, to the limitation described at 9.02). Moreover, under the rule of *Taft v. Bowers* (4.01), any unrealized appreciation in the value of the stock also will be treated as belonging to the child, even though such appreciation occurred before the gift was made. The tax law makes no effort to tax the dividends or the appreciation back to the donor merely because the property belonged to him originally. Hence, the reduction of overall family tax obligations through gifts of income-producing property is a common expedient to which those who have wealth may freely resort.

But what about those who don't—those whose income is derived from personal efforts rather than property ownership? If dividends, interest and rents can be shifted by outright gift of the underlying property, what about wages, salaries and fees? One cannot give away one's skills very easily, yet there is something disturbing in the conclusion that income-splitting is a device available to property owners alone. Can the fruits of personal services be shifted? If not, what justifies or at least explains the apparent discrimination? Even with respect to property-owners, there may be questions of a troublesome nature when the gift is other than a simple outright transfer of all substantial rights. Suppose, for example, that the owner of income-producing property transfers it to another family member but retains a right to revoke the transfer and take the property back whenever he chooses. Will the property be regarded as belonging to the transferee for tax purposes, or will the transferor's revocation right be considered the equivalent of continued ownership? The law must decide how far the property owner should have to go in the direction of an outright transfer to assure that the income from a gift of property will be attributed to someone beside himself. Here, as in the case of gifts of personal service income, there appear to be *two* candidates for taxability, each with a significant link to the income in question. And as no legal basis exists for apportioning the income between them, it is evidently necessary for the law to choose one candidate to the exclusion of the other. The question, of course, is which.

The development of legal principles governing choice of taxable person was largely left to judicial construction during the early days of the income tax. Between 1930 and 1940 the Supreme Court decided a substantial number of cases involving income attribution, largely under the authority of what is now § 61. These early cases generally favored the government (with certain significant exceptions). While their results were "correct" in the sense that any other set of outcomes would have put taxpayers in a position to render the progressive rate structure a virtual nullity, the Court's use of § 61 for this purpose was, shall we say, creative. The section defines gross income but actually says nothing directly about *whom* the income belongs to. Yet the alternative to judicial rule-making (at least until Congress should act) would have been to allow taxpayers to make the choice of taxable person *for themselves,* and thus to minimize their tax burdens more or less at will.

The discussion that follows is divided into two sections. Section 8 digests the early cases and shows how the Supreme Court formulated "common law" attribution principles under the general authority of § 61. These decisions became the basis for subsequent legislative action, particularly in the fields of trusts and family partnerships. But while partly displaced by specific Code provisions, the early decisions continue to have application in many situations not expressly covered by statute, and for this reason they are part of the basic professional vocabulary of every tax specialist. Section 9 considers some of the statutory rules on income attribution: 9.01 takes up the subject of gifts in trust, now largely dealt with by detailed Code provisions; 9.02 describes newly enacted rules on the unearned income of minors; 9.03 examines family business associations, especially family partnerships. Brief reference to another statutory "solution"—the split-income joint-return procedure which is available to husbands and wives—is made in the subsection immediately following, with further details at 9.04, while the Code treatment of alimony—considerably refined by recent legislation—is described at 9.05.

SECTION 8.   THE EARLY CASES

8.01   Gifts of Personal Service Income;   Lucas v. Earl;   Poe v. Seaborn.

(a) Redirected salary. In *Lucas v. Earl,*[1] the taxpayer, a lawyer, entered into a contract with his wife which provided that the future income earned by either spouse would be treated as belonging equally to both. In 1920 and 1921—long before the enactment of the present joint-return procedure for husbands and wives—the taxpayer earned salary and fees, presumably in substantial amounts, of which one-half was paid over to his wife pursuant to the contract. The question presented was whether the taxpayer should be required to include in his gross income the entire amount of the salary and fees, or only the one-half portion that he retained. Stressing that the income-splitting agreement was valid and binding under state law, the taxpayer argued that the aim of the Code was to tax income only if beneficially received. Since his wife possessed the absolute right to receive and enjoy one-half of the income under the contract, the taxpayer urged that that share must be regarded as "hers" within the meaning of § 61, and that only the half retained could be treated as "his."

1.   281 U.S. 111 (1930).

179

Speaking through Justice Holmes, the Supreme Court held that the assignment of unearned wages is ineffective under the federal income tax to shift income to the assignee, whatever its effect as a matter of ordinary contract law. Without denying the validity of the contract and the wife's legal claim to one-half the income, the Court held that the intent of the statute was to "tax salaries to those who earned them"—in this case, of course, the husband. This statutory purpose could not be "escaped" through the medium of "anticipatory arrangements ... however skillfully devised." Regardless of the parties' motives—that is, even if they had no intent to avoid taxes—"the fruits" of the taxpayer's labor could not be "attributed to a different tree from that on which they grew." In effect, it was the exercise of the taxpayer's income-producing skills, rather than the actual receipt of the pay envelope by the donee, which must be considered as determinative.

The *Earl* decision thus limits the candidates for taxability in personal service cases to one. Earl was denied the freedom to make his *own* choice of taxable person; rather, that choice was made for him through the imposition of a rule of attribution which ties service-income to the person who earns it. By contrast, income in the form of property appreciation may, under § 1015(a) and the holding in *Taft v. Bowers* (4.01), be shifted from donor to donee at the taxpayer's sole discretion. Thus the owner of appreciated property may decide for himself whether to sell the property and include the gain in his own income, or give it away and shift the gain to the donee. The taxpayer in *Earl* sought a similar discretion as to personal earnings by arguing that beneficial receipt should be regarded as the sole criterion of taxability. Had the Court agreed, the result would be to permit a taxpayer to make his own decision as to whether he, or someone else, should be taxed on his ordinary employment income. Since other family members will often confront lower marginal rates than the taxpayer himself, in many cases the taxpayer would simply designate such others to receive, and pay the tax on, a portion of his annual earnings.

This suggests, of course, that it was not so much fruits-and-trees—that ghastly metaphor—which concerned the Court in *Earl* as it was the prospect of a wholesale "escape" from the progressive rate schedule. The issue, after all, was *who* should be taxed—Mr. or Mrs.—on the one-half share of salary and fees, not whether such income should be taxed at all or be taxed to the parties twice. If the government had lost in its effort to attribute the income to Mr. Earl, then surely Mrs. Earl would have had to include the amounts in her income for the years in question; having won, the government must then concede that the receipts were excludable by Mrs.

Earl as gifts under § 102(a) since it was clear that the assignment was gratuitous. Accordingly, the government's only interest in the matter was to prevent the taxpayer from effectively reducing the applicable rate of tax by splitting his salary income with his wife. Not merely wives, of course, but minor children and perhaps other family dependents could be made parties to contracts like Earl's, thus further multiplying the width of the income tax brackets. Since the great bulk of family income comes from personal services, a government defeat in *Earl* would seriously have damaged the entire concept of graduated rates. While it may be true that taxpayers are free to reduce their taxes by legal means—"everybody does so, rich or poor; and all do right ..."[2]—still nothing could have been less consistent with Congressional intent than Earl's attempt to deflate the rate structure. Hence the government's victory in *Earl* was really inevitable, whether Earl the man be viewed as fruit or tree.

Having succeeded so well in the *Earl* case (the Court's decision was unanimous), the government might reasonably have expected an equally favorable outcome in *Poe v. Seaborn,*[3] a case decided only a few weeks later and raising issues of a similar character. In *Seaborn,* the taxpayer and his wife were residents of the State of Washington, under whose community property laws the income of either spouse, whether from property or from services, was treated as belonging equally to the other. At the same time the state law gave the husband legal power to manage and dispose of the community's assets in any way he chose, "short of committing a fraud on his wife's rights." For the year 1927 Seaborn and his wife each filed a separate return containing one-half of the family income, which comprised Seaborn's salary, plus interest, dividends and gains from the sale of real estate. Despite *Lucas v. Earl,* the Court held that the local law was effective for federal tax purposes and sustained the taxpayer in reporting only half of the salary and property income in his return. The Court pointed out that in *Earl* the salary income would have belonged to the husband alone in the absence of the contract entered into with his wife. Here, by contrast, "the earnings are never the property of the husband, but that of the community," owing to the operation of the state law.

Considerations of legal title, which in *Earl* were described as "attenuated subtleties," thus proved determinative in *Seaborn.* The decision presumably reflected the Court's reluctance to allow local property institutions of long-standing to be subordinated by

---

2. L. Hand, J. in *Comm'r v. Newman,* 159 F.2d 848, 850–1 (2d Cir.1947).   **3.** 282 U.S. 101 (1930).

the federal tax law, especially as Congress must have been aware of the community property laws at the time the federal income tax first was enacted. In addition, the element of tax-avoidance, with which the Court was surely concerned in *Earl,* was less urgent in *Seaborn* for at least three reasons. In the first place, the splitting of income was accomplished by operation of law rather than through voluntary contract, and hence was confined to residents of the small handful of community property states. Taxpayers could emigrate from common law to community property jurisdictions in an effort to obtain split-income benefits, but it was unlikely that the tax saving would be great enough to induce many to undertake the pains of relocation. Second, the scope of the income-splitting permitted under *Seaborn* was limited to husband and wife; the "community" to which the income belonged did not include minor children or other dependents. Hence *Seaborn* authorized *doubling* the width of the tax brackets, but no more. Finally, the effect of the community property laws was fixed and permanent. The wife was taxed on half the community income as long as the marriage lasted no matter what her income from separate sources—property acquired prior to marriage or by inheritance or gift from others—so that even if income-splitting proved disadvantageous in a given year, the parties could do nothing to reverse it. By contrast, contractual arrangements might be revoked and restored from time to time in the light of anticipated changes in the spouses' separate income.

Yet even when these differences are noted, the plain fact is that *Seaborn* injected an element of geographical discrimination into the taxation of family income—most especially personal service income. From the standpoint of national tax policy, such discrimination was highly undesirable. And despite its concern for local property law systems, *Seaborn* in effect encouraged a number of common-law states to adopt, or prepare to adopt, the law of community property as a means of extending the same federal tax benefits to their citizens. The effort was not always successful. In *Commissioner v. Harmon,*[4] the Court ruled that a husband's earnings continued to be taxable to him despite the adoption of a community property law by the state of Oklahoma. As the state's community system was elective rather than mandatory, the income-splitting was found to result from the taxpayer's voluntary action in electing to have the community rules apply; thus *Earl* rather than *Seaborn* was held to be controlling.

4.　323 U.S. 44 (1944).

Against this background of threatened widescale changes in state property laws, Congress in 1948 acted to equalize the status of married couples living in common law and in community property states. The Code was amended to authorize *all* married couples to aggregate their income and deductions on a joint return, and to pay a tax equal to twice what a single person would pay on one-half of their combined taxable income. The effect was virtually the same as if all the states in the Union had adopted the community property system at one stroke, although *federal* enactment of the income-splitting joint return "meant that the political credit for reducing taxes was concentrated on Congress rather than dispersed among the state legislatures." [5]

Joint-returns are considered in more detail at 9.04. It suffices here to note simply that the consequence of the 1948 legislation was to eliminate the discriminatory effect of *Seaborn* and to place all married couples on a parity as far as income-splitting is concerned.[6]

(b) Services in kind. The *Earl* case involved an effort by the taxpayer to reduce his taxes by redirecting fees earned from a third party (Earl's clients or employer) to his wife. *Earl* blocked this attempt by requiring that earned income be attributed to the person who performs the services, even though the cash itself is paid over to an assignee. But suppose a taxpayer makes a gift of personal service income "in kind." For example, suppose the taxpayer performs services of a commercial nature for another member of his family and refuses to accept compensation for his work. The effect, quite obviously, is to increase the net income of the "donee" and to reduce that of the taxpayer-donor. Since there is thus, potentially, a shift of personal service income between related individuals, does *Earl* require that the cash value of the taxpayer's services be included in his own income (and excluded or deducted from that of the donee)?

The answer really cannot be delivered in a single breath. In general, however, the *Earl* doctrine has *not* been extended to uncompensated services, even though the effect of such arrangements may be to transfer earned income from higher to lower-bracket family members. The reason, quite simply, is sheer impossibility; the *Earl* doctrine would become unbearably burdensome if it were stretched to cover every instance in which one family member performed uncompensated services for another. Thus,

---

5. Bittker, *Federal Income Taxation and the Family,* 27 Stanford L.Rev. 1389 (1975).

6. See Surrey, *Federal Taxation of the Family—The Revenue Act of 1948,* 61 Harv.L.Rev. 1097 (1948).

suppose a father manages his child's securities, or suppose an adult son manages an apartment building belonging to his elderly parents—in each case, of course, without charging a fee for the services performed. Those services, though not without value, are likely to be relatively modest, to be carried out separately from the performer's full-time occupation, and in any case would be viewed by the parties as a function of ordinary familial obligation. It is virtually inconceivable that the *Earl* decision was intended to authorize the government to attach a cash value to every gratuitous intra-family service, and equally unlikely that the government would wish to exercise such an authority if it existed.

It is probably fair to say, then, that taxpayers may perform uncompensated services for other family members without fear of attribution under *Earl*. And this conclusion probably holds true even if the services are much more than modest—as where the father undertakes to manage a corporation or a partnership business which is owned by his children. This does not mean that Earl, the lawyer, could have shifted half his income to his wife by purporting to be her employee—that is, by contracting to work for a fixed wage or a percentage of receipts. Since Mrs. Earl presumably had nothing to contribute to the "firm," the employment undoubtedly would have been disregarded as a sham and all of the income taxed to Earl on the ground that no true employment relationship had been created. But if Mrs. Earl contributed vital services—if she, too, were a lawyer, for example—or if the business required substantial capital which Mrs. Earl supplied, then, as stated, the principles of income-attribution apparently would not prevent Earl from minimizing the family's taxes by accepting less than full compensation for his services.

The distinction between "redirected income," "sham employment," and "services in kind" has given the Service difficulty in cases where the beneficiary of the uncompensated service is a charity. As noted at 7.03, contributions to charity of money or other property are deductible by the giver. Under § 170(b), however, the amount deductible in any taxable year may not exceed 50% of the donor's adjusted gross income. Although § 170 says nothing directly about gifts of services, by implication uncompensated personal services are "allowed" in unlimited amount—not through specific deduction, to be sure, but by permitting the "volunteer" to exclude the value of the services rendered from his gross income. Charity work, whether in the form of direct assistance (a doctor working without pay for a clinic, say) or of fund-raising activities, is obviously widespread, yet no one has ever supposed that such efforts result in anything but excludable imputed income to the individual. This implied exclusion is not subject to the percentage limitation which applies to the deduction for gifts of money or other property; in effect, the value of the services is not taken into the volunteer's income in the first place.

In several published rulings, the Service has tried to distinguish for this purpose between redirected fees, which it regards as gifts of property, and services in kind. In Rev.Rul. 71,[6a] the Service held that the percentage limitation of § 170(b) would apply where an entertainer arranged with his sponsor or employer to pay his performance fee directly to his favorite charity. Where, however, the charity itself sponsored the performance or entertainment, the fact that the entertainer contributed his services free of charge would not result in taxable income to him. In effect, therefore, no limitation would be imposed on the amount he could exclude. Whether in a given case the charity was in fact the entertainer's employer *pro tem,* or was merely the beneficiary of income earned from third parties, was a question of "substance," "good faith," and "reality"—whatever those terms might mean.

The charitable-donee problem is only one example of the difficulty the Service has had over the years in coping with, and limiting, the implied exclusion for services-in-kind. Another important instance can be seen in the long drawn-out struggle over the tax status of family partnerships. The latter topic (which was finally dealt with by specific legislation) is taken up at 9.03, below.

8.02 Assignment of Deferred Income: Helvering v. Eubank. In *Earl,* as has been seen, the taxpayer made an assignment of salary and fees for legal services to be rendered in the future. The assignee's receipt was thus dependent on the assignor's willingness to go on working. If the assignor at any time decided to retire, take a vacation or otherwise substitute leisure for income-producing effort, the assignee's right to receive cash payments would obviously come to a halt. In this sense the gift of income in *Earl* was revocable by action (or inaction) of the assignor and remained subject to his control both as to time of realization and as to magnitude. To be sure, the Holmes opinion makes nothing of this circumstance, stressing instead the simple connection between taxability and personal effort. Still, it could be argued that a different result might have been reached in *Earl* if the taxpayer had assigned to his wife a claim derived from services *already completed.* In the latter event the assigned claim would have had a value in the assignee's hands which was independent of

6a. 1953–1 C.B. 18. *And see,* G.C.M. 27026, 1951–2 C.B. 7.

the assignor's future efforts; it would be "property" like cash or securities, and hence, perhaps, like them assignable.

In *Helvering v. Eubank*,[7] the taxpayer on the termination of his insurance agency assigned to a family trust his right to receive renewal commissions which he had earned through the sale of insurance policies in earlier years. Since the taxpayer was on the cash method of accounting, the commissions would not be taxed to him until actually received in cash. The commissions were subsequently collected by the trustee and held for the benefit of other family members. The question presented was whether the commissions, when received, were includable in the taxpayer's income despite the assignment, or were taxable to the assignee. The court of appeals held that the assignment was effective to shift the income to the latter. It conceded that an individual could not "escape taxation upon his compensation in the year in which he earns it." That, presumably, was the rule of the *Earl* case. "But when a taxpayer who makes his income tax return on a cash basis assigns a right to money payable in the future for work already performed ... he transfers a property right, and the money, when received by the assignee, is not income taxable to the assignor."

On appeal, the Supreme Court reversed. In a brief opinion, the Court held that a mere power to collect the commissions, which was all the assignee had received from the assignor, was insufficient to shift the income to the assignee for tax purposes. Accordingly, the renewal commissions were taxable to the assignor himself in the year received by the assignee. The Court did not suggest that the assignment by itself produced income to the taxpayer— that would be a rule of realization rather than one of mere attribution. It refused, however, to agree that personal service income, which for some reason (*e.g.*, the taxpayer's accounting method) is not includable in the year in which the services are rendered, thereby becomes "property" which can be shifted to another taxpayer by gratuitous assignment. Although Justice Stone's opinion is somewhat cryptic, the Court apparently felt that the donee was merely a passive repository whose relationship to the income was too weak to support a claim of ownership.

Taken together, the *Earl* and *Eubank* cases bar the assignment (for tax purposes, that is) of most kinds of conventional compensation rights. Thus a typical executive pay package would include (i) a current annual salary, plus (ii) a promise of further payments for a period of years following the executive's retirement. *Earl* makes clear that the current salary element will be taxed to the executive

7. 311 U.S. 122 (1940).

in full despite a prior agreement with his employer to pay a portion of it to other family members. *Eubank* makes equally clear that the executive will be taxed on the retirement benefits, when paid, even though the right to receive those benefits is assigned to another in advance of payment, and even though inclusion is deferred by reason of the taxpayer's accounting method or other applicable rules of realization.

Yet despite their considerable impact in the personal compensation field, there is a closely related area—that of self-created property rights—in which the rule of *Earl* and *Eubank* simply doesn't work. Suppose a well-known artist paints a landscape, puts a frame around it, and gives it to his son. The painting is worth, say, $10,000 at the date of the gift. The donee is tempted to sell the painting at once—there are plenty of bidders—but on reflection decides to hold the canvas for a while in the hope of a better price. It turns out that the decision was a wise one: the art market improves substantially, and the painting is finally sold by the son for $25,000. If we assume a zero basis for the painting, then there is $25,000 of income which plainly has to be taxed to someone. But to whom—the artistic father or the shrewdly calculating son? If we concentrate solely on the connection between taxability and personal effort, a theoretically correct answer can easily be given. Since $10,000 is traceable to the father's work as an artist and $15,000 to the son's shrewd calculation, the $25,000 of income should be attributed in precisely the same proportion, *i.e.,* $10,000 to the father, and $15,000 to the son. Each would thus recognize his own particular contribution to the total and the *Eubank* rule would be given a properly refined application.

The difficulty with this solution is that income-attribution rules are nearly always applied on an all-or-nothing basis. Apportionment (which would necessitate a hindsight valuation of the painting at the date of the gift) is not authorized by the statute and has never been attempted by the courts, while the only logical alternative—to treat the gift itself as a taxable event—is contrary to the present understanding of the realization requirement. Only one of the two candidates for taxability can be chosen, and under the decided cases it will evidently be the son. As compared with the donee in *Eubank* the son obviously has more than a mere "power to collect." He owns the painting, may decide when or whether to dispose of it, and negotiates the price and terms of sale. These elements of personal discretion are sufficiently material to cause the son to be treated as the source of the income. It follows that self-created property rights—which would also include patents and copyrights—are effectively assignable for tax purposes despite the element of personal services on the part of the assignor.

Taking the matter a short step further, suppose an author or inventor transfers his copyright or patent to a publisher or manufacturer under a royalty arrangement and then assigns the royalty contract to a donee. Since the donee thereby acquires no more than a "power to collect," one would tend to suppose that the royalties, when paid, would be taxable to the donor. To be sure, an assignment of the copyright or patent itself would be effective for tax purposes—the donee, like the son with the painting, is free to exercise his own discretion with respect to the disposition of the property (selling or retaining the movie rights in a book, exploiting an invention directly or selling it for a lump sum, and so on). But where the copyright or patent has already been disposed of by the donor, it seems reasonable to expect the *Eubank* case to be controlling. The courts, however, have held that because a prior assignment of the copyright or patent would suffice to shift the taxable income to the donee, a subsequent gift of the royalty contract must be treated similarly.[8] In extended form the reasoning is that (1) a copyright or patent is effectively assignable because it is "property" rather than a mere personal service claim; (2) a royalty contract derived from the transfer of a copyright or patent is therefore also "property"; and hence (3) *Eubank* does not apply. What has happened, of course, is that the problem of apportioning taxable income which led to the exception for self-created rights in the first place has been transformed into a short-hand distinction between "property" and "services." So altered, the exception has been applied to cases in which there is really *no* apportionment problem whatever—cases, that is, in which the donee has no discretion and contributes nothing to the production of the income that is finally realized.

8.03 Gifts of Income From Property—Horst, Blair and Schaffner.

(a) The Horst case. Assume that a taxpayer—call him F for father—purchases a $1,000 5% coupon bond on January 1. The bond matures in twenty years and interest is payable annually. Suppose that F at once detaches and gives to S, his son, the first year's coupon, which entitles S to collect $50 in cash on December 31. At a discount rate of 5%, the value of S's coupon at the date of

---

8. *Heim v. Fitzpatrick*, 262 F.2d 887 (2d Cir.1959). Compare *Strauss v. Comm'r*, 168 F.2d 441 (2d Cir.1948), involving an unsuccessful attempt to assign contingent deferred compensation rights and presumably controlled by *Eubank*.

the gift is $47.60. Since bond and coupon together are worth $1,000, the present value of F's bond (coupon detached) is necessarily $952.40. When it matures, on December 31, the coupon will of course be worth $50. By the same date F's bond plus the remaining coupons will have recovered in value to $1,000. Thus—

	Value of coupon/bond on Jan. 1	Value of coupon/bond on Dec. 31	Increase in owner's net worth	Cash Received
S	$ 47.60	$ 50	$ 2.40	$50
F	952.40	1,000	47.60	–0–

In these circumstances, how much should F and S include in their respective gross incomes for the taxable year?

Not one, not two, but three possible answers can be given:

Answer 1: Follow the cash flow. Since S receives $50 in cash on Dec. 31, while F receives nothing, tax the entire interest-payment to S. To be sure, F has enjoyed an increase in net worth during the taxable year of $47.60, but as this increase is in the form of implicit income rather than cash, there might be hardship in imposing on F an obligation to pay the tax. By contrast, S has funds in hand with which to meet that obligation. As noted in discussing the *Gavit* case (see 4.02), where two candidates for taxability appear, one with cash and the other with implicit income only, there is a certain practical wisdom in choosing the former to bear the burden of the outlay.

Answer 2: Disregard the gift of the coupon entirely. The coupon is nothing more than a right to collect $50 on Dec. 31; and since F could as well have collected the payment himself and then transferred the cash to S by gift, tax F on $50, and S on nothing. Under this approach F is treated as the constructive owner of the coupon throughout the taxable year. The $50 of interest received by S is attributed to F, even though the latter received no cash whatever.

Answer 3: Follow the net worth increase. Since S's net worth increases by $2.40 during the taxable year, while F's net worth increases by $47.60, tax the $50 of interest to S and F in the same proportions. This, surely, would be the actual result if, instead of a detached coupon worth $47.60, F had given S a 5% savings account containing $47.60 in cash, and at the same time had deposited $952.40 in a savings account of his own. S would then earn and be taxed on interest of $2.40 over the year, while F would earn and be taxed on $47.60. Arguably, the tax outcomes should be alike whether F chooses to invest in 5% government bonds or in savings accounts of equivalent yield.

Each of the three answers is plausible, I think. Which is best depends on one's criteria:

Answer 1—tax S on $50, F on 0—finds support in the Supreme Court's decision in *Irwin v. Gavit,* the facts of which are in many respects similar to those of our hypothetical (see 4.02). The issue in *Gavit* was whether the annual income of a testamentary trust should be attributed to the income beneficiary, to whom it was distributed, or be excluded as a gift or inheritance. By likely implication, if the income beneficiary were *not* taxed on all the current trust income, then the amount excluded would have to be taxed to the remainderman of the trust. The latter step could be justified on the ground that the value of the remainder interest increases with the passage of time, much as does the value of F's bond in our illustration. Faced, in effect, with two candidates for taxability, the Court in *Gavit* chose the income beneficiary rather than the remainderman, presumably because the former received the actual cash distribution from the trust.

Returning to our bond-and-coupon hypothetical, one can easily view S as the income beneficiary (though for one year only), F as the remainderman, the coupon as the annual income, and the bond as the corpus of a "trust." If the *Gavit* precedent were regarded as controlling, the result, of course, would be $50 of taxable income to S and zero to F—which is just what the taxpayer in *Horst* contended.

Answer 2—tax F on $50, S on 0—is the one which the Supreme Court actually gave in *Helvering v. Horst.*[9] In a lengthy opinion by Justice Stone, the Court held that the current interest payments on the taxpayer's bonds were includable in the taxpayer's income despite his annual gifts of the coupons to his son. In effect, the Court taxed F, the "remainderman," on the income from the property, and by implication viewed S, who actually collected the income at the year-end, as the recipient of an excludable gift. The result in *Horst* was thus exactly opposite to the outcome in *Gavit,* but the Supreme Court's opinion is of little help in understanding why. Justice Stone's opinion is largely and murkily preoccupied with the question of realization. The Court struggles—without success, I should say—to find a rationale in the notion that because the donor obtained personal satisfaction from the act of giving, the gifts themselves should be regarded as a realization of taxable income. Yet it is plain that the Court did not intend to alter the settled rule that a gift of appreciated property does not result in a

9. 311 U.S. 112 (1940).

realization by the donor, so that the still unanswered question is why the transfer of a bond-coupon should be treated differently.

Confusing verbiage aside, it has long been obvious that the critical element in the *Horst* case is not the gift of the annual coupons but the donor's continued retention of the bond. This can easily be seen if we ask whether the result in *Horst,* or in our illustration, would be the same if F, having given the first coupon to S, then promptly gave the bond itself with the remaining coupons to his daughter (D). Since F was taxed on the interest received by S when F was the owner of the bond, should we now expect that D will take F's place and be taxed in the same way because *she* has become the bond-owner? Unless *Horst* was meant to overrule *Gavit,* which is nowhere indicated, the answer is clearly no. The tax-pattern established by the earlier decision would now take hold: S, the "income beneficiary," would be taxed on the interest represented by the bond coupon, while D, the "remainder-man," would be entitled to the gift exclusion and would be taxed on nothing. Both of the candidates for taxability are donees in this version, and the choice between them falls on S. Since in *Horst* the outcome is reversed, one deduces that it is the presence of F, the donor, as a candidate for taxability that makes the vital difference. Whereas in *Gavit* the donor is out of the picture, in *Horst* he is obviously very much in it, and indeed the arrangement is one which he himself has created.

But why should it matter whether the part of "remainderman" is played by a donee or by the donor himself? The answer is that by holding on to the bond and the remaining coupons, the donor retains the power to direct and redirect the flow of property income at frequent intervals, and thus in effect to reduce the applicable tax-rate to a minimum. In our illustration, as in the *Horst* case, the donor gave away the coupon for a single year only. Once that year had ended, he would of course be free to keep the next year's interest-payment for himself, or to assign it to the same donee again, or to choose another donee if he wished. The same range of choices would be available in each succeeding year, so that the donor would effectively have reserved a power to redistribute the income annually among all the members of his family, including himself. In making this yearly choice, one would expect the donor to assign the income to the possessor of the lowest marginal rate of tax, everything else being equal. It is true that F could *always* shift the future interest income to a donee of his own selection by giving away the entire bond. That step, however, would permanently vest the income in the new owner, and in the course of time the donee might well move into a tax bracket no lower than the donor's. But if the choice of donee is permitted to be made on an annual basis, then each year presents the donor with a fresh opportunity to assess the impact of the rate structure on the several members of his family and to make the choice that minimizes the family's tax obligations.

The *Horst* decision blocks the device just mentioned by treating short-term gifts of income as ineffective for tax purposes. The power to redistribute property income at brief intervals, if retained by the donor, is treated as equivalent to the ownership of the income itself. Realization—at least in the ordinary understanding of that term—is not especially relevant; the bond interest when received by S is taxable to F just as if the latter had actually received it at the year-end. Essentially, the tax-shifting effort fails in *Horst* because the donor's control over the flow of income is so substantial that his prior ownership is viewed as continuing despite the gift. As in *Earl,* the taxpayer is denied the right to make his own choice of taxable person. The choice is made for him, so to speak, through the medium of a rule which attributes the income to the donor as long as he retains ownership of the underlying property.

These comments may also serve to explain why the *Horst* decision taxes F on the entire interest payment of $50 instead of limiting the attributed amount to $47.60—the actual increase in F's net worth—as Answer 3 would prescribe. The conception that underpins the holding in *Horst* is one of continued ownership on the part of the donor, not merely of the bond which he owns in fact, but of the coupon which legally belongs to the donee. To tax F on $47.60 only would be to concede that the gift of the coupon had actually been effective to separate the income and remainder interests in the property. Were this concession made, however, the force of the *Gavit* precedent would be felt, and it would then become difficult to avoid the tax-pattern approved in the earlier decision. Putting the matter differently, *Gavit* apparently requires that *all* the income from a gift of property be taxed to the income-beneficiary in situations involving an *effective* division of beneficial ownership. To escape this consequence, the Court in *Horst* was obliged to find that where the gift of income is of brief duration, and the donor himself reserves the remainder, then for the purpose of income-attribution no true division of beneficial ownership has been accomplished and all the income "belongs" to the donor. Answer 3—the middle position—is simply unavailable.

(b) Blair and Schaffner. The *Horst* case involved what is commonly referred to as a gift of a carved-out interest—a part of the taxpayer's property is carved out and transferred to the donee,

but the remaining part is retained by the donor. As already suggested, the significance of this factor is that it leaves the donor free to make temporary and periodic allocations of taxable income. The progressive rate structure is obviously vulnerable to such practices, but the *Horst* decision furnishes the Treasury with a powerful means of defense.

The importance of "carving-out" in the field of income-attribution can be seen by comparing the Supreme Court's decisions in *Blair v. Commissioner* [10] and *Harrison v. Schaffner.* [11] Both *Blair* and *Schaffner* involved assignments of rights to trust income, yet the taxpayer succeeded in *Blair* but failed in *Schaffner.* The reason, presumably, is that the element of carving out was absent in the former case and present in the latter.

In *Blair* the life-tenant of a testamentary trust assigned to his children specified dollar interests in the income of the trust. Although the donor retained the unassigned portion of the trust income for himself, the donees' interests were to continue for the duration of the life estate and were thus coterminous with the donor's. The Service contended that the gifts were only of a "right to receive . . . income" and hence should be taxed to the donor. The Court, however, held the *donees* taxable. In *Schaffner,* the income beneficiary of a trust also assigned to her children specified dollar amounts of trust income, but here the amounts assigned were to be paid out of the income of the trust for the following year. Thereafter, and for all subsequent years, the trust income would again be paid to the donor. This time the Court held the *donor* taxable, despite the taxpayer's contention that the gifts were of "property" and hence taxable to the donees.

Both *Blair* and *Schaffner* are generally assumed to be correct and likewise mutually consistent. The assignment in *Blair* was of a permanent interest in the donor's property—once given away the donees' fractional interests could never revest in the donor because the gifts were to last as long as the life estate itself. The donor's power to control the income stream represented by his life estate was to that extent terminated and could never be revived. Essentially, the gifts in *Blair* resembled the transfer by a stockholder of a portion of his shares, or the transfer by a building-owner of an undivided interest in his real estate; in either such event, the dividends or the rents from the property transferred would undoubtedly be taxable to the donee. To be sure, the life estate was itself a right to taxable income. Yet the life estate was all the property the donor had, and as the fractional interests were as-

10. 300 U.S. 5 (1937).   **11.** 312 U.S. 579 (1941).

signed without reversion the assignment was entitled to the same effect as the assignment of any other property.

In *Schaffner,* by contrast, the taxpayer transferred one out of a series of income payments—very much as if the stockholder or the real estate owner gave away one year's dividends or one year's rents. As in *Horst,* the transferor was free to dispose of the subsequent payments in any way he chose, designating other recipients from time to time or retaining such payments for himself. No permanent addition was made to the donee's taxable income: the donor could reassess his tax position at the end of the year and make a new judgment in the light of foreseeable circumstances. The gift was thus a temporary income allocation, a carving-out, and it is precisely this which the *Horst* decision condemns.

A loose end: The *Schaffner* case involved a "wasting asset"— an asset of limited duration whose value is zero at the end of its useful life—and for this reason presents a somewhat weaker case for attribution than *Horst* itself. Suppose a taxpayer buys a 10-year lease for $50,000 under which he is to receive 10 annual payments of $7,500. Using the straight-line method of amortization, the first and each succeeding payment will include $2,500 of income plus $5,000 of return of capital. Suppose the taxpayer gives the *first* of the series of payments to his son. The son will receive not only $2,500 of income (otherwise taxable to the donor) but $5,000 of the donor's invested capital. As far as the $5,000 of capital is concerned, it is lost to the donor and can never again be used by him to generate disposable income. Whereas in *Horst* the bond-owner's principal was restored once the coupon-year had passed, here the opportunity to redirect the yield on a portion of the donor's capital has been terminated. Hence, perhaps the gift should be regarded as a transfer of "underlying property" rather than of a mere right to income. In effect, however, the *Schaffner* case rejects this argument, because it extends the prohibition against "carving-out" to wasting as well as non-wasting assets, or, rather, ignores the difference between the two.

Suppose, in the same hypothetical, that after nine years have passed the lease-owner gives the *last* of the 10 rental payments to his son. Although the effect seems exactly the same from every standpoint, there is no carving-out and the gift would most likely be effective for tax purposes. Once the first nine payments have been received, the tenth payment is "all the property the donor has." The fatal element of a reversion is lacking.

8.04　Gifts in Trust—Corliss, Wells and Clifford.　The trust device is exceedingly useful from the standpoint of a donor of property who wishes to retain elements of control over the disposition of his gift.　As compared with a transfer of property to an individual donee, a gift in trust enables the grantor to determine the beneficial ownership of the property over more than one generation by providing for life estates with remainders to descendants. In addition, the distribution of trust assets, whether income or corpus, can be flexibly arranged by authorizing the trustee to make payments in varying proportions to any member of a class—say the grantor's children—or even to retain and accumulate the trust income in a given year if that seems preferable.　The grantor, moreover, may reserve a right to receive or apply the income for his own benefit, or to recover the corpus on termination of an income interest granted to another, or even, as in *Corliss v. Bowers,* to revoke the trust and restore the trust property to his personal ownership.　Finally—again as compared with a gift to an individual—the creator of a trust is able to appoint the manager of the property by designating a person of responsibility and skill in the handling of investments—a bank, a lawyer, a friend, even himself— to serve as trustee.　These elements of flexibility and discretion are difficult or impossible to create when property is simply given outright to an individual donee—there really are no viable legal means of limiting a donee's right to deal with the property as he himself sees fit when the gift is in outright form.

Yet the very flexibility of the trust device means that lines must be drawn between gifts in trust that are effective for tax purposes because they sufficiently resemble outright gifts to be treated in the same way, and gifts in trust that are ineffective because the grantor's interest continues to predominate.　Thus, how far must the grantor go in the direction of a complete surrender of his personal authority over the trust property before trust income will be treated as belonging to the beneficiaries?　Put otherwise, what rights and interests may the grantor retain without continuing to be regarded as the substantial owner of the property transferred?　This issue obviously arises only with respect to lifetime or *inter vivos* trusts.　While testamentary trusts also present choice of taxable person questions (see 4.02), the candidates for taxability are necessarily restricted to the living beneficiaries and do not include the grantor-decedent.

The Supreme Court's early decisions in the field of lifetime trusts can be treated more briefly than the cases discussed in the preceding subsections because gifts in trust are now governed entirely by specific statutory provisions.　Indeed, Congress showed an inclination at a very early point to resolve trust attribution problems by legislative enactment, and as the dissent in the *Clifford* case shows it was possible even then to argue with some force that Congress intended "trusts and estates" to be wholly free from the judicial rule-making process that had been applied to individuals under the authority of § 61. The Court majority rejected this limitation in *Clifford,* but when Congress in 1954 adopted the detailed statutory coverage referred to above it expressly provided that the new Code sections should have exclusive application. Hence, unlike *Earl, Horst* and *Blair,* which continue to be the governing authorities in the area of gifts to individuals, the cases discussed next should be read chiefly as background for the present-day statutory treatment of gifts in trust described at 9.01, below.

The Revenue Act of 1924 contained two statutory provisions relating to the attribution of trust income to trust grantors. The first—now embodied in Code § 676(a)—provided that a grantor would be taxed on trust income if he retained a power, exercisable alone or with a nonbeneficiary of the trust, to revest the trust corpus in himself. The second—the forerunner of present § 677(a)(3)—provided for the taxation of the grantor where the trust income could, in the discretion of any person, be distributed to the grantor or accumulated for his benefit, or applied to the payment of premiums of insurance on the grantor's life. In *Corliss v. Bowers,*[12] the taxpayer had created a revocable trust for the benefit of his wife and children. Sustaining the constitutionality of the first of the two provisions mentioned above, the Supreme Court held that the grantor's power to revoke the trust and thus to stop payment to the income beneficiary was equivalent to actual ownership of the trust property. With reference to taxation, said the Court, "if a man disposes of a fund in such a way that another is allowed to enjoy the income which it is in the power of the first to appropriate it does not matter whether the permission is given by assent or by failure to express dissent. The income that is subject to a man's unfettered command and that he is free to enjoy at his own option may be taxed to him as income, whether he sees fit to enjoy it or not."

In *Burnet v. Wells,*[13] the taxpayer had transferred to an irrevocable trust certain property the income from which was to be used to pay the premiums for an insurance policy on the grantor's life. On the grantor's death the policy proceeds were to be collected by the trustee (who also presumably owned the policy) and invested

---

12. 281 U.S. 376 (1930).   **13.** 289 U.S. 670 (1933).

for the benefit of the grantor's daughter. Conceding that it applied by its terms, the taxpayer argued that the second of the two 1924 amendments was unconstitutional insofar as it taxed a grantor on trust income applied to the payment of insurance premiums because it thereby sought to tax one who (quoting the dissent) "retained no vestige of title to, interest in, or control over the property transferred to the trustee." Once again the Supreme Court held for the government, although only by a vote of 5–4. An insured person, it found, is under an obligation—moral if not legal—to continue to pay the premiums on his life insurance, and Congress therefore could reasonably determine that the use of trust income for that purpose conveyed a taxable benefit to the grantor. "Even if not a duty, it [insurance] is a common item in the family budget, kept up very often at cost of painful sacrifice . . . . It will be a vain effort at persuasion to argue to the average man that a trust created by a father to pay premiums of life insurance for the use of sons and daughters is not a benefit to the one who will have to pay the premiums if the policies are not to lapse." The dissenting Justices argued fervently that the grantor had actually severed all connection with the trust property and that the statutory amendment was unconstitutional because it sought to tax "the income of A [the trustee or the beneficiary] as the income of B [the grantor]."

Viewed in hindsight, neither *Corliss* nor *Wells* involved an especially startling expansion of the ordinary concept of "income". As respects revocable trusts, the grantor could be taxed because he had control of the trust, and therefore of its earnings, even though the income was actually received by the beneficiary. The income was his if he wanted it; the beneficiary had nothing that could not be taken back by the grantor at will. The element of "unfettered command", at least when exercisable by the grantor in his own favor, was sufficient to support a taxable link between the grantor and the trust. Insurance trusts obviously present a harder case, but as a grantor is clearly taxable if trust income is used to meet his legal support obligations—his children's medical bills, for example—it also seems reasonable for Congress to have regarded life insurance premiums as belonging in the same category. Presumably the grantor was willing to maintain the premiums out of his own funds originally, and the trust was simply an irrevocable commitment of income to the same purpose.

Although *Corliss* and *Wells* were thus decided on the basis of specific statutory provisions, the Supreme Court's decision in *Helvering v. Clifford* [14] shows that the Court continued to believe that

14. 309 U.S. 331 (1940).

its own authority under § 61 had not been preempted by Congressional action in the trust field.　In *Clifford,* the grantor created a trust for the benefit of his wife.　The trust was to terminate at the end of five years and the corpus was then to be paid over to the grantor himself as remainderman.　The grantor also appointed himself to be the sole trustee with broad management powers and with a power to distribute the trust income to his wife or to accumulate it for her benefit.　In fact, the trust income was annually distributed to the grantor's wife.　Although the trust arrangement was plainly not within either of the two subsections mentioned above, the Court held that the grantor was the owner of the trust for purposes of § 61 and hence taxable on the trust income.　"[T]he short duration of the trust, the fact that the wife was the beneficiary, and the retention of control over the corpus by the [taxpayer]" all led "irresistibly" to that conclusion.　The trust, said the Court, was "at best a temporary reallocation of income within an intimate family group.　Since the income remains in the family and since the husband retains control over the investment, he has rather complete assurance that the trust will not effect any substantial change in his economic position . . . .　[W]hen the benefits flowing to him directly through the wife are added to the legal rights he retained, the aggregate may be said to be a fair equivalent of what he previously had . . . ."

Justice Douglas' opinion stressed the point that "no one fact is normally decisive" in determining whether the grantor or the beneficiary should be treated as the "owner" of the trust.　As in *Horst* the short-term nature of the beneficiary's income interest was surely a major factor in the outcome—it is as if the bond-owner had detached five annual coupons while retaining the bond—but the Court was plainly unwilling to isolate that circumstance and state that it, by itself, was either necessary or sufficient.　The same, of course, was true of the other significant elements which linked the corpus to the grantor—the grantor's power to accumulate or distribute the trust income at his discretion, his broad powers of management, and the fact that the trust income was to go to the grantor's wife.　The Court's approach was to aggregate these factors, thus avoiding the need to give precise weight to any particular criterion.　Most commentators, perhaps, would have guessed that the short-term feature was critical and indeed was *both* necessary and sufficient.　But no one could be certain.　The power to accumulate—to "compel" the beneficiary to save the trust income during the five-year term—was an important element of control; perhaps it, too, could be regarded as equivalent to ownership.　Management powers seemed somewhat less significant, and trusts for the benefit of one's wife were reasonably common; yet when these factors were joined together the totality might suffice to meet the Court's conception of continued ownership. Once again, the "aggregative" approach placed the matter in substantial doubt.

Some commentators applauded, while others condemned, the *Clifford* decision for its vagueness and elasticity. The Treasury responded to *Clifford* by issuing detailed regulations in which the significance of various possible factors was weighed and sorted out in an effort to provide reasonable guidelines for taxpayers and their advisors. The Regulations emphasized individual elements of the trust arrangement—duration of the trust, extent of the grantor's control, power to manage in his own interest—rather than the balancing of factors which the Court had seemed to approve, and the lower courts were by no means always friendly to the government's position. The scope of the *Clifford* decision being uncertain, it became evident in time that a statutory solution was required. As noted above, Congress in 1954 provided that solution in the form of a set of detailed Code provisions [15] which effectively put an end to "judicial balancing" in this field. While the *Clifford* case was thus superseded by Congressional action, it remains true that the present statutory treatment owes much of its inspiration to that decision, and the case itself, along with *Earl* and *Horst,* is something of a high point in the history of the Supreme Court's confrontation with the problem of income-attribution.

8.05 Summary of Attribution Principles. The income-attribution cases are really simpler than they look. On the whole, the Supreme Court's opinions in this field are over-long and confusing—*Horst, Clifford, Blair* could all have been handled much more briefly, especially the first-named. *Eubank,* on the other hand, is really too brief and cryptic, and at all events should have drawn its precedent from the *Earl* decision rather than claiming to be indistinguishable from *Horst. Earl* itself, finally, would have been a better opinion if Holmes had omitted the fruit-and-tree metaphor, both for literary and for conceptual reasons.[16] The problem throughout, perhaps, was how the Court could aid in developing a set of anti-tax avoidance rules—how it could act to give protection to the graduated rate structure—without directly admitting that it was engaged in judicial law-making. Operating under a limited mandate, the Court sought to safeguard the rates by manipulating the legal concepts of "income," "property," and "ownership" in-

---

15. § 671 *et seq.*

16. The *Earl* opinion has been described as "late vintage Holmes, magisterial in tone, studded with quotable phrases, and devoid of analysis." Bittker, *Federal Income Taxation and the Family,* 27 Stanford L.Rev. 1389, 1401 (1975).

stead of making bald utterances about tax-avoidance. But the quoted terms are inherently confusing and indefinite; they can be used to mean almost anything. In a sense, therefore, in summarizing the attribution rules, it is better and simpler to stress the *results* of the decided cases than to linger over the reasoning.

Taking this approach, the decisional law of income-attribution can be restated as follows:

(1) *Personal service income* is taxable to the person who does the work, no matter whom he designates to receive the pay envelope. This is true whether the services are to be rendered in the future, as in *Earl,* or have already been completed at the time the designation is made, as in *Eubank.* But there are exceptions:

(a) Uncompensated services—services in kind—are apparently allowed to be excluded from the taxpayer's income in most cases. The general rule of *Earl* is not applied here and the value of the uncompensated service is treated in the same way as imputed income. As will be seen at 9.02, however, this exclusion is in turn reversed where the taxpayer is a member of a family partnership, though not where he is an employee of a family corporation.

(b) Patents, copyrights and the like are free of the general rule even though plainly a product of personal efforts. The statute does not provide for the apportionment of income between donor and donee, and as both parties may reasonably claim to have made a contribution to the income ultimately realized on disposition of the asset, the general rule gives way to considerations of feasibility and permits the donee to report all the income as his own.

(2) Gifts of *income-producing property,* as in *Blair,* are effective to shift the future income to the donee for tax purposes. Here, too, there are exceptions:

(a) The donor remains taxable if he has a right to take the property back, as in *Corliss,* or to use the income for himself or to meet his own obligations, as in *Wells.*

(b) The donor remains taxable if he has a right to alter the identity of—that is, to redesignate—the donee in his own discretion. A short-term gift of property, as in *Clifford,* or a gift consisting of a limited number of income-payments drawn from a larger series, as in *Horst* and *Schaffner,* is ineffective to relieve the donor of tax.

(c) Somewhat indefinitely—*Clifford*—the reservation by a donor of powers to manage and dispose of trust property may be treated as equivalent to continued ownership. As stated, the scope of this exception and the meaning of continued "ownership" are now reflected with reasonable clarity in a group of specific statutory provisions which supersede the *Clifford* decision.

Even as oversimplified, the above rules suggest that property—stocks, bonds, real estate—is treated more favorably under the tax law than personal services. While he was barred from assigning a single coupon only, the father in *Horst* was obviously free, if he wished, to shift the interest income to his son by giving away the entire bond. Apart from the restriction on short-term transfers and the like, income from investments can readily be divided among the members of a family by making gifts (including gifts in trust) of the underlying property itself. No equivalent division is possible with respect to service income. With minor exceptions there appears to be no way to assign the fruits of personal effort; wage and salary earners are simply stuck with the progressive rates. To be sure, there is a difference in administrability. While it is easy enough to link wages to wage-earners, any effort to reallocate property income to donors would run into near-hopeless problems of tracing and identification. But this in itself hardly answers the basic criticism.

There may, however, be another way of looking at the whole question. It could be said that what the law does in this field is simply to prohibit the shifting of *pre-tax* income, while allowing the transfer of savings. Thus, suppose a lawyer earns fees of $100,000 and pays tax at a rate of 30%. *Earl* makes it impossible for the lawyer to give the fees away before paying his income tax of $30,000. Once the tax is paid, however, and the lawyer meets his own living expenses, he is free to do what he likes with the amount that is left. The sense one has of discrimination against earned income as opposed to income from property may ease a bit if we reflect that "property" is simply the taxpayer's earned income *after tax*. There is a tendency to think of personal service income and "property" as always belonging to two different and distinct individuals or to two different *classes* of individuals. Not so, of course, and perhaps one gets a different feeling about the problem of discrimination and favoritism if the legal rules are put this way: A taxpayer who derives income through personal efforts must pay the tax thereon; he can, however, give his savings to his kids.

SECTION 9. STATUTORY TREATMENT OF INCOME ATTRIBUTION

9.01 Grantor Trusts. The present statutory treatment of trusts (and estates) can be viewed in two parts. The first—contained in Subparts A–D of Subchapter J—pertains to ordinary or conventional trusts in which the grantor retains no significant interest and the trust income is taxed to the named beneficiaries or the trustee. All testamentary trusts necessarily fall into this class; so do most *inter vivos* trusts, because there is little point in creating a lifetime trust if the income from the trust property continues to be taxed to the grantor. Although trusts are treated as independent taxable entities by the Code (taxable under a separate rate schedule), it is not the intention thereby to increase the taxes of those who use the trust device. In computing its annual taxable income, therefore, the trust is permitted to take a *special deduction* for distributions made to its beneficiaries. This means that the beneficiaries and not the trust are taxed on the income distributed during the year; the trust serves merely as a "conduit" through which taxable income flows into the hands of the individual recipients.

The trust itself is taxed only if the trustee accumulates the trust income in a given year instead of distributing it. As noted, the trust pays taxes, roughly, as if it were an individual taxpayer. But even when accumulations occur, the trust income will be taxed only once, and ultimately at the beneficiary's individual marginal rate. This is accomplished by the so-called throwback rule. Under that rule, through use of an averaging device, any previously accumulated income which is finally distributed to a beneficiary— *e.g.,* on termination of the trust—is taxed as if it had been distributed in the earlier year in which it was earned by the trust instead of being accumulated. The taxes previously collected from the trust are then credited to the beneficiary and are regarded as having been paid by the trustee in partial or complete satisfaction of the beneficiary's individual tax liability. Thus, the beneficiary alone is taxed in the end, though on a deferred basis.[17]

---

17. Such deferral would be of benefit if trust accumulations were taxed to the trust at a lower current rate than that applicable to the beneficiary. To reduce this possible advantage, the 1986 Act adopted a revised rate schedule for trusts (and estates). Under § 1(e), (as amended in 1993), only the first $1,500 of trust income is subject to the 15% marginal rate; the 28% rate applies between $1,500 and $3,500; the 31% rate above $3,500; the 36% rate above $5,500; and the 39.6% rate above $7.500. There is, thus, little benefit in accumulating trust income; hence the throwback rule, practically speaking, loses much of its importance.

The second element of the statutory scheme appears in Subpart E of Subchapter J. It is concerned exclusively with so-called grantor trusts, and represents the legislative solution to the problems created by *Clifford*. Only *inter vivos* trusts are affected, quite obviously, since the aim of the Code at this point is to prevent living grantors from avoiding tax by shifting income to other family members while still retaining an interest in or a power over the property placed in trust. Where that interest or power is considered to be substantial, the Code in effect ignores the separate existence of the trust and treats the grantor as if he continued to own the property directly. As noted earlier, the intention of Congress was to overcome the uncertainties of the *Clifford* case through specific legislation and to place the entire question of grantor trusts outside the scope of judicial construction under § 61(a). Accordingly, § 671 provides that the statutory rules described below are exclusive with respect to whether trust income is taxable to a grantor "solely on the grounds of his dominion or control over the trust." This element of exclusivity does not, however, supersede or preempt other standing rules of income-attribution such as those approved in the *Earl* and *Horst* cases. Thus, an attempted assignment of personal service income to a trust, though not alluded to in Subpart E, would still be ineffective as an income-shifting device because "dominion or control over the trust" is not the basis of the assignor's liability under those circumstances. But when the issue is of the *Clifford* variety—*i.e.*, whether the grantor's interest in the trust is so substantial as to be the equivalent of continued ownership—the specific statutory provisions are given exclusive application.

From the standpoint of a trust grantor, the *Clifford* rules operate to set the minimum conditions for income-shifting. As suggested above, there is little reason to create a lifetime trust that *offends* the statutory limitations: if trust income continued to be taxed to the grantor because he had retained an interest in or power over the trust property, then the grantor might as well have kept the property in his own hands to start with—why bother with a trust at all? By the same token, there is no compelling reason for the grantor to give up a greater interest in the trust property than the Code specifically demands. Having surrendered whatever rights he must in order to shift income to the lower-bracket beneficiary, the grantor can if he wishes (and presumably would) reserve to himself all the remaining elements of ownership. Thus the main object in creating a lifetime trust—often the only object— is to reduce the family tax burden. To achieve that end the grantor would usually do as much as, but also as little as, the statutory rules—now to be summarized—require.

(a) Reversionary interests. Code § 673 picks up the principal feature of the *Clifford* case by providing that a grantor is treated as the owner of the trust property whenever he (or his spouse) retains a reversionary interest in income or corpus having a value in excess of 5% of the trust property. The 5% limitation is a 1986 Act addition. Under the far more liberal (read weaker) restriction of prior law, the grantor continued to be taxed on trust income if he retained a reversionary interest which might reasonably be expected to take effect "in possession or enjoyment" within 10 years of the creation of the trust. But if the reversion could take effect only after 10 years—say at the end of 10 years plus one day—§ 673 did not apply and trust income was taxable to the beneficiary (if distributed, or, if accumulated, to the trust). In effect, income-shifting was permitted even though the underlying property was likely to be returned to the grantor during his lifetime. Evidently, Congress considered that 10 years was a long enough period to protect against the bracket manipulation that is illustrated by the *Horst* case. Focusing on relative ownership rights, moreover, the holder of a 10-year income interest actually "owns" a larger proportion of the trust property than the holder of the reversion. At an 8% interest rate, for example, the present value of a reversion to take effect at the end of 10 years is worth about 46% of the value of the trust property—less than half—so that, in a sense, more of the property "belongs" to the donee-income beneficiary of a 10-year trust than to the grantor-reversioner. If relative degree of ownership is what counts in this field, then perhaps the 10-year rule could be defended "analytically." In any case, as stated, 10-year trusts—which enabled grantors to shift income to family dependents, while at the same time assuring recovery of the property once the dependent ceased to be such—were often recommended to donors of a cautious mentality, and were apparently very widely used.

Convinced that the reversionary-interest trust involved an improper separation of income from ownership, Congress in 1986 repealed the 10-year rule and substituted the rigorous 5% limitation mentioned above. To see just *how* rigorous (again assuming an 8% interest rate), the 5% rule means that a retained reversion cannot take effect for nearly 40 years if grantor trust status is to be avoided. Quite obviously, therefore, a near complete divestiture of interest on the part of the grantor is now required, and reversionary-interest trusts, for practical purposes, are a thing of the past. The new rule applies, moreover, whether the reversion takes effect after a term of years or on the death of an income beneficiary (other than the death of a child during minority), so that a trust to pay the income to an aged parent for life, remainder to the grantor, will henceforth always be treated as a grantor trust. Under prior law, reversions taking effect at the income beneficiary's death (no matter what his age) were excepted from the 10-year limitation.

(b) *Income for grantor's benefit.* Code § 677(a)—whose constitutionality was upheld in *Burnet v. Wells*—treats the grantor as the "owner" if the trust income is or may be distributed to or accumulated for the benefit of the grantor or his spouse, or applied to the payment of premiums on an insurance policy on the grantor's life. The grantor is taxed under these circumstances where the power to dispose of trust income resides in the grantor himself, in a nonadverse party, or in both, provided that the approval of an adverse party is not required. The term "adverse party" is defined as one having an economic interest in the trust that would be adversely affected by the exercise of the power.

In *Helvering v. Stuart* [18] the Supreme Court held under the predecessor of § 677(a) that the income of a trust which could be used for the support and maintenance of the grantor's minor children was taxable to the grantor whether used for that purpose or not. § 677(b) was enacted as a response to the *Stuart* decision. It provides that the grantor is not taxed merely because the trust income *may* be applied to the support of his dependents; the grantor is taxed, however, to the extent the income is so applied. Trusts which empower the trustee to accumulate for the benefit of minor children or to expend trust income for the children's support are a common family savings device, and their usefulness is obviously enhanced by § 677(b). Still, the latter provision does enable the trust grantor to avoid ownership while still retaining a right to use trust income to meet his own legal obligations, and for this reason it may be viewed as somewhat out of step with the treatment of insurance trusts in § 677(a).

(c) *Revocability and powers to control enjoyment.* §§ 676(a) and 674(a) tax the grantor where he (or a non-adverse party) retains substantial powers of disposition over the income or corpus of the trust. The former section is simply the current version of the revocable trust provision which was approved in *Corliss v. Bowers*—a grantor who retains power to revoke the trust is treated as the owner of the trust property. Both sections are coordinated with the 5% rule of § 673: the grantor is not taxed currently if the retained power cannot affect the trust for a period such that the

18.   317 U.S. 154 (1942).

grantor would not be treated as the owner if the power were a reversionary interest.

§ 674 is of major importance insofar as the details of trust draftsmanship are concerned, and it is also here that the most difficult and debatable legislative judgments were made by Congress. The section begins in subsection (a) by treating the grantor as the owner of the trust if the beneficial enjoyment of corpus or income is subject to a power of disposition exercisable by anyone other than an adverse party, but then goes on in subsections (b)–(d) to list the exceptions which actually define the scope of the general rule. The exceptions are of two sorts—those which apply regardless of whom the grantor appoints to serve as trustee, and those which apply where the trustee is "independent", *i.e.*, neither the grantor himself nor anyone related or subordinate to the grantor. If the grantor wishes to serve as trustee himself or to appoint a related or subordinate party, the powers permitted to be granted to the trustee without causing the grantor to be taxed are the limited discretionary powers described in subsection (b); if the grantor appoints an independent trustee, the much broader powers described in subsection (c) will be permitted. The choice is thus "essentially between giving the trustee the grantor really prefers limited discretionary powers and giving a trustee selected from a restricted list broader discretionary powers." [19]

Among the more important powers which the grantor himself may exercise as trustee under § 674(b) are the power to invade corpus for a current income beneficiary if chargeable to that beneficiary's share, and the power to accumulate income for a current income beneficiary provided the accumulations are ultimately payable to the beneficiary himself or his estate or appointees. In effect the grantor may retain a power either to advance or to postpone the beneficiary's receipt of income or corpus, such power to be exercisable in the grantor's sole discretion or in the discretion of any person he selects. A trust for the benefit of the grantor's child, with powers in the trustee to invade corpus or accumulate income for the child's benefit, is thus not regarded as "owned" by the grantor even if he appoints himself the trustee.

If the grantor is willing to appoint an "independent trustee"— which may include not only a corporate fiduciary (a bank or trust company) but the grantor's lawyer or accountant—§ 674(c) permits him (without adverse tax consequences) to create what is called a

---

19. Westfall, *Trust Grantors and Section 674: Adventures in Income Tax*   *Avoidance,* 60 Col.L.Rev. 326 (1960).

spray trust. Not only can the trust corpus be advanced or the income accumulated, but the trustee is free to decide which person among a class of beneficiaries (*e.g.*, the grantor's children) will actually receive the income or corpus from time to time and in what proportions.

Both provisions can be (and have been) criticised as excessively liberal to trust grantors. The permission to accumulate income in § 674(b) enables the grantor to choose for himself whether the trust or the beneficiary shall bear the tax on current trust income, and while any accumulations will ultimately be taxed to the beneficiary when the latter receives them, it may be advantageous to "use" the trustee's bracket rate in the meanwhile and thus in effect obtain the benefit of tax-deferral.[20] The permission to choose *among* beneficiaries in § 674(c) obviously enables the trustee to do precisely what was condemned in the *Horst* case, namely, to allocate the trust income to the lowest marginal ratepayer or to distribute it in a manner which equalizes the taxable income of the beneficiaries. Moreover, the "independence" from grantor influence which is presumed to reside in the bosom of the grantor's banker, lawyer or accountant may be more apparent than real in many cases.

As compared with an outright gift, where the property-income is permanently vested in an identifiable donee, §§ 674(b) and (c) thus allow the grantor to end his own tax liability without making a definite choice of the person to whom the property income will be attributed thereafter. Hence if we assume that outright gifts represent the basic model of permissible tax-shifting, the rules of § 674 are something of a departure in the direction of more discretion and more liberal treatment for property owners and their families.

(d) Persons other than grantor treated as owner. § 678(a), which embodies prior case law,[20a] provides that a person other than the grantor will be treated as the owner of a trust if such person has sole power to vest the corpus or income in himself, whether or not exercised. Like the other statutory provisions in this area, § 678(a) displaces § 61(a) and has exclusive application. However, it is narrower in scope than the sections which provide for taxing grantors. A trust created by the taxpayer's father, say, which empowers the taxpayer to distribute trust income to his wife or to accumulate it for the benefit of his children would not be treated as owned by the taxpayer since he lacks the power to obtain the

---

20. Less so now than previously, as explained in Note 17, above.

20a. *See Mallinckrodt v. Nunan,* 146 F.2d 1 (8th Cir.1945).

income for himself directly. The same arrangement, if created by the taxpayer himself with property acquired from his father by gift or inheritance, would run afoul of § 677(a), so that in effect the parties are rewarded for their foresight.

A loose end: The use of interest-free demand loans (instead of revocable gifts) to shift income from high- to low-bracket family member was reportedly much resorted to prior to the addition in 1984 of § 7872. While the device itself seems rather transparent, the general view appeared to be that such arrangements had no income tax consequences for either borrower or lender. A parent, for example, faced with tuition and related costs of $10,000 a year for his college-student child, might lend the child $100,000 on a non-interest bearing note. Although theoretically free to do otherwise, the well-behaving child would invest the funds in a 10% U.S. Treasury bond, pay his own college expenses, and then hand the bond over to his parent in repayment of the loan on graduation day. While the bond interest would be taxed annually to the child (who would presumably have little other income), the parent in effect would have succeeded in excluding from his own gross income the otherwise nondeductible cost of the child's college education.

The 1984 provision—subject to a *de minimis* exception and other conditions—deals with family loans by imputing an interest payment from child to parent and then treating the interest actually forgone as a gift-back from parent to child. Thus, the child would first include the Treasury bond interest in his gross income and then deduct an imputed interest payment to the parent. The parent would include the imputed interest in *his* gross income and would then be deemed to have returned that sum to the child as a nondeductible gift. The result, quite obviously, is the same as it would be if the parent had purchased the bond for himself, received the interest, and then made a gift to the child of the latter amount.

Code § 7872 applies as well to interest-free loans between corporations and shareholders. In the corporate-shareholder context, however, the imputation concept is designed to assure that the Treasury bond interest will be taxed at *both* levels—as it would be if the corporation simply bought the bond itself and then distributed the bond interest to the shareholder as a dividend. Accordingly, if we substitute corporation for parent and shareholder for child in the above illustration, the results under § 7872 are (1) inclusion of the Treasury bond interest in the shareholder's gross income followed by the deduction of an imputed interest payment to the corporation, (2) inclusion of the imputed interest payment in the corporation's gross income, and (3) payment of an imputed dividend to the shareholder by the corporation equal to the interest actually forgone. The imputed dividend, though taxable to the shareholder, is not deductible by the corporation. When the dust has settled, therefore, one finds that an amount equal to the bond interest will have been taxed once at the corporate level and again to the shareholder, which is just what our double-tax system requires.

9.02 Unearned Income of Minors. As already generally observed, the problem of income-attribution arises, essentially, because the Code treats the taxpayer and each member of his family as a separate taxable person. Except for spouses, who normally file jointly, each family member calculates his or her own taxable income based on the rules of attribution described above, computes tax, and files his or her own individual tax return. The attribution rules are designed to prohibit the assignment of personal service income and to limit an assignor's discretion in the case of property gifts, but the tax law does not attempt to deal with family income-splitting by redefining the taxable unit. The notion that parents and children might be viewed as a single taxpayer, however plausible, is not one that has ever been seriously considered by Congress, perhaps because the question of when a child ceases to be a "child" and becomes an independent adult with a separate household is really one of fact rather than legal definition.

Without departing from this principle of separate taxability, the 1986 Act did, in a limited way, take a step towards family unity. Under § 1(g), the net unearned income (dividends, interest, etc.) of a child who is under the age of 14 is taxed to the child as if included in his parent's income. In effect, the child's net unearned income is taxed under the new provision at the parent's rather than the child's applicable rate. The aim, quite obviously, is to prevent high-bracket parents from shifting income into the hands of low-bracket children through gifts of securities and other investment property—gifts which, under a normal application of the income-attribution rules, would achieve precisely that result. By way of *de minimis* exclusion, the term *"net* unearned income" means unearned income less the sum of $500 plus the greater of (1) expenses actually incurred in producing such income or (2) $500 of the standard deduction. Generally, therefore, the first $1,000 of unearned income is free of the parental rate-attribution rule. The child's "earned" income—newspaper routes, TV sit-com roles—is still taxed to the child independently, but (changing prior law) the child is not entitled to a separate personal exemption if the child is eligible to be claimed as a dependent on its parents' return.

Both the House and the Senate versions of § 1(g) limited parental rate-attribution to unearned income from property transferred by the parents themselves. Somewhat surprisingly, the Senate-House Conference dropped this limitation and extended the so-called "kiddie-tax" to all unearned income of the child, even though derived from non-parental sources. The most likely non-parental sources are, of course, grandparents, so that in effect generation-skipping transfers (whether by gift or bequest) are included as well. While the cut-off at age 14 is a bit puzzling, presumably the definitional question mentioned earlier can be answered with confidence as to this age group since children under 14 are virtually certain to be dependent members of the parental household.

As indicated, § 1(g) operates—has effect—in all cases where the income from property transferred by gift is taxable to the *donee* under the customary income-attribution rules. A typical instance would be a *non*-grantor trust—for example, a trust to pay the annual income to a named beneficiary, with the grantor having no reversionary interest and retaining no discretionary powers with respect to income or corpus. Under prior law, the trust income would "belong" to the beneficiary, whatever his age, and would be taxed at the beneficiary's marginal rate. Under § 1(g), while such income is still taxed to the beneficiary, the tax that is payable is determined by reference to his parents' marginal rate, assuming the beneficiary is under age 14. This is true, as noted, whether the grantor of the trust is the beneficiary's parent or someone else, and would be true even if the trust were testamentary rather than *inter vivos*.

Final question: Why didn't Congress simply tax the child's unearned income directly to the parents by including such income in the parents' return (under § 1(g)(7) the parents may elect to include it but are not required to do so)? The answer—fairly obvious, I suppose—is that the parents do not have legal access to the child's income to pay the tax, and could conceivably find their own resources insufficient for that purpose. Hence, the income is taxed to the child, though at the parents' marginal rate, which makes the child's assets available for tax payment.

9.03　Family Business Associations.

(a) Partnerships. As suggested at 7.01(b), the Supreme Court experienced considerable difficulty in the early days in applying the principles of *Clifford* and *Earl* to family partnerships. The issues were reviewed by the Court on two separate occasions—first in

Commissioner v. Tower,[21] then again in *Commissioner v. Culbertson* [22]—and in neither instance could the Court generate an opinion which was sufficiently clear and definite to settle recurring controversies between taxpayers and the government. In the end, Congress legislated a set of operating rules for family partnerships by enacting § 704(e). These rules have worked reasonably satisfactorily over the years; family partnership taxation is no longer the raging problem it used to be. Even so, it may be worthwhile to see just why it was that the Supreme Court found the general question of income-attribution so hard to handle in the family business context—why, that is, the customary attribution rules that had been formulated by the Court in other situations proved not to be self-executing here.

Suppose a taxpayer owns and operates a business—say a cattle ranch, as in the *Culbertson* case—in which capital (livestock, grazing land), as well as the taxpayer's personal services, are both income-producing factors. The taxpayer has heretofore operated the ranch as a sole proprietorship, but he now decides to reconstitute the business as a partnership by assigning to each of his three children a 25% interest in the capital and income of the enterprise. Father and children execute a partnership agreement under which each is to receive one quarter of the net income annually as well as one quarter of the partnership capital in the event of sale or dissolution. The father retains the right to manage the ranch, including the right to decide what proportion of the partnership profits is to be distributed each year and what proportion is to be retained and reinvested in additional tangible assets.

Since the father will continue as manager, he is of course entitled to a salary for his labors. But that, too, ultimately, is within his discretion. Quite obviously, any salary that he does take will, like wages paid to other employees, reduce the partnership's net income and hence be reflected in lower income-shares for the partners (*i.e.,* himself and the children). If for some reason he chooses to forgo his salary in a given year, then, equally obviously, partnership net income and individual shares will be increased. Thus, if the salary forgone is $100,000, each partner will enjoy a $25,000 increase in his or her partnership share; in effect, the father "recoups" one-quarter, but gives up three-quarters, of the compensation he could have claimed.

It is important to note that partnerships, unlike corporations, are *not* treated as separate taxable entities. Partnership net in-

21. 327 U.S. 280 (1946).   22. 337 U.S. 733 (1949).

come is determined in roughly the usual way—by deducting business expenses from gross income. The net figure is then included in the gross income of the individual partners—whether or not actually distributed—in accordance with their agreement, which is 25% each in our example.

Prior to the enactment of § 704(e), the Internal Revenue Service sought in cases like the above to treat *all* of the partnership income as taxable to the donor-partner under the attribution principles established in *Clifford* and *Earl*. Initially, at least, the Supreme Court was receptive to the government's approach. In the *Tower* case, the Court appeared to hold that family partnerships would not be recognized for tax purposes unless the donee-partner contributed either (a) "vital services" or (b) "original capital" to the firm. If the donee performed no service, as was frequently true, and if the donee's capital interest had been acquired by gift from the taxpayer, then the partnership would be ignored. In *Culbertson*, however, the Court implied that the foregoing was too narrow an interpretation of its earlier decisions, and asserted that what really counted in determining whether a family partnership should enjoy recognition was whether the parties had a "bona fide intent" to form a partnership. If "the partners joined together in good faith to conduct a business, having agreed that the services or capital to be contributed presently by each is of such value to the partnership that the contributor should participate in the distribution of profits, that is sufficient ...." While this declaration was apparently intended to liberalize the treatment of family partnerships, the Court did not make clear what it regarded as the criteria of "good faith" for this purpose; moreover, the presence of four concurring opinions raised doubt about the finality of the Court's position. At all events, the *Culbertson* decision reportedly had little practical effect in advancing the resolution of disputes in this field, and the tax status of family partnerships continued to be litigated until Congress finally legislated a solution.

On hindsight, one surmises that there were two reasons for the Court's inability to establish settled rules of income-attribution for family partnerships. The first—essentially reflecting uncertainty about the effect of the *Clifford* case—arose from the fact that partnerships, being operating businesses, necessarily involved a commingling of assets belonging to the donee *and* the donor. In exercising his management powers over the partnership business, the donor might be expected to make decisions about his own share of partnership income, and hence also about the donee's, which reflected the outlook of an executive-entrepreneur rather than a conventional fiduciary. In particular, he might decide to retain and reinvest all the annual partnership profits in excess of his salary, so that the donee-partner would receive absolutely nothing until the donor finally decided to sell the business, or retired or died. Viewed from one standpoint, therefore, although the gift of a partnership interest was in a formal sense "complete", the donor's status as managing partner would enable him to deprive the donee of independent ownership and control as long as the donor, acting in his own interest, chose to keep the partnership alive. Whether this fell within the ban of *Clifford,* or was to be treated as an effective transfer under *Blair,* was, perhaps, a matter for doubt in the absence of a specific statutory rule.

The second uncertainty—possibly even more important than the first—concerned the application of the *Earl* decision. As stated previously, while *Earl* prohibited the assignment of personal service income in the form of salaries or fees earned from third parties, the same prohibition apparently did not apply to uncompensated services—that is, to transfers of personal service income in kind. But while the traditional exclusion for intra-family services was appropriate, or inevitable, in the case of incidental management assistance—a father managing his child's securities—it might well appear to go too far in cases where the uncompensated labor represented the taxpayer's full-time occupation. The difficulty, however, was that *Earl* itself contained no intrinsic means of distinguishing between major and minor transfers of service income, or between full-time professional activity and mere family favors. Lacking a basis for making that distinction, the Court perhaps felt that it could not authorize an extension of *Earl* to family partnerships without at the same time committing itself to the absurd proposition that all intrafamily services were taxable to the performer.

The "bona fide" requirement of *Culbertson* may be understood as a rough effort to cope with the difficulties just mentioned. The insistence upon a contribution by the donee-partner of capital or services as a condition of "good faith" was, seemingly, an attempt to apply the philosophy of *Clifford* and *Earl* with a broadsword by converting the entire question into one of "intent." But this approach proved inadequate. Not only was the meaning of good faith unclear, but the broadsword treatment made it difficult to separate effective gifts of property from ineffective gifts of services, although that distinction otherwise prevailed throughout the income-attribution field.

Congress responded to the confusion by enacting what is now § 704(e), which preempts the prior case law. Briefly described, § 704(e) permits gifts of partnership interests to be treated as complete for tax purposes despite the retention of substantial management powers by the donor. The donor's motive in making the gift no longer has significance. From the taxpayer's standpoint, therefore, the *Clifford* question has been favorably resolved. At the same time, however, § 704(e) prevents "deflection" of personal service income to the donee by requiring an allowance of reasonable compensation for the donor's services. The *Earl* doctrine is thus applied to uncompensated services, but the application is limited to family partnerships and does not intrude on the traditional exclusion described above. The overall effect is to treat gifts of partnership interests like gifts of any other property. The property element is capable of transfer, very much like stock or real estate, while the service element is subjected to a rule of attribution. While the latter feature might have been expected to generate a good many disputes about the value of the donor-partner's services, in fact there has been relatively little litigation under § 704(e) to date, and it seems clear that the Service no longer views the problem as especially serious.

(b) Corporations. § 704(e) is, I think, about the only place in the Code where Congress has required that employees not be *underpaid* for tax purposes. § 162(a) limits the business-expense allowance for salaries and wages to a "reasonable" amount, but that provision, as has been seen, is generally understood to bar the deduction by an employer of payments that are excessive. It has rarely been interpreted to require the imputation of *additional* salary where the employee's compensation is too low by market standards. Since the ranching business in *Culbertson* could as easily have been carried on in corporate form—with Culbertson giving his children stock in a corporation instead of interests in a partnership—why didn't Congress extend the rule of § 704(e) to family corporations as well as family partnerships? As matters stand now (and have always stood), the only defense the Treasury has against income-shifting through the medium of under- or uncompensated services by a corporate employee is the general rule regarding personal service income laid down in *Lucas v. Earl*. As already noted, however, the courts apparently do not read the *Earl* case as extending to services "in kind," and the result is that under present law Culbertson almost certainly could avoid personal tax on his services by incorporating the ranch and refusing to accept a salary for his work.

The justification, or at least the explanation, for this outcome is slightly complex and not especially satisfying. As noted earlier, corporate income is subject to a two-level tax. It is taxed once at the corporate level when realized, and then again at the shareholder level when distributed as a dividend (net of the corporate tax). Thus, if Culbertson—now chief executive of the family corporation—chooses to forgo all or a part of his annual salary with a view to increasing the returns to the other family stockholders, the salary forgone will be taxed both to the corporation and to the stockholders (himself, perhaps, included) when the net amount is paid out in dividends. Depending on rates, the overall tax bite may still be less than if the same amount were paid to Culbertson in salary and then transferred to the donee by gift, but it is sure to be greater (just because of the double tax) than it would be if the family partnership device were used. Possibly, then, the omission of anything equivalent to § 704(e) in the family corporation area can be explained on the ground that there is simply less tax-avoidance to worry about.

Probably, though, the real explanation for the omission lies in a Congressional policy to aid the growth and expansion of small businesses, at least if carried on in corporate form. Thus, suppose the ranch-corporation chooses to *retain* its after-tax earnings for reinvestment in additional livestock instead of paying those earnings out as dividends. In such event, the salary forgone by Culbertson will be taxed to the corporation only. Under the present rate schedule, corporate taxable income up to $10 million is taxed at a rate of 34%, above that level at a rate of 35%. The topmost individual rate, nearly 40%, is thus obviously *higher* than the corporate rates, and in earlier postwar periods (until 1964 the maximum individual rate was over 90%) the difference between individual and corporate rates was greater still. In the absence of a statutory equivalent of § 704(e), therefore, Culbertson can arrange to have the business income taxed at the lower prevailing corporate rates by simply electing to reinvest that income in additional corporate assets instead of drawing it out as salary. Stated differently, if Culbertson decides to use a portion of his "savings"—the excess of his "true" salary over the amount needed for personal living expenses—to expand his ranch, the tax law permits him to do so at a bargain rate of tax. Quite obviously, the benefit is available only if the company retains its income and expands. The retained income may still be subject to a shareholder-level tax some day—if the stock is later sold at a gain, for example—but that day could be very distant and may not even dawn within the lifetimes of existing stockholders.

All of this suggests that from the standpoint of small businesses, the separate corporate tax has been a conscious subsidy device. Congress has really *expected* small corporations to be used as tax-deferral mechanisms; the absence of a corporate version of § 704(e) reflects a legislative intention to assist their growth by permitting the stockowner-entrepreneur to shift personal income to the company. As long as the business is in an accumulation phase, therefore, its income will enjoy the benefit of a reduced tax-rate if the corporate form is chosen.

§ 704(e) shows that Congress does not intend quite the same benefit to be available to family partnerships. While income derived from partnership *capital* can be shifted to family donees and accumulated at their lower marginal rates, income derived from the donor's personal *services* cannot. The reason for the limitation, perhaps, is that since partnerships and partners are not subject to a double tax on business earnings, the donee-partners' lower rates would apply whether the salary income forgone by the donor were reinvested in additional business assets or simply withdrawn by the partners for their personal use. The purpose of the "subsidy"— expansion of the enterprise—could not be assured, therefore. Moreover, individual donees (children) would often be taxable at even lower rates than those that apply to corporate income, and perhaps the latter concession is as far as Congress wished to go.

The whole scheme is absurdly clumsy, and complicated far beyond the above description.[23] My object here, however, is merely to explain why personal service income can be shifted in a corporate setting more or less without question, when so much judicial and legislative effort has been directed at preventing the same kind of shifting in the case of family partnerships.

I should add that the relationship between corporate and individual tax rates has been slightly tumultuous in recent years. Thus, the Revenue Act of 1986 reduced corporate rates substantially but cut individual rates more sharply still. As a consequence, the tax focus for smaller, closely-held businesses underwent a major change. With the top marginal rate for individuals down to 28% (in 1986) and the corporate rate pegged at 34%, the advantage of

---

23. See Bittker and Eustice, *Federal Income Taxation of Corporations and* *Shareholders* (1987) Ch. 1.

paying a corporate rather than an individual tax on business earnings obviously disappeared. The consequence was that most closely-held companies simply ceased to pay the corporate tax—whether by liquidating and then resuming their operations in the form of partnerships or sole proprietorships or, more often, by taking advantage of Subchapter S. Subchapter S (Code § 1361 et seq.) permits a corporation with no more than 35 shareholders to elect to be taxed as a partnership or proprietorship, which means, generally speaking, that company earnings are taxed directly to the individual shareholders, no corporate tax being due. Prior to 1986, as noted, companies wanting to retain their earnings would usually have found it inadvisable to make a Subchapter S election, because the individual tax rate was higher than the corporate tax rate. That relationship having been reversed by the 1986 Act, the S–election became well-nigh universal for closely-held companies and the corporate tax became a tax on public (or at least larger) companies only.

The 1993 Act returns the corporate-individual rate relationship to what it was before 1986. As stated, the top individual rate is now nearly 40%, while the corporate rate remains at 34% for most closely-held companies. Presumably, therefore, that clicking sound one hears is the sound of Subchapter S elections being revoked, although the current spread—only 6 points at most—together with uncertainty about future rate-levels (the S–election, once revoked, cannot be revived for 5 years) may cause some taxpayers to hesitate and await further developments.

9.04 Joint Returns; Taxation of Married and Single Persons. As indicated at 8.01, married persons since 1948 have been permitted to split their incomes by filing joint returns. The 1948 legislation overcame the advantage which residents of community property states enjoyed by reason of the Supreme Court's decision in *Poe v. Seaborn,* and in effect extended the same split-income benefit to all married taxpayers irrespective of residence. The statutory scheme is a simple one. Husband and wife may (and almost all do) file a joint return on which their income and deductions are aggregated. Joint returns can, of course, be filed even though one spouse has no income or deductions whatever. Under the original joint-return procedure, the tax on a joint return was determined by (a) computing a tax at the customary rate on one-half of the couple's taxable income, and then (b) doubling the tax so computed. The effect was that the marginal tax rate applicable to the husband and wife was the same as that of a single person with only half as much income. If a married couple had $40,000 of taxable income, the marginal rate of tax on the last dollar would be the same as that for a single person with only $20,000 of taxable income.

Given a sharply progressive rate structure, however, this income-splitting procedure necessarily meant that single persons paid substantially higher taxes than married couples at the *same* income levels. While two married couples with $40,000 of income would pay the same tax whether they lived in California or New York, a single person earning $40,000 would pay much more than either. Some degree of difference between marrieds and singles can no doubt be justified—the same $40,000 income stream supports *two* people in the case of a married couple—but presumably this element should be reflected in a higher standard deduction for couples and an additional personal exemption rather than by doubling the width of the tax brackets. In 1969, accordingly, Congress took steps to reduce the disparity in tax burden between marrieds and singles by establishing a separate rate schedule for each group in § 1(a) and § 1(c), respectively.[24] This had no substantive effect on married taxpayers (whose tax liabilities were unchanged), but for single taxpayers the effect was to lower the rates generally, with the principal beneficiaries being individuals in the middle and upper brackets where the disparity between marrieds and singles had been the largest.

The relationship between the tax status of single persons and the tax status of married persons actually makes a lot of trouble for the income tax—especially so once progressivity is restored to the rate-structure.[25] One would of course prefer that the tax law be "neutral" in its effect on the decision to marry or not to marry, but the fact is that it is not. Marriage, as such, entails a tax "bonus" in many instances but also entails a tax "penalty" in others, both being a function of the rate-structure and both for the most part being unavoidable. The "bonus" element is straightforward. Assuming that A has positive taxable income while B has none, the tax due on A's earnings under § 1(c) when A is single will obviously be greater than the tax due under § 1(a) after A and B have

24. The higher tax on single than on married taxpayers that resulted from the adoption of income-splitting in 1948 led Congress in 1951 to extend relief to those single persons—widowers with children, for example—who maintained a family household for their dependents. Under § 1(b), a special rate schedule applies to so-called "heads of house-holds" which is roughly midway between that applicable to married couples and that applicable to single taxpayers.

25. Bittker, *Federal Income Taxation and the Family,* 27 Stanford L.Rev. 1389 (1975). And see Gann, *Abandoning Marital Status as a Factor in Allocating Income Tax Burdens,* 59 Texas L.Rev. 1 (1980).

become a married couple, the "bonus" being the difference between the two. Thus, where there is only one family bread-winner, the tax liability for that individual as a single person and for that individual as a married person is as follows (for the year 1993):

	Tax Liability	
A's Taxable Income	**A Single**	**A Married**
$ 25,000	$ 4,127	$ 3,750
75,000	18,772	16,203
150,000	43,772	39,528
300,000	99,572	95,328

By contrast, where A and B are both employed and each has earnings that are not greatly different from the other's, the effect of combining the spouses' taxable income under the present rate-structure is to *increase* their overall tax liability relative to what that liability would have been had they remained single. To take just one example, assume that A and B are both fifth-year associates at a well-known law firm and that each receives a salary of $125,000. Under current tax rates, personal exemptions and standard deduction, each would owe tax of about $32,600 as a single person, or $65,200 for the two together. Married and with a combined income of $250,000, A's and B's liability on a joint return rises to about $71,600. The marriage "penalty" is thus roughly $6,400—not peanuts even for these good folks.

Both the marriage "bonus" and the marriage "penalty" are undesirable phenomena if we believe that the tax law ought properly to be neutral as far as choice of marital status is concerned. Unfortunately, nothing much can be done about the problem as long as the Code maintains a progressive rate-structure *and* requires that married couples with the same total income—whether earned by one spouse alone or by both spouses equally—pay the same amount of tax. Put otherwise, an income tax system cannot at one and the same time have (a) progressive marginal rates, (b) equal taxation of married couples with equal marital income, and (c) neutrality as between single status and married status. A tax system that wants (c) will have to give up either (a) or (b)—it can't contain all three elements simultaneously.

9.05 Alimony and Separate Maintenance. Prior to 1942, alimony payments made by a husband to his ex-wife were neither taxable to the wife nor deductible by the husband. No statutory authorization existed for a deduction (plainly, such payments were not business expenses), and the wife's receipt was held not to be "income" within the meaning of § 61. §§ 71(a) and 215(a), which reversed this pattern, were chiefly intended to afford relief to husbands who, on occasion, found that their tax equalled or even exceeded the income that was left after making alimony payments. § 71(a) provides that alimony and separate maintenance shall, in general, be included in the wife's gross income; § 215(a) allows a corresponding deduction to the husband for payments taxable to the wife under § 71.[26] § 682 extends the same statutory scheme to trust arrangements by excluding from the husband's income, and including in the wife's, amounts received from an alimony trust. Taken together, these provisions can best be seen as a determination with respect to choice of taxable person rather than as rules relating to the definition of income or expense. In effect, the husband is treated as a conduit for gross income that legally belongs to the wife under the divorce decree. As a corollary, § 62(10) provides that alimony payments made by a husband shall be deducted from his *gross* income in computing his adjusted gross income: deduction, thus, is permitted even if the husband does not elect to itemize his personal expenses, *i.e.*, just as if the payments were excluded from his income to begin with.

The largest single interpretative problem in the alimony field has been that of distinguishing between alimony payments and property settlements. Conceptually (if not always actually), the obligation to pay alimony is an annual charge against the husband's pre-tax income and entails a redirection of that pre-tax income to his former wife. So viewed, the inclusion-deduction pattern of §§ 71 and 215 seems appropriate, even obvious, for the reasons mentioned above. Property settlements, by contrast, though also an important feature in many divorces, constitute a division between the spouses of family savings. Such savings, in turn, represent the family's accumulated wealth *after* paying income taxes. It is evident that the division of family savings between husband and wife should result in neither taxable income for the wife nor a deduction for the husband—any more than would a transfer of property from the husband to any other family member. The overturning of the *Davis* case (see 5.04) is, of course, consistent with the latter proposition.

The distinguishing characteristics of alimony, as opposed to property settlements, would normally be fairly clear. While alimony is always paid in cash, is made in recognition of the husband's legal support obligation, is paid at regular intervals, and is likely to continue only until the wife's remarriage (or until the death of either spouse), property settlements usually are carried out all at once or over a brief period, may include non-cash assets such as

---

26. Code § 7701(a)(17) provides, in effect, that if wife pays alimony to husband, then for "husband" read "wife" and for "wife" read "husband."

stock or real estate, and are usually not contingent on subsequent events (*i.e.*, the wife normally gets her share of family property even if she remarries immediately). The inclusion-deduction regime is right for transactions falling into the first category, wrong for those in the second.

But, inevitably, instances arise in which the arrangement between the spouses possesses mixed elements. Thus, the divorce agreement may refer to payments for "support"—normally alimony—but limit the payment period to a specified number of years, or contain a dollar ceiling, or require that payments be continued for a stated period despite death or remarriage. In the same way, property settlements may entail a long-term payout—as where the husband in effect pays the wife for her share of the family business in annual cash installments over an extended period—and thus resemble alimony. The Code definition of "alimony" was complex and uncertain prior to 1984; the decided cases in the field were numerous, and the spouses themselves often took conflicting positions—the husband seeking to deduct under § 215, but the wife unwilling to include under § 71—with the Service then being obliged to litigate in order to avoid a whipsaw.

Having been urged by the Treasury and the bar to clarify matters, Congress in the 1984 Act adopted a new set of definitional principles which (with further amendments in 1986) have the considerable merit of simplicity. Under present § 71, payments will qualify as "alimony"—deductible by the husband, includable by the wife—if they are in cash, are made pursuant to a divorce or separation instrument, and terminate at the death of the payee-spouse. The requirement of prior law that alimony payments arise out of the husband's obligation of support as established by State law—a requirement which placed the Treasury somewhat at the mercy of the local divorce courts [27]—is entirely omitted. Also, overruling prior case law, the amended Section provides that so much of an alimony payment as is subject to reduction on the happening of a contingency involving a child (*e.g.*, the child's attaining a certain age) shall be treated as "child support" and hence neither deductible by the husband nor includable by the wife.

Finally, while the amended alimony definition contains no specific duration requirement—payments may be regarded as "alimony" even though scheduled to continue only briefly—§ 71(f) contains a so-called recapture rule which applies where the payment-schedule is front-end loaded, *i.e.*, large payments at the very beginning and much smaller payments or none at all thereafter. If

27. See *Beard v. Comm'r,* 77 T.C. 1275 (1981).

payments made in the first two years and deducted by the husband as "alimony" are deemed excessive relative to the payment made in the third year, the excess amount, determined under a statutory formula, is required to be added back to the husband's income and is then allowed as a deduction to the wife. The aim, quite obviously, is to prevent what is really a lump-sum property settlement from masquerading as periodic alimony where the payor's applicable marginal rate is higher than the payee's. If payments cease during the three-year period by reason of the death of either spouse or the wife's remarriage—events that are involuntary or at least not prearranged by the spouses—the recapture rule does not apply.

Part D: TAX ACCOUNTING

Code § 446(a) provides that "taxable income shall be computed under the method of accounting on the basis of which the taxpayer regularly computes his income in keeping his books." This provision reflects the general approach of tax accounting. It indicates, as might be expected, that tax accounting largely depends upon and accepts the principles of ordinary commercial accounting. There are, however, some important differences, and by and large it is the areas of divergence, rather than the similarities between the two systems, which are taken up in this brief Part. In some instances these differences are the product of administrative and other policy considerations peculiarly relevant to taxation; in others (the tax treatment of prepaid income would be an example; see 12.02) they appear merely to be the result of doubtful reasoning on the part of the courts and the Internal Revenue Service.

Although extensive, freedom to choose a method of accounting is not unlimited. § 446(b) broadly authorizes the Commissioner to reject, or at least contest, the taxpayer's accounting practice if that practice does not "clearly reflect income." Much of the litigation described in Sections 11 and 12 entails an application of that standard. In general, the courts have tended to regard the subject of accounting as "administrative," and have shown a considerable willingness to follow the Commissioner's lead on close questions. This, in turn, has prompted Congress, from time to time, to adopt provisions aimed at relieving particular hardship situations. Overall, this pattern of judicial caution and Congressional liberalization has led to a steady, but also a painfully slow, improvement in the applicable rules.

In a sense, the precise timing of revenues and expenses is more important for tax-accounting purposes than it is for general accounting purposes. Allocation of borderline items to one period rather than another in the company's financial statements can, if necessary, be explained to investors and other interested persons by means of footnotes to the income statement or the balance sheet. When the accounting decision is one that has to be reflected on an income tax return, however, the stake is an increase or reduction in the taxpayer's actual cash tax obligations, with mere explanation being secondary. Accordingly, the conflicts are likely to be sharper in a tax setting, particularly when there has been a rise or decline in rate-levels as between two taxable years, or when an individual

223

taxpayer, by reason of a change in his income, faces higher marginal rates in one taxable period than in another.

This Part is divided into three sections. Section 10 deals with the annual accounting requirement—the requirement that income be determined and reported at fixed intervals of a year. Sections 11 and 12 describe the principal accounting methods used by individual and business taxpayers, namely, the cash and the accrual methods of accounting. The effort, as usual, is to concentrate on the questions that have occasioned controversy, and to emphasize major elements of the tax accounting system rather than details.

SECTION 10. ANNUAL ACCOUNTING

10.01 Loss Carryovers—Burnet v. Sanford & Brooks. Code § 441 provides, in effect, that the taxpayer's taxable income shall be computed on the basis of his "annual accounting period." For almost all individuals the annual accounting period is simply the calendar year; corporations and other business taxpayers frequently use fiscal years—say July 1 to June 30—which may conform to the normal cycle of their manufacturing or marketing activities. In either case the taxpayer's income is determined and reported at 12-month intervals, and his tax is assessed and paid on the basis of events occurring between the beginning and the end of each such period. While the taxpayer's true income cannot really be ascertained until his economic existence is over, it is obvious that no functioning tax system could afford to wait for its collections until the end of an individual's lifetime or until the termination of a business enterprise. Income and taxes must be reported and paid periodically, and the 12-month unit is familiar to almost every taxpayer. But even so, there is something artificial about this attempt to cut the flow of economic activity into segments for the purpose of making annual tax payments, and distortions—sometimes serious distortions—necessarily result.

Roughly speaking, the history of the annual accounting requirement is one of literal enforcement by the courts, followed in a few important instances by the enactment of specific relief legislation. Compared, for example, with the innovative role it played in the field of income-attribution (Part C), the Supreme Court has been notably cautious and conservative in its approach to accounting problems. (Put differently, the Court mainly followed the government's lead in both areas.) Mindful that the Treasury was required to process and audit millions of tax returns annually, the Court in its early decisions was plainly reluctant to apply the income definition under § 61 in ways that might complicate the needs of practical tax administration. As a result, the somewhat delicate task of balancing more equity against heavier administrative burdens was largely, and wisely, left to Congress and the Treasury.

In *Burnet v. Sanford & Brooks Co.,*[1] the taxpayer had entered into a dredging contract with the United States, but ultimately abandoned the undertaking and sued the government for breach of warranty. Between 1913 and 1916 the taxpayer incurred expenses of $176,000 in excess of the payments received under the contract. In 1920, as a result of the lawsuit, the taxpayer recovered the excess expenses of $176,000, plus $16,000 of interest conceded to be taxable. The taxpayer apparently had other sources of revenue during the periods affected because it reported a positive net income for the year 1914. For 1913, 1915 and 1916, however, it reported net losses from business operations after deducting the expenses just mentioned.

The question presented was whether the award received in 1920 was includable in the taxpayer's gross income for that year (when, apparently, it had no deductible business expenses). The taxpayer argued that as the dredging contract had produced no profit whatever, the amount received in 1920 could not be "income" within the meaning of the 16th Amendment. Since, however, the requirement of annual accounting could not simply be dismissed, the taxpayer proposed three alternative mechanisms by which its prior losses could be given proper recognition: (i) allow the operating losses sustained in 1913–15–16 to be carried forward as an offset against the award received in 1920; or (ii) treat the dredging contract as a unitary transaction, with the excess expenses being added back to the income of the earlier years and the award being excluded from that of the later; or (iii) treat the earlier outlays as capital expenditures (or as "loans" to the government) which could later be charged off against the award. Each of these devices, in the taxpayer's view, would succeed in recognizing the absence of gain under the contract, and would do so without detracting from the integrity of the annual accounting requirement.

Reversing the court of appeals, the Supreme Court sustained the Commissioner in treating the award as fully taxable in 1920. The Court held that each accounting period must be regarded as a discrete unit for tax purposes, and found that "income" under the Constitution could properly be understood to refer to accessions taking place solely within the taxable year. Annual accounting, said the Court, was a familiar practice prior to the adoption of the

1.   282 U.S. 359 (1931).

16th Amendment; the Amendment did not require Congress to adopt a system of transactional rather than periodic reporting, even if the former were deemed practicable. The Court did not indicate whether a line would have to be drawn at *some* point—suppose, *e.g.,* that Congress attempted to impose an accounting period of a month or a week or a day. It was plain, however, that an annual time-unit posed no such problem.

In reality, although the taxpayer's claim had strong appeal from the standpoint of equity, the Court was simply unwilling to take a position with respect to the meaning of "income" whose effect would be to keep alive the tax returns of prior years. The proposal to permit earlier losses to be carried forward, if accepted, would have meant that prior returns *never* could be finally retired and discarded; the proposal to treat the contract as a unitary transaction,[2] or to recharacterize the prior expense deductions as capital expenditures or loans, might mean that earlier returns would often have to be reopened and subjected to a second audit procedure. The Court presumably felt that any device which increased the burdens of administration by requiring that prior tax returns be revived or reaudited would have to be the product of a legislative, rather than a judicial, initiative.

In fact, Congress did act to mitigate the effect of the annual accounting rule (though not quite soon enough to help Sanford & Brooks) by adopting the net operating loss carryover provisions of § 172. Under that section, losses incurred in business now can be carried back to the 3 years preceding the loss year, and then forward for the 15 succeeding years, as a deduction from the positive income of each of those prior or subsequent periods. In effect, a 19-year span is covered if one includes the loss year itself. Companies which experience fluctuating profits and losses—say a $500 net operating loss in Year 1 followed by $1,000 of profit in Year 2—are thus treated the same in overall terms as companies with a flat income stream, that is, with $250 of profit in both years. Since interperiod loss-offsets are important to an equitable tax system, most would agree that the averaging period should be limited only by considerations of administrative feasibility.

Alternating profit and loss years are more likely to occur in the case of corporate than individual taxpayers. Most individuals derive their incomes from personal services, so that "losses"—in the

---

2. An election to report on the completed-contract method of accounting actually was available to the taxpayer, if made in advance. No doubt assuming that its expenses would be offset annual-ly by adequate progress payments from the government, the taxpayer did not make the election. The Court, in effect, refused to permit the election to be made on a hindsight basis.

sense of an excess of business expenses over personal earnings—are unlikely to arise even if the individual is unemployed. The Code does not generally permit a carryover of unused personal expenses or dependency allowances. On the other hand, individuals may suffer hardship under the annual accounting requirement solely by reason of the progressive rate structure. An author, for example, who receives sizeable royalties in the year in which his best-selling novel is published may have earned little or nothing in earlier years when the book was being written. While the progressive tax concept assumes a higher marginal tax rate on higher levels of income, plainly there would be inequity if those whose incomes fluctuate widely were required to pay much heavier taxes than those who earn at a steady pace. Prior to 1986, the individual rate structure was fairly steeply progressive, and the Code, accordingly, extended relief to taxpayers with fluctuating income by means of a 4-year averaging device. Under former §§ 1301–1305, if a taxpayer's income in the current year exceeded 140% of his average income for the preceding 3 years, the excess was taxed as if it had been earned in equal installments over the 4-year span. The marginal tax-rate applicable to the excess income, then, became the rate that would have applied had such income been spread out evenly over the 4 years instead of being "bunched" into a single taxable period.

However reasonable in concept, the averaging rules proved rather complex in operation, especially where the taxpayer's marital status changed during the affected period. Also, it was not clear that the eligibility requirements always succeeded in confining the benefits of averaging to taxpayers with fluctuating income as intended. Thus, the beneficiaries of income-averaging sometimes turned out to be taxpayers who had enjoyed a sudden but *sustained* increase in earnings, such as students entering upon their "real" careers following graduation. Critics of the averaging provisions also pointed out that the rules dealt with only one inequitable situation, that is, a series of low-income years followed by a high income year. Nothing was done for taxpayers experiencing a sharp *decline* in income following a period of high earnings (*e.g.,* out-of-work executives), although such taxpayers similarly presented an appealing case for relief.

Instead of improving it, the 1986 Act simply eliminated the individual income-averaging system by repealing the relevant Code sections. That decision has the merit of simplicity, and with the reduction in tax-rates and the adoption of a far less progressive rate structure, the need for an averaging system has obviously declined. Income fluctuations are less likely to produce marginal rate differences; and when they do occur, such differences are likely to be less severe than formerly. The "author" mentioned above may still pay higher taxes than a salary-earner whose income is relatively stable, but Congress evidently deemed the disparity too small (and infrequent) to justify a complex statutory remedy.

10.02　Claim of Right. § 172 provides a considerable measure of averaging to offset the harsh effect of the annual accounting system. It does not, however, purport to cope with the somewhat narrower class of problems which are usually referred to as "transactional." The Supreme Court's decision in *North American Oil Consolidated v. Burnet* [3] provides the background. In *North American,* the company, upon the entry of a lower court decree in 1917, received income from the operation of certain oil properties whose ownership had previously been disputed. The income had been earned in 1916 but was paid over to a receiver until the dispute should be resolved. The lower court decree was appealed, and finally affirmed in 1922. Since tax rates apparently were lower both in 1916 and in 1922 than in 1917, the taxpayer argued that the income should be taxed either in 1916 when it was earned or in 1922 when the taxpayer's right to the funds was finally established. But the Supreme Court sustained the Commissioner in treating 1917 as the proper year for inclusion. In 1916, the taxpayer had nothing more than a disputed claim. In 1917, however, it actually received the cash income, which it then held under a "claim of right" and without restriction as to use. Accordingly, the income properly became taxable in that year, even though its ultimate ownership continued to be disputed, and even though the taxpayer might still have been "adjudged liable to restore its equivalent" in 1922. In effect, current inclusion was required where the taxpayer (a) received the funds in question, (b) treated them as its own, and (c) conceded no offsetting obligation. While *borrowed* money is not taxable owing to the borrower's obligation to repay (3.01), the fact that a receipt is subject to dispute or other contingencies which extend beyond the taxable year does not create a similar basis for exclusion.

Like *Sanford & Brooks,* the *North American* decision can best be explained and defended on practical grounds. Although it might be fairer to wait until contingencies affecting the receipt are resolved, the Treasury has a plausible interest in immediate taxation. Postponement creates the risk that the taxpayers might become insolvent before the tax is paid. In addition, the task of deciding when income has attained an appropriate level of "certainty" would

3.　286 U.S. 417 (1932).

be administratively burdensome. Although the last appeal from the lower court decree was exhausted in 1922, North American might still have feared a legal attack on some collateral ground which it could have cited as reason for a further delay in reporting the income. Quite obviously, actual receipt of the disputed funds is an event that is easier to identify than the final resolution of a controversy.

But while the claim of right doctrine makes practical sense, it does create a possibility of hardship in those cases in which the contingencies are finally resolved *against* the taxpayer and the disputed income has to be surrendered to another claimant. In *U.S. v. Lewis,*[4] the taxpayer-employee received a bonus of $22,000 in 1944 which he reported as income for that year. In 1946, pursuant to a state court judgment that the bonus had been computed improperly, he returned $11,000 to his employer. Claiming that the excess bonus had been received under a mistake of fact, the taxpayer sought to reopen his 1944 return and recompute his tax for that year by excluding the excess amount. The Supreme Court, however, relying on the *North American* decision, held that the full bonus was taxable in 1944 under the claim of right doctrine. Claim of right, said the Court, was a rule of finality which was deeply rooted in the tax system, and no exception could be permitted merely because the taxpayer was "mistaken as to the validity of his claim."

Actually, the claim of right doctrine need not have been invoked at all in the *Lewis* case. The taxpayer's right to the bonus was not disputed in 1944, so that inclusion of the income in that year was not in doubt and, indeed, was never contested by the taxpayer. What the taxpayer sought was not postponement (as in *North American*), but an opportunity to treat the earlier receipt and the later repayment as a single, unified transaction for tax purposes. While the government conceded that the repayment of the excess bonus would be deductible in 1946, it is evident that the taxpayer's applicable tax-rate was higher in 1944 when the bonus was received. Hence the tax saved in the later period would be less than the tax paid on the prior inclusion. The taxpayer argued, in

---

4. 340 U.S. 590 (1951). Somewhat by contrast, in *Arrowsmith v. Comm'r,* 344 U.S. 6 (1952), the taxpayer-stockholder had properly reported his gain on the liquidation of his corporation as capital gain. In a subsequent year, the taxpayer, as transferee of the corporate assets, was obliged to pay a judgment rendered against the corporation. Although the outlay was technically an ordinary loss owing to the absence of a sale or exchange, the Court upheld the Commissioner in treating it as a capital loss on the ground that the payment of the corporate debt was related to the prior liquidation and hence took its character from the earlier transaction.

effect, that his tax liability for 1944 should be reduced to take account of the subsequent loss. In the absence of specific legislative authorization, however, the Court refused to apply a transactional approach in taxing the bonus income, and held, instead, that the receipt and the repayment must be reflected in separate taxable years.

In 1954, Congress reacted to the hardship evident in *Lewis* and similar cases by adding § 1341 to the Code. Briefly, if an item was included in income in a taxable year because of the claim of right doctrine, and if in a later year it is established that the taxpayer did not have an unrestricted right to the item, so that a deduction exceeding $3,000 is allowable, the tax for the later year will be whichever of the following is the lesser: (a) the tax in the later year computed with the deduction, or (b) the tax in the later year without the deduction, but reduced by the amount by which the tax in the earlier year would have been decreased if the item in question had been excluded from the earlier year's income. In effect, the taxpayer can be in no worse a position than if the item had never been included in his gross income—essentially, the taxpayer's position in *Lewis.*

§ 1341 thus leaves the basic claim of right doctrine intact; the *North American* rule is still applicable for the purpose of determining *when* unsettled income is required to be included for tax purposes. The section reverses the outcome in *Lewis,* however, by authorizing a reduction in the earlier year's tax (in effect) where an item included in one taxable period becomes deductible in another.

10.03   The Tax Benefit Rule. What about the converse of the *Lewis* pattern? Suppose a taxpayer (Lewis' employer, say) properly deducts an outlay in one year and then in a later year reclaims and recovers the same amount? Under the so-called tax benefit rule—largely a judicial creation but one of long-standing— the subsequent recovery is included in the taxpayer's income, provided that the earlier deduction produced a tax saving in the prior period. Stated somewhat technically, if the deduction of an item offsets taxable income, then the item itself (the claim against Lewis) takes a basis in the taxpayer's hands of zero. When it is "exchanged" for cash, the taxpayer realizes reportable gain equal to the amount received.

Some odd applications of the rule have arisen. In *Alice Phelan Sullivan Corp. v. U.S.,*[5] the taxpayer in 1939 and 1940 contributed two parcels of real estate to charity and deducted the value of the contributions from its income. The gifts were conditioned on the

---

5.   180 Ct.Cl. 659, 381 F.2d 399 (1967).

property's being used for religious or educational purposes. In 1957, the donee decided not to use the gifts and returned the properties to the taxpayer. The Court of Claims sustained the Commissioner in requiring the taxpayer to include the properties in its income for 1957 at a value equal to the amounts deducted as charitable contributions in the earlier years. While the return to a taxpayer of his own property—*e.g.*, the repayment of a loan— normally does not produce taxable income, "the principle is well engrained in our tax law that the return or recovery of property that was once the subject of an income tax deduction must be treated as income in the year of its recovery."

As with the *Lewis* decision (*i.e.*, before the enactment of § 1341), the *Sullivan* case stops short of adopting a complete transactional solution to the problem of prior deduction and subsequent inclusion. Tax rates in 1939–40 when the real estate was contributed to charity were well below the rates that prevailed in 1957 when the property was recovered, so that from the taxpayer's standpoint the overall "transaction" produced a net tax loss. The same consequence would occur, of course, if the taxpayer's applicable bracket rate changed from one year to the other even though the rate schedule itself remained constant. In an earlier decision involving similar facts [6] the Court of Claims had applied the tax benefit rule to require the taxpayer merely to repay the taxes previously saved—in effect, employing a kind of common-law version of § 1341. But in *Sullivan* the court reversed this aspect of its prior decision on the ground that statutory authority for it was lacking.[7]

Although the "recovery" concept stressed in *Sullivan* is indeed familiar and "engrained," the Service, with support from the Supreme Court, has applied the tax benefit rule in broader terms than the word "recovery" suggests. In *Bliss Dairy*,[8] the taxpayer-corporation had purchased cattle feed for use in its operations and deducted the full cost of the feed in the year of purchase. The company was liquidated in the following taxable year and among the assets distributed to its shareholders was a substantial portion

---

6. *Perry v. U.S.*, 142 Ct.Cl. 7, 160 F.Supp. 270 (1958).

7. Under § 111, if a deduction produced *no* tax benefit when taken because the taxpayer reported a loss for that year at least equal to the amount deducted, then the subsequent recovery of the item deducted will be excluded from the taxpayer's income in the later year. § 186 added to the Code in 1969, specifically extends the latter rule to damages received for breach of contract or fiduciary duty (as well as antitrust injury and patent infringement), and would thus apparently provide complete relief for the taxpayer in *Sanford v. Brooks*.

8. Decided together with *Hillsboro National Bank v. Comm'r*, 460 U.S. 370 (1983).

of the feed just mentioned.   Code § 336 (since amended) then provided that a corporation shall recognize no gain on distributing its assets in liquidation even though the property distributed has a basis in the corporation's hands that is lower than the value of such property at the distribution date.   Since Bliss had already deducted its cost, the basis of the unused cattle feed was zero; its value was about $60,000.

Sustaining the government, the Court held that the value of the unused feed should be included in the corporation's income and reported on its final return despite the non-recognition rule of § 336.   In taking an expense deduction for the cattle feed, the taxpayer in a sense warranted that the feed would be used, or consumed, in its business; such use, in turn, would one day generate gross income to match the earlier deduction.   By liquidating, as it were, in mid-stream, the taxpayer had obviously eliminated the latter feature of the transaction; no matching income would ever materialize, because the cattle feed had been withdrawn from the taxpayer's business.   While the expense deduction might have been proper when taken, subsequent events—the liquidation— proved "fundamentally inconsistent" with its original justification. Accordingly, the cost of the cattle feed must be restored to the company's income—added back to profits—and the prior tax benefit surrendered.

Though a bit of a tangle, Justice O'Connor's opinion in *Bliss* reaches a reasonable and expectable result.[9]   The decision does, however, confirm that the tax benefit rule goes beyond the limited "recovery" situation dealt with in *Sullivan* and operates as a kind of recapture or reconciliation principle as well.

SECTION 11.   THE CASH METHOD

As noted earlier, the cash receipts and disbursements method of accounting is used by almost all individual wage and salary earners.   It is used, also, by a good many personal service companies and other small-scale enterprises in which inventories are not substantial.[9a]   Compared with the accrual method of accounting, which often requires that income and expense items be recognized prior to (or after) their receipt or payment, the cash method has the merit of simplicity.   The recognition of income and expense is governed by the chronology of cash receipt and disbursement;

---

9.   *See* White, *An Essay on the Conceptual Foundations of the Tax Benefit Rule,* 82 Mich.L.Rev. 485 (1984).

9a.   § 448(b), added in 1986, expressly prohibits use of the cash method by larger corporations and certain other entities.

revenues and expenditures are recognized at the time cash is received or paid out regardless of when the claims or obligations actually arose. The result, among other things, is that bookkeeping and accounting duties are minimized; indeed, for most cash method taxpayers, all "accounting" is done in the family checkbook.

Perhaps the main interpretative problem that has arisen in connection with the cash method is the treatment of deferred compensation. If an executive, in addition to a cash salary, receives a promise from his employer to make further payments after the executive retires, is the value of that promise currently includable in the executive's income along with the salary, or can it be deferred until actual payment takes place? *Cash* method seems to imply deferral, but perhaps the employer's promise (like the endowment policy at 1.02) should be regarded as the *equivalent* of cash and hence be taxed currently at its discounted value. This and related issues are examined in the subsection next following.

A converse problem is considered at 11.02. If expenses are normally recognized by cash method taxpayers at the time actual outlays are made, what should be the treatment of expenses that are paid in advance, say a three-year fire insurance premium? May a taxpayer accelerate his expense deductions by making pre-payments? Or does the capital expenditure rule restrict the operation of the cash method and require the taxpayer to amortize the insurance premium over the three-year period? As with the deferred compensation problem, the question here is how to reconcile the premise which underlies the cash method—that net income for the taxable year shall be determined by reference to receipts and disbursements—with the broad statutory requirement that the taxpayer's accounting method shall "clearly reflect" his annual income.

11.01 Constructive Receipt and Cash Equivalency. The Treasury, in Regulations of long standing, has made it clear that in determining gross income under the cash method, a taxpayer may not look solely to the *cash* that he has realized, nor even solely to his *actual* receipts. "Generally, under the cash method . . ., all items which constitute gross income (whether in the form of cash, property, or services) are to be included for the taxable year in which actually or constructively received." Regs. § 1.446–1(c)(1). Two enlargements are thus implied: receipt may be constructive as well as actual; and includable income may take other forms than cash. Neither extension is surprising, yet both tend to blur the simple concept of cash method accounting.

(a) Constructive receipt. Briefly stated, the constructive receipt doctrine prescribes that a taxpayer may not postpone income that is available to him merely by failing to exercise his power to collect it. An employee whose year-end wages have been made available cannot avoid inclusion by waiting until the next year to pick up his pay envelope; a lawyer cannot return his client's check with a request to pay the fee in a later period. Once the receipt is earned and within the taxpayer's control, it is includable despite his efforts to delay it. Any other rule would put wage and fee earners in a position to defer their income more or less at will and thereby achieve a kind of homemade averaging outside the specific limits of the statute.

The constructive receipt doctrine is a "rule of law" for determining when income is taxable, which means that taxpayers, as well as the Commissioner, may invoke it. In *Hyland v. Commissioner,*[10] the taxpayer was the chief executive and controlling stockholder of a personal service corporation. He performed services for the corporation in 1942 but received no actual cash salary in that year. Although the company's board of directors had approved a salary allocable to 1942 of about $35,000, the amount was not actually paid until 1943. While the taxpayer's original return for 1942 did not include the salary item, in an *amended* return filed some years later, he did report the $35,000 as 1942 income and excluded it from income for 1943. We may assume that the taxpayer's applicable tax rate turned out to be lower in the earlier than in the later period.

The taxpayer argued that in view of his control of the corporation, and in view also of the board's resolution, the salary was constructively received by him in 1942. He stressed that he could have reduced the salary to possession in that year simply by causing the corporation to issue a check. The Court of Appeals, nevertheless, sustained the Commissioner in taxing the salary in 1943. It held that the constructive receipt doctrine would not be applied merely because the taxpayer, as controlling stockholder, could have directed the company's treasurer to make the salary payment. That argument, said the Court, would prove too much, for it would mean that in every close corporation the corporate earnings would be "constructively received" by persons having the power to compel their distribution. But as corporations and shareholders are assumed to be separate taxable persons, mere power or control could not be taken as equivalent to the exercise thereof. Not the power to cause the board to act, therefore, but an actual

10. 175 F.2d 422 (2d Cir.1949).

crediting or setting aside of the funds in question would be necessary to support inclusion.

In a sense, of course, the position urged by the taxpayer in *Hyland* was one that most taxpayers would oppose, because it threatened a privilege long regarded by the owner-managers of closely held corporations as their birthright (though, as noted at 9.03(b), of less practical importance now than formerly). Thus, under present law a shareholder-executive in a small company may entirely or partially forgo his annual salary. The amount forgone will then be taxed to the corporation; it will not be "imputed" to the individual merely because his services would reasonably entitle him to take down an equivalent amount. In the alternative, the executive may draw his full salary, pay the individual tax, and then reinvest the money in the corporate business by lending it back or buying additional stock. In short, the owner-manager may elect, annually, to pay tax *either* at the corporate *or* at his individual rate on that portion of his salary (actual or constructive) which he desires to leave in the company's hands for use in the business.

Quite obviously, had the "constructive receipt" argument succeeded in *Hyland,* there would at least have been a danger that the Commissioner would take the resulting "rule of law" as authority to *require* owner-managers to include a reasonable salary in their gross incomes under all circumstances. But such an authority would be contrary to the accepted (if unstated) legislative scheme just described and would represent a departure from existing practice. The Commissioner has plainly recognized the intent of Congress in this respect: although the *Hyland* opinion left open the possibility that the *government* "might successfully invoke the doctrine of constructive receipt against the sole stockholder of a one-man corporation," with rare exceptions the Commissioner has not attempted, under either the constructive receipt doctrine or the income-attribution rules, to impute taxable salaries to controlling shareholders.

(b) Deferred compensation. A major distinction between the cash and the accrual method of accounting arises in connection with the treatment of accounts receivable. Amounts due from clients, customers, or employers are not included in a cash method taxpayer's income until actually received in cash; by contrast, accrual method taxpayers normally report such items when the services are completed or the merchandise is shipped and the amount due has been billed or invoiced. Suppose, for example, that a salesman earns commissions for goods sold during the current year, but the commissions are actually paid in the following year. If the salesman is on the cash method, the commissions will be

includable in the later period even though they were fully earned in the first year and their amount was undisputed. If the salesman used the accrual method, the commissions would be taxed in the earlier period even though actual payment was made subsequently. Assume in either case that the commissions are paid by the taxpayer's employer in due course—that is, early in the second year. Then, as between the two, the cash method salesman enjoys the relatively modest advantage of a one-year deferral of tax. This results because the cash method excuses the taxpayer from currently reporting items which happen to be outstanding at the close of the taxable year, and also incidentally allows the taxpayer to associate his cash inflows with his tax payment obligations.

The illustration just given assumes that the delay in payment of the salesman's commissions is merely a year-end phenomenon and not a conscious effort to reduce taxes. But suppose the deferral has been carefully prearranged between the salesman and his employer, and suppose also that the period of delay is much longer than a single year. Anticipating that his bracket-rate will be lower after his retirement, the salesman and his employer enter into a deferred compensation agreement which provides that a portion of the salesman's annual earnings will be withheld by the employer and paid out in installments after the salesman reaches retirement age. Perhaps the agreement even provides for imputed interest on the amounts withheld, as if the funds were deposited in a savings account for the salesman's benefit. If this arrangement succeeds from a tax standpoint—that is, if inclusion is deferred until actual payments begin—the salesman will have postponed his taxes for a relatively substantial period, and will have obtained the further advantage of the lower post-retirement rates. In effect, the cash method of accounting, whose chief aim is to simplify the taxpayer's bookkeeping, will thus have been converted into an *ad hoc* averaging device.

The Commissioner has attacked deferred compensation arrangements under both a constructive receipt and an economic benefit theory. His success, however, has been limited. In *Commissioner v. Oates*,[11] for example, the taxpayer, an insurance agent, was entitled on the termination of his agency to receive renewal commissions as they were earned over the succeeding 9-year period. The commissions were expected to be relatively high for the first few years, and then to decrease owing to the lapse of policies and other factors, finally reaching a low point by the end of the 9-year term. Prior to the commencement of payments and before any

---

11. 207 F.2d 711 (7th Cir.1953).

amounts were actually due, the taxpayer and his employer entered into a new agreement which provided that the renewal commissions would be paid in fixed monthly installments over a 15-year period at the rate of $1,000 a month. While the commissions earned by the taxpayer during the first year of the contract were nearly $50,000, he received and reported only the lesser amount to which the revised agreement entitled him.

Holding that neither the constructive receipt nor the economic benefit theory applied, the court of appeals rejected the Commissioner's effort to annually tax the full amount of the commissions earned. As to constructive receipt, the court found that doctrine applicable only to compensation *already* due and payable. While a taxpayer could not turn his back on income which was actually tendered to him, this did not mean that he was barred from arranging for the deferral of compensation in *advance* of the time it was earned. As to "economic benefit," the court rejected the argument that each year's earned commissions were effectively realized by the taxpayer, and then applied to the purchase of the $1,000-a-month annuity. Finding that the amended contract "was in the nature of a novation" rather than an exchange, the court held that only the actual cash payments received by the taxpayer could be treated as "realized" in any taxable year.

The *Oates* decision can be contrasted with the so-called "endowment policy case" mentioned at 1.02, above. There, it was stated that an employee would be taxed *currently* on the value of an annuity or endowment policy purchased *from* an insurance company *by* the taxpayer's employer, the policy to be turned over to the taxpayer at the date of his retirement. In *Oates,* the taxpayer also received a promise of future payments in the form of an annuity issued by an insurance company, but, as it happened, the insurance company itself was the taxpayer's employer. The *Oates* decision shows that the unconditional promise of the *employer,* even though itself a sound insurance company, to pay compensation in the future will not give rise to a constructive receipt or a taxable economic benefit to a cash method employee. But if the employer substitutes for its own promise either a fund outside its control or the unconditional obligation of a third party, that act does give rise to current income for the reason that the fund or the obligation is regarded as the equivalent of cash.

Having largely failed in its effort to treat deferred compensation arrangements as currently taxable, the Service in a 1960 ruling conceded the major elements of the controversy, and held, in effect, that conventional, unfunded deferred compensation agreements would be given their intended effect for tax purposes. In Rev.Rul.

60–31,[12] an executive was employed under an agreement which provided for an annual salary plus deferred compensation, the latter to be paid after termination of the executive's employment. The deferred payment obligation was annually credited on the employer's books and, once credited, was nonforfeitable. The Service ruled that the executive would be taxable only when he received the deferred amounts, because a "mere promise to pay, not represented by notes or secured in any way, is not regarded as a receipt of income within the intendment of the cash receipts and disbursements method."

While the deferred compensation field has been fairly stable since the issuance of Rev.Rul. 60–31, it may still be of some interest—perhaps only archaeological—to ask why the Commissioner should have succeeded so well (in cases like *Lucas v. Earl* and *Helvering v. Eubank:* see 7.01, 7.02) in preventing the assignment of earned income to other taxable *persons,* while largely failing to prevent the assignment of such income to other taxable *periods.* Briefly put, why did the government win in *Eubank,* but lose in *Oates,* when both cases entailed an effort by an insurance agent to minimize the impact of the progressive rate structure through an assignment or restructuring of his renewal commissions? The answer, most probably, is that the question of taxable person was not thought to be constrained by accounting rules to the same degree as the question of taxable period. In *Eubank,* the courts and the Service were at liberty to invent rules of income attribution under the general authority of § 61. Whether the assigned renewal commissions should be attributed to Eubank or to his assignee was not hedged in by fixed accounting principles, and hence the courts were free to regard the question as open. By contrast, the taxpayer in *Oates* could draw support from the cash method itself, which apparently contains no intrinsic distinction between short-term, involuntary deferrals and deferrals which are extended and also prearranged. To tax *both* currently, however, would virtually be to abrogate the cash method of accounting.

More generally, it may simply be that the courts have intuitively favored the idea of self-help income-*averaging*—which does, after all, appeal to one's sense of equity—while viewing income-*splitting* as a dangerous avoidance device and one with a wide potential for mischief.

11.02 Prepaid Expenses. For reasons already made clear, the acceleration of expense deductions normally benefits a taxpayer by permitting him to defer his taxes to later periods. As indicated

---

12. 1960–1 C.B. 174.

at 6.02, this factor largely explains why disputes arise between taxpayers and the Commissioner over the scope of the capital expenditure limitation in § 263. If an outlay for certain equipment is treated as an expense under § 162, it is currently deductible and reduces this year's tax. If the outlay is treated as a capital expenditure under § 263, it must be recovered through depreciation over the useful life of the equipment. Taxpayers almost always prefer immediate deduction to deferral.

On the whole, the question of deductible expense or nondeductible capital expenditure is unaffected by the taxpayer's accounting method. Cash and accrual method taxpayers both are required to capitalize the cost of assets having an extended useful life, and to recover such cost through depreciation allowances under § 167. A contrary rule, one which permitted cash method taxpayers to deduct currently the full cost of long-lived assets merely because an actual cash outlay had been made, would obviously result in serious distortions of taxable income. Accordingly, despite some increase in record-keeping complexity, cash method taxpayers are no less subject to the capital expenditure limitation than taxpayers using the accrual method.

The same limitation also generally applies to the prepayment of expenses, though there have been occasional lapses in the decided cases and even the administrative rulings. By and large, prepayments of insurance premiums, rents, compensation and the like are currently deductible only to the extent that the "asset" or service so acquired is exhausted during the taxable year. The unused portion of the premiums, rent, etc. is required to be prorated, or amortized, over the years to which the benefit relates.

It is, perhaps, not wholly clear whether § 263, which limits the deduction of expenses otherwise allowable under § 162, applies in a similar fashion to taxes and interest "paid or accrued within the taxable year" under §§ 163 and 164. Arguably, the latter provisions authorize cash method taxpayers to take a current deduction for the items thus *specifically* named even where a substantial prepayment is made. Whether for this or some other reason, the Service at an early date ruled that interest paid in advance for a 5-year period by a cash method taxpayer was fully deductible in the year of payment. This ruling, however, invited substantial tax-avoidance through the prepayment of interest on real estate mortgages by high-bracket taxpayers, and as a result, in 1968 the Service revoked its prior position on the ground that the deduction of prepaid interest did not clearly reflect taxable income.[13] Under the later ruling, prepaid interest had to be amortized over the period to which it actually related if the prepayment was for a period of more than 12 months beyond the close of the current year. In 1976, Congress put an end to even this limited concession by adding § 461(g), which requires cash method taxpayers to capitalize all prepaid interest (other than in connection with home mortgage loans) and to deduct such interest ratably over the period of the loan.

Apart from prepaid interest, cash method taxpayers engaged in farming have been permitted, under long-standing administrative regulations, to treat as current expenses a wide variety of costs which other taxpayers would have to capitalize. Although intended merely to simplify the bookkeeping chores of ordinary working farmers, these rules have sometimes been converted into lucrative tax-shelter arrangements by high-income individuals—doctors, dentists, movie-stars—who have never driven a tractor or milked a cow. A brain surgeon, for example, who appears to be having an especially good year might choose to invest in a so-called cattle feeding partnership. The partnership prepays the cost of the feed for the cattle in the *current* year, allowing the doctor to deduct his share of the prepayment. The cattle are sold in the *following* year, and the doctor then reports his share of the gain. Since his income is lower in the second year than in the first, the good doctor achieves a spreading and deferral of the first year's high earnings. Other syndicated farming shelters have also been popular. Thus, deferral *plus* conversion of ordinary income into capital gain has been achieved by investing in orchards, vineyards, and the like. Maintenance and other growing costs are currently deductible by the investor, while the later sale of the land and orchard produces a capital gain.

Added to the Code in 1976, and since expanded, §§ 263A and 464 attempt to distinguish between taxpayers who are actively engaged in farming as a business, and taxpayers who passively invest in widely held farm "syndicates" with a view to exploiting the farm-accounting rules for the purpose of sheltering income derived from other sources. Briefly, the provisions mentioned require farming syndicates to deduct the cost of feed, fertilizer, etc. only when actually consumed. In addition, the cultivation and maintenance expenses of groves, orchards and vineyards are now required to be capitalized to the extent that such expenses are

---

13. Rev.Rul. 68–643, 1968–2 C.B. 76. *Interest,* 16 U.C.L.A.L.Rev. 36 (1968). And see, Asimow, *Principle and Prepaid*

incurred before the property becomes productive. In effect, therefore, deferral through the anticipation of expense deductions is sharply curtailed.

SECTION 12. THE ACCRUAL METHOD

From an accountant's standpoint, the determination of periodic income is essentially a process of "timing" the recognition of revenue and "matching" against such revenue the expense items which are related thereto. The cash method of accounting makes no scientific effort either to "time" or to "match," because under it the recognition of revenue and expense turns largely on the accidental factor of receipt or disbursement. Subject to the modifications described in the preceding Section, receivables and payables are recognized only when reduced to cash. While this simple method is suitable for individuals rendering personal services, for corporations and other taxpayers which engage in the sale of merchandise, whether as manufacturers or distributors, and which extend credit to their customers and receive credit from their suppliers, a satisfactory determination of annual income requires the more refined techniques of accrual. Almost all businesses of any substantial size, therefore, use the accrual method of accounting in respect to the recognition of revenues and expenses. In addition, taxpayers engaged in the production or purchase and sale of goods are specifically required by Code § 471 to use opening and closing inventories in computing the cost of goods sold.

Briefly described, *accrual* is a technique for recognizing revenue items prior to their receipt in cash and for recognizing expense items prior to their actual payment. Thus, accounts receivable— amounts owed to the taxpayer by its customers—and accounts payable—amounts owed by the taxpayer to its suppliers—are both taken into account at the time the obligation becomes fixed, even though payment is not received or made until a later period. *Deferment*—which is no less a part of the prescribed technique where ordinary commercial accounting is concerned—is a device for postponing the recognition of revenues received in advance, and of expenses paid in advance, for services to be rendered or goods to be delivered in the future. Suppose, for example, that a lessor receives 5 years' prepaid rents from his lessee. On the lessee's side, the advance rentals are required to be capitalized and prorated over the 5-year term. Tax and commercial accounting principles here converge. On the lessor's side, commercial accounting would similarly require that the advance receipt be deferred through credit to a liability account, and then included year-by-year in the lessor's

241

income. As will be seen, however, tax accounting follows a different course at this point. In effect, tax accounting puts the lessor on the cash method for this limited purpose and requires him to include the full prepayment in the year of receipt.

The sections that follow examine three important issues. Section 12.01 takes up the timing and matching of receipts and expenditures by accrual method taxpayers, and in particular the treatment of items that are disputed or uncertain. Section 12.02 gives more detailed attention to the above-mentioned question of deferment, as well as the related topic of reserves for estimated expenses. Finally, 12.03 explains and illustrates the use of inventory techniques in determining the cost of goods sold.

12.01 Recognition of Income and Expenses; Disputed Items.

(a) Timing of revenues and expenditures. For accrual method taxpayers, the recognition of *income* depends on when the taxpayer's right to receive the item becomes fixed and determinable. In *Lucas v. North Texas Lumber Co.,*[14] the taxpayer, a sawmill operator, gave another concern a 10-day option to purchase its timber lands for a specified price. The option was exercised on December 30, 1916, at which time the taxpayer ceased operations and withdrew its employees from the land. Deeds to the property were delivered to the purchaser on January 5, 1917, and on that date the purchase price was paid and the transaction closed. The taxpayer, on the accrual method, sought to report its profit in 1916, while the Commissioner asserted that the appropriate year for inclusion was 1917. Rates, of course, were substantially higher in 1917, a war year, than in 1916. Finding that title to the land did not pass to the vendee until 1917, and that no unconditional liability to pay the purchase price arose until the deeds were delivered, the Supreme Court held that the taxpayer's gain could not be included in the earlier year despite its use of the accrual method.

The *North Texas Lumber* case is generally cited for the proposition that accrual of income is not permitted or required until goods or services have been transferred or performed, even where customers' orders are booked and a binding sale contract has been entered into at a fixed price. Thus, accrual based on contracts for future delivery presumably is improper. On the other hand, the rule as stated has not been applied inflexibly, and accrual of income has been permitted on a contract rather than a "sales" basis where the taxpayer has followed a consistent practice over an extended period

14. 281 U.S. 11 (1930).

of time. It can be argued, indeed, that *North Texas Lumber* was not really an accounting decision at all. The transaction involved a one-time transfer of fixed assets (not a recurring sale of goods), and the issue posed was when such transactions should be regarded as closed. The rule announced—that realization occurs on delivery of the property sold, even though the obligation to deliver became binding in a previous period—is one that probably applies to all casual sales of property, regardless of the seller's accounting method.

Moving to the recognition of *expenses* by accrual method taxpayers, the Supreme Court in *U.S. v. Anderson* [15] confirmed that expense items are to be deducted not when cash happens to change hands, but when "all the events" occur which establish the taxpayer's liability to make the payment and the amount due can be determined with reasonable accuracy. In *Anderson,* the taxpayer, a munitions manufacturer, incurred a special profits tax on munitions manufactured by it in 1916. The tax became due and was paid in 1917, and the taxpayer sought to deduct the tax-payment from its income in the later rather than the earlier year. Once again, income tax rates were higher in 1917 than in 1916. The taxpayer argued that taxes do not accrue until they are assessed, and that the assessment date, 1917, was therefore the proper time for deduction. The Court, however, held that the munitions tax must be deducted in 1916. Conceding that taxes technically do not become a *legal* liability until assessed, the Court found, nevertheless, that all the events necessary to fix and determine the taxpayer's obligation had occurred in the earlier period. In an accounting sense, therefore, the taxes had accrued.

Superficially, perhaps, the *Anderson* decision seems inconsistent with the holding in *North Texas Lumber.* If recognition of income had to await the actual delivery of the timberland in *North Texas Lumber,* then perhaps the recognition of expense should have had to await the actual assessment of the munitions tax in *Anderson.* If the all-events test required passage of title to the land, it might also have been expected to require assessment of the tax. Actually, however, the two cases are aimed at somewhat different goals. In *North Texas Lumber* the Court's objective was to establish a practical rule for the *recognition* of revenues by accrual method taxpayers; in general, the decision requires that revenues be recognized when goods are shipped to the buyer, neither earlier nor later. *Anderson,* by contrast, is chiefly interested in *matching* expenses with the particular revenues with which

15. 269 U.S. 422 (1926).

those expenses happen to be associated; the Court's aim was to assure that the taxpayer's gross income and related expenses would be reported in the *same* taxable period. The all-events test was rather a clumsy verbal locution for attaining the two different ends in view, but the results reached by the Court were satisfactory on the whole and are consistent with normal accounting practice.

In *U.S. v. General Dynamics Corp.*,[16] the taxpayer maintained health insurance for covered employees (some 56,000, apparently) through a self-insured program under which it paid medical claims out of its own funds. Employees who had received medical services during the year would file claims for reimbursement under the plan; such claims would then be reviewed for eligibility and coverage by employee-benefit personnel and, if approved, would be paid by the taxpayer in due course. Because there was typically some delay between the time an employee received medical treatment and the time the employee submitted his claim for reimbursement, it always happened that a proportion of the current year's reimbursable claims would not actually have been filed with benefit personnel by the year-end and, hence, would not be approved and paid until the following year or perhaps even the year after that. The taxpayer sought to accrue and deduct the full amount paid, due, and estimated to be due for medical services received by its employees during the current taxable year. The amount so deducted included (a) payments actually made and (b) claims approved for payment—the figures for those two categories being known with certainty. Also, however, the accrual included (c) claims not yet filed at year-end but for which a reasonable estimate could be made on the basis of the company's statistical and actuarial experience for prior periods. The government raised no question about categories (a) and (b), but it rejected the company's effort to accrue amounts attributed to category (c) on the ground that, as to the latter, the requirements of the all-events test had not been met.

In a somewhat confusing opinion (and with three dissents), the Supreme Court sustained the government's position under the all-events standard. The Court appeared to accept as reasonable the company's estimate of the dollar amount that its late-filing employees would ultimately become entitled to. Nevertheless, it refused to agree that the fact of liability could be "firmly established" prior to the time that an employee actually filed a claim. Some individuals covered by the medical plan and plainly entitled to reimbursement might simply fail to file their claims, whether "through

---

16. 481 U.S. 239 (1987), discussed in Jensen, *The Supreme Court and the Timing of Deductions for Accrual–Basis* *Taxpayers,* 22 Georgia L.Rev. 229 (1988).

oversight, procrastination, confusion over the coverage provided, or fear of disclosure to the employer of the extent or nature of the services received". Such failure, said the Court, was more than a "remote and speculative possibility". Hence, the act of filing must be seen not as a mere technicality or ministerial detail, but as "the last link in the chain of events creating liability for purposes of the 'all events' test."

Actually, and despite the Court's contrary assertion, the possibility that an employee might fail (through oversight, etc.) to file a reimbursement claim does seem pretty remote, or at least quite unlikely, for the obvious reason that anyone who thinks himself entitled to reimbursement—especially for a sizeable doctor's bill—is almost certainly going to ask for it. Rejection of a doubtful claim by the benefit staff following review seems a good deal more likely in a given instance, and one might have thought that if anything qualified as a "last link" it would be the stamp of approval that turned a pending claim into a right to payment. Linkage aside, perhaps the easiest way to explain the *General Dynamics* decision is to say that it follows precedent in refusing to sanction expense accruals on the basis of statistical or actuarial estimates of liability (absent express statutory authorization). As suggested at 12.02, the Code and the decided cases generally deny deduction for additions to reserves for *estimated* expenses, even where the estimate is reasonable and likely to be fairly accurate. Such conservatism in tax accounting can be criticized, but the pattern of legal development in this area—administrative and judicial disallowance, followed in a few specific instances by legislative relief—is quite clear-cut. Though the facts in *General Dynamics* may have been closer to the line of allowability than those present in various earlier decisions, in the end the asserted accrual *was* based on a statistical estimate and for that reason, probably, had to be denied.

(b) Disputed items. In *North Texas Lumber* and *Anderson* the income and expense items in question were uncontested. The taxpayer's right to receive payment for the sale of land, or its liability to pay the federal munitions tax, as well as the amounts thereof, were clear. Suppose, however, that a taxpayer's claim to income or liability for expense is subject to dispute. What is the effect of the dispute on its obligation under the accrual method to include or deduct the item prior to payment?

In *Continental Tie & Lumber Co. v. U.S.*,[17] the taxpayer, under legislation enacted in 1920, became entitled to an award from the federal government for losses resulting from government control of

17. 286 U.S. 290 (1932).

its railroad operations during World War I. Actual payment was not made until 1923, however, because it took that long for the Interstate Commerce Commission to promulgate regulations and make a determination of the amount to which the taxpayer was entitled. Finding that the taxpayer's right to an award was "fixed" by the passage of the 1920 legislation, and that data on its books would have enabled it to compute the amount due with reasonable accuracy, the Supreme Court held that the award should have been accrued and reported in 1920 despite the delay in payment.

The *Continental Tie* decision is usually taken to imply a distinction between disputes as to whether an obligation is owing to the taxpayer at all and disputes as to the amount of an obligation conceded to be due. Disputes as to basic liability delay inclusion; disputes as to amount do not, if a reasonable estimate can be made. The distinction is not especially realistic, and probably the better rule would be to require accrual only to the extent of the amount agreed to by the obligor, while permitting delay as to the disputed balance.

The holding in *Continental Tie* can be contrasted with that in *North American Oil,* which also involved the inclusion of uncertain income by an accrual method taxpayer. In *North American Oil,* the taxpayer was required to include income at the time it was received in cash despite a very lively dispute over the taxpayer's right to retain it. In *Continental Tie,* the award was required to be accrued prior to payment even though there was uncertainty as to the amount. Taking the two decisions together, the effect is a construction of "accrual" which plainly favors the *earlier* inclusion of uncertain items and in that respect coincides with the tax-collector's convenience. As noted at 10.02, however, the possibility of hardship to the taxpayer has been reduced by the addition to the Code of § 1341, which now affords "transactional" relief where the taxpayer discovers in a later year that he had no right to all or a part of the previously included income.

The general rule governing the accrual of uncertain income—that no inclusion is required as long as the item is unpaid and the other party disputes his basic liability to the taxpayer—has its counterpart on the deduction side. In *Dixie Pine Products Co. v. Commissioner,*[18] the Supreme Court denied the taxpayer's right to accrue unpaid state gasoline taxes in the year incurred, because the taxpayer then contested its liability for such taxes on the ground that the chemical used in its business was not gasoline within the meaning of the state law. Going still further, in *U.S. v. Consolidat-*

18.   320 U.S. 516 (1944).

ed Edison Co.,[19] the Court held that a contested state tax could not be accrued as a deduction even when paid, since all the events necessary to fix the taxpayer's liability would not have occurred until the contest had terminated and the taxpayer's liability was resolved. Congress found the *Consolidated Edison* decision harsh and in 1964 overruled it by adding § 461(f), which provides for the deduction of disputed items in the year paid even though the taxpayer continues to contest his liability after the payment is made. If the taxpayer's liability later turns out to be less than the amount paid, the difference is taken back into income at that time, assuming the earlier deduction resulted in a tax benefit (see 10.03).

A loose end: As indicated, the all-events test is generally taken to mean that an expense item must be accrued when the taxpayer's liability is fixed and the amount is reasonably determinable. But suppose the expense item, though fixed and determinable, relates to services or property that is to be provided to (or by) the taxpayer in a future period. Thus, suppose a company on the accrual method contractually obligates itself to pay another concern $1 million for certain repair and clean-up work that it knows it will require in the future. The work is to be done, and the payment is to be made, 15 years from today. Since both liability and amount are fixed, the all-events test would literally seem to be satisfied.[20] Does this mean that the taxpayer can accrue and deduct the full $1 million in the *current* taxable year even though the work itself is not to be performed and paid for until much later?

Prior to 1984, the answer may well have been yes—in which case the all-events test would have generated a sizeable financial benefit for the taxpayer in question. Assuming a 40% tax rate, the $1 million deduction would be worth $400,000 in current tax savings. Such savings invested at an after-tax rate of 6% for 15 years would grow to about $1 million by the end of that period, and the latter sum could then be used by the taxpayer to meet its obligation under the contract. In effect, the repair work would have cost the taxpayer nothing: by deducting the entire expense in Year 1 (though without actually paying anything until Year 15), the taxpayer would have succeeded in shifting the full cost of the contract to the Treasury. Logic, of course, suggests that if the all-

---

19. 366 U.S. 380 (1961).

20. *U.S. v. Hughes Properties, Inc.,* 476 U.S. 593 (1986); and see *Mooney Aircraft, Inc. v. U.S.,* 420 F.2d 400 (5th Cir.1969), discussed in Gunn, *Matching of Costs and Revenues As a Goal of Tax Accounting,* 4 Va. Tax Rev. 1 (1984).

events test did indeed permit an accrual in Year 1, the allowable deduction should have been limited to the *present value* of the future $1 million outlay, or $400,000. Assuming the same 40% tax rate applied in year 15, the advantage of accruing in advance of payment would then be eliminated. Thus, the tax saving realized by deducting $400,000 today ($160,000) is simply the present value (at 6%) of the tax saving to be realized at the end of 15 years ($400,000); hence, the taxpayer would be indifferent between deducting now and deducting later (he could not, of course, do both). While this solution presumably handles the problem, the difficulty from a purely legal standpoint is that no statutory authority exists for imposing a present-value limitation on accruable amounts.

To prevent avoidance through premature accruals, Congress in 1984 modified the definition of "all-events" by adding § 461(h) to the Code. The new subsection provides, in general, that the all-events test shall not be regarded as satisfied until the year in which "economic performance" occurs with respect to an accrual-method taxpayer's liability. Hence, deduction of the $1 million contract obligation would be permitted in Year 15 when the work in question was actually performed, but not in Year 1 when the contract was entered into.

12.02 Advance Receipts and Reserves for Estimated Expenses. An important area of divergence between accounting rules as applied for tax purposes and generally accepted accounting principles involves the treatment of prepaid income. For many years the Treasury has insisted that payments for services to be performed in later years are taxable in the year received even though they are in large part unearned at that time. Generally accepted accounting principles would require that the taxpayer defer the inclusion of advance receipts until the year or years in which the services are performed and the income is actually earned.

The Supreme Court has steadfastly supported the Treasury's position. In *American Automobile Association v. U.S.,*[21] the Court sustained the government's refusal to permit deferment by holding that advance membership dues received by the automobile club were includable in the year of receipt, although the period of an individual's membership almost always extended into the following year. The Court found that the club's allocation of dues on a monthly basis was "artificial" because it bore no necessary relationship to the particular time or times when a member might actually require road services. Accordingly, the club's allocation system did not so clearly reflect income as to be binding on the

---

21.　367 U.S. 687 (1961).

Treasury. In *Schlude v. Commissioner,*[22] involving prepayments for dancing lessons, the Court again required full inclusion in the year of receipt. The taxpayer had carefully allocated its students' fees to the periods when the dancing lessons, which could be taken at times arranged by the students themselves, were actually given, thus apparently meeting the requirement of accuracy laid down in the *AAA* decision. The Court, however, found the allocation effort still inadequate. Since students who had paid their fees might allow their contract rights to lapse, "the studio was uncertain [at the end of each taxable year] whether none, some or all of the remaining lessons would be rendered."

Though generally regarded as unjustified from an accounting standpoint, the Service's insistence on full inclusion of advance payments has a certain practical merit. Administration is obviously simplified because it is easier to identify the taxable event as the receipt of cash than to work out precise and reliable rules for deferral. In addition, the Treasury is not obliged to wait until later years for its tax collections, in the meanwhile taking an unsecured risk that the taxpayer may ultimately be unable to pay. Here, as at other points in the field of accounting, the Supreme Court has shown itself willing to subordinate equity and accuracy of income measurement to the apparent demands of practical tax administration, though it is notable that the *AAA* and *Schlude* cases were both decided by 5–4 majorities.

Despite its convenience, the tax accounting rule for prepaid income has long been criticized on the ground that it distorts income by requiring inclusion of the unearned portion of a receipt. Advance receipts, it can be argued, are much like loans. While "repayment" is to be made in the form of taxable services, the resulting income ought properly to be deferred until those services have been performed. More serious, perhaps, is the hardship which the taxpayer may suffer by being forced to bunch in a single year income which is actually attributable to two or more taxable periods. Since (as shown below) the deduction of reserves for estimated expenses is not generally permitted, the taxpayer may not offset the prepaid income by related expenses which are expected to be incurred in subsequent years. And even if the taxpayer prepays those future expenses, such prepayment is treated as a deferred expense comparable to a capital expenditure and is required to be prorated over the periods to which it relates.

Recognizing the force of these criticisms, Congress in 1954 attempted to harmonize the rules of tax and commercial accounting

22. 372 U.S. 128 (1963).

by enacting a provision—§ 452—which allowed accrual method taxpayers to defer prepaid income to the year or years in which it was actually earned. The period of deferral, generally, was limited to five years. It was quickly discovered, however, that revenue losses during the period of transition from the old to the new rules were likely to be unacceptably large, and § 452 was therefore retroactively repealed. In 1958, and again in 1961, Congress enacted provisions which authorized deferral for specific types of prepaid income: § 455 permits the deferral of prepaid subscriptions for magazines and other periodicals; § 456 overcomes the result in the *AAA* case by allowing the postponement of prepaid dues received by membership organizations such as automobile clubs. In addition, in 1971 the Service modified its administrative practice by announcing that it would approve a limited deferral for payments received in one year for services to be rendered before the end of the following year.[23] Instead of reporting such items when received, an accrual method taxpayer may include them in the next succeeding taxable year or when the services are actually performed, whichever is first. Apart from this administrative concession, and with the statutory exceptions for subscription fees and membership dues, the general case law described above presumably still applies.

Very much the same pattern of case-law and statutory development shows up in the area of reserves for estimated expenses. Generally accepted accounting principles normally require that liability reserves be set up to take account of probable expenses which relate to current income but which have not become fixed and unconditional by the close of the taxable year. Tax accounting, on the other hand, with certain limited statutory exceptions (of which the most important is the reserve for bad debts permitted by § 166(c)), apparently denies a deduction for such reserves. Thus, deductions have been denied for reserves for estimated personal injury claims, for probable maintenance and service guaranties, for estimated refunds, cancellations, and so on. Tax accounting, here, has followed the strict rule that no accrual of expense will be permitted unless the taxpayer's obligation is fixed on the basis of events in existence at the end of the taxable period. The Service, presumably, has been concerned that a more lenient approach would lead to excessive pessimism as to future liabilities in years of high tax rates, and has preferred to forbid the accrual of reserves rather than attempt to deal with taxpayer's estimates on a case-by-case basis.

23. Rev.Proc. 71–21, 1971–2 C.B. 549.

Once again, as with prepaid income, Congress tried in 1954 to bring tax and commercial accounting rules together. § 462 authorized the deduction of an addition to reserves for estimated expenses, provided the amount could be estimated reasonably accurately on the basis of prior experience. Again, however, it became apparent that the revenue losses in transitional years had not been sufficiently anticipated, and the new provision was promptly and retroactively repealed.

A loose end: Not often has the Commissioner taken such a decisive beating in a tax accounting case as the one he recently absorbed in *Commissioner v. Indianapolis Power & Light Co.*[24] The *IPL* case had been reviewed by no fewer than 28 judges (including the full Tax Court) by the time it came to a close, yet the Commissioner was unable to persuade even one that his position on the law was correct. Why did he put up such a struggle? The answer, I suppose, is that the legal issue involved—the taxability of customer security-deposits—affected a very large number of the country's public utilities, including most particularly your local and long-distance telephone companies. The Commissioner's persistence in fighting the *IPL* case is thus presumably to be explained by the sizeable amounts of potentially taxable income that must have been at stake, together, perhaps, with an exasperated sense that form was impeding a true perception of substance.

The rather straightforward question in *IPL* was whether a cash deposit required and received by the taxpayer, an electric utility, from certain of its customers should be regarded as an advance payment for services to be rendered in the future or as a mere security-deposit. Ultimately, the issue was one of timing. If viewed as an advance payment, the deposit would be taxable to IPL in the year received under the *AAA* decision but then would be deductible or excludable by IPL in the later year in which it was refunded to the customer or applied against an outstanding bill. If viewed as a security-deposit, the deposit would be treated as a loan, in effect, and would only become taxable if and when later applied to the payment of the customer's bill. IPL did not require deposits from all of its customers—only those whose creditworthiness was in doubt—and it was obligated by local law to pay interest to each depositor. On the other hand, the funds deposited were not segregated or set apart in a special account but were presumably added to and used by IPL as part of its general working capital. As

---

24.　493 U.S. 203 (1990).

of 1975, IPL held something like $1 million in untaxed customers' deposits, and one supposes that the net amount (and hence, in the Service's view, the amount of income being deferred) tended to increase from year to year.

Once a customer had established good credit standing by paying his bills regularly, or on termination of the customer's service, IPL would refund the deposit by check if the customer's account was paid up. In the alternative, at the customer's option, IPL would apply the deposit to any outstanding balance. If the customer's account was delinquent, IPL could of course apply the deposit without the customer's consent. In fact, depositors chose, or were compelled, to apply their deposits to outstanding balances nearly 90% of the time (in whole or part).[25]

Following an earlier ruling, the Commissioner sought to distinguish customer deposits securing the utility's property interest—possible damage to meters, for example—and deposits securing the customer's obligation to make payment to the utility for services rendered. Only the former would be regarded as a "true security deposit", while the latter would be treated as a taxable advance payment. In response, IPL argued that a refundable deposit was just that—a refundable deposit—whether it secured an obligation to compensate for damage to physical property or secured the customer's obligation to pay his electric bills when due.

Affirming a unanimous decision of the Court of Appeals, which had affirmed a unanimous decision of the Tax Court, the Supreme Court held for the taxpayer on the ground that a customer never gave up his legal right to recover his deposit and could always insist upon full repayment in cash (if his bill was paid up). "So long as the customer fulfills his legal obligation to make timely payments," said Justice Blackmun, "his deposit ultimately is to be refunded, and both the timing and method of that refund are largely within the control of the customer." Accordingly, the depositor must be regarded as a creditor and the deposit as a loan. To be sure, only a small minority of customers actually demanded refunds. For most, the deposit ultimately *became* a payment for services by being credited against the monthly bill, and I think we can assume that those IPL customers whom the company classified as credit risks never thought of their deposits as anything *but* advance payments. It remained true, however, that a customer could recover his deposit if he chose. Some did—not many, but some—and that circumstance turned out to be insuperable as far as the Commissioner was concerned.

25.　88 T.C. 969.

12.03 Use of Inventories. Under generally accepted accounting principles, a business which derives profits from the sale of goods must, in determining its income at the end of the year, divide its merchandise costs between those costs which are properly allocable to the current year's operations and those costs which should be deferred to subsequent periods. Formerly, accountants placed emphasis upon the balance sheet showing as the primary objective of inventory pricing, and hence the problem was principally one of valuation. At the present, however, the emphasis is upon income determination, that is, upon the matching of appropriate costs against related revenues. As stated by the American Institute of Certified Public Accountants, "in accounting for the goods in the inventory at any point of time, the major objective of inventory pricing is the matching of appropriate costs against revenues in order that there may be a proper determination of the realized income. Thus, the inventory at any given date is the balance of costs applicable to goods on hand remaining after the matching of absorbed costs with concurrent revenues."

For tax purposes also, the objective of inventory valuation and inventory identification (that is, the matching of inventory cost against related revenue) is that of clearly reflecting income. Thus, § 471 provides that inventories are to be used whenever they are necessary in order clearly to determine the income of any taxpayer. According to the Regulations, inventories of merchandise on hand at the beginning and end of every taxable year must be taken in all cases in which the production, purchase or sale of merchandise is an income-producing factor. The use of inventories does not of itself represent a separate and distinct method of accounting. Rather, it is a component of the over-all accounting procedure whose essential purpose is to establish the cost of goods sold as a step towards determination of the taxpayer's gross income from business operations.

There are two authorized methods of valuing or pricing inventories for tax purposes. These are (1) the cost method and (2) the use of "cost or market, whichever is lower." As respects the further problem of identifying items included in inventories, the general requirement is that the "first-in, first-out" (FIFO) rule be used. However, taxpayers may also identify inventory under the "last-in, first-out" (LIFO) rule, if a specific election to employ LIFO is made in accordance with the requirements of § 472. FIFO and LIFO are briefly described in the paragraphs following. A comprehensive illustration is provided at the end.

(a) The "First-in, First-out" (FIFO) method. Where inventory is identified in accordance with the FIFO rule, it is assumed that

the goods first acquired are sold first and hence that the goods in the closing inventory are those most recently purchased. In conjunction with FIFO, the taxpayer may utilize either the cost or "cost or market" method of inventory valuation. The effects of these methods are summarized below.

1. *Cost.* Under this method, the value of each unit of merchandise is determined on the basis of its actual cost, with additions for freight, handling, and similar expenses. Use of the cost method in conjunction with FIFO may result in fairly wide fluctuations in income, depending on fluctuations in price levels. Thus, profits tend to be greater in a rising market, and in a falling market losses tend to be greater (or profits tend to be less), than where the "cost or market" method is used or where the cost method is tied in with the LIFO formula. Despite these effects, the use of "cost" in conjunction with FIFO presents, in many cases, a profit or loss picture which is closer to actual results. This is especially so if, as in the case of merchandise subject to deterioration, the goods on hand at the close of the taxable year are in fact those most recently purchased or produced. If the taxpayer's business is one that is characterized by fairly stable prices, the cost method normally recommends itself as being the simplest to use.

2. *Cost or Market.* Where inventory is valued on the basis of cost or market, whichever is lower, the taxpayer must first determine the cost of items on hand at the closing inventory date and then compare such cost with the market value of identical items on the same date. The lower of the two values is taken as the closing inventory value. For the purpose of subsequent inventories, the value of the closing inventory at market will be deemed to be its cost in the opening inventory of the succeeding taxable year. Use of the cost or market method may be desirable where market prices fluctuate considerably. In the case of a falling market, this method, as compared with the cost method under FIFO, tends to reduce income for the year in question: the value of closing inventory is reduced to market, creating a higher cost of goods sold, which in turn results in a lower gross income figure. However, income for the following year will necessarily be greater than it would be under the cost method, since, as stated, the closing inventory value of the preceding year becomes the opening inventory of the following year.

In the case of a rising market, the use of "cost or market" produces no different result than the simple cost method, since market value is used only when it is lower than cost. Hence, while the cost or market method anticipates losses in a falling market, additional profits are not anticipated in a rising market. The cost or market method may, in general, be used only in conjunction with the FIFO method.

(b) *The "Last-in, First-out" (LIFO) method.* The LIFO method of inventory identification has been available to all taxpayers on an elective basis since 1939. Under LIFO, the taxpayer is permitted to assume that the goods last purchased were the goods first sold, and thus to value his closing inventory as if it were composed of the earliest purchases. Under LIFO, inventories must be valued at cost. Since the LIFO method assumes that the goods sold during the year are the goods most recently purchased, it has the effect of stabilizing income by minimizing the impact of price level changes upon inventory valuation. Profits are kept down on a rising market, while during a period of declining prices profits are likely to appear where otherwise losses might be shown. In contrast, the use of FIFO, whether in conjunction with cost or with cost or market, tends to accentuate profits on a rising market and to reduce profits or increase losses when prices decline. From the taxpayer's standpoint, the LIFO method produces best results during a period of rising prices, unless it becomes necessary to liquidate existing low-cost inventory. In the latter event, the deferred profits representing unrealized inventory appreciation will be "bunched" in the single year of liquidation. The Code has in the past provided limited relief in cases of involuntary liquidations of LIFO inventory due to war conditions, but otherwise simply leaves the taxpayer to assume this risk. As indicated above, for tax purposes LIFO inventory must be valued at cost; the cost or market method is not permitted. This, of course, means that an election to employ LIFO would be decidedly inadvisable in a period of declining prices, since the losses inherent in the earlier high-cost inventory would be deferred instead of realized. Efforts to permit the use of LIFO in conjunction with the cost or market method have consistently been opposed by the Treasury.

(c) *Comparison of principal methods.* The following example illustrates in simple fashion the difference in gross profits under FIFO (using either cost method or cost or market method) and under LIFO. It will be noted that the "First Year" involves a rising market and the "Second Year" a falling market for the taxpayer's product. As indicated above, the cost method in conjunction with FIFO tends to accentuate both profits and losses in a sharply fluctuating market. The cost or market method under FIFO produces a like result in a rising market, while in a falling market, as compared with the simple cost method, it tends to anticipate inventory losses and hence produces increased losses (or reduced profits). Finally, as compared with the cost and cost or market methods under FIFO, the LIFO method produces smaller profits in a rising market as well as smaller losses (or even profits) in a falling market and thus has a stabilizing effect upon income during periods of fluctuating prices.

Assumed Facts

First year:
 Purchases:
  (1) 100 units at $50 per unit $5,000
  (2) 75 units at $75 per unit   5,625
  (3) 125 units at $100 per unit   12,500
                  $23,125

 Sales:
  200 units at $100 average price $20,000
 Inventory December 31:
  100 units, with a market value of $110 per unit

Second year:
 Purchases:
  (1) 75 units at $100 per unit $7,500
  (2) 50 units at $80 per unit   4,000
  (3) 100 units at $45 per unit   4,500
                  $16,000

 Sales:
  225 units at $75 average price $16,875
 Inventory December 31:
  100 units, with a market value of $35 per unit

Difference in Gross Profits

	FIFO		LIFO
	Cost	Cost or Market	
First year:			
Purchases	$23,125	$23,125	$23,125
Closing inventory	10,000	10,000	5,000
Cost of goods sold	$13,125	$13,125	$18,125
Sales	20,000	20,000	20,000
GROSS PROFIT	$ 6,875	$ 6,875	$ 1,875
Second year:			
Opening inventory	$10,000	$10,000	$5,000
Purchases	16,000	16,000	16,000
Total	$26,000	$26,000	$21,000
Closing inventory	4,500	3,500	5,000
Cost of goods sold	$21,500	$22,500	$16,000
Sales	16,875	16,875	16,875
GROSS PROFIT (OR LOSS)	($ 4,625)	($ 5,625)	$ 875

Part E: RECOGNITION OF GAINS AND LOSSES—SELECTED ISSUES

Enough has been said about the computation of gains and losses from sales of property to require at this point no more than a brief recapitulation of Code nomenclature. § 1001(a) provides that "gain or loss" shall be the difference between the "amount realized" from a "sale or other disposition of property" and the taxpayer's "adjusted basis" for the property sold. The term "amount realized" is defined in § 1001(b) to include not only cash but the "fair market value" of any other property received, so that by implication the receipt of consideration in kind is regarded as a realization which generates gain or loss. § 1011 states that "adjusted basis" means "basis"—usually "cost" as provided in § 1012, but capable of a good many special formulations (see 13.01 next following, for example) depending on the circumstances—as "adjusted" under § 1016. § 1016 contains a long list of required additions to or subtractions from original cost which are designed to give effect to inclusions, exclusions, deductions or disallowances prescribed by other substantive Code provisions. Of the adjustments listed in the section the most important for the discussion below is that contained in subsection (a)(2), which provides that the basis of depreciable property (such as buildings and machinery) shall be reduced from year to year by the amount allowable as a deduction for "exhaustion, wear and tear, obsolescence, amortization, and depletion."

Having thus determined the amount of gain or loss by simple computation, the next question would be whether or not the gain or loss had been "realized" as a result of the event that occurred. Although the Code says nothing directly about the realization requirement, it is well understood that "mere" property appreciation or decline is not regarded as a realization of gain or loss. As stated earlier, the income tax is a tax on transactions, not on income as such. Largely because of its ambiguous and artificial character, the realization requirement has generated a good many difficult problems of interpretation. A sampling of these was offered in Section 5, above, and the present Part adds some further illustrations.

Assuming there *is* a realization in the form of a "sale" of property for cash or an "exchange" of one property for another, § 1002 then requires that the realized gain or loss be "recognized" (unless otherwise provided) and reflected in the taxpayer's gross income under § 61.[1] While "realization" and "recognition" generally run together, there are a number of transactions which involve a clear realization of gain or loss but for which the Code specifically provides *non* -recognition (sometimes optionally). Leasehold terminations (5.03) and "involuntary conversions" (2.04) are examples that have already been considered. In these and other instances Congress evidently considered that the realization rule or the income definition created hardships when rigorously applied, and it chose instead to protect the gain or the income from immediate recognition or inclusion. In other situations—like-kind exchanges, for example, and certain corporate mergers—the "exchange" is regarded as involving no real alteration in the character of the taxpayer's investment despite a technical or formal change, and again immediate recognition of gain or loss is specifically avoided. In most non-recognition cases, the taxpayer's basis in his original property is carried over to the newly acquired property. The overall effect, then, is a deferral of the gain or loss, rather than total forgiveness or permanent disallowance.

Assuming all of these preliminary considerations are disposed of—*i.e.,* there is a realization of gain or loss and it is not deferred by a non-recognition provision of any sort—the next and final question would be whether the special regime that has been established for *capital* gains and losses is applicable because of the nature of the asset sold. In the past, this issue vastly overshadowed the others in importance and complexity. Though less important now, it remains relevant (as well as complex) and is probably better dealt with in a separate Part. Hence our treatment of property sales is carried out in two steps, with the present Part E being given over to realization and recognition questions (largely involving real estate transactions) and Part F being devoted entirely to capital gains and losses.

SECTION 13. TRANSACTIONS IN MORTGAGED PROPERTY

Almost all real estate purchases, I suppose, are financed by mortgage loans, whether obtained from a bank or other institutional lender or from the seller of the property himself if he is willing to hold the purchaser's obligation. The property acquired stands as security for the loan, and in the event of a default in payment of

---

1. As indicated at 6.06, losses are deductible only if specific authorization can be found therefor, *e.g.,* in § 165. Losses from the sale of property held for personal use—say the family auto—are not allowed; but see discussion at 15.02, below.

interest or principal by the borrower-mortgagor the lender-mortgagee may foreclose on the security, dispose of it at auction and apply the proceeds to the debt. Any excess of foreclosure proceeds over the amount due (there rarely is any) is returned to the debtor. Any deficiency can be enforced against the debtor's other assets if (as would almost always be true in the case of a home-buyer) the debtor assumes personal liability for the loan. If no such personal liability is provided for (as noted below, commercial property mortgages are often nonrecourse, meaning that the lender's sole security is the property itself), then the deficiency simply becomes the lender's loss.

The mortgage-loan itself is usually repayable—amortizable—in equal installments (monthly, quarterly, etc.) over a stated term of years. As has been noted (2.02), the early amortization payments consist largely of interest on the outstanding principal, while the later payments consist largely of principal itself. If the property-owner sells his property before the mortgage has been fully amortized, the sale proceeds go first to satisfy the mortgage debt—the mortgagee being in the status of a senior security-holder—with only the balance going to the mortgagor, the owner of the equity. In some instances, especially where commercial property is concerned, the new purchaser will simply assume (or take the property subject to) the outstanding mortgage and carry out the established amortization schedule, in which event the residual cash component goes entirely to the equity-owner. The amount received by the equity-owner after satisfaction or assumption of the mortgage would reflect his initial cash investment in the property plus subsequent payments of mortgage principal, plus or minus any change in market value during the period of his ownership.

The subsection that follows raises an important tax question which relates in particular to mortgages on commercial property. In brief, the question is whether an investor who purchases real estate on the basis of a nonrecourse mortgage can take depreciation in the same way, and in the same amount, as if the purchase was entirely self-financed. The answer is affirmative, as will be seen, and on it, to a considerable degree, rests the much-publicized contemporary phenomenon called the "tax shelter."

Mortgages are considered further in connection with the realization requirement at 13.03 and 13.04. The question of what constitutes a borrowing is revived with respect to sale-and-leaseback transactions at 15.01.

13.01 Nonrecourse Debt and the Depreciation Allowance; The *Crane* Rule. It may have occurred to the reader at various points that debt plays a peculiarly controversial role in the tax law, and this is nowhere truer than in regard to its effect on the depreciation allowance. As suggested just above, most commercial real estate investments—apartment buildings, office buildings, shopping centers—are financed in substantial part by nonrecourse mortgage loans, that is, loans which the investor-borrower is not personally liable to repay. The investor draws on his own resources for, say, 20% of the purchase price (or construction cost) of the property, and the mortgage lender, perhaps a bank or insurance company, supplies the balance of 80%. The mortgagee can foreclose on the property itself in the event of a default, but it cannot recover against the investor individually. The investor's risk is therefore limited to his equity; he can lose no more than his 20% out-of-pocket investment. If the property falls in value to less than the outstanding mortgage balance and is then foreclosed upon, the unpaid mortgage principal becomes the lender's loss alone.

Under these circumstances, should the investor be permitted to include the amount borrowed in the basis of the property for purposes of computing annual depreciation? Or should his basis be limited to his equity investment, on the ground, presumably, that the investor assumed no personal liability for the mortgage debt? As will be seen, the *overall* allowance for depreciation is the same under either approach. What differs is the scheduling of the allowance—larger in the early years if the mortgage is included in basis, smaller in the early years if it is not—and hence the timing of taxable income. At stake, as usual, is the anticipation or deferral of the property-owner's tax obligations, a factor which is said to be of major importance in promoting real estate investment.

Actually, the Supreme Court pretty well settled the issue more than forty years ago by holding in the *Crane* case that the "amount realized" by a seller of mortgaged property included both the cash received from the buyer and the face amount of the mortgage to which the property was subject.[2] The seller, it was said, had received a benefit by being relieved of the mortgage indebtedness, and hence her gain was computed by subtracting her basis in the property from the total of the cash received *plus* the mortgage. The Court was not directly concerned with the determination of "basis" under § 1012, or "adjusted basis" under § 1011(a); but the implication was clear and unavoidable. If mortgage indebtedness is included in "amount realized" when property is sold, then it must also be reflected in the seller's "adjusted basis" when acquired. To see why, assume an investor purchases an acre of land

2. *Crane v. Comm'r,* 331 U.S. 1 (1947).

for $4,000, paying $1,000 out of his own resources and borrowing the balance of $3,000 on a mortgage. A year later, after $200 has been paid on the mortgage principal, the property is sold for an amount exactly equal to its original purchase price, $4,000, the buyer paying $1,200 in cash and assuming the mortgage balance of $2,800. Under *Crane,* the amount realized by the seller is $4,000, that is, the cash received plus the mortgage assumed by the buyer. Since the seller has obviously realized no gain or loss on the transaction, it must be the case that his basis is also $4,000 and includes both cash investment and mortgage balance as well. If the mortgage were excluded from the seller's basis, a taxable gain of $2,800 would result; but this would plainly be improper as there has been no change in the value of the land during his ownership.

The effect of the *Crane* rule on the computation of gain or loss on sale of the property is thus entirely negligible. As long as the mortgage indebtedness is accorded symmetrical treatment, as long as it is dealt with in the same way at both ends of the transaction, the choice between inclusion and exclusion of the mortgage debt is a matter of no importance. As will have been surmised, however, gain or loss on sale is not the only relevant tax calculation. If the property is depreciable (the land mentioned above was not), the choice between inclusion and exclusion directly affects the size of the annual depreciation allowance, and that indeed turns out to be its real significance.

The Court of Appeals' decision in *Parker v. Delaney* [3] will serve as an illustration of what has just been said. Simplifying the facts, the taxpayer had acquired an apartment building in Year 1 with a cash investment of zero but subject to an unassumed mortgage of $273,000. Using the latter figure as his "cost," the taxpayer took depreciation deductions totalling $45,000 during the 10-year period of his ownership and paid $14,000 on the principal of the mortgage. In Year 11 he disposed of the property—actually, he abandoned it to the mortgagee—for no cash but still subject to an outstanding mortgage balance of $259,000 (that is, $273,000 less the $14,000 he had paid back). The taxpayer's adjusted basis for the property at that date was $228,000—$273,000 (original cost) less $45,000 of depreciation. Finding that the mortgage balance represented an "amount realized" in accordance with the *Crane* decision, the court held that the taxpayer had a taxable gain of $31,000—$259,000, the amount realized by the taxpayer, less his basis of $228,000—even though the disposition involved no cash receipt whatever.

---

3. 186 F.2d 455 (1st Cir.1950).

In a concurring opinion, Judge Magruder took the trouble to show how the calculation might have been carried out if the *Crane* case had been decided differently. Under a more "natural" reading of § 1001(b), he argued, the "amount realized" in the *Parker* case would properly be *zero* since the taxpayer had received no cash consideration when he quitclaimed the property to the mortgagee. By the same token the taxpayer's basis could not exceed $14,000— his cash payments on the mortgage principal—which would then have to be reduced by the $45,000 that had been allowed to him as depreciation. His adjusted basis would therefore be a negative figure, ($31,000), and when this was subtracted from the amount realized, zero, the resulting positive number, $31,000, would be recognized as taxable gain. The outcome would thus be identical to that arrived at by the court majority, but it would be reached without the artificial construction of "amount realized" which had been resorted to in *Crane*.

To summarize, the alternative calculations in *Parker v. Delaney* are as follows:

		Majority	**Magruder**
1.	Original cost	$273,000	$ –0–
2.	Addition to basis	–0–	14,000
3.	Depreciation allowed	(45,000)	(45,000)
4.	Adjusted basis	228,000	(31,000)
5.	Amount realized	259,000	–0–
6.	Gain recognized (5 − 4)	$ 31,000	$ 31,000

Neat, to be sure, but why bother? Why did Magruder go through a recalculation using a different formula when his final result was just the same as the majority's? The answer appears to be this: although compelled in this case to give effect to the $45,000 of depreciation deductions already allowed to the taxpayer in earlier years, Magruder apparently felt that the depreciation should have been limited to the taxpayer's cash investment in the property—that is, to the $14,000 which had actually been paid by the taxpayer to reduce the original mortgage principal. In effect, Magruder thought that the mortgage (for which the taxpayer was not personally liable) should have been excluded from the calculation for all purposes. If this had been done, the taxpayer's total depreciation allowance would have been only $14,000, and his basis as well as the amount realized and gain recognized on disposition of the property would all have been zero. To be sure, the net result is still the same in overall terms: under Magruder's scheme, $14,000 of deductions would offset $14,000 of investment; under the *Crane* rule, $45,000 of deductions were balanced by $14,000 of investment plus $31,000 of taxable gain. But the *timing* of both deductions and the taxable gain is very different. Under Magruder's approach, only $14,000 would be deductible between Years 1 and 10, with nothing taken into income in Year 11. Under *Crane,* $45,000 was deducted between Years 1 and 10, with $31,000 taxed in Year 11. For the usual reason—namely, that tax-payments are postponed when deductions are accelerated—taxpayers will always prefer the *Crane* approach to Magruder's alternative, and it is the *Crane* system which the law applies today.

But (resorting to our usual inquiry) which of the two approaches is correct as an original matter? Should nonrecourse mortgage indebtedness be included in determining the taxpayer's basis for depreciation purposes, or should it be excluded? At this point, I think, a further systematic illustration of the two "rules" will be useful. Judge Magruder's opinion is too brief for us to know exactly what procedure he intended to support, but the one attributed to him below seems consistent with his language and intent. Repeating the illustration used at 6.07(d), assume that the taxpayer purchases an asset—this time a "building"—with a useful life of 5 years and with no expected salvage value. The cost of the building is $4,000 and, for simplicity, assume that the entire purchase price is borrowed from a bank on an 8% mortgage. The annual mortgage amortization requirement is $1,000, which is allocated between interest and principal in accordance with the following schedule:

Year:	1	2	3	4	5	Total
Interest	$320	260	210	140	70	$1,000
Principal	$680	740	790	860	930	$4,000

Finally, assume that the investor anticipates net rents from the property (he has already found a lessee) of $1,200 a year for the five-year period.

Under an "ideal" system, the investor's annual taxable income would be $1,200 less the sum of (a) the annual interest payment to the bank and (b) the "true" cost of operating the building for the year, otherwise known as "depreciation." As already argued (see 6.07(d)), the correct way of computing annual depreciation is to compare the present value of anticipated cash-flows at the beginning of the taxable year with the present value of such cash-flows at the end of that year. The difference is the taxpayer's true cost of operation. Under this method of depreciation—previously referred to as the sinking-fund method—the annual depreciation allowance is lower in the earlier years and higher in the later years where anticipated cash flows are level. Annual income follows an inverse pattern. The above mortgage amortization schedule reflects precisely this approach from the bank's standpoint: the repayment of mortgage principal (equivalent to depreciation) starts low and steadily rises, while the interest component (equivalent to income) starts high and steadily declines.

Our real-estate investor is really in the same position as the bank vis-a-vis his own lessee, except that *he* anticipates an annual payment of $1,200. As shown at 6.07(d), the resulting allocation between income and principal recovery is as follows:

Year:	1	2	3	4	5	Total
Income	$627	513	410	295	155	$2,000
Principal	$573	687	790	905	1,045	$4,000

If allowable depreciation followed *this* schedule, the investor's annual taxable income would be higher at the beginning, and lower at the end, of the five-year term. Thus—

Taxable Income—Sinking Fund

Year:	1	2	3	4	5	Total
Net rents	$1,200	1,200	1,200	1,200	1,200	$6,000
Interest	320	260	210	140	70	1,000
Depreciation	573	687	790	905	1,045	4,000
Taxable Income	$307	253	200	155	85	$1,000

How close does either the *Crane* or the Magruder approach come to approximating these "ideal" results?

Under the *Crane* rule the investor's basis for his property is equal to its cost of $4,000 even though the entire purchase price was supplied by the lender. Using the straight-line method of depreciation, the annual depreciation allowance is therefore $800 (5 × $800 = $4,000). The investor's annual taxable income—deducting interest and depreciation from net rents—would then be as follows:

Taxable Income—Crane

Year:	1	2	3	4	5	Total
Net rents	$1,200	1,200	1,200	1,200	1,200	$6,000
Interest	320	260	210	140	70	1,000
Depreciation	800	800	800	800	800	4,000
Taxable Income	$ 80	140	190	260	330	$1,000

As predicted, the *Crane* rule produces lower taxable income in the early years, higher in the later—although the "ideal" trend is in the opposite direction. The investor's true taxable income in Year 1 is equal to the net cash received after the payment to the bank—$1,200 minus $1,000, or $200—plus the excess of his principal repayment over the cost of operation—$680 minus $573, or $107—for a total of $307. But *Crane* taxes him on only $80, so that $227 of Year 1 income is effectively deferred. The deferral in Year 2 is of $113; in Year 3 it is $10. These deferred amounts are picked up in Years 4 and 5, of course, but in the meanwhile the taxpayer has enjoyed the usual benefit of tax-postponement. Furthermore, his annual cash flow for the first three years—$200 a year—is greater than his taxable income in each of those years, a fact which leaves the taxpayer feeling pleased indeed.

By contrast, Magruder's approach—or, at least, the one generally attributed to him—is to include borrowed funds in basis only to the extent of principal actually repaid. Thus, the initial principal repayment of $680 would be recovered over a 5-year period at the straight-line rate of $136 a year. Year 2's principal repayment of $740 would be recovered over the remaining 4 years of the building's useful life at a rate of $185 a year, so that depreciation for Year 2 would be $136 carried over from Year 1 plus Year 2's $185, a total of $321. This would continue until in Year 5 all the unrecovered amounts from the earlier years, plus the entire principal payment made in Year 5, would be deducted as "depreciation." On this scheme, the investor's taxable income would be as follows:

Taxable Income—Magruder

Year:	1	2	3	4	5	Total
Net rents	$1,200	1,200	1,200	1,200	1,200	$6,000
Interest	320	260	210	140	70	1,000
Depreciation	136	321	584	1,014	1,945	4,000
Taxable Income	$744	619	406	46	(815)	$1,000

Magruder's trend—higher taxable income in the early years, lower in the later—is in the same direction as the "ideal," but it is pretty clear that the downward progression from Year 1 to Year 5 is far too steep. Income is being unduly anticipated, depreciation unduly deferred. The proof is that if the taxpayer sold the property at the start of Year 2 he would receive $3,427 from the buyer— *i.e.* the sum of the present values of the remaining four rental payments. He would then pay the bank the principal he still owed, $4,000 less $680 paid the first year, or $3,320. This would leave a net "amount realized" of $107. The taxpayer's basis, however, would be $544—the $680 paid in, less Year 1 depreciation of $136— so that the sale would actually generate a loss of $437—$544 less $107. It is evident, however, that there has been no change in the property's real value and that the "loss" is merely a bookkeeping artifact. Indeed, the loss of $437 is simply the difference between Magruder's Year 1 taxable income of $744 and the "ideal" Year 1 income of $307.

All of these dreary numbers really serve to show that the source of the distortion in cases like *Parker v. Delaney* is not the *Crane* rule and the treatment of debt but the failure (or inability) to require an appropriate method of depreciation.[4] Quite obviously, if the sinking-fund method were used, the results under *Crane* would be the same as those of the "ideal" system. Annual income would then be measured accurately, and the inclusion of debt in the taxpayer's basis would be harmless. But since depreciation is overstated in the earlier years (even under the straightline method), the *Crane* rule seems to open the way to (really, it just does nothing to restrain) the postponement of taxable income. Magruder's approach, by excluding debt from the taxpayer's basis, prevents such postponement—but the corrective is plainly excessive.

A final point (already much discussed at 6.05, above) should be noted. Even if the depreciation allowance is regarded as untouchable, Congress could still (if it wished) achieve results equivalent to the "ideal" by requiring a deferral of the taxpayer's annual interest deductions. Thus, if interest deductions of $227 the first year, $113 the second and $10 the third had to be deferred to the fourth and fifth years, the benefit of anticipating depreciation in the three earlier periods would obviously be washed out. As my illustration implies, however, the law fully recognizes the economic "fact" that the deductible interest component in the taxpayer's annual mortgage payments is higher at the start of the 5-year period ($320) than at the end (only $70). The consequence is that the taxpayer gets the best of both worlds: interest deductions are correctly computed (which means higher deductions in the earlier years), while depreciation allowances are incorrectly computed (which *also* means higher deductions in the earlier years). By contrast, as the reader may recall, the Code sometimes insists on symmetrical treatment of borrowing costs where the asset acquired with the borrowed funds qualifies for a tax preference. § 265, for example, disallows deductions for interest on funds borrowed to purchase tax-exempt municipal bonds; § 264 does the same in connection with single-premium insurance contracts; § 163(d) restricts the deduction of so-called "investment interest." No similar limitation exists with respect to interest on funds borrowed to purchase depreciable property, although, as already mentioned, permitting depreciation to be overstated is the practical equivalent of exempting a substantial portion of the income generated by such property from tax.

4. See Surrey, McDaniel and Pechman, *Federal Tax Reform for 1976* (1976), p. 19.

I do not mean to suggest that the conflict, or difference, between the two deduction schedules is accidental or that Congress is unaware of it. In adopting ACRS—which allows a taxpayer to recover the cost of depreciable property over a much shorter period than the useful life of the property itself—Congress specifically intended to encourage—indeed, to subsidize—investment in plant and equipment. Deferring interest deductions so as to match the deferral of income resulting from over-rapid depreciation would simply be a way of cancelling the subsidy, since almost all businesses borrow to finance their purchases of plant and equipment. In effect, then, the existing incentive "system" is of a twofold nature: on the one hand, it allows depreciation to be deducted in excess of actual economic cost; on the other, it imposes no corresponding restriction on the deductibility of related interest expense.

Tax shelters represent an extreme example of the twofold system just described. Having permitted the shelter device to spread and flourish to a remarkable degree, Congress finally took decisive action in 1986 by imposing restrictions on the deductibility of so-called passive activity losses. Those restrictions, with related background, are discussed in the section next following.

13.02 Tax Shelters: The "At-Risk" and "Passive Activity Loss" Limitations.

Commencing in the 1960's and continuing at an accelerated pace for some twenty years or so, tax shelters for high-income individuals became a major industry in this country and, in the view of many, a national scandal. Typically through the medium of real estate limited partnerships, top-bracket taxpayers were able, pretty much at will, to reduce their regular tax obligations to very low levels, if not indeed to zero. Public awareness of the tax-shelter phenomenon finally appeared to grow to some degree, and it may be that the willingness of Congress to adopt the 1986 reform legislation after decades of resistance or indifference can in part be traced to a general perception that high-paid people were systematically and habitually avoiding their apparent tax obligations by participating in legally sanctioned shelter arrangements.

In conventional form, the shelter consists of highly leveraged real estate in which individual investors participate as limited partners. The limited partners make initial cash payments to the shelter promoter which are largely absorbed by commissions, fees and similar charges, while the cost of the property itself is financed through a mortgage loan from a bank, insurance company or other institution. The loan is nonrecourse, but, under the *Crane* rule, the limited partners are entitled to treat the borrowed amount as if it were a personal loan and, hence, to include the indebtedness in basis. Rents received by the partnership are then expected to cover mortgage principal and interest requirements plus management fees. Sometimes, but not always, there is a small annual cash return to the investors.

As I attempt to illustrate below, the combination of (a) accelerated depreciation and (b) deductible interest on the nonrecourse mortgage loan inevitably generates substantial "losses" during the earlier years of the enterprise. Such losses are of course tax artifacts. If true economic depreciation were substituted for accelerated depreciation, then, usually, the enterprise would operate at or close to a break-even level—there would be no deductible "loss" to report—and the investment from the standpoint of the limited partners would have little purpose. The same result would arise if (while leaving accelerated depreciation untouched) otherwise deductible interest were deferred or disallowed as under Code § 265(a)(2). In fact, however, neither limitation was imposed. Instead, high-bracket taxpayers were enabled (encouraged) to combine tax-exempt income with tax-deductible borrowing and, by so doing, to reduce their taxable income to a minimum. The "loss" resulting from the shelter investment would be offset against income from other sources (chiefly personal services), even though the taxpayer himself would have lost little or nothing in economic terms.

(a) At-Risk. The 1986 Act made a threefold attack on tax-shelters—real estate shelters especially—by (1) substantially lengthening the depreciable lives of residential and commercial real estate, (2) partially extending the at-risk requirement (described below) to real estate investment, and most important (3) adopting "passive activity loss" rules which severely limit an individual taxpayer's ability to offset shelter losses against income from other sources. The first of these anti-shelter elements—longer depreciable lives—can be mentioned briefly: under § 168(c), residential real estate is assigned a 27.5-year and commercial real estate a 39–year useful life (increased from 31.5 by the 1993 Act), as compared with much shorter useful life periods under prior law. Since, as shown at 6.09, accelerated depreciation equals partial tax-exemption, the stretch-out of useful lives reduces the tax benefits that real estate investors have enjoyed in the past.

The "at-risk" requirement—added to the Code in 1976 and applicable to all depreciable property *other* than real estate—operates as a further limitation on tax shelters. In effect, § 465 withdraws or dilutes the *Crane* rule by restricting the amount of deductible loss from the ownership of depreciable property to the total amount of the taxpayer's economic investment—the amount he has "at risk." In turn, a taxpayer is considered at risk only with respect to the cash (or other property) that he has actually drawn from his own resources. Borrowed funds are deemed to be at risk if the taxpayer is personally liable for the debt or the debt is secured by his personal assets, but nonrecourse loans are *not* included. The investor cannot deduct any more than the amount placed at risk under this definition, and the amount so deducted reduces his investment correspondingly.

Before the adoption of § 465, tax shelter promotions involved not only real estate but many other kinds of large-scale depreciable assets—airplanes, computers, box-cars, river barges, motion pictures, mining rights, what-not. The shelter elements consisted of the usual dynamic duo—quick depreciation plus deductible interest on nonrecourse indebtedness, with resulting "losses" to the individual investors in the early years. With the adoption of § 465, non-real estate shelters (box-cars, etc.) pretty much lost their appeal. The reason, of course, was that investors would generally be unwilling to assume *personal* liability for shelter debt, which might run to 99% of the entire cost of the property. As stated, however, § 465 specifically omitted to cover real estate. For better or worse, Congress was persuaded that the public interest justified special incentives for housing and construction, including the continuation of the *Crane* rule. The real estate industry benefited most handsomely; with equipment shelters effectively ruled out, real estate became, and for some ten years remained, the only shelter game in town.

In 1985, the Treasury proposed that "at-risk" be extended to include real estate as well as other depreciable property, and in the 1986 Act Congress did modify the real estate exception, though in a limited manner only. Nonrecourse loans from *outside* lenders—banks and other institutions—continue to be free of "at-risk": in effect, with respect to conventional institutional financing, the *Crane* rule applies as before and investors are still entitled to include such third-party debt for the purpose calculating deductible losses. With respect to *inside* financing, however—that is, loans made by promoters or by the seller of the property—"at risk" credit is allowed to the buyer-investors only if the latter are personally liable for the debt. Congress was aware that lender-sellers sometimes make nonrecourse purchase-money "loans" well in excess of the true value of the property sold with no real intention of ever collecting the principal amount of such loans—while investors, with no threat of personal liability, welcome such value inflation as a source of additional depreciation deductions.

As noted above, however, once personal liability is required the investor will lose enthusiasm for the scheme just described unless he somehow trusts the lender never to enforce his claim. By contrast, third-party lenders—banks, etc.—are much less likely to make loans that exceed the property's true value and much more likely to seek full repayment of the loan when due. Concerned to prevent abuse of the *Crane* rule, Congress extended the "at-risk" requirement to promoters' and sellers' loans but, in effect, excluded bona fide third-party financing.

(b) Passive Activity Losses. The most significant step taken by Congress towards eliminating real estate tax-shelters was the addition in 1986 of § 469, which segregates so-called "passive activity losses" and bars their use as an offset against income from unrelated sources. As stated, the purpose of shelter investment is to create artificial losses (resulting, largely, from high leverage and over-rapid depreciation) that can be deducted from gross income generally. In limiting the deduction of passive losses to income from similarly "passive" sources, the 1986 Code provision in effect denies their use as an offset against personal service and other active business income, as well as against "portfolio" income such as dividends, interest and capital gains. The evident consequence is that real property investments of which the chief aim is to generate "losses," but which are otherwise without positive economic value, must cease to have appeal.

An illustration (oversimplified) may help to show both how conventional tax shelters have been used in the past and how the "passive activity loss" rules now operate to inhibit them. As in 13.01 above, assume that a taxpayer buys a "building" for $4,000, borrowing the entire purchase price from a third party-lender at an interest rate of 8%. The loan, which is nonrecourse, is repayable in equal annual installments of $1,000 over 5 years. Once again, the interest/principal schedule is as follows:

Year:	1	2	3	4	5	Total
Interest	$320	260	210	140	70	$1,000
Principal	$680	740	790	860	930	$4,000

In our earlier illustration, the taxpayer was able to find a lessee who rented the property for $1,200 a year, so that the investment generated a positive annual cash-flow of $200 and evidently made sense in purely economic terms. Suppose, however, that we eliminate such economic benefit by stipulating that the lessee will pay rent of only $1,000 a year; in effect, the taxpayer is to serve merely as a pipeline from the lessee to the lender, receiving $1,000 from the former as rent and paying $1,000 to the latter as interest and principal, but netting nothing for himself.[4a]

Apart from taxes (and a hope that the property may appreciate) the arrangement is altogether pointless; but if we stir in (a) the *Crane* rule, (b) straight-line depreciation and (c) annual interest deductions, we will have cooked up a very serviceable little tax shelter. Thus, obviously—

Year:	1	2	3	4	5	Total
Net rents	$1,000	1,000	1,000	1,000	1,000	$5,000
Interest	320	260	210	140	70	1,000
Depreciation	800	800	800	800	800	4,000
Taxable Income/ (Loss)	$ (120)	(60)	(10)	60	130	-0-

Assuming he expects to have income from other sources and to pay tax at a rate of (say) 30% throughout the 5-year period, then— § 469 aside—the taxpayer will save $36 (30% of $120) in taxes the first year by offsetting his "loss" against such other income, $18 the second year and $3 the third—a total tax-saving of $57. In all three years his after-tax income will exceed his pre-tax income, while his economic income will be unaffected. The taxes saved in years 1–3 will have to be repaid in Years 4 and 5, but, as usual, there is a tangible and substantial benefit in deferring to later periods taxes otherwise due currently.[4b]

When Year 4 does finally arrive, moreover, the taxpayer (if he is lucky and the property *has* appreciated) may be able to sell the shelter for an amount sufficient to reimburse the tax then due on his built-in gain. Such gain would necessarily be equal to the

---

4a. Admittedly—see 6.09(b)—there would be a question as to whether the "lease" qualified as such for tax purposes. It almost surely would if the taxpayer made some equity investment to begin with and had some expectation of a residual value at the end of the term. Adding these factors would complicate the example without really changing the results; however, a *caveat* is in order.

4b. Familiar question: Why did the lender agree to this deal instead of acquiring the depreciable property directly? The lender, after all, has to report full economic income—$320 the first year, $260 the second, etc.—because he owns a financial asset (the borrower's mortgage note) and receives taxable interest. If the lender had invested in the building instead of the mortgage, his taxable income after depreciation would be only $200 ($1,000 − $800) in the first and each succeeding year. In effect, the lender has permitted the borrower to enjoy the benefit of income-deferral—a total of $190 over years 1–3—while enduring the penalty of income-anticipation himself. But why would he do that? The answer—already suggested at 6.02 in discussing *Starr's Estate*— must be that the lender confronts lower tax rates than the borrower under a graduated rate structure or for some reason is wholly or partially exempt from tax. For a consideration—brokerage commission, higher interest rate— the lender is willing and eager to sell his advantageous tax position to the borrower and the borrower is happy to buy it. As always, it takes two to shelter; and as always, the only loser is the Treasury.

income previously deferred, that is, $190. Under the rule of *Parker v. Delaney*, the taxpayer, on disposing of the property, would be treated as realizing the remaining mortgage debt—$860 + 930 = $1,790—while his basis would have been reduced to $1,600 ($4,000 − (3 × $800)). Hence his gain (for tax purposes) would be $190 and his tax, as stated, would be $57 at the assumed 30% rate. To recoup the $57 he would need to sell the property for $81.42 above the mortgage debt ($81.42 − (.30 × $81.42) = $57)—in which event the shelter would have worked out very well indeed.

New § 469 effectively eliminates the shelter benefits just described by imposing a kind of quarantine on the so-called "passive activity losses" recorded in Years 1–3. The term "passive activity" refers to any business activity in which the taxpayer does not "materially participate." Rental activities are treated as "passive" (unless, under a 1993 amendment, the taxpayer is engaged in such activities on essentially a full-time basis), and the owner of a limited partnership interest is treated as being engaged in a "passive activity" irrespective of his actual participation. A "passive activity loss"—determined by taking into account all items of deduction attributable to the passive activity, including interest on mortgage indebtedness—is not disallowed, but is deductible only against income from that or another passive activity, with indefinite carryforward. As already emphasized, neither personal service income, nor active business income, nor income from securities investments, is treated as passive activity income, and hence none of these taxable receipts can be offset by shelter "losses." A full-scale segregation is thus accomplished. Tax shelters are banished to a separate schedule, in effect, and are not allowed to mix with other elements of the individual's tax-return.

The work-out of all this in our illustrative case should be easy to surmise. Assuming the taxpayer has no other passive activity income, the losses incurred in Years 1–3 will offset nothing in those years but can be carried forward to offset any passive activity income that materializes in subsequent periods—presumably, in Years 4 and 5. Such suspended losses are also deductible if and when the taxpayer disposes of the shelter activity. Thus, as indicated, the taxpayer in our illustration must realize a gain of at least $190—the difference between the unpaid mortgage principal and his adjusted basis—if he disposes of the property at the start of Year 4. Since his prior losses would have produced no tax benefit owing to the "passive activity" restriction, it would be improper to tax his equally artificial gain at that point and the losses then serve to eliminate that gain.

The new provision bristles with interpretative difficulties—
what constitutes "material participation" is only the most obvious—and the Regulations issued by the Treasury are both lengthy
and complex. However, as suggested at 6.05 in connection with
our discussion of tax arbitrage (of which real estate shelters are
simply an example), it is essentially the presence of an exempt
income-source—here, over-rapid cost recovery—that is responsible
for the problem.

One last reminder may be in order. As just shown, new § 469
prevents taxpayers from combining quick depreciation with interest
deductions so as to create artificial losses that can be used to offset
income from unrelated sources. It does not, however, in any way
restrict the "internal sheltering" that was illustrated in the preceding Section. There, the taxpayer, having rented his property to a
lessee for $1,200 a year, was able to defer a substantial proportion
of his true economic income ($227 in Year 1, $113 in Year 2, etc.) to
later periods through a combination of allowable depreciation and
interest deductions. Although income is thus understated for tax
purposes, § 469, aimed solely at restricting losses, obviously has no
application. Put otherwise, § 469 does not increase taxable income
by cutting back on the depreciation and interest deductions as such;
rather, it *limits* the shelter-effect to the positive income generated
by the investment itself.

13.03 Mortgage of Appreciated Property—The Woodsam Case.

Suppose an investor purchased certain commercial real estate—say a small office building—some years ago at a cost of
$100,000. Real estate prices having steadily climbed, the property
today has a value of $350,000. The investor, needing money for a
wholly separate purpose, now decides to raise some cash by placing
a mortgage on the property. To keep matters simple (even if
slightly unrealistic), assume the investor is able to borrow an
amount equal to the entire value of the property, that is, $350,000.
He is of course prepared to put the property up as security, but he
does not wish to be personally liable for the debt or to make other
of his assets available to the lender in case of default. Prospective
mortgagees, it turns out, are eager for the business, and the
investor is able to obtain the funds he wants by issuing a nonrecourse mortgage. As already explained, if default occurs, the
debt can be satisfied through foreclosure of the property itself, but
the mortgagee can make no claim for any deficiency against the
debtor individually, whatever the value of the other assets in his
portfolio.

The mortgage transaction purports to be a loan, of course, and loans (even secured loans) are not usually regarded as realizations. But isn't this situation somewhat different? In view of the absence of personal liability, can't it reasonably be argued that the investor has in fact realized a gain to the extent that the mortgage proceeds exceed his basis in the property? The investor, after all, has withdrawn $350,000 in cash—$250,000 more than his original investment. To be sure, if the property continues to appreciate, he will presumably elect to make the amortization payments on schedule. But if the market shifts around and the value of the property declines, he can simply abandon the property to the lender without personal obligation for the deficiency. The investor has thus terminated his risk on the downside and has converted the property's appreciation into cash. Accordingly, why not regard the mortgage transaction as a sale and treat the excess of "amount realized" over basis as a taxable gain?

If this view were accepted, the investor would recognize gain of $250,000 immediately. If the property were sold outright in a later year for, say, $400,000, the investor would have a further taxable gain of $50,000. The entire appreciation would thus have been taxed in two stages: $250,000 at the time the mortgage was issued and $50,000 later on. By comparison, if the mortgage transaction is *not* treated as a realization, then nothing is taxed currently and the gain of $300,000 is deferred until the later year when the property is sold.

This now-familiar contrast between anticipation and deferral suggests that taxpayers would generally resist realization in the circumstances given. In the *Woodsam* case,[5] however, it was the taxpayer who argued *for* realization and the government which successfully opposed it. The reason for the switch in positions, evidently, is that the year in which the mortgage loan was made and the alleged realization took place was barred to the government by the statute of limitations. This, however, did not prevent the taxpayer from arguing that a taxable (but not a tax-collectable) realization had occurred at that point, and that the basis of the property at the time it was subsequently sold—which was the transaction at issue—should be increased to reflect the earlier event. The government—perhaps anxious to avoid a whipsaw in this and in all the similar cases which would at once have been brought forward—argued that neither a realization *nor* a step-up in basis had taken place in the earlier period. The Court agreed. Stressing that the mortgagee remained a mere creditor and that the

5. *Woodsam Associates, Inc. v. Comm'r*, 198 F.2d 357 (2d Cir.1952).

taxpayer as equity-owner would get the benefit of any further property appreciation, the court refused to treat the nonrecourse loan differently from a loan with personal liability; it therefore held that the mortgage was not a "disposition" which produced a taxable gain. As a result, the taxpayer's entire gain was taxed in the year of sale, which was still open under the statute of limitations.

From one standpoint the *Woodsam* case is merely another illustration of the ambiguous nature of the realization requirement. The decision could, I think, as easily have gone for the taxpayer as for the Treasury. A nonrecourse mortgage loan can quite respectably be viewed *either* as (i) a conventional borrowing plus a right in the borrower to "put" the property to the lender (by defaulting on the loan) in the event the value of the property should decline, or (ii) a conventional sale plus a right in the seller to "call" the property (by amortizing the mortgage) in the event the value of the property should rise. Either characterization is plausible, and one suspects that the court may have been led to accept the first and reject the second as much because it found the taxpayer's argument "novel" as because of any fundamental perceptions about the concept of realization. Perhaps the court was also moved by administrative considerations: a holding for the taxpayer might have obliged the Service to examine the financial condition of all borrowers, even including those who do assume personal liability for their debts. If the borrower's resources are negligible apart from the property pledged, as where the borrower is a corporation with no other substantial assets, the practical effect is roughly the same as if the loan were made on a non-recourse basis, and perhaps a realization would have to be found in both cases. As suggested at 3.01 in connection with stockholder borrowing, however, the task of distinguishing loans from non-loans is burdensome, and it is no doubt usually best avoided if possible.

At all events, we can now combine the *Crane* and *Woodsam* cases in a single illustration. Suppose a taxpayer purchases an apartment building for $4,000, paying $1,000 out of his own funds and borrowing the balance of $3,000 on a nonrecourse mortgage. The property subsequently appreciates to $10,000 and the taxpayer, as in *Woodsam*, borrows an additional $6,000 by adding that amount to the mortgage. What is the taxpayer's basis for the property? Answer: $4,000. The subsequent borrowing of $6,000 represents untaxed property appreciation and is not included in the taxpayer's basis. That, in effect, is the holding in *Woodsam*. The earlier borrowing of $3,000 is part of his original cost, however, and *is* included in basis under *Crane*. If the property appreciated no

275

further and were finally sold for $10,000—the taxpayer receiving $1,000 cash and the mortgage, now $9,000, being assumed by the buyer—the "amount realized" would be the full $10,000. The later as well as the earlier borrowing would be included for this purpose and the taxpayer would recognize a gain of $6,000. The latter outcome is arithmetically correct since the taxpayer has realized a total of $7,000 cash as against an initial cash investment of only $1,000.

Crane and Woodsam thus apparently differ in their effect on the computation of basis. Initial borrowing is included in basis under *Crane,* while subsequent borrowing is excluded from basis under *Woodsam* owing to the absence of a taxable realization. In practical effect, however, this difference will often prove illusory. Thus in the illustration just given suppose that the $6,000 subsequently borrowed is invested in a *second* apartment building. The taxpayer will then be allowed depreciation on a total property cost of $10,000—$4,000 for the old property under *Crane,* and $6,000 for the new property *despite* the absence of a realization under *Woodsam.* In effect the limitation described in the preceding paragraph—no step-up in basis without a taxable realization—has been evaded: although the basis of the old property is unaffected by the subsequent borrowing, there is obviously nothing to stop the taxpayer from reinvesting the borrowed funds in another depreciable asset. *Crane* and *Woodsam* thus *both* operate to permit taxpayers to include untaxed capital in property basis—one directly, the other indirectly. From the government's standpoint, therefore, the *Woodsam* case creates (or confirms) a sizeable loophole, and it might very well have been better if the decision had gone the other way.

Indeed, there is irony (of a sort that occurs often in the tax field; see *Taft v. Bowers* at 4.01) in the fact that the government was the *winning* litigant in the *Crane* and *Woodsam* cases. In each case the particular issue concerned the proper method of computing gain on the final sale of property. In *Crane* the government had to argue *for* the inclusion of the purchase-money mortgage in the amount realized by the taxpayer; in *Woodsam* it had to argue *against* the notion that subsequent mortgaging might constitute a realization. The government won in both instances, but the victories have cost it plenty.

13.04   Dispositions of Encumbered Assets—*Tufts* and *Diedrich.*

(a) Excessively mortgaged property. Despite some ambiguity in the opinion itself, tax commentators, I think, have generally felt

that the Supreme Court's decision in *Crane* stands for a simple principle of tax-symmetry. If a nonrecourse mortgage is included in the property-owner's basis for purposes of computing annual depreciation, then the unpaid balance of that mortgage must be included as well in determining "amount realized." Put differently, if the tax law treats nonrecourse debt as a real cost when property is acquired, then, to be consistent, "relief" from such debt has to be treated as a real benefit when the property is sold. *Parker v. Delaney* so holds, and notwithstanding Judge Magruder's contrasting view, the general question is now settled beyond argument.

Both in *Crane* and in *Parker v. Delaney,* however, the courts assumed that the property—real estate in each case—had a market value that was at least equal to the amount of the unpaid mortgage at the time the property was disposed of. Even apart from tax-symmetry considerations, therefore, it was more or less reasonable to say that the taxpayer had been "relieved" of the full mortgage debt when the property (subject to the mortgage) was transferred to another. But suppose, in a given case, that the securing property is worth *less* than the mortgage debt. In that circumstance, a taxpayer who is not personally liable would have no economic reason to satisfy the debt in full; threatened with foreclosure, the taxpayer could simply abandon the property to the mortgagee. Paying a lender $100 to retain title to property worth only $99 is hardly sensible as long as the lender's security is limited to the property itself. If the property is disposed of at that point, isn't the measure of "relief," and hence the "amount realized," the lower value of the property rather than the full amount of the debt?

The Supreme Court furnished a negative answer in *Commissioner v. Tufts,*[6] decided in 1983. Rounding and simplifying, the taxpayers in *Tufts* borrowed $1.85 million to construct an apartment building. They made no cash investment of their own and their debt was evidenced by a nonrecourse note secured by a mortgage on the building. Over the next two years the taxpayers took depreciation (and other) deductions of $450,000, which reduced their basis in the building to $1.4 million. Unable to operate the building profitably, and having repaid none of the loan principal, they sold the property (perhaps at the insistence of the mortgagee) to another investor. The latter paid the taxpayers nothing in cash but took the building subject to the mortgage. On the date of the sale, the fair market value of the property was not greater than the taxpayers' adjusted basis of $1.4 million. Since the value

---

6.   461 U.S. 300 (1983).

of the property represented the limit of their liability, the taxpayers argued that no more than $1.4 million could be included in "amount realized" and, hence, that no gain should be recognized on the transaction.

Finding that *Crane* "stands for the ... proposition ... that a non-recourse loan should be treated as a true loan," the Court held that the taxpayers had realized the full unpaid balance of the mortgage debt—$1.85 million—and, accordingly, must recognize a taxable gain of $450,000. The taxpayers, said the Court, had included the loan in their basis "on the understanding" (*i.e.,* for tax purposes) that they had an obligation to repay the full amount. When the obligation was relieved, they necessarily "realize[d] value to that extent under § 1001(b)." Accordingly, in determining amount realized, "the fair market value of the property ... becomes irrelevant." In effect, borrowing with personal liability and borrowing without personal liability are to be treated alike for this purpose.

The decision in *Tufts,* as has been said,[7] is entirely unremarkable once the need for tax symmetry is acknowledged, and indeed the final outcome is merely a repeat of the result reached in *Parker v. Delaney.* As in the earlier case, the appropriate measure of gain in *Tufts* was the difference between the deductions allowed, $450,000, and the amount invested by the taxpayers, $0. To be sure, there was an economic loss to someone—the property did fall in value from $1.85 to $1.4. The true loser, however, was not Tufts but the mortgage-lender, which (except that it was a federal agency) would appropriately recognize the loss if and when it finally foreclosed.

In a concurring opinion, Justice O'Connor proposed another— and in some respects a more coherent—way of analyzing the *Tufts* transaction. Drawing on a thoughtful *amicus* brief, O'Connor suggested that the transfer of excessively mortgaged property might be viewed as a twofold event consisting of (a) a sale of the asset itself, the apartment building, for its actual market value of $1.4, and (b) use of the constructive proceeds (again, $1.4) to satisfy the taxpayers' debt of $1.85. The sale, on this view, would generate *no* taxable gain, because the amount realized by the taxpayers was no greater than their adjusted basis for the building. The debt repayment, however, would result in $450,000 of "cancellation of indebtedness income" in accordance with the rule of the *Kirby Lumber* case (3.02). The *amount* of income to be recognized— $450,000—would be no different from that recognized by the Court majority, but it happens that cancellation of indebtedness income is

7. Andrews,—*On Beyond Tufts,* 61 Taxes 949 (1983).

"ordinary" while gain from the disposition of an apartment building is likely to be capital gain, taxable at a bargain rate. The Court majority conceded that the concurring view might be justified if the issue were *de novo,* but it concluded that, under existing authority, the extinguishment of debt must be regarded as part of the property sale itself and could not be viewed as a separate transaction between the borrower and lender.

A final *Tufts* -related issue—really, a limitation on the scope of the *Tufts* decision—should be mentioned. Having convinced the Court that the original mortgage loan of $1.85 must be treated as an "amount realized" by the property sellers, is the Commissioner also bound to treat the property buyer—Tufts' vendee—as having an equivalent "cost" of $1.85? If so, property having little actual value but subject to large nonrecourse indebtedness (the larger the better, indeed) would become attractive to investors solely as a source of depreciation and accrued interest deductions. Thus, a high-bracket taxpayer might be eager to acquire such property even though he never expected either to realize a penny of rents or to see the property increase in value, and *certainly* never intended to pay off the mortgage debt. His sole aim would be to obtain the tax benefits that derive from the ownership of a depreciable asset whose "cost" for tax purposes would include the full amount of the unassumed mortgage. For its part the mortgagee would often be content with small annual interest payments (as stated, no payments on mortgage principal would ever be made), since foreclosure might gain it even less.

Probably, however, where property is *known* to be worth less than the nonrecourse debt at the time the property is acquired, the purchaser's basis should be limited to the lower value figure—$1.4 in the *Tufts* case. To be sure, *Crane* held that non-recourse debt is to be treated as a real cost to the purchaser of encumbered property despite the absence of personal liability. But this assumes that the "debt" is real debt—that an investor would, or might, be willing to incur the obligation for objective economic reasons. Quite obviously, however, no one would be willing to pay more for property, or borrow more to buy it, than the property was actually worth. It follows that if (as with Tufts' vendee) the nonrecourse mortgage exceeds the value of the property *when acquired,* such excess should not be regarded as real indebtedness and should not be included in the buyer's "cost."

Assuming (with some support from the decided cases [8]) that the conclusion just stated is correct, what happens when Tufts' vendee

8. *Pleasant Summit Land Corp. v. Comm'r,* 863 F.2d 263 (3d Cir.1988);   and see, *Franklin's Estate v. Comm'r,* 544 F.2d 1045 (9th Cir.1976). The issue

sells the property—still subject, say, to the original mortgage of $1.85—to yet another purchaser? At that point the rule of symmetry should take hold. Having been allowed a "cost" of $1.4, Tufts' vendee should be treated as having realized the same amount on sale, and this would be true even if, by then, the market value of the property had declined still further.

Summarizing, it turns out that the value of property subject to a nonrecourse mortgage is highly relevant in determining a purchaser's "cost" at the time the property is acquired, but altogether irrelevant in determining his "amount realized" when the same property is sold. At acquisition, the question is whether the nonrecourse obligation is or is not true debt, and for this purpose value matters. On sale, the only applicable principle is one of tax-symmetry, and for this purpose value couldn't matter less.

(b) Conditional gifts. The *Diedrich* case,[9] decided by the Supreme Court in 1982, raises yet another question about the application of the *Crane* rule—namely, whether (or how) the rule affects *gifts* of encumbered property. As background, suppose a taxpayer owns stock with a basis of $20 and a value of $100. Pledging the stock as sole security, the taxpayer borrows an amount equal to the appreciation—$80—and then gives the stock, subject to the indebtedness, to another family member. Although gifts are not in themselves realization events, it is obvious here that the taxpayer is partly a giver but partly also a seller. *Tufts* makes it clear that a transfer of encumbered property generates an "amount realized"— just as if the transferee had paid cash instead of taking on the debt—and the courts have had little difficulty in finding, under the facts assumed, that the transaction is a sale as well as a gift.[10] Having invested $20 in the asset transferred, having borrowed $80 in cash with no personal obligation to repay, and having terminated his interest in the asset by conveying it to someone else, the transferor plainly falls within the *Tufts* rule and gain recognition follows. This is true even though the transaction involves family members: as indicated throughout Part C, the Code does *not* employ a systematic notion of family unity—spouses as well as parents and children are viewed as separate persons for tax purposes—so that a sale of property by one family member to another is, in general, treated the same as a transaction between strangers.

is discussed in Jensen, *The Unanswered Question in Tufts: What Was the Purchaser's Basis*, 10 Va.Tax Rev. 455 (1991).

9. *Diedrich v. Comm'r*, 457 U.S. 191 (1982).

10. *Estate of Levine v. Comm'r*, 634 F.2d 12 (2d Cir.1980).

Though it seems a bit grudging, donors frequently make gifts of property on condition that the donee pay the resulting federal gift tax, which, under § 2502(d), is expressly made a legal liability of the donor. In many cases, presumably, the donee is obliged to sell the property to obtain the necessary funds. Assuming that the donee—a child, say, or a trust—is in a lower bracket than the donor, however, any gain thereby realized will be taxed at a lower rate than would apply if the donor had sold the property himself to pay the gift tax or had borrowed against the property and then transferred it to the donee subject to the debt. The question, obviously, is whether the conditional gift device actually succeeds in shifting the potential gain to the donee, or whether the "condition"—payment by the donee of the donor's gift tax obligation—turns the gift itself into a taxable event.

In *Diedrich,* the taxpayer made a conditional gift to his children of stock having a basis in his hands of $50,000 and fair market value of $300,000. The federal gift tax, which the children agreed to pay, was $60,000. Resolving a conflict among the circuits, the Supreme Court held that the assumption of gift tax liability by the donees produced a measurable economic benefit to the donor and hence should be regarded as the equivalent of cash consideration. Although the donor's aim was to make a gift—really a *net* gift—it was also his intent, in adding the payment condition, to be relieved of a personal tax obligation. Citing both *Old Colony* and *Crane,* the Court sustained the Commissioner in treating the property transfer as part gift and part sale.

With the Court's approval, the Commissioner calculated Diedrich's gain under § 1001(a) by simply subtracting his property basis, $50,000, from the gift tax obligation assumed by the donees, $60,000. The taxable gain was thus $10,000—an odd result, in a way, because it is less (by a factor of five) than the gain the taxpayer would have recognized if he had sold just enough stock to pay the gift tax himself. Had he followed the latter course, the taxpayer would have had to sell $60,000 worth of stock, which would be one-fifth ($60,000/$300,000) of his total shares. His basis for the shares sold—one-fifth of $50,000—would have been $10,000 and the gain recognized ($60,000 − $10,000) would therefore have been $50,000. In effect, while persuading the Court that part-gift/part-sale was the right way to characterize conditional gifts, the Commissioner used a computational formula—allocating all of the transferor's cost to the "sale" element—that may still make it advantageous to employ the conditional gift device. Indeed, had the gift tax liability been no greater than Diedrich's basis, there would have been no taxable gain whatever under the Commissioner's formula despite $250,000 of value appreciation in the property transferred.

A loose end: Using the same numbers, what would be the basis of the stock in the hands of Diedrich's donee? Total appreciation was $250,000. Since the donor was held to have recognized a gain of $10,000 on the transfer, the donee's basis just *has* to be a number such that an immediate sale of the stock for $300,000 will generate recognition to the donee of the remaining $240,000 of untaxed appreciation. Sure enough: in the case of part gift/part sale transactions, the Regulations [11] provide that the basis of the property in the hands of the donee shall be the amount paid for the property (here $60,000) or the donor's basis (here $50,000), whichever is greater. It follows that the donee's basis in *Diedrich* is $60,000, and a prompt sale of the stock for $300,000 will indeed produce further taxable gain of $240,000.

Shall we go on? Suppose the donor's basis in *Diedrich* had been $100,000, so that the amount of unrealized appreciation was only $200,000. Since the gift tax liability assumed by the donee, $60,000, would then be less than the donor's basis, the donor would recognize no gain or loss on the transfer; in effect, the donor would simply have recouped a portion of his $100,000 investment. As above, the donee's basis would be the amount paid for the property ($60,000) or the donor's basis ($100,000), whichever was greater. The donee's basis would thus be $100,000 and a prompt sale of the stock for $300,000 would generate taxable gain of $200,000—once again the right result.

SECTION 14. DEFERRED PAYMENT TRANSACTIONS

14.01 In General. The tax treatment of deferred payment transactions has been a vexing problem for the income tax virtually from the beginning. In general, and apart from any specific legislative intervention, sales of property on a deferred payment basis should be treated no differently from sales of property for a single lump-sum payment. The buyer's promise to pay stated amounts in the future—usually represented by notes or other evidence of indebtedness—normally has an ascertainable market value, and this market value constitutes an "amount realized" by

----

11. Regs. § 1.1015–4(a). For transfers made after 1976, the donee's basis would be increased by the proportion of the gift tax that is attributable to the net appreciation in the value of the gift. Code § 1015(d)(6).

the seller. The difference between that amount and his basis would be the measure of the seller's gain or loss. To illustrate, suppose a taxpayer owns an apartment building with an adjusted basis of $20,000 and a fair market value of $100,000. He sells the property to another investor for $10,000 cash and a $90,000 mortgage payable in 9 equal annual installments with interest at 12%. Assuming that the fair market value of the mortgage is equal to its face amount, the taxpayer would be treated as having realized $100,000 in the year of sale and would therefore recognize and pay tax on his entire gain of $80,000. In effect, the mortgage debt would be viewed as payment for the property sold—the equivalent of cash—and the transaction would be viewed as "closed" even though the greater part of the purchase price is not to be received in cash until later years. Having recognized his gain in full, the taxpayer would hold the mortgage at a basis of $90,000, and the annual amortization payments made by the buyer would be allocated in part to taxable interest and in part to what would now be a tax-paid capital investment in the buyer's indebtedness.

The "income" definition and the concept of "amount realized" thus make no generic distinction between sales for cash and sales for future payments—in effect, realization does not depend on the medium of exchange. Yet despite this general approach, one cannot help, I think, feeling some uneasiness about the idea of treating a "mere" claim to future payments as the equivalent of money. In the first place, the seller may have difficulty obtaining the funds to pay the tax liability that arises from the sale. Assuming that the $80,000 gain above is taxed at a rate of (say) 30%, the seller would owe a current tax of $24,000. As this exceeds the $10,000 cash down-payment received from the buyer in the year of sale, the seller may be compelled to dispose of the mortgage or of other assets, or to borrow himself, to obtain the balance. Such actions may well be costly and contrary to his preference (although, of course, paying taxes is always contrary to one's preference). Second, although a conventional real estate mortgage is easy to value, suppose the deferred payment claim is secured by some relatively unfamiliar type of property—say a patent or a business interest—or is merely a personal obligation of the buyer. Or suppose it is contingent in amount. Since no active market for such claims exists, the danger of an erroneous valuation is obviously considerable and the taxpayer may suffer if the value assigned to the claim by appraisal turns out to be too high.

As might be expected, the tax law has developed a response to both of the problems just mentioned—one a statutory relief provision (the installment sale method), the other a judicial creation (the "fair market value" rule). Both are described in the paragraphs that follow. Where applicable, each enables a taxpayer who has made a deferred payment sale to postpone recognition until the buyer's obligation has actually been reduced to cash. The two postponement schemes operate differently, however, and as will be seen each provides a "solution" that goes somewhat beyond the problem to be solved.

14.02 The Installment Method. Substantially revised and expanded by Congress in 1980, Code § 453 now provides, as a general rule, that gains from deferred payment transactions involving real estate and other investment property shall be spread out proportionately over the entire payment period. In the illustration above, one-tenth of the total purchase price of the building—$10,000 out of a total of $100,000—was received in cash in the year of sale. Accordingly, only $8,000 of the seller's $80,000 gain ($\frac{1}{10} \times$ $80,000) will be taxed in that year. As the mortgage principal is payable at the rate of $10,000 a year in each of the succeeding 9 years, a like proportion of the gain will be recognized as each installment is received. The seller's tax will, of course, be payable on the same schedule, *i.e.*, $2,400 in the year of sale and $2,400 each year thereafter, assuming again a tax rate of 30%. Cash receipts are thus at all times in excess of the tax due.

In the past the installment method of reporting gain was elective—taxpayers wanting installment treatment had to say so specifically when filing their tax returns. The election was hedged about with various restrictions, but given the advantages of deferred recognition the great majority of deferred payment sellers did in fact so elect. Recognizing this, Congress in 1980 changed the law to make installment treatment the *general* rule, and it also eliminated most of the conditions that had applied to the elective provision. Under the amended section taxpayers are still free to elect *out* of the installment method and recognize their full gains in the year of sale, but unless a very special reason exists (*e.g.*, a loss carryforward that is due to expire in the same year) presumably few will choose to do so.

Most commentators have approved the 1980 legislation on grounds of simplification. It may be worth observing, nevertheless, that § 453, when applicable, actually results in a *reduction* of tax liability and thus has consequences for the taxpayer that are substantive, not merely procedural. If the property-seller in the illustration above had sold his building for $100,000 cash, his tax liability of $24,000 would have been payable at once. Having sold on the installment method, his tax is payable at the rate of $2,400 a year over a 10-year period. The present value of the latter obligation, discounted at an after-tax rate of (say) 8%, is only about $16,100. Hence, it can be said that § 453 has effectively reduced the seller's tax by some $7,900.

Whether the section *should* have this consequence can, perhaps, be questioned. The apparently benign object of § 453 is to make it easier for installment sellers to pay their taxes by associating gain recognition with the receipt of cash. In resorting to the technique of income-deferral, however, the section in effect imposes different burdens on taxpayers who otherwise appear to be similarly situated. Thus, property sellers who desire or are willing to invest in their vendee's installment obligations are taxed at one "rate," while those who sell for cash because they prefer to invest the funds received in securities issued by other borrowers are taxed at another and higher rate, everything else being equal. But no reason in policy justifies discriminating between the two sets of investors (nor, perhaps, were the consequences of deferral fully appreciated by Congress when it adopted § 453). Discrimination could be avoided if the successive tax payments carried interest like other "loans"—that is, if the Treasury were treated as a lender entitled to interest on the delayed tax collections—and § 453 relief would then be limited in a way that appears to conform to its goal. The statute does not require interest, however, and therefore the installment method serves not merely to associate tax outflows with cash inflows, but also to reduce the installment seller's tax cost in absolute terms.[12]

14.03 The "Fair Market Value" Rule. The installment method works well mechanically where, as in a conventional real estate sale, the buyer's payment obligations are fixed and determined. If the overall purchase price, the term of the indebtedness, and the amount of the annual payments are all established in advance, calculation of the gain component in each installment is simple and straightforward. But suppose the sale is subject to contingencies so that the price or the payment period is uncertain. The owner of a patent, for example, might transfer his rights to a manufacturer in consideration of the latter's promise to pay a percentage of the sales of the patented article for a stated period of years, but with no fixed maximum amount; or the deal might call for payment of a percentage of sales until a stated total had been reached, but with no fixed limit of time. In *Burnet v. Logan*,[13] as

---

12. The 1987 Act amended Code § 453A with respect to installment sales of business and rental real property with a selling price greater than $150,000. Under the amended provision, if the total amount of the seller's installment receivables at year-end exceeds $5 million, interest will be charged by the government on the deferred taxes attributable to the excess.

13. 283 U.S. 404 (1931).

will be seen, the transaction was limited neither in time nor amount—payments were to continue as long as the property, a mine, went on producing revenues for the buyer.

How, if at all, should the installment method be applied in these circumstances? More particularly, how should the seller's basis be apportioned when the total, or the term, or the size of the annual installments is uncertain? In *Logan,* the taxpayer owned stock in a corporation whose principal asset was a fractional interest in a large iron ore mine. In 1916 all of the company's stock was sold to another concern for $2,200,000 in cash—the taxpayer's share was $137,000—plus an agreement to pay the sellers a royalty of 60 cents for each ton of ore taken from the mine. From 1917 to 1920, the years at issue in the case, the taxpayer received payments averaging about $9,000 annually under the royalty contract. The question presented was whether, or to what extent, the annual royalty payments should be included in her gross income.

The government took the position that the 1916 stock sale was a "closed" transaction, a completed disposition of the taxpayer's shares. The royalty contract was found to have a value as of 1916 of $1,900,000 based on the estimated number of tons of ore in the mine and the estimated period (45 years) over which the ore was likely to be extracted. Thus, argued the government, the taxpayer's share of the contract's estimated value, about $120,000, plus her share of the initial cash payment represented the amount realized on the exchange, and the difference between this and her basis for the stock should have been recognized as gain (or loss) in 1916. The royalty contract would then have had a basis in the taxpayer's hands of $120,000, because that was the value assigned to it for the purpose of computing gain (or loss) on the sale of the stock. With an expected payout period of 45 years, each annual royalty payment received under the contract should have been treated as recovery of capital to the extent of $2,667 ($120,000/45), with the balance being included in taxable income. Since royalty payments in the years 1917–20 averaged about $9,000, the included portion of each payment would thus, in the government's view, have been about $6,333.

Holding that nothing was includable in the taxpayer's income for the years in question, the Supreme Court rejected the government's effort at valuation and found that the royalty contract had no ascertainable fair market value when received in exchange for the taxpayer's stock. Although the 1916 transaction was a "sale," the amount realized was indeterminate and the transaction was therefore "not a closed one." This meant (a) that no gain or loss was recognized by the taxpayer in 1916 when the sale took place (the initial cash payment was less than her basis for the stock), and (b) that no income would be taxed to the seller until the annual royalty payments (plus the initial cash payment) exceeded her stock basis, an event which apparently would not occur for a good many years in the future. To be sure, an interest in the same contract had been valued for estate tax purposes on the death of the taxpayer's mother, but in that context a value *had* to be established because the estate tax is imposed once and for all on the occasion of death. Income tax not collected currently can be collected in the future, however, and the Supreme Court therefore decided that it would be better to await the resolution of contingent events than to anticipate them by resort to "estimates, assumptions and speculation."

The *Logan* decision thus establishes that an exchange of property for a contingent payment contract will be regarded as an "open" transaction if the contract claim lacks an ascertainable fair market value. To be sure, this would occur, as the Service has said, only in "rare and unusual cases." *Logan* should not be regarded as holding that the absence of a fixed principal amount suffices by itself to render every contingent payment right indeterminate as to present worth; in particular, mineral interests, including royalty rights, are at present usually considered to be capable of valuation. Still, cases do arise in which the uncertainties affecting a buyer's obligation are so considerable, or the commercial field to which it relates is so unfamiliar, that the contract right is deemed beyond reliable appraisal. Closely-held businesses, for example, are often sold on a contingent-payment basis, as where the sole stockholder of X Corporation sells his shares for $100,000 cash plus 10% of the corporation's profits for each of the next five years. Very likely in such a case, the percentage payment right would be viewed as having no currently ascertainable fair market value, so that the seller's gain (or loss) would not be fully recognized in the year of sale.

The decision not to recognize gain (or loss) immediately can, perhaps, be defended on the ground that contingent payment obligations are simply too uncertain to value. It is less obvious, however, why the seller should be permitted to defer recognition until his *entire* property basis has been recovered. Suppose, in the example just above, that the stock seller has a basis for his X shares of $250,000. If the 10% payments go along at an annual rate of about $75,000, *Logan* allows the seller to offset his basis against the down-payment plus each of the next two years' percentage payments, and thus to report no gain until the fourth year of the six-year contract. From the seller's standpoint this is an even better outcome than that afforded by § 453. While the installment sale election also avoids immediate recognition, it does require that the taxpayer's gain be taken into account ratably as cash installments are received. As noted, § 453 reflects a purpose to relate cash inflows to tax outflows—hence the ratable inclusion. By contrast, the *Logan* rule emphasizes the element of risk in the transaction, and responds by deferring gain until the taxpayer's cost has been returned in full.

Long dissatisfied with the *Logan* result, the Treasury in 1980 persuaded Congress to amend § 453 so as to permit contingent payment transactions to be treated as installment sales, with the Treasury itself being authorized to substitute ratable cost-recovery rules for the "front-end" procedure authorized by *Logan*. Thus, in a case in which the payout period is fixed but the maximum amount to be paid is uncertain, the Regulations [14] now require that basis recovery be spread out equally over the stated payment period—in the example above, one-sixth of the stockowner's $250,000 basis, or $41,667, would be offset against each of the six payments to be received. Where maximum amount is fixed but term of payment is indefinite, each annual receipt will be allocated in the same proportion that the seller's basis bears to the maximum amount payable, with the balance being taxable gain. If, as in *Logan,* both maximum price and payout period are uncertain, the Regulations establish an arbitrary term—15 years—over which cost-recovery will be spread. In all such cases, any unrecovered cost will be allowed to the seller as a loss when the contract comes to an end.

Do these new rules mean that *Logan* has at long last been interred? Apparently not: the election-out alternative remains available under amended § 453, and while its use will be rare in the case of *conventional* installment sales, it may be that contingent payment sellers, preferring front-end to ratable cost-recovery, will attempt to avoid § 453 by electing "open" transaction treatment under *Logan*. Although the Committee Reports which accompanied the 1980 legislation express hostility to *Logan* and seem to intend that front-end cost-recovery shall no longer be available, the amendments as enacted simply fail to carry that intention out. The revised section does not expressly preempt the *Logan* rule— hence, arguably, the rule lives on as an electable alternative. On the other hand, the courts may now be led to treat the initial valuation problem more rigorously than they have in the past, so that contingent payment sellers who do elect out will run a greater

---

14. Regs. § 15a.453–1(c).

risk than heretofore that the buyer's obligation will be found to have an ascertainable value. In the latter event, of course, gain would be recognized in full in the year of sale and even ratable recovery would be foreclosed. Perhaps, therefore, the election-out gamble would seem unattractive to most contingent sellers.[15]

SECTION 15.   NON–RECOGNITION TRANSACTIONS

The Code extends non-recognition to a variety of transactions which would otherwise result in taxable gain or allowable loss. Some of these have already been mentioned (see 2.04, 3.02, and 5.03, for example); others are discussed in the subsections that follow. As usual where gain or loss is required or permitted to go unrecognized, the basis of the property received or acquired is "adjusted" so as to insure that the taxpayer's gain or loss will be picked up later. The effect—as the reader well knows—is to postpone tax-payment in the case of unrecognized gains, and to accelerate tax-payment in the case of unrecognized losses. I need hardly add that taxpayers usually like non-recognition where gain is concerned (though, as in *Woodsam,* recognition and a step-up in basis may sometimes be preferred), but almost always dislike non-recognition when the effect is to defer a loss.

Non-recognition transactions can be divided, very roughly, into three categories:

(1) Continuity-of-investment cases, where non-recognition normally applies to gains and losses alike. Exchanges of tangible assets (real estate, used equipment) for other tangible assets of like kind are a major example; corporate mergers (most emphatically not discussed herein; see Preface) are another. In these limited but important situations the Code evidently considers the new investment to be a mere continuation of the old, an alteration in form or identity but not in substance. Hence, the exchange of old property for new, though undeniably a realization, is deemed an inappropriate occasion for final reckoning of gain or loss.

(2) Hardship situations, where non-recognition is usually confined to gains. Leasehold terminations, involuntary conversions, sales of personal residences and various other transactions which for one reason or another are thought unusually onerous are to be found in this category. Non-recognition is supplied by way of "relief" in these circumstances and the taxpayer's gain is permitted to be deferred.

---

15. Ginsburg, *Future Payment Sales After the 1980 Revision Act,* 39   N.Y.U.Tax Inst. (1981), Ch. 43.

(3) Tax-avoidance "schemes," where non-recognition applies to losses only. Wash sales—the sale and repurchase of the same security within a 30-day period—and sales of property between family members and other related parties belong to this group. The taxpayer is thought to be manipulating or exploiting the realization requirement by making a spurious disposition of his property, and the Code reacts by disallowing the loss that would otherwise result. In the case of wash sales, § 1091 requires that the security repurchased take the basis of the security sold, so that the loss deduction is postponed until a bona fide disposition is made. In the case of related-party sales under § 267, by contrast, the purchaser's basis for purposes of computing loss is his actual cost rather than the seller's basis. Hence, as with gifts (see 4.02), the loss deduction is permanently disallowed.

The subsections that follow draw a representative from each of the first two categories named above. Like-kind exchanges are discussed in 15.01, and personal residence transactions at 15.02.

15.01 Like-Kind Exchanges. § 1031(a) provides that gain or loss will not be recognized if business property (other than inventory) or investment property (other than stocks and bonds) is exchanged for other business or investment property of like kind. Apart from ordinary equipment transactions—a used truck for a new one—where the trade-in allowance would otherwise frequently generate small amounts of taxable gain or allowable loss, the section's principal application is to real estate swaps in which two building owners simply exchange their properties one for the other. Gain or loss usually would be considerable in such cases, and there is clearly a realization. At this point, however, the Code chooses to emphasize the continuous character of the taxpayer's economic behavior—still an investor and still in real estate—and treats the exchange as an inappropriate occasion for recognition. As noted, corporate securities are excluded from § 1031: presumably one security is not sufficiently "like" another when the real assets which they represent are considered, and in any event the exchange of securities could so easily be arranged that ordinary stock market gains would soon attain a near-exempt status for many investors. Even as to real estate, etc., § 1031 is strictly limited to exchanges in kind; recognition cannot be avoided if property is initially sold for cash, even though the proceeds of sale are promptly reinvested in other property of like kind.

The aim of § 1031 is to postpone the recognition of gains and losses, not to forgive them completely. This objective is accomplished, as usual, by requiring that the basis of the old property be substituted for the new. If A owns an apartment building with a basis of $60 and a value of $100 which he exchanges for another apartment building of equal value, his basis for the acquired property is the same as that of the property surrendered, $60. The $40 of appreciation that was realized but not recognized on the exchange will be taxed if and when the acquired property is sold for cash or exchanged for dissimilar property. The effect is simply a "rollover" of his original property investment, which can be repeated as often as new opportunities for exchange arise.

§ 1031 does not prohibit the receipt of cash "boot" in connection with a like-kind exchange, and indeed it is likely that some cash is paid in most cases as a way of making up differences in value between the properties exchanged. Postponement is still permitted as to the like-kind element, but gains (though not losses) are recognized to the extent of the cash. If A in the illustration above exchanges his old building worth $100 for a new apartment building worth only $90, and also receives $10 in cash, § 1031 still applies to the exchange but now A recognizes a gain of $10. Under § 1031(d), his basis for the new building is $60: his old basis, $60, plus recognized gain, $10, minus cash received, $10. Thus the unrecognized balance of A's original property appreciation, $30, remains as potential gain to be taxed when the new building is finally disposed of. In effect, A's "investment" has been increased from $60 to $70 because $10 was taxed on the exchange; but $10 is now represented by cash (which necessarily has a "basis" equal to its face amount), while $60 is represented by the new apartment building.

Suppose, in the last example, that A's basis for his original building had been greater than its current market value, say $120. As losses are not recognized under § 1031 (losses are deferred *despite* the receipt of money), the $10 cash would be applied to reduce A's basis for the new building to $110. He would then still have a loss potential of $20 ($110–$90), which is equal to the decline in value of the old building.

If property is exchanged subject to a mortgage, § 1031(b) treats the mortgage as money, and gain is recognized to the transferor to the extent thereof. Thus, suppose A purchased the original apartment building for $40 cash, subject to a $20 nonrecourse mortgage. His basis under the *Crane* rule would then be $60. Suppose that the building appreciates in value to $100. If A now exchanges the old building for a new unmortgaged property worth $80 he realizes $100—the value of the new property, $80, plus the $20 mortgage assumed by the transferee. Since the mortgage assumption is treated as money, A would recognize a gain of $20 on the exchange. His basis for the new property would be $60—*i.e.,* basis in the old building, $60, plus the gain recognized, $20, less the "money" received, $20—which properly leaves $20 of appreciation still to be recognized when the new building is sold. While the arithmetic is correct, it is not entirely clear why § 1031 requires recognition of gain in these circumstances. A has withdrawn no cash at any stage, and as the object of the provision is to defer recognition until the original property is converted to money or other dissimilar assets, it would seem consistent for A to recognize no gain on the mortgage transfer and to take the new property at a basis of $40. The section follows a different course, however, and since mortgages are likely to be present in most real estate transactions, one suspects that relatively few such exchanges occur without gain recognition in some amount.

Non-recognition may, of course, be undesirable from the taxpayer's standpoint. As noted, losses are not recognized on an exchange of like property, so that taxpayers owning real estate (or other qualifying property) which has declined in value would normally prefer to dispose of their property for cash, recognize their losses, and then reinvest the proceeds in new property at a basis equal to its actual cost. Despite prompt or even simultaneous reinvestment, the intervening cash "step" is apparently enough to avoid the application of § 1031. The Treasury accepts (and will insist where gain has been realized) that a prior cash sale voids the jurisdictional requirement of the section.

Nevertheless, the government has sought to deny loss recognition in one related context—so-called sale-and-leaseback transactions—despite the existence of an apparent sale for cash. In the leading case, *Jordan Marsh Co. v. Commissioner*,[16] the taxpayer, owner of a large department store, conveyed its real estate—land and building—to certain investors for $2,300,000 in cash, and then entered into a 30-year lease of the same property with the vendees. Claiming that the transaction was an outright sale, the taxpayer sought to deduct as a loss the difference between its adjusted basis for the property and the cash received. The Commissioner disallowed the deduction on the ground that the transaction represented an exchange of like property—a fee interest for a long-term lease— plus cash to boot. The Treasury Regulations under § 1031 provided (and the taxpayer apparently accepted) that a leasehold of 30 years or more was the equivalent of a fee interest. Although plainly contemplating the exchange of a fee in Blackacre for a 30-year leasehold in Whiteacre, the Regulations were not expressly limited to cases involving different properties, and the government

---

16.   269 F.2d 453 (2d Cir.1959).

could therefore argue that the present transaction also constituted a like-kind exchange.

The court held for the taxpayer and allowed the loss. The price paid for the property by the vendees concededly represented its full fair market value. Moreover, the rentals for which the taxpayer was obligated under the lease were "full and normal," so that the leasehold had no "capital value"—no value in excess of the present value of the rents payable—in the taxpayer's hands. The taxpayer thus received nothing of value apart from the cash, and hence there was nothing to which § 1031 could actually apply. The court concluded that the transaction must therefore be characterized as a "sale" rather than a tax-free "exchange." At all events, the court noted, the "strained" construction given by the government to the word "exchange"—a transfer of property in return for a lesser interest in the *same* property—was unlikely to have been intended by Congress when it adopted § 1031.

But should the government have relied on § 1031 in the first place? Apart from tax consequences, most businessmen probably regard leasebacks as an alternative to mortgage financing, a transaction which does not result in the realization of gain or loss. Why, after all, should a company which already owns an asset and wants to continue to use it sell that asset and lease it back? The only possible answer is: to raise capital *without* surrendering the property. In that respect leasebacks and mortgage loans are quite alike: like a borrower, the seller-lessee receives an amount in cash which it must amortize with interest over the term of the lease; and like a borrower, it remains in possession of the property for an extended period of time. Changes in the value of the property—the ups and downs of the real estate market—are largely borne by the lessee, so that its prior interest in the property cannot really be said to have been terminated, any more than can the interest of a mortgagor.

But, on the other hand, the resemblance to a mortgage loan is not a perfect one. The lease does not go on forever, and if the property can be expected to have some residual value when the lease finally terminates, then that residual value will belong to the buyer-lessor. While a borrower recovers clear title to its property once the loan has been fully amortized, a seller-lessee relinquishes the property to the buyer and has nothing left on termination of the leasehold except an opportunity to renegotiate for an extension of the lease. Undeniably, the reversionary interest—the value of the property when the lease expires—has been transferred by the former owner and now belongs to the buyer-lessor.

293

Just which of these factors—continued possession of the property or transfer of the reversionary interest—should be regarded as determinative if the issue is framed in terms of "sale or loan" is obviously open to debate.   At the least, however, it seems less artificial, less "strained," to put the question in that way than to search for a possible application of § 1031.   Actually, the leaseback seems to involve *mixed* elements of sale and loan, and perhaps one way to resolve the ambiguity for tax purposes would be to have it both ways.   The sale-oriented and the loan-oriented elements of the arrangement can both be respected if the transaction is viewed, quite simply, as a sale of the reverter and a loan for the balance.   A portion of the vendor's gain or loss would then be recognized immediately—that attributable to the sale of the reversionary interest—while the balance of its property cost would be taken into account through depreciation (or amortization) over the term of the lease.   To illustrate, suppose Jordan Marsh has an adjusted basis for its property of $3,000,000.   It estimates that at the end of 30 years it can get $50,000 for the salvage value of the building plus $950,000 for the land, a total of $1,000,000.   The present value at 5% of $1,000,000 "due" in 30 years is about $230,000.   If the property is now "sold" for $2,300,000 subject to a 30-year leaseback, then 1/10th of the cash proceeds ($230,000/$2,300,000) can be attributed to the reversionary interest.   Using the same ratio, Jordan Marsh's basis for the reversionary interest is 1/10th of $3,000,000 or $300,000.[17]   Hence the taxpayer's recognized loss would be limited to the difference between that figure and $230,-000, or $70,000.   Having thus offset $300,000 of its original adjusted basis of $3,000,000, the balance of $2,700,000 would be recoverable through depreciation (or amortization) at the rate of $90,000 a year over the 30-year term.

Quite obviously, § 1031 does not come into play at all under the suggested approach.   Instead, the sale-and-leaseback is characterized as part-sale and part-loan, with each element being given the independent consequence it seems to deserve.   By contrast, the court in *Jordan Marsh* would allow an immediate loss of $700,000 in the illustration just given, while the Treasury, stressing the like-kind factor, would allow no loss whatever.

15.02   Sale of a Personal Residence.   Apart from the special relief provisions described below, the tax treatment of personal residence transactions is simple and straightforward (as well as illogical).   Thus, gain from the sale of a residence is includable in

17. *I.e.* $\dfrac{x}{\$3,000,000} = \dfrac{\$\ 230,000}{\$2,300,000}$ where x is the basis of the reversionary interest.

the seller's income (almost always as capital gain) while losses are treated as "personal" and are disallowed. A taxpayer who buys a house for $50,000 and later sells it for $70,000 has $20,000 of taxable gain. If the house were sold for $30,000, the taxpayer's apparent loss would be $20,000, but since a personal residence is neither business nor investment property under § 165(c), the loss would be non-deductible. As shown at 6.06, there are occasional disputes about whether residential property is held for personal use or for investment, but where the seller himself has occupied the residence up to or close to the date of sale the issue will almost always be resolved in favor of "personal."

What may be questioned somewhat more fundamentally [18] is whether the Code calculates gain correctly in the case of residence transactions, and whether, by the same token, it is proper to disallow *all* losses from sales of residences on the ground that they are "personal." To see what sort of criticism can be offered, it will be useful to recapitulate—briefly and by illustration—some of what was said earlier (see 1.03 and 7.04) about imputed rents and the depreciation allowance. Suppose a taxpayer pays $50,000 for a personal residence which has an estimated useful life of 25 years. As noted previously, the imputed rental value of the property— make it 12% annually, or $6,000—is excluded from the home-owner's gross income by long-standing administrative rule. At the same time, however, the taxpayer is permitted to take no deprecia-tion on the house because a personal residence does not qualify under § 167 as property used in business or held for the production of income. The depreciation deduction would otherwise be $2,000 a year ($50,000/25) if computed on the straight-line method. The law thus affords the taxpayer a *net* exclusion for imputed rent of $4,000—gross imputed rent of $6,000 less disallowed depreciation of $2,000—and presumably this can be taken as the intended limit of the homeowner's tax preference.

If annual depreciation of $2,000 *were* allowed on the taxpayer's residence, his basis for the purpose of computing gain or loss on sale would of course be adjusted—that is, reduced—by an equiva-lent amount under § 1016(a)(2). The adjustment, as has been seen, is necessary in order to prevent the taxpayer from taking double credit for the same expenditure. Thus, the taxpayer's basis at the end of 5 years would be reduced to $40,000 *if* annual depreciation of $2,000 had been allowed to him over the 5-year period. As depreciation is not allowed, however, § 1016(a)(2) does not apply. Hence no adjustment is made to the taxpayer's basis,

18. Epstein, *The Consumption and Loss of Personal Property Under the In-* ternal Revenue Code, 23 Stanford L.Rev. 454 (1971).

which remains at $50,000 throughout the period of his ownership. Suppose, then, that the taxpayer sells the house at the end of the fifth year for an amount exactly equal to his original purchase price—that is, $50,000. In effect, the property (which is now 5 years older than when he bought it) has appreciated in value over the period in question and the taxpayer has made a gain of $10,000—the difference between the sale price of $50,000 and the anticipated value of the residence of $40,000. But as his basis is also $50,000, the taxpayer realizes no *taxable* gain even if he gives up homeownership entirely at this point and invests the sale proceeds in other types of assets.

It turns out that a basis adjustment would have been appropriate after all. Although the Code disallows annual depreciation *during* the 5-year term, by failing at the same time to reduce the basis of the property to $40,000 it gives the taxpayer a lump-sum credit when the property is sold exactly equal to the depreciation disallowed. This omission (presumably) results from a belief that basis adjustment is solely a corollary to the *allowance* of depreciation deductions. In fact, however, the taxpayer's basis should also be adjusted as a corollary to the *disallowance* of depreciation. Putting the matter another way, consistency of treatment requires that the disallowance of annual depreciation on a personal residence also be reflected in an annual basis reduction, unless for some reason it is intended to reverse the disallowance when the residence is disposed of.

Very much the same sort of comment can be made about losses. Thus, suppose that the taxpayer sells the property for only $30,000 at the end of 5 years. Although market forces have deprived the taxpayer of $10,000 (again, the difference between the anticipated value of $40,000 and the amount realized of $30,000), the entire loss is disallowed as "personal." Yet, if the purpose of the Code is merely to prevent the taxpayer from deducting the cost of earning tax-free income—which the disallowance of annual depreciation would suggest—the correct approach would be to reduce the basis of the property to $40,000, but then to permit the difference between that figure and the amount realized to be recognized as a capital loss. In brief, the disallowance of "true" losses means that the prior exclusion of imputed rents is to that extent rescinded. By contrast, the non-recognition of "true" gains means that the prior exclusion is to that extent enlarged.

Having foisted these theoretical considerations on the reader, I must now disclose that the taxation of residence transactions is actually dominated by Code §§ 121 and 1034, the former a 1978 addition. Under § 1034, gain from the sale of a personal residence is not recognized if the taxpayer buys a new residence within a 2-year period (before or after), provided that the cost of the new residence is at least equal to the sale price of the old. If less costly, gain is recognized up to the amount of the difference. As with like-kind exchanges, the basis of the new residence is adjusted to reflect the gain not recognized, so that in effect such gain is merely deferred. § 121, however, goes much further by permitting taxpayers age 55 and over to exclude, on a one-time elective basis, up to $125,000 of gain from the sale of a residence if the seller has occupied the residence for at least three out of the preceding five years. Older homeowners whose children have decamped and who can now make do with smaller quarters thus receive a handsome tax benefit when they sell the family home. Like § 1034, § 121 reflects the perception that sales of personal residences often result from more or less involuntary factors—changes in employment or in family size—and that gains may largely be attributable to inflation. Still, the $125,000 figure seems generous even by current standards, and the two provisions together—deferral for younger homeowners and a sizeable exclusion for older ones—should mean that the majority of residence transactions will be subject to no tax at all. In many cases, of course, the family residence will be kept until the senior generation passes on, upon which event the basis of the property in the hands of the decendents' heirs steps up under § 1014 (see 4.01) and any prior appreciation is eliminated for tax purposes.

Part F: CAPITAL GAINS AND LOSSES

SECTION 16. INTRODUCTION

16.01 Recent History; Repeal and Reinstatement.
Apart from a brief interval during the late 1980's, our law has consistently awarded a "preference" to long-term capital gains, either by exempting a portion of such gains from tax or by taxing such gains at a bargain rate. Before the 1986 Act, old § 1202, now repealed, allowed individual taxpayers to deduct from gross income 60% of their net long-term capital gains—chiefly, gains from the sale of securities and real estate held for more than 6 months—and pay tax on the balance of 40% only. A taxpayer subject to the top marginal rate of 50% (prior to 1987) thus saved 30 cents on every dollar of income that met the statutory definition of a long-term capital gain. If, for example, the taxpayer enjoyed a bit of luck on the stock market and realized a $10,000 gain from the sale of securities, § 1202 would reduce his taxable gain to $4,000 and his tax would be only $2,000. In effect, the law enhanced the taxpayer's reward by excusing him from tax on 60% of the gain—a tangible benefit of 50% of $6,000 or $3,000. If the same $10,000 were received as ordinary income, *e.g.*, wages or business profits, the tax bite would of course be the full amount of $5,000 (assuming, again, the old 50% top rate).

In 1986, Congress reduced the top marginal rate for individual taxpayers to 28%, largely eliminated progressivity from the rate-structure, and simply repealed § 1202. The effect of the latter step was to require capital gains to be included in gross income in full and to tax such gains at the same top rate—28%—as income from ordinary sources. The element of "preference" thus disappeared entirely. Congressional tax-writers were of course aware that the preponderance of capital gains goes to high-bracket taxpayers: having cut the top individual rate nearly in half, it was felt that the "need" (as the Senate Committee put it) to maintain a reduced rate for capital gains no longer existed and, hence, that ordinary income and capital gains could be taxed alike. Much the same conclusion was reached with respect to corporate taxpayers. Under pre–1986 law, corporate capital gains were subject to a so-called alternative tax which was nearly 20 points lower than the 46% rate then generally applicable to corporate taxable income. With the regular corporate rate reduced by the 1986 Act to 34% (the present 35% rate is a 1993 change), Congress thought it proper to repeal the alternative tax and leave all corporate income, including capital gains, to be taxed at the regular corporate rate.

Despite repeal of the capital gain preference, Congress kept in place all of the complex definitional and computational paraphernalia described in the Sections following, so that taxpayers were (and are) still required to distinguish capital gains and losses from *ordinary* gains and losses. Congress' reasons for retaining (instead of wiping out) the whole burdensome statutory scheme were chiefly two. In the first place, it was thought important to protect the revenues by restricting the deductibility of capital *losses*. As noted much earlier (5.01, 5.05), the realization—and hence the timing—of investment gains and losses is largely voluntary: a taxpayer can sell his property this year, next year, or never. Because only *realized* gains are subject to tax, a permission to offset investment losses against ordinary income would prompt taxpayers to realize their losses immediately while postponing the realization of their gains, with possibly damaging consequences to the fisc. Thus, a taxpayer owning stock X which has appreciated in value by $100,-000 and stock Y which has declined in value by $100,000 (and whose net worth is therefore unchanged) might well elect to sell Y but retain X and use his Y loss to eliminate tax on his salary or business income. To prevent this outcome, the 1986 Act continued the prior law restriction contained in Code § 1211. In effect, realized capital losses can be offset only against realized capital gains (plus $3,000 of ordinary income). The Y loss thus produces a significant tax benefit for the taxpayer only if and when he realizes the X gain (or of course any other capital gain).

Beyond the concern about losses, Congress wished to make it very clear that the elimination of the capital gain preference was indissolubly linked to the reduction in regular tax rates that represented the centerpiece of the 1986 Code revision, and in particular to the act of establishing 28% as the top individual rate. Obviously intending that 28% be fixed as the maximum rate on long-term capital gains even if, or especially if, budgetary considerations should later make it necessary to raise ordinary rates, the Conference Committee report that accompanied the 1986 Act contained this solemn warning:

"This conference agreement follows the Senate amendment [in repealing the 60% capital gain deduction] . . .

"The current statutory structure for capital gains is [however] retained in the Code to facilitate reinstatement of a capital gains rate differential if there is a future tax rate increase."

For better or worse, Congress remained true to its own prescription when it increased rates in 1993. Under Code § 1(h), net capital gains (*i.e.*, the excess of long-term gains over short-term losses) can be taxed at a rate no greater than 28% no matter how much income a taxpayer has from other sources. Hence, an individual whose 1993 income, including capital gains, would otherwise be subject to tax at a rate of 31%, 36% or 39.6% now (a) subtracts his net capital gains and computes tax on the ordinary income that remains (presumably at the higher rates), and then (b) adds to that liability a tax equal to 28% of such net capital gains. In effect, for taxpayers with high levels of ordinary income plus capital gains, § 1(h) limits to 28% the rate applicable to the long-term capital gain component, thus affording the taxpayer a 3–point, an 8–point, or an 11.6–point break, depending on the marginal rate that would otherwise apply.[1] The 1993 Act made no change in the treatment of corporate capital gains, which continue to be taxed at the regularly applicable corporate rates.

Whether the capital gain preference is wise or unwise as a matter of national economic policy has been debated by tax specialists for decades, and perhaps the safest thing to say is that the question is debatable. What cannot be denied, however, is that the decision to treat capital gains in a special way adds substantially to the complexity of the federal income tax. The effect of this is felt by students, who are obliged to devote much more study time to the material that follows than might otherwise be required, by practicing lawyers, who must now (or again) engage in "planning" their clients' transactions so as to maximize capital gain and minimize ordinary income, and by the Internal Revenue Service itself, which has the task of policing the relevant statutory distinctions. According to a Service publication, that particular task—determining when capital gain treatment is appropriate and when it is not—has absorbed more administrative time and effort on the part of government personnel than any other *single* feature of the Internal

---

1. In the 1993 Act, Congress added an entirely new and different § 1202, which afford especially favorable treatment to gains from the sale of so-called qualified small business stock. A qualified small business is one whose gross assets do not exceed $50 million and which engages in any trade or business other than the performance of personal or financial services. Subject to various conditions, the new provision permits individual taxpayers to exclude 50% of such gains up to the greater of 10 times the taxpayer's basis in the stock or $10 million, with the includable 50% still being eligible for the customary 28% rate-limitation. Obviously intended to encourage people who are prepared to risk their money in new ventures, § 1202 requires that the stock be acquired by the taxpayer on its original issuance by the corporation itself, not through subsequent purchase.

Revenue Code. Wise or otherwise, the capital gain preference comes at a high cost to the system.

16.02 Legislative Purpose. With only one brief intermission, preferential treatment for capital gains has been a major feature of the federal income tax since 1922. Generally speaking, it applies to long-term gains from sales of investment property and permits those gains to be taxed at substantially lower effective rates than the rates that apply to "ordinary" income. As noted in the preceding Section, prior to 1986 this was accomplished by means of a special provision under which individual taxpayers could deduct from gross income 60% of their capital gains and pay tax on the balance of 40% only. At present, the preference is reflected somewhat more modestly in a rate differential: under Code § 1(h) the maximum tax-rate for long-term capital gains is 28%, while the marginal rates for ordinary income rise to 39.6% at the very top.

How can this long-standing tax concession be explained? What justifies the special treatment of investment gains? Curiously in view of its significance to the revenues, the capital gain preference has never received a systematic exposition in any official source. Congressional committee reports, debates, etc., contain little on the subject of underlying policy, apart from occasional references to "fairness", "incentives", and the like. Building on what few scraps of legislative background can be found, however, the courts and the commentators have seemed to perceive that the aim of the capital gain preference is twofold: first, to prevent the "bunching" of accrued property appreciation; and second, to assure, or at least to foster, the mobility of invested capital. Whether these factors really have been primary in the collective mind of Congress is quite uncertain, though, and it may well be that other considerations—persistent inflation, for example, or a desire to encourage risk-taking, or even a primitive sense that capital appreciation is not the same as "income"—have had an influence on the legislative outlook as well. The absence of a clearly articulated set of policy objectives has been criticized by many.[2] Among other things, it has apparently kept Congress from setting up a detailed and explicit statutory classification system for capital assets. Unsure of its own goals, Congress has provided an incomplete picture of what belongs in the class of "capital assets", leaving to the courts and the Service the task of developing the further content of that term through case-by-case analysis. As the discussion in Section 17 will show, this effort has largely been directed at *limiting* the scope of the capital asset

2. See Surrey, *Definitional Problems*   L.Rev. 985 (1956).
in Capital Gain Taxation, 69 Harv.

definition—a difficult undertaking without clear statutory guidance—and most would agree that it has not worked out as well as might be wished.

In *Burnet v. Harmel*,[3] the Supreme Court stated that the purpose of the capital gain section was "to relieve the taxpayer from ... excessive tax burdens on gains resulting from a conversion of capital investments, and to remove the deterrent effect of those burdens on such conversions." As suggested above, the Court presumably had two problems in mind, both arising from the act of "conversion" or realization. In the first place, gain realized on a sale of property may of course reflect appreciation which has built up or accrued over a period of many years. If stock is purchased at $100 a share in Year 1 and is finally sold in Year 5 for $150, the $50 gain then realized may be the sum of a series of unrealized gains which accrued over the five-year period. Since, historically, our rate-structure has been progressive, if we include the entire $50 in Year 5 just because the stock happened to be sold in that year, the investor's tax could be considerably greater than if the gain had been taken into account ratably over the five-year holding period. This, arguably, would be unjust and "excessive." Realization, after all, is a rule of administrative convenience, and it ought not of itself to be the cause of higher tax burdens. Accordingly, preferential treatment can be seen as a rough-and-ready way of mitigating the impact of progressive rates on income that is "bunched" into a single taxable year.

The second problem alluded to in *Harmel*—usually referred to as the "locked-in" effect—is evidently forward rather than backward looking. Thus, suppose an investor who owns an appreciated asset identifies another investment property which seems to offer higher returns than the one he now holds. Apart from the effect of taxation, the investor would sell his existing property and reinvest the proceeds in the new, higher-yielding asset whose existence and potential he has presumably spent time and money to discover. But, on the other hand, if he sells his appreciated property he has to pay an immediate tax on the gain. If he holds it, however, that tax can be postponed indefinitely—even death does not result in a taxable realization. As a result, the higher expected yield from the new property has got to be reduced, in effect, by the tax cost of disposing of the old, and when this calculation is made it may turn out that the new opportunity is not sufficiently profitable to make the switch worthwhile. The taxpayer is thus locked into his

---

3. 287 U.S. 103 (1932).

existing investment by the prospect of a tax on the sale, and his capital is deprived of the mobility which it ought ideally to possess.

Once again, therefore, the capital gain preference operates to mitigate the "deterrent" effect of the realization rule by making it less costly for those who own appreciated property to switch into other assets when their investment judgment dictates that they should, and in that respect the mobility of capital is improved.

Assuming that *Harmel* was correct, or largely correct, in its summary of the goals that Congress had in mind when it adopted the capital gain rules, does either objective really justify the preference (whether in its recent or its present form)? "Relief from bunched income" is plainly the weaker of the two supports.[4] While there is a good deal to be said *for* relief from bunching, there is very little to be said in favor of using either the old 60% deduction or the present rate differential as a means of providing that relief. In the illustration above, the taxpayer's gain was assumed to have accrued over a 5-year period. If we regard it as unfair to include the entire gain in the fifth year alone, then the obvious remedy is to require the taxpayer to pay a tax in the fifth year equal to the tax that would have been paid had the gain been included in income as it accrued. This might, accidentally, be the same as a tax on 40% of the gain under prior law or a tax at a marginal rate of 28% under present law, but in many instances it would be a good deal higher. To take an extreme case, suppose the taxpayer was in the topmost rate-bracket in each of the five years without regard to the unrealized property appreciation. In that event his gain would have been taxed at the top-bracket rate even if *annual* inclusion of the unrealized appreciation had been required. The "bunching" of the gain into the fifth year would have occasioned no increase in overall tax liability; hence no "relief" would be needed. In effect, if our object is to simulate the year-by-year accrual of the property appreciation, the best way to do it is, simply, to spread the gain back over the 5-year period. Neither the old special deduction nor the present rate differential accomplishes this result and hence neither can be said to be an adequate substitute for an explicit spread-back rule or an averaging device.

On a more detailed level, the 6-month holding period requirement which for many years defined "long-term" capital gain was obviously inconsistent with the idea of "relief from bunching." Under the 6-month rule, a taxpayer enjoyed preferential treatment

---

4. See Blum, *A Handy Summary of the Capital Gains Arguments,* 25 Taxes 247 (1957).

with respect to gain on property that was bought and sold within the space of a single taxable year; hence no "bunching" could have occurred. While the holding period was subsequently increased to a full year, the possibility that a taxpayer might have purchased a security at the start of Year 1, watched the security rise during the course of that year, and then realized his gain by selling the security at the start of Year 2, hardly presents a compelling case for relief. The same kind of inconsistency can be observed in connection with installment sales and other deferred payment transactions. The permission to defer gain beyond the year of sale by itself enables the taxpayer to spread his income over more than one taxable period. Yet, as will be seen (17.05), the capital gain preference is fully available to installment sellers. Thus, even if Congress initially had "relief from bunching" in mind, it has made no systematic effort to distinguish between taxpayers actually needing such relief and others.

The "mobility of capital" argument has considerably more force as a justification for tax relief, but it still is unclear why a special deduction or a rate differential is an appropriate way to respond to it. If one takes seriously the notion that taxing property gains "deters" investors from transferring capital to more profitable uses, then the correct response would seem to lie in one of two mutually exclusive directions. Thus, (a) we could refrain from taxing property gains *at all* if the taxpayer promptly reinvests the proceeds of sale in other long-lived assets. Under this approach, the taxpayer would be permitted, in effect, to roll over his capital investments free of tax. As with like-kind exchanges or residence transactions (15.01, 15.02), his original basis would be continued in the new investment property, and the deterrent effect of gain taxation would be removed entirely.[5] In the alternative, (b) we could tax property gains at ordinary rates *as they accrue,* without waiting for an act of realization. The taxpayer would then obtain no advantage from postponing the sale of his appreciated property, because the annual appreciation (or decline) would be taxed (or deducted) at the year-end anyway. There would thus be no reason to refrain from switching investments if better opportunities came along.

As compared with either of these "extreme" solutions—rollover or annual accrual—the special deduction technique so long embodied in the Code seems a weak and inadequate compromise, and the present rate differential is obviously no better. Capital

---

5. See C. Blum, *Rollover: An Alternative Treatment of Capital Gains,* 41   Tax L.Rev. 383 (1986).

gains were and are still subject to a substantial (even though reduced) measure of taxation; hence realization, which is at the heart of the problem, continues to deter the making of individually and socially desirable investment choices. At the same time, taxpayers who do realize capital gains get the benefit of the reduced rate of tax even when the gain is *not* reinvested and the proceeds of sale are expended on consumption. Reinvestment is not a condition of the capital gain preference; hence the preference is not confined to those who do actually reinvest their profits.

Regarding capital losses, the present treatment—for the most part, permitting capital losses to offset only capital gains—is also a function of the realization requirement. As noted earlier, because only realized gains are subject to tax, a permission to deduct losses from other income would encourage taxpayers to realize their losses immediately while postponing the realization of their gains, with a resulting loss to the revenues. The restricted deductibility of capital losses, however, means that less successful investors—those who experience more losses than gains on a lifetime basis—are compelled to make a tax sacrifice for the benefit of more successful investors. The latter get the advantage of postponing their gains *until* realized, while the former "pay" for this advantage by forgoing a full deduction for their losses even *when* realized.[6]

———————

A loose end: Lacking any better opportunity, this may be the place to point out that the federal income tax in a sense discriminates against savers, as compared with consumers, by imposing what some would call a *double* tax on savings. Income, however derived, is taxed to an individual *once* when he earns or receives it. If the amount that remains is expended on consumption goods— food, lodging, entertainment, etc.—no further tax is imposed on the individual with respect to that original receipt. If, however, the individual chooses to "expend" his after-tax income on corporate shares, government bonds or other assets which produce further income, then that further income will of course be subject to a further tax. Savers are thus taxed *twice;* consumers only once.

To illustrate: Assume C and S, individuals, live in a country which at present imposes no income tax whatever. Each earns $1,000. C, a consumer, chooses to expend his $1,000 on a vacation. S, a saver, expends his $1,000 on a 6% bond with a view to receiving annual interest of $60 to use in future periods. Since

6. *See* Warren, *The Deductibility by Individuals of Capital Losses under the*   *Federal Income Tax,* 40 U.Chi.L.Rev. 291 (1973).

they live in a tax-free world, both individuals get what they want for the same dollar expenditure.

Now assume that their country adopts an income tax of 50%. How much must C and S earn in order to acquire, respectively, a $1,000 vacation and a $60-a-year income stream? As to C, the answer is obviously $2,000. Since the vacation is not a deductible expense, it has to be purchased out of after-tax income. With the new 50% income tax in force, C will have to earn $2,000 in order to have $1,000 left for his annual trip to Florida. But what about S? The bond purchase *also* is not deductible—taxpayers are no more allowed to deduct amounts expended on "savings" than they are amounts expended on "consumption". At the same time, however, the interest on S's bond will *itself* be subject to the 50% income tax. In effect, earnings devoted to the purchase of an income-stream, *and* the income-stream itself, are *both* included in income. This means that S will actually have to earn $4,000 in order to be in the same position that he occupied before the new tax was enacted. Thus the $4,000 would be reduced by the 50% tax to $2,000. The $2,000 that remained would then be used to buy a 6% bond yielding interest of $120 a year. The $120 of annual interest would *also* be taxed at the 50% rate, leaving a net after-tax income-stream of $60. In this sense, therefore, while C the consumer is required to earn only $2,000 because he pays the 50% income tax just once, S the saver is required to earn $4,000 because his savings are subjected to a double imposition.[7]

Does all this provide any justification for a capital gain preference? Not in any explicit way, certainly. In the first place, as already observed, the capital gain preference applies without regard to whether gains are expended on consumption goods or reinvested in other capital assets. Hence the preference is not confined to savers. It is the *source* of the income—realized capital appreciation—rather than the destination of the proceeds which attracts the favored treatment. Second, and by the same token, the preference is not available for savings generally. Taxpayers whose income derives from personal services are taxed on such income at the full ordinary rates even if they spend none of it and save it all. Once again, source is the determining criterion. Personal service income is always taxed at ordinary rates no matter what expenditure choice the taxpayer then elects to make.

---

7. A now-classic exchange of views on this topic appears in Andrews, *A Consumption–Type or Cash Flow Personal Income Tax,* 87 Harv.L.Rev. 1113 (1974), and Warren, *Fairness and a Consump-* *tion–Type or Cash Flow Personal Income Tax,* 88 Harv.L.Rev. 931 (1975). And see Fried, *Fairness and the Consumption Tax,* 44 Stanford L.Rev. 961 (1992).

Still—and conceding that the point is more intuitive than rational—I suspect that there remains in the minds of many a dim sense that capital appreciation is not truly "income". If so, the feeling may ultimately trace to a hunch that capital gains, more often than not, are held back from the ordinary flow of consumption expenditure and reinvested in new or additional income-producing assets. Perhaps, then, favored treatment represents an oblique and unsystematic response to the problem of discrimination illustrated in the comparison of C and S, above. If capital gainers are also savers—typically, if not always—then maybe the capital gain preference is intended to mitigate the double-tax on savings by treating the larger part of such gain as if it lacked the taxable characteristics of "income."

16.03 Mechanics of Computation. The computation of tax on capital gains and losses, though detailed, is reasonably straightforward and can be summarized fairly briefly. To begin with, § 1222 divides capital gains and losses into two classes—long-term and short-term. Long-term gain or loss is defined to mean gain or loss from the sale or exchange of capital assets held for more than 1 year; short-term gain or loss refers to gain or loss from the sale of capital assets held for 1 year or less. Net long-term gains are treated "preferentially"; net short-term gains are simply taxed at ordinary rates.

For individual taxpayers, the long-term capital gain preference is in the form of a 28% rate limitation. The relevant Code provision is § 1(h), which actually provides two alternative procedures for computing tax on long-term capital gains. The statutory purpose is to assure (i) that the 28% rate-maximum is never exceeded and (ii) that the lower 15% rate will apply to the extent that the taxpayer's long-term capital gain would otherwise fall within the 15% bracket. In effect, if taxable income other than long-term gain exceeds the 15% bracket, the taxpayer pays tax on such income at the regular rates—which, as stated, may rise to 39.6%—and then adds a 28% tax on the long-term capital gain. If taxable income is within the 15% bracket, he pays tax at the 15% rate on such taxable income plus so much of his long-term capital gain as is needed to fill that bracket up, and then adds a 28% tax on any additional long-term gain.

In general, capital losses can be offset only against capital gains. Any excess or unused capital loss for the current year can be carried forward to subsequent taxable years without time limitation. In order to minimize record-keeping where the unused capital loss is relatively small, § 1211 permits individual taxpayers to

307

offset capital losses (whether short-term or long-term) against ordinary income up to $3,000 annually.

The calculation of short-term and long-term capital gains and losses is carried out through the "netting" procedure set forth in § 1222. As stated, the section begins by distinguishing short-term from long-term gains and losses by reference to the 1–year holding period. It then directs the taxpayer to net the gains and losses in each category separately. If one category shows a net loss and the other a net gain, the net loss and the net gain are netted against each other. This means that short-term loss may offset long-term gain or, equally, that long-term loss may offset short-term gain. There are then these possible outcomes:

(1) Net gains in both categories, in which case the net short-term gain is taxed as ordinary income, while the net long-term gain is dealt with under § 1(h) and may be subject to the 28% rate limitation;

(2) Net losses in both categories, in which case the net losses are combined and can be offset against up to $3,000 of ordinary income (with unlimited carryforward);

(3) Net loss in one category and net gain in the other, in which case the loss in the former category (whether short or long) is offset against the gain in the latter category (whether short or long). Having combined the two categories—

(a) If there is an excess of short-term gain over long-term loss, the excess is a short-term gain and is taxed as ordinary income;

(b) If there is an excess of long-term gain over short-term loss, the excess is a long-term gain and is dealt with under § 1(h), as described above;

(c) If the net loss in either category exceeds the net gain in the other, the excess (loss) is offset against $3,000 of ordinary income, with unlimited carryforward.

By way of simple illustration, assume that the taxpayers, a married couple, have salary income of $150,000, a long-term capital gain of $55,000, a long-term capital loss of $10,000, and a short-term capital loss of $5,000. Assume also that the taxpayers are entitled to two personal exemptions and take the standard deduction. Their tax liability for the year would be determined as follows:

Salary		$150,000
Long-term capital gain	$55,000	
Long-term capital loss	(10,000)	
Net long-term capital gain	$45,000	
Net short-term capital loss	(5,000)	
Net capital gain (§ 1222(11))		40,000
Gross income		$190,000
Personal exemptions, $4,700, plus standard deduction, $6,200		(10,900)
Taxable income		$179,100
Taxable income reduced by $40,000 net capital gain		$139,100
Tax on $139,100 under § 1(a)		$ 35,650
Tax on net capital gain under § 1(h) (28% of $40,000)		11,200
Total tax liability		$ 46,850

Without the § 1(h) rate-limitation the taxpayers' total tax liability would be about $50,000, so the saving—nearly $3,200—is modest though not insignificant.

So much for mechanics, on to strategy:

If the reader has ever had an investment account with a brokerage company, he almost certainly will have received a "Year–End Tax Planning" letter of which the aim is to alert him to the possibility of saving taxes by realizing gains and losses on securities in his portfolio. The strategic alternatives are fairly numerous and depend on which categories of gains and losses have already been realized during the taxable year and which categories remain unrealized. As a kind of self-administered test, assume that an investor has already realized $10,000 of long-term gain during the current taxable year. He also has in his portfolio $10,000 of unrealized long-term loss on stock X, and $10,000 of unrealized short-term gain on stock Y. He has decided, as a matter of investment judgment, to sell both stock X and stock Y, but he does not care whether he sells one or both just before the end of the current year or just after the start of the new year. From a tax standpoint, what should he do? The answer, of course, is that he should hold on to both stocks until the current year ends, and sell both after the new year begins. If he sold both stocks before the end of the current year, the long-term loss on stock X would offset the long-term gain already realized, and the investor would be left with a short-term gain on stock Y, which would be taxed at ordinary rates. The same would be true if he sold stock X this year and sold stock Y next year, except that the short-term gain would be taxed a year later. If he sells both X and Y in the new year, however, the long-term loss on X will offset the short-term gain on Y. The gain realized in the current year is then taxable without offset, but since it is of the long-term variety it qualifies for the 28% rate-limitation under § 1(h) and the investor can congratulate himself for his shrewd year-end maneuvering.

SECTION 17. JUDICIAL DEVELOPMENT OF THE CAPITAL ASSET DEFINITION

17.01 General Comment. As the sections that follow will suggest, the Supreme Court has played an unusually active role in developing—really, limiting—the scope of the capital asset definition. With some exceptions, the Court's effort over the years has been to narrow the category of transactions qualifying as sales of capital assets and thereby to prevent that category from occupying a larger part of the tax universe than seemed consistent with Congressional intent. The need for judicial activism in this area resulted, in part, from the curious, upside-down way in which the Code itself defines the term "capital asset." Thus, § 1221 *begins* with the broad assertion that "capital asset means property held by the taxpayer (whether or not connected with his trade or business)". The key word in this phrase obviously is "property," a word which contains no inherent or intrinsic limitations, and which, therefore, could be understood to embrace rights, claims and interests of any and every description. Taken literally, the statute seems to contemplate a world that includes nothing *but* capital assets, and speaks as if all transactions and dealings qualified for capital gain or loss treatment. To be sure, five classes of property—among them, business inventory and salary claims—are at once excluded from the definition of a capital asset, thus, in effect, being typed as "ordinary". Yet the existence of these specific exclusions, which appear in §§ 1221(1)–(5), seems to strengthen the possibility that all *non*-excluded items may be swept into the capital asset category.

Plainly, however, Congress did not intend that the federal income tax should primarily be a capital gain tax. The capital asset definition was meant to apply to investment property—securities and real estate—which is capable of appreciating in value over an extended period of ownership. Other kinds of assets or claims, especially those which do not customarily reflect long-term changes in value, are expected to be covered by the "normal" operation of the income tax and to be taxed at customary rates. In the latter category would be recurring income of all sorts, whether from business, services or investment itself, as well as a nearly limitless variety of income-items which do not fit so neatly into familiar compartments. In effect, if Congressional intention is the guide, then ordinary income should be the general rule and capital gain should be the exception.

This section considers some of the major cases in which the courts have undertaken to interpret the capital asset definition. Consistent principles have not always been easy to articulate, because the original aim of Congress in enacting the capital gain provisions is nowhere set forth in comprehensive terms. As the quotation from *Burnet v. Harmel* suggests, however, the courts have assumed that capital gain was intended chiefly to serve as an averaging and anti-deterrent device. It has also been assumed that income from business or professional activities, as well as recurring investment income such as dividends, interest and rents, are to be viewed as falling *outside* the favored category. But while these assumptions are necessary and plausible, their implementation in particular cases often has been difficult. As in the income-attribution field, the courts have been compelled to invent and manipulate doctrinal concepts in order to reach results which they could regard as consistent with legislative intent. The concept of "property" has sometimes been utilized to this end, as has the notion that some kinds of economic interests are merely a "substitute for future ordinary income." In addition, since capital gain or loss is described in § 1222 as resulting from the "sale or exchange" of a capital asset, ordinary or capital treatment occasionally has turned on whether a particular transaction qualified, or failed to qualify, as a "sale or exchange." Judicial opinions are frequently opaque, however, and in that respect they reflect the courts' uncertainty about underlying Congressional goals.

17.02 Everyday Business Activities. The profits and losses realized by a business enterprise through the sale of its products to customers are obviously *ordinary* profits and losses. This is true whether the enterprise is a corporation, taxable at the separate rates set forth in § 11, or a partnership or proprietorship whose net income or loss is taken into account directly by the individual partners or proprietor. Everyday business income, together with wages, salaries, dividends, interest and rent, accounts for the great bulk of taxable income, and it plainly falls outside the category of capital gain or loss. § 1221(1), discussed in some detail at 18.01, makes this conclusion clear by excluding business "inventory" from the capital asset definition, thus insuring that day-to-day merchandise transactions will have no claim to capital gain treatment. Real and depreciable property used in business—land and buildings, machinery and equipment—is likewise denied capital asset status by § 1221(2). As will be seen at 18.02, however, these so-called fixed assets are subject to a special regime under § 1231, which does permit capital gain in limited measure.

But what about other kinds of business assets—securities, leases, franchises, trade-names, "goodwill" and other intangibles—which do not fit neatly within the excluded classes of "inventory" or of real and depreciable property, but which also may be a source of gain or loss to the enterprise?   § 1221 says nothing directly about these residual items, so that at least one approach would be to view the catch-all clause as conferring capital asset status on all of them more or less by default. The test, quite simply, would be whether the asset in question—say, a franchise or a license—is specifically excluded by § 1221(1) or (2). If not, then even though it is used in business, and even though business activity commonly yields ordinary gains and losses, the gain or loss in this instance must be capital because the asset literally constitutes "property" within the terms of § 1221.

The Supreme Court has tackled the issue in question—whether business assets not specifically excepted from the capital asset definition are, as a consequence, necessarily within it—in two widely separated decisions, *Corn Products Refining Co. v. Commissioner*,[8] decided in 1955, and *Arkansas Best Corporation v. Commissioner*,[9] decided in 1988. The former, as will be seen, was a sort of *tour de force* in which the Court substantially expanded the category of *non*-capital assets to include property acquired for a purpose integral to the taxpayer's everyday business, even though not squarely within a statutory exception. The latter, in contrast, may be read as a somewhat embarrassed attempt, inspired by three decades of unhappy experience with the former, to refocus the problem in narrower terms.

In *Corn Products* the taxpayer was a large manufacturer of corn starch, syrup, sugar and related products. It typically accepted orders from its customers under which shipment of merchandise was to be made within 30 days at a set price. Since its storage facilities were limited, the taxpayer was sometimes obliged to purchase raw materials in the spot market, and on occasion, when weather conditions had caused a sudden increase in spot prices, it evidently found that customers' orders could only be filled at a loss. To deal with this problem, the company embarked on a regular program of buying corn futures—contracts which entitled it to purchase a fixed amount of corn at a future date at a fixed price. If the price of corn thereafter rose, the company would be protected:

8. 350 U.S. 46 (1955).   9. 485 U.S. 212 (1988).

it could either take delivery under the futures contracts if it had an actual need for raw materials, or else sell the contracts at a gain and reimburse itself for any increase in the spot market price.

In 1940 the taxpayer realized a gain of $680,000 from the sale of futures contracts; in 1942 it sustained a loss of $110,000. Finding that the taxpayer had a "business" as distinguished from an "investment" purpose in purchasing the corn futures, the Supreme Court held that the gains (and losses) were ordinary and hence taxable at the regular corporate rate. The futures, in the Court's view, had played an "integral part" in the taxpayer's business by protecting it "against a price increase in its principal raw material and [assuring] a ready supply for manufacturing requirements." Profits and losses arising from the "everyday operation of the business" must be regarded as ordinary, therefore, because Congress did not intend to award preferential treatment to transactions that are a "normal source of business income."

As noted, the Court rejected the taxpayer's argument that the corn futures were entitled to capital asset status merely because they qualified as "property". That term, it said, must be narrowly construed. At the same time, the Court appeared to concede that the futures were neither "inventory" in a conventional sense nor stock-in-trade within the meaning of § 1221(1). In effect, therefore, by a strong handling of the statute, the Court *created* a class of property—property acquired for a purpose integral to the taxpayer's business—which it found to be constructively excepted from the capital asset definition. The Court did not say that *all* business assets must be treated as ordinary, and presumably the reference to "everyday" operations was intended to imply a distinction between recurring transactions and others. It did, however, apparently establish that the statutory exceptions were not exhaustive and that in cases not covered by a specific exception the question of "capital or ordinary" could not be answered without additional analysis of the taxpayer's purpose or intent.

Though *Corn Products* was undoubtedly correct in outcome, emphasizing the taxpayer's motive for acquiring property has led to much uncertainty in application. The treatment of securities—stocks, bonds and the like—has been especially troublesome. In *Commissioner v. Bagley & Sewall Co.*[10] for example, the taxpayer entered into a construction contract with a foreign government for the manufacture of certain machinery, and was required under the contract to deposit U.S. Government bonds as security for its performance. The taxpayer purchased the bonds for this purpose

10.   221 F.2d 944 (2d Cir.1955).

at a cost of $820,000 and then, immediately after completing the contract, resold the bonds at a $15,000 loss. The court of appeals held that the loss was allowable in full as a deduction from ordinary income. Although the bonds were obviously "property", the factual background made it clear that their purchase "was a reasonable and necessary act in the conduct of [the taxpayer's manufacturing] business," and that "no investment was intended." Accordingly, the taxpayer was upheld in treating the $15,000 bond loss as "a deductible business expense [under § 162], or business loss [under § 165], properly taken in the instant year since that was the first time the reason for holding the bonds disappeared and the extent of the loss could be accurately measured." Dissenting, Judge Frank argued that the exceptions in § 1221(1)–(5) were exclusive, that the court had no power to broaden those exceptions through "judicial amendment", and, hence, that the taxpayer's loss should have been treated as a capital loss offsettable solely against capital gains.

Subsequent cases, most of them involving stock or other securities acquired to achieve a business goal of some sort, have tended to apply the *Corn Products* rationale quite broadly. In *Booth Newspapers,*[11] for example, ordinary loss treatment was allowed where the taxpayer, a publisher, sold the stock of a newsprint manufacturer which it had originally purchased during a paper shortage in order to secure a long-term source of supply. The court found the stock to be a non-capital asset on the ground that the taxpayer had a "business purpose" in making the original purchase, although the same result might have been reached by characterizing the stock as a substitute for raw materials and hence as "inventory" under § 1221(1). Other decisions have carried the business purpose rationale to more surprising lengths. Thus, an ordinary loss result was reached where the taxpayer originally bought securities in another firm in order to have access to new technologies,[12] and, in yet another case, where a holding company's purpose in acquiring the stock of a subsidiary was to protect its own business reputation.[13] In these and like decisions, the stock or securities, though lacking the close relationship to current inventory that was present in *Corn Products* itself, were found to have been purchased for business rather than investment reasons and for that reason alone were held to have ordinary status under the rationale employed in *Corn Products*. In a few instances where the securities finally sold at a loss had been held for an extended period of time, the courts

---

11. *Booth Newspapers, Inc. v. U.S.,* 303 F.2d 916 (Ct.Cl.1962).

12. *Schlumberger Tech. Corp. v. U.S.,* 443 F.2d 1115 (5th Cir.1971).

13. *Campbell Taggart, Inc. v. U.S.,* 744 F.2d 442 (5th Cir.1984).

have denied ordinary loss treatment on the ground that the taxpayer's original business purpose had later been displaced by a purpose to hold for investment; in other cases (at least prior to *Arkansas Best*) the courts have attempted to distinguish between securities acquired for the purpose of protecting the taxpayer's existing business (ordinary) and acquisitions aimed at expanding into new business areas (capital). Some courts, also, have found themselves enmeshed in the difference between "predominant" and "substantial" business motivation, with the outcomes in particular cases turning on highly tenuous elements of proof. Once again, the emphasis on motive and intent has made it difficult to insure uniform administration of the capital gain and loss provisions where business taxpayers are concerned.

The administrative problem has been aggravated, from one standpoint, by the fact that the *Corn Products* "rule" has been regarded as a "rule of law" available to taxpayers as well as the government and applicable to gains and losses alike. Not surprisingly, therefore, as just suggested, most of the litigated cases involving an application of the *Corn Products* doctrine are cases in which the security or other asset is disposed of at a *loss*. Asserting that the property was acquired for business-related rather than investment-related reasons, the taxpayer reports the loss as a deduction from ordinary income. When the very same property appreciates, on the other hand, the taxpayer is likely to find that investment motives were predominant and will report his profit as a capital gain. Had the bonds in *Bagley & Sewall* gone up, for example, the gain would almost surely have shown up as a routine capital gain on the taxpayer's return, where only a very sharp-eyed revenue agent would be likely to have thought of challenging it. Hence, ironically, the *Corn Products* doctrine has served chiefly as a justification for ordinary loss treatment; rarely has it produced ordinary treatment on the gain side.

In view of these difficulties, many commentators have suggested that the Court would have been better advised had it reached the result it did in *Corn Products* on a narrower ground; namely, that the corn futures were merely a substitute, or "surrogate", for the taxpayer's principal raw material. Under standard accounting practice, the term "inventory" generally refers to property at all stages of production and makes no distinction between raw materials, work in process and finished goods. Corn actually on hand in the taxpayer's warehouse would therefore be regarded as inventory for accounting and presumably for tax purposes. While the futures represented a contractual right to purchase corn rather than being the raw material itself, it is obviously no great leap to regard the two as practical equivalents and on that basis to treat the futures contracts as actual inventory within § 1221(1). Taking that approach, there would be no need to consider the taxpayer's motive, purpose or intent, because gains and losses from the sale of futures would be ordinary under a plausible construction of the inventory exception.

Had the Court followed this simpler course, one important consequence would have been to permit the Service to insist that securities be "included in inventory" at the time of their original purchase if the taxpayer intended to claim ordinary treatment thereafter. In effect, taxpayers would be required, as a matter of tax accounting, to declare the status of the security—whether ordinary or capital—when it was initially acquired, rather than after it had been disposed of. Gains and losses would then be treated alike and "optional" or hindsight classification would be foreclosed. More than anything else, perhaps, it was the "potential for such abuse"—the taxpayer asserting that its original motive had been investment-related when the property was later sold at a gain, but business-related when it was later sold at a loss—that led the Supreme Court in *Arkansas Best* to declare (after thirty-odd years) that its *Corn Products* opinion had been misunderstood and that the prevailing interpretation was "too expansive".

In *Arkansas Best,* the taxpayer, a holding company, in 1968 acquired as an investment 65% of the stock of a commercial bank. The bank did reasonably well at first but beginning in 1972, as the local real estate market declined, the bank developed financial difficulties and was classified as a "problem bank" by federal examiners. During the "problem" period, which extended through 1974, the taxpayer (together with other shareholders) contributed substantial amounts of capital to the bank and received additional shares. The taxpayer sold the greater part of its bank stock in 1975 and, as a result, reported and claimed deduction for an ordinary loss of about $10 million. The Tax Court, purporting to apply *Corn Products,* held that the bank stock purchased by the taxpayer *prior* to 1972 had been acquired with an "investment" goal in view—*i.e.,* the taxpayer thought the stock was undervalued and would appreciate—while the stock acquired through capital contribution *after* 1972 had been acquired "exclusively for business purposes"—*i.e.,* to preserve the taxpayer's business reputation by preventing the bank (of which the taxpayer was the controlling shareholder) from failing. It followed, on this view, that the taxpayer's stock loss was a capital loss to the extent attributable to the pre–1972 shares, but ordinary to the extent attributable to the shares acquired during the later period.

Rejecting the Tax Court (and affirming the Eighth Circuit), the Supreme Court held that *all* of the taxpayer's bank stock, whenever acquired, was a capital asset and that no portion of the taxpayer's loss could be treated as ordinary. The Court expressly disapproved the expansive interpretation that *Corn Products* had received in *Booth Newspapers* and other lower court cases. Justice Marshall admitted, or conceded, that the opinion in *Corn Products* may not have made clear whether the ordinary-income result "was based on a narrow reading of the phrase 'property held by the taxpayer' [in § 1221], or on a broad reading of the inventory exclusion of [§ 1221(1)]." Now, however, and in order to resolve any uncertainty on that score, the Court was prepared to assert that *Corn Products* should properly have been interpreted as "involving an application of § 1221's inventory exception" rather than as an effort "to create a general exemption from capital-asset status for assets acquired for business purposes." While the corn futures were not "actual inventory", they were plainly a part of the taxpayer's inventory-purchase program and as such were mere substitutes or surrogates for the corn inventory itself. It followed that the *Corn Products* "doctrine" could be of no benefit to the taxpayer in *Arkansas Best*. The bank shares were not in any sense inventory in the taxpayer's hands—the taxpayer was obviously not a dealer in securities—and hence the taxpayer's loss, whether attributable to the shares acquired for investment or to the shares acquired for a business-related purpose, was a capital loss.

Having overruled the *Booth Newspapers* line of decisions, at least as to rationale, *Arkansas Best* presumably also rejects the reasoning in *Bagley & Sewall* and requires that we approve Judge Frank's dissenting view instead. The question would not (or would no longer) be whether Bagley & Sewall had acquired the bonds for a business rather than an investment purpose. Rather, the pertinent question would be whether the loss was in some way a surrogate or substitute for a business expense—presumably the cost of procuring a performance bond—that would otherwise be allowable under § 162. Pretty plainly, it was not. To be sure, a contractor that undertakes a large construction project would almost always be required to post a bond in order to secure its performance obligations under the contract. The bond would normally be obtained from a surety company to which the taxpayer would pay an insurance premium, such premium being deductible as an ordinary and necessary business expense. But if, in lieu of a surety bond, the taxpayer posts security of its own, using its own capital for that purpose and acting as a self-insurer, then it seems fair to say that the taxpayer has earned the insurance premium for itself. In effect, the taxpayer has both "paid" (to itself) and "received" (from itself) an imputed premium, the two steps together simply producing a wash as far as the taxpayer's return is concerned. The customary bond-premium outlay associated with contract performance is thus effectively taken account of for tax purposes; hence an ordinary deduction on the ground that the company's loss was functionally equivalent to a business expense would not be justified.

Putting it differently, the loss sustained by the taxpayer in *Bagley & Sewall* was the result of a chance decline in the Treasury bond market and had nothing to do with the cost of performing the contract as such. While the bonds were admittedly acquired for a business-related reason, *Arkansas Best* makes it clear that "business purpose" no longer serves as the operative criterion. That being so, capital rather than ordinary loss treatment would (now) appear to have been appropriate.

17.03 Substitute for Future Income.

(a) Carved-out interests; Hort and Lake. Suppose a taxpayer buys a share of stock for $100, with the expectation that the future cash dividends will be $8 a year. Subsequently, corporate profits having increased, the annual dividend expectation goes up to $10, and the stock itself appreciates to $125. If the taxpayer now elects to sell the stock, he will, of course, recognize a $25 gain, and since corporate stock, normally, is a capital asset, the gain will be taxed as capital gain. On the other hand, if the taxpayer chooses to hold the stock and receive the annual dividends, he will have $10 a year of ordinary income. Such dividends will be included in his income without an offset of basis, moreover, because the tax law, which follows accounting concepts here, does not permit the cost of securities, land or other non-wasting assets to be recovered until the property is finally disposed of.

All this, of course, is well understood. Whatever the merits from a policy standpoint, the Code makes a sharp distinction between gain that is realized on a sale of property and income received in the form of periodic yield. The former is taxed as capital gain, the latter as ordinary income. In formal and practical terms the distinction is an easy one to administer, because the difference between selling a share of stock and retaining the stock in one's portfolio is obvious on its face.

But suppose the above stock-owner attempts to steer a middle course. Not wanting to sell his stock, but needing cash for current expenses, he sells to another investor his right to receive the annual dividends from the stock for the next five years. At an appropriate rate of discount—say 8%—the present value of $10 a year for five years is $40, and that is what the taxpayer gets from the vendee. In return, the taxpayer notifies his broker to pay over all dividends to the vendee until the five-year term has ended.

How should the $40 payment be taxed? The question—which has a wicked odor of fruit-and-tree about it—is really not very difficult, because the risk of widescale tax-avoidance if the "sale" were allowed to qualify as a capital transaction has simply been too great to bear. Thus, suppose the transaction *were* treated as a sale of a capital asset. The result, presumably, would be three-fold: (a) The taxpayer would be entitled to offset a proportionate part of his $100 basis against the proceeds of sale. Since the five-year dividend right represents 40/125ths of the total value of the stock, its "basis" would be 40/125ths of $100, or $32, and the taxpayer's gain on the transaction would be only $8, *i.e.,* $40 minus $32. (b) The $8 gain would be treated as capital gain. And (c), the taxpayer's remaining basis for the stock would be reduced to $68—$100 minus the $32 already recovered. If the stock were still worth $125 at the end of the five-year term and were then sold, the taxpayer would recognize a further capital gain of $57, *i.e.,* $125 minus $68. Total income from the stock investment over the five-year period would thus have been $65—dividend prepayment of $40 plus sale price of $125, less $100 original cost—and *all* of it would have been taxed as capital gain.

Plainly, however, if these outcomes were adopted by the law, all taxpayers owning stock or other income-producing property would be free (and, in effect, encouraged) to convert their ordinary investment income into capital gain by selling, or discounting, such income in advance of payment. Once the period covered by the advance sale had passed, the property-owner could *again* dispose of the future income for a term of years, and again report the "gain" as capital. By this process of anticipation (in itself a distortion of normal behavior), all periodic investment income could be converted into capital gain contrary to the evident intent of Congress.

Arguably, also, the status of the taxpayer in the illustration above is closer to—"more like"—that of an investor who retains his shares and receives his dividends in the normal way than it is to one who sells his shares outright. Again assuming that the stock continues to be worth $125 when the five-year period covered by the advance sale is over, the picture that emerges is as follows: Immediately prior to the advance sale the taxpayer owns stock with a market value of $125. Immediately after the advance sale he owns $40 cash plus a reversionary interest in the stock worth $85 ($125 less $40). The reversionary interest then rises in value year-by-year, until, at the end of the fifth year, the taxpayer resumes full ownership of the stock, which *still* has a value of $125. The $25 of stock appreciation that was present at the beginning of the five-year period thus remains *unrealized* ; in addition, the taxpayer has enjoyed a periodic economic "gain" through the annual increase in the value of his reverter.

In these respects, the advance-seller's position is similar to that of the "normal" dividend recipient: both own appreciated property at the end of the five-year term, and both have enjoyed a periodic addition to wealth. Presumably, therefore, both should be treated alike. In fact, as the *Hort* and *Lake* cases suggest, the courts *would* treat both alike, with the single exception that the advance-seller, having chosen to convert his dividend right to cash, would be taxed in the year the advance payment was received instead of at annual intervals. It might, indeed, be better to avoid even this dissimilarity, and to allow the advance payment to be taxed on a prorated basis over the five-year period. The rules of tax accounting (see 12.02) generally do not permit the deferral of cash receipts, however, and while this rigidity in accounting practice may be regrettable, it is not a matter that can be dealt with through the capital gain provisions except at the risk of considerable tax-avoidance.

In *Hort v. Commissioner,*[14] the taxpayer inherited a building, of which the main floor had been leased to a bank for a period of 15 years at an annual rental of $25,000. Subsequently, when the lease still had some 13 years to run, the bank notified the taxpayer that it wished to terminate its occupancy. Office rents had declined sharply by reason of the Depression, and in any event the bank no longer found it profitable to maintain a branch in the taxpayer's building. After negotiations, the taxpayer agreed to cancel the lease in consideration of a cash payment by the bank of $140,000.

The taxpayer reported a *loss* from the transaction of $21,000. The lease (in his view) had a separate basis of $257,000, which was said to be the discounted value of the rents due from the bank for the 13 years remaining. The amount realized on the cancellation was calculated to be only $236,000, *i.e.,* the cash payment of $140,000 plus $96,000 representing the *reduced* rental value of the premises for the same 13-year period. Rejecting this approach, the Commissioner not only disallowed the loss, but treated the $140,-000 payment as ordinary income.

In a brief opinion, the Supreme Court sustained the Commissioner in all respects. Cancellation of the lease, it said, "involved nothing more than the relinquishment of the right to future rental

14.   313 U.S. 28 (1941).

payments in return for a present substitute payment and possession of the leased premises." Since those future rents would have been taxed as ordinary income if received in the normal course, the "substitute" payment could be treated no differently. As respects the claimed loss, moreover, the Court concluded that it would not be consistent to allow the taxpayer a separate basis for the lease. If the taxpayer had suffered an economic injury because of the lease cancellation, that injury "would become a deductible loss only when its extent had been fixed by a closed transaction," that is, by a sale of the underlying real estate itself.

While the "substitute for future income" language is in some respects overbroad, the Court's intention in *Hort* is reasonably clear. Quite simply, the Court's aim was to deny (a) capital treatment, and (b) an offsetting basis, to one who disposes of a right to future income which has been carved out of a larger estate. In effect, the sale of an income right, unaccompanied by a disposition of the underlying property, results in ordinary income to the seller equal in amount to the entire proceeds of the sale. The "substitute" language, in the view of most commentators, was merely a shorthand way of asserting that carved-out interests do not qualify as capital assets and do not absorb any portion of the taxpayer's property basis.

The *Hort* decision is generally cited as the leading and definitive authority for the carved-out interest rule. Yet it might be noted that the case itself involved the *cancellation* of a lease by the lessee rather than the sale of a lease to a third party, and I think it can be argued that the former transaction, as compared with the latter, really does not present quite the same compelling case for ordinary treatment. Where a lease is sold by the lessor to a third party, some (perhaps all) of the amount received by the seller must be a substitute for future rental payments that would otherwise be taxed at ordinary rates. In practical effect, the transaction is equivalent to the sale of an account receivable, *i.e.,* the rent due under the lease. The buyer simply acquires the right to receive a series of cash payments, and hence the amount he pays the seller for that receivable will be the same whether rents have gone up or down in the market and whether the lease is burdensome or advantageous to the lessee. A payment for cancellation, by contrast, involves the vacating of the premises by the original lessee— the lease has plainly grown burdensome—with the lessor then presumably re-leasing the premises to another party at a lower figure and reporting the new rental-stream as ordinary income. The payment received by the lessor can thus be identified as, and really cannot be anything but, a premium attributable to a change in the market value of the leased premises. In effect, Hort's lease went up in value because rents dropped, just as a bond goes up in value when interest rates fall. If the bank repurchased or redeemed its own previously issued *bonds* at a premium—the bondholder recovering his original principal plus the premium amount— the bondholder's gain would be a capital gain. Arguably, the bank's act in repurchasing or cancelling its lease (which, from the bank's standpoint, is just another kind of IOU) should be viewed in equivalent terms: the lessor likewise recovers his original principal (the leased premises) plus a premium for giving up the lease (in *Hort,* $140,000). If a bond-redemption generates capital gain to a bondholder, why not a lease-redemption to a lease-holder? In essence, the two seem quite alike. But whatever the strength of this position, the Supreme Court in *Hort* obviously viewed the sale and the cancellation of a lease as indistinguishable for tax purposes—equally to be regarded as an act of carving-out—and it is clear at present that lease-cancellation payments are ordinary income to a lessor.

In *Commissioner v. P.G. Lake, Inc.,*[15] the Supreme Court extended the rule of the *Hort* case to transactions involving mineral properties—perhaps the one field in which sales of carved-out interests do commonly serve as a device for financing acquisition and exploitation activities. In *Lake,* the taxpayer-corporation owned the working-interest in two oil leases. In exchange for the cancellation of a debt, it assigned to its creditor a right to receive the sum of $600,000 out of the proceeds of future sales of oil. The parties anticipated that the payout would take about three years, a period substantially shorter than the useful life of the working-interest itself. The Fifth Circuit found the assignment to be a sale of a capital asset on the ground that the assigned oil-payment right constituted an "interest in land" under local law. The Supreme Court reversed. "The substance of what was received," it said, "was the present value of income which the recipient would otherwise obtain in the future. In short, consideration was paid for the right to receive future income, not for an increase in the value of the income-producing property."

As in *Hort,* the quoted language is broader than it needed to be, because the Court's aim, again, was merely to assure that carved-out interests would be treated as ordinary. Thus, capital gain treatment would presumably have been sustained if the life of the oil-payment and the life of the working-interest had been

---

15.   356 U.S. 260 (1958).

coterminous, since then the fatal element of carving-out would have been absent.

(b) Sale of a life estate. As suggested, the issues raised in *Hort* and *Lake* have an element of fruit-and-tree about them, and it is not surprising to discover that the Supreme Court found it useful in those cases to draw analogies from the older income-attribution cases. Thus, *Hort* cites *Horst,* and *Lake* draws heavily on *Clifford, Horst, and Schaffner.* The reason is fairly plain. In the income-attribution cases, the Court's aim was to prevent property-owners from shifting tax to lower-bracket donees through short-term assignments of income. In *Hort* and *Lake,* the aim was to prevent the conversion of ordinary income into capital gain through use of a similar device. In both areas, though for somewhat different reasons, the Court sought to block what it regarded as a subversion of Congressional intent, and in both the preventive rule was one which required that the underlying property be completely disposed of (whether through gift or sale) before the desired tax benefit would be allowed.

In one well-known instance, however, this practice of placing reliance on the income-attribution cases proved slightly disastrous. In *McAllister v. Commissioner,*[16] the taxpayer sold her life estate in a testamentary trust to the trust's remainderman for $55,000 cash. Asserting that her basis in the life estate, computed actuarially, was about $63,000, the taxpayer reported a capital loss from the sale of $8,000. Much as he had in *Hort,* the Commissioner disallowed the loss and treated the entire $55,000 as ordinary income.

With one dissent, the Second Circuit held for the taxpayer. Judge Clark, for the majority, reasoned that the issue "reduce[d] itself to the question whether the case [was] within the rule of Blair v. Commissioner . . ., or that of Hort v. Commissioner . . . ." In *Blair,* he noted, the Supreme Court had held that the gift of a life estate represented "the assignment of a property right in a trust." Hence, the donee rather than the donor was taxable on the trust income received thereafter. *Blair,* said Clark, was "indistinguishable from the present case," because here, as there, the taxpayer transferred her entire interest in the property. By contrast, had Mrs. McAllister attempted to sell the income for a few years only— had she, as in *Hort,* engaged in a carving out—the transaction would be viewed as mere income anticipation, and the Commissioner's position would be sustained.

Dissenting, Judge Frank argued that the *Blair* decision was not determinative: the fact that the *donor* of a life estate was held not

16.   157 F.2d 235 (2d Cir.1946).

taxable under § 61(a) on trust income received by the donee did not, in his view, establish that the *seller* of a life estate was to be treated as having disposed of a capital asset within the meaning of § 1221. *Hort* rather than *Blair* was the relevant authority, he thought, because the sale of a life estate, like the cancellation of a lease, "resemble[d] the advance payment of dividends, interest, or salaries." As in *Hort,* the sale was merely a substitute for future income, and hence the proceeds should have been taxed at ordinary rates.

Once again, it is important to emphasize that there were really *two* issues before the court in *McAllister:* (1) whether Mrs. McAllister could report a *loss* from the transaction, and (2) whether in any event the life estate was a capital asset in her hands. As stated, Judge Clark resolved both questions favorably to the taxpayer, because the absence of a carving-out convinced him that the case was controlled by *Blair.*

The decision in *McAllister* almost certainly was wrong. To see why, it will be useful to remind ourselves of the rules that govern the taxation of trust income where the life-tenant *retains* her life estate and receives annual distribution from the trust in a "normal" manner. As indicated at 4.02, under the "system" approved by the Supreme Court in *Irwin v. Gavit,* the life tenant is taxed on *all* the trust income during the term of the trust, and is *not* allowed an offset for amortization. The remainderman, on the other hand, includes nothing in his income either annually or on the termination of the trust. At the death of the life-tenant, the remainderman takes over the trust property at a basis equal to its full basis in the hands of the trustee, just as if the remainderman had been the sole legatee. To illustrate, assume that a decedent leaves property in trust (life estate to A, remainder to B) with a basis and value at death of $100,000. The property is expected to yield income of $8,000 a year. Based on A's life-expectancy (say 12 years), the present value of her interest in the trust is $60,000; that of the remainderman $40,000. Under *Gavit,* A will include the full $8,000 of trust income every year throughout her lifetime. B will include nothing, and when the trust terminates at A's death B will take the trust property at a basis of $100,000. The *Gavit* "system" is thus one in which the exclusion for gifts and bequests—and hence the *entire* basis in the property—goes to the remainderman alone. All the taxable income—and hence *none* of the basis—goes to the life tenant.

Apparently unaware of *Gavit,* the court in *McAllister* disregarded the system just described insofar as the life-tenant was concerned. The decision, in effect, permits A to take credit for a proportionate share of the basis of the trust property where the life estate is *sold,* but does (and of course can do) nothing to limit the remainderman's claim to the full basis of the property when the trust terminates. The result is an *over*-recovery of basis. If A sells her life-estate for $60,000 immediately after the decedent's death, she has no gain or loss under *McAllister* because her basis for the life-estate is held to be $60,000. When the trust terminates, B's basis for the trust property under *Gavit* becomes $100,000. Thus, 160% of the property's basis will ultimately be recovered by its beneficial owners, which is obviously an erroneous outcome.

The error becomes even clearer when one observes that the effect of *McAllister* is to eliminate entirely a substantial proportion of the taxable income of the trust. This follows from the fact that the *purchaser* of the life estate (in *McAllister* the remainderman himself) is entitled to amortize his cost over the expected term of the interest he has purchased—12 years in our illustration. The purchaser stands apart from the relationship between the life-tenant and remainderman; he is an "unrelated" investor who has actually laid out $60,000 for a wasting asset, and that outlay is properly recoverable by him through amortization deductions at the rate of $5,000 a year. In overall terms, therefore, $60,000 of trust income will be taxed to *nobody.*

The *Blair* case, of course, did not entail the same consequence. While the donee of the life estate became taxable on the trust income (no doubt at a lower marginal rate than the donor), the Supreme Court did not suggest that the life estate acquired a basis in the donee's hands by reason of the gift, or that any change occurred in the normal operation of the *Gavit* rules. Income-shifting was approved in *Blair* because of the absence of a carving-out, but this holding had, or should have had, no bearing on the treatment of amounts realized on *sales* of life estates. In emphasizing *Blair* and overlooking *Gavit,* Judge Clark simply fastened on the wrong income-attribution rule.

A similar set of observations can be made about the second question raised in *McAllister*—whether the life estate was a capital asset in the hands of the life tenant. Even if Judge Clark had gotten the basis problem right—which would have meant giving the life tenant a basis of zero—it would have been inconsistent with *Hort* and *Gavit* to treat the proceeds of sale as capital gain. The aim of *Gavit,* really, is to simplify the taxation of trust income by treating the life-tenant and the remainderman as if they were one individual. Under *Hort,* if an individual property-owner sells an income interest for a term of years but retains the underlying property, the proceeds of sale are taxable as ordinary income because the transaction is viewed as a carving-out. By plausible analogy, the same should be true if a life estate is sold separately from the remainder, because *Gavit* integrates the life-tenant and the remainderman for tax purposes. If, however, the life estate is held to be a capital asset, then, in effect, the ordinary income thrown off by the trust will be $60,000 less than it should be, and a clear advantage arises in creating split interests in property as compared with outright gifts or bequests.

The *McAllister* problem was finally dealt with by Congress in 1969 through the addition to the Code of § 1001(e). Curiously, however, § 1001(e) is limited to the basis aspect: the subsection provides that for purposes of computing gain or loss, a term interest in property shall have no basis in the hands of a donee or heir, except where the sale of the term interest is part of a transaction in which all beneficial interests are disposed of. No change was made as respects the capital asset status of the life estate, however, so that if the illustrative transaction took place now, the taxpayer would presumably have $60,000 of capital gain. Apparently, Congress was persuaded that sellers of life estates (often, perhaps, older people) would suffer hardship if the proceeds of sale were taxed all in one year as ordinary income, and having corrected the computation of basis, was willing to continue favored treatment as respects the resultant gain.

(c) Other contract rights. Right or wrong, the *Hort* and *McAllister* decisions show that the courts do not treat all transactions involving contract claims alike. In *Hort,* the element of carving-out led to ordinary treatment; in *McAllister,* the assumed absence of that element led to capital gain. In other cases, especially when employment rights are concerned, the courts have sometimes resolved definitional issues by finding that the contract sold or cancelled lacked or possessed the status of "property"; in still others, the factor of "sale or exchange" has been seen as critical. Overall, the treatment of contract rights is exceedingly untidy; the decided cases are hard to line up in a consistent fashion, and judicial reasoning is often unclear. Much of the blame belongs to Congress. Here, as in the *Corn Products* area, the need is for a detailed statutory classification which effectively separates capital from non-capital transactions. Uncertain of its own goals in the capital gain field, however, Congress has preferred to leave the matter to the courts.

Leasehold interests. As already noted in connection with *Hort,* a *lessor* normally has ordinary income on the sale or cancellation of a lease. *Hort,* obviously, was a case in which rental values had *fallen* after the lease was entered into; the lease had grown onerous to the lessee, who paid the lessor a cash sum to be free of it.   But suppose that the real estate market had moved in the other direction, that rental values had increased, and that the rental called for in the lease had become a bargain by current standards. The lease would then have been economically burdensome to Hort, the lessor.   If Hort had paid $140,000 to the lessee for the cancellation of the lease, or if the lessee had sold its rights to occupy the building to a third party, would the lessee have had ordinary income also?   The answer, apparently, is no.   The courts have held, as to *lessees,* that the sale or surrender of a lease results in capital gain.[17]   In the lessee's hands, it is said, the leasehold is a substantial interest in real estate, not merely a claim to future income. Whereas the amount received by Hort, a lessor, for cancellation of the lease was held a substitute for future rents, the amount paid to a lessee for surrendering *its* interest in a lease is regarded as received in exchange for a property right which qualifies as a capital asset.

As usual, however, distinctions based on the "substitute for ordinary income" doctrine are not very satisfying.   A lessee who is the beneficiary of a favorable lease enjoys a saving of annual rents which will be reflected in higher net income from the business operations conducted on the leased premises.   Since rentals are otherwise fully deductible, the saving is merely an addition to the ordinary income which the lessee will realize through occupancy. If this benefit is bought up by the lessor, or is sold to a third party, the payment received is as much and as clearly a "substitute for future income" as the payment that is made to a lessor when the fact-pattern is reversed.

Probably, though, the "substitution" doctrine is nothing more than judicial shorthand, just as is the fruit-and-tree doctrine in the income-attribution field.   The real, or at least the best, reason for distinguishing between lessors and lessees resides in the presence (in one case) and the absence (in the other) of the familiar element of carving out.   Once again, a lessor who disposes of his interest in a lease *still* owns the underlying income-producing property—land or building—after the disposition.   He therefore retains the ability, on the expiration of each successive lease, to *repeat* the process of making an advance disposition of his right to future rentals.   If such advance dispositions were accorded capital gain treatment, then all of the property-owner's ordinary rental income could be converted into capital gain.   By contrast, a lessee owns only cash

---

17. *E.g., Comm'r v. McCue Brothers & Drummond, Inc.,* 210 F.2d 752 (2d   Cir.1954). And see Code § 1241.

following the disposition of a lease, and thus lacks the opportunity to again dispose of his rights in the same leasehold. The tax law reflects this difference, in effect, by treating the leasehold as a mere substitute for ordinary income when it is the *lessor* who sells or surrenders the lease. Where the *lessee* is concerned, however, the leasehold turns out to be substantial "property".

Employment contracts, agencies, distributorships, etc. Suppose the manager of a baseball team is dismissed by his club at the end of the first year of a two-year contract. The contract calls for a salary of $300,000 a year, and the manager, after negotiation, agrees to accept $100,000 for releasing the club from its remaining obligation. Is the $100,000 payment capital gain, or is it ordinary income?

The courts have held consistently that payments made to an employee for the surrender of his employment contract are ordinary.[18] Although the decisions sometimes rest on the ground that the contract cancellation is not a "sale or exchange," or that an employment contract is not "property," it seems likely that the courts have been influenced chiefly by the feeling that employment and personal service is simply not an appropriate context for capital gain. Possibly, also, there is an analogy between the position of the baseball manager in the illustration above and the position of a lessor of real estate. The manager receives a payment for cancellation of his contract because his services are now worth less to the club than when the contract was entered into, but he is also free to accept similar employment elsewhere. In *Hort,* the lessor received a premium from his lessee because rental values had declined, and, again, was free to re-lease the property to another tenant. If ordinary income was required to be recognized in *Hort* (for reasons relating generally to the carved-out interest limitation), perhaps the same principle justifies ordinary treatment for employees (*i.e.,* lessors of services) when an employment contract is terminated. It would also seem to follow that if an employ*ee* is like a less*or,* then an employ*er* is like a less*ee.* Hence, if the baseball club sold a player's contract to another team for cash, presumably its gain would be capital.

Once we leave real estate leases and employment agreements, however, the treatment of contract termination payments becomes uncertain. It has been held, for example, that amounts received by a taxpayer on the transfer of an agency contract giving the taxpayer an exclusive right to represent a popular singer were ordinary. Viewing the agency agreement as essentially similar to an employ-

---

18. *E.g., McFall v. Comm'r,* 34 B.T.A. 108 (1936).

ment contract, the Tax Court found that the right to represent a client was not a capital asset.[19] The Fifth Circuit, on the other hand, has held that the sale of a right to service mortgage accounts by collecting payments and performing other duties on behalf of the mortgage-holder, an insurance company, did entail the transfer of a capital asset.[20] The court apparently felt that the service contract was a major structural element of the taxpayer's business, and not merely a right to earn employment income. Code § 1241 specifically provides that the cancellation of a distributorship agreement shall be treated as a "sale or exchange" in cases in which "the distributor has a substantial capital investment in the distributorship." Although the section deals only with the sale or exchange requirement, it was evidently Congress' intent to afford capital gain where a distributorship which involved a significant outlay by the taxpayer is sold or terminated. The proper treatment of contracts which cannot easily be classified as employment contracts, but which do not meet the capital investment test of § 1241, is thereby left in doubt.

Among the most interesting of the many decisions in the contracts field is *Commissioner v. Ferrer.*[21] As a matter of incidental history, the Second Circuit prior to *Ferrer* had distinguished fairly sharply between real-estate leases and other contract rights. Thus, as noted earlier, the court found capital gain upon a lessee's surrender of its lease to the lessor, but also found ordinary income upon the cancellation of an exclusive distributorship,[22] the sale of exclusive agency rights,[23] and the termination of an exclusive right to buy the output of a coal mine. In the last of these cases, *Commissioner v. Pittston Co.,*[24] the court held that the taxpayer's contractual right to acquire the mine output at a predetermined price lacked the quality of a substantial property interest, in part because the taxpayer's sole remedy would have been in money damages had the mine owner elected to breach the contract by selling coal to third parties. In this respect, the court said, the taxpayer's status differed from that of a lessee whose rights in the leased premises are enforceable in equity and thus constitute an interest in the property itself. A dissenting opinion argued that the output contract was the equivalent of a lease of the mining property and, hence, should have been treated as a capital asset.

---

19. *General Artists Corp. v. Comm'r,* 17 T.C. 1517 (1952), affirmed 205 F.2d 360 (2d Cir.1953).

20. *Nelson Weaver Realty Corp. v. Comm'r,* 307 F.2d 897 (5th Cir.1962).

21. 304 F.2d 125 (2d Cir.1962).

22. *Comm'r v. Starr Brothers,* 204 F.2d 673 (2d Cir.1953).

23. *General Artists Corp. v. Comm'r,* supra note 13.

24. 252 F.2d 344 (2d Cir.1958).

The "substantial property" test was also stressed in *Ferrer.* The taxpayer, a well-known actor, had entered into a dramatic production contract with the author of a novel called *Moulin Rouge.* The contract gave Ferrer (1) the right to produce and present a play based on the novel, (2) the right to veto any disposition of movie rights prior to the time the play had run for a specified period, and (3) the right to receive 40% of any motion picture proceeds if the play was in fact produced and the movie rights were sold thereafter. Before a play could get underway, however, Ferrer received an offer from John Huston to do a movie based on *Moulin Rouge* in which Ferrer would play the lead. As part of the deal, Huston insisted that Ferrer consent to either "an annulment or conveyance" of the dramatic production contract between himself and the novelist. Ferrer agreed and entered into a new contract with Huston. Under the new contract, Ferrer was to receive a salary for performing the role of Toulouse-Lautrec, plus a stated percentage of the motion picture distribution profits. The latter was said to be in consideration for the surrender by Ferrer of the original dramatic production contract. In 1953, in addition to the salary, which he reported as ordinary income, Ferrer received $180,000 as his percentage of the distribution profits. The issue in the case, simply, was whether the percentage payment should be treated as ordinary income or capital gain.

The Tax Court found as a fact that the percentage payment was *not* mere personal service income, but had truly been received in exchange for Ferrer's assignment of the dramatic production contract. The contract, in turn, was held to be a capital asset, and hence the entire payment was treated as capital gain. On appeal by the Commissioner, the Second Circuit declined to reverse the lower court's findings on the personal service issue. It did, however, reassess the character of the contract rights which Ferrer had acquired and then released, by treating each as a separate economic interest in the novel. On this basis, the court decided that right (1)—the right to produce a play—was analogous to a lease of the story property, Ferrer being the lessee, because equitable relief would have been available had the contract been breached; and that right (2)—the veto power—was equivalent to an "encumbrance" which equity would also protect if necessary. However, as to right (3)—the right to share in the proceeds of any sale to the movies—the court found that this element did *not* rise to the status of an "equitable interest" in property, but merely represented a claim to "a percentage of certain avails ... as further income from the lease of the play." Right (3), in the court's view, was comparable to the right of a lessee to receive from his lessor "a percentage of what the lessor obtained from other tenants attracted to the building by the lessee's operations"; in effect, the movie rights would become valuable if the play was a success. Since such percentage payments would be ordinary income to the lessee if received during the term of the lease, a sale of the lessee's right thereto for a lump-sum payment produced ordinary income as well. Accordingly, rights (1) and (2) were given capital asset status, while right (3) was held to be ordinary. The case was then remanded to the Tax Court for an allocation of the percentage money among these several interests.

Judge Friendly's opinion in *Ferrer* is skillfully devised and plausible. Even so, one can question whether it was truly appropriate to treat each of the taxpayer's contract rights as a separate unit, instead of viewing the contract, as the Tax Court had, as one single economic interest. Suppose, to use the court's leasehold analogy, that a lessee is entitled to occupy certain premises for a term of years. The lease provides for a stated annual rental, but provides also that this stated rental is to be reduced by payment to the lessee of a percentage of the rents received by the lessor from other tenants in the same building. In exchange for a lump-sum, the lessee now surrenders his entire leasehold interest, including his right to rent reduction payments. It seems quite clear that such a transaction would produce capital gain. There might be doubt about the result if the lessee sold off the right to percentage payments by itself and retained the lease, but where the leasehold is disposed of as well there seems to be no reason to deny capital gain treatment once it is conceded that a lease is a capital asset. In *Ferrer* the "lessee" retained nothing, and certainly the right to share in the motion picture proceeds was a part of the overall lease arrangement, not an independently acquired interest. It is difficult to see, therefore, why right (3) should have been carved out of the basic contract and treated as if disposed of for a separate consideration when that was simply not the case, except as this construction may have been necessary to reach the desired result.

One suspects that at bottom this complex decision reflects an unstated compromise which traces back to the basic issue of personal services. Constrained by the Tax Court's negative finding on that question, the court nevertheless managed, through a deft manipulation of the lease analogy, to sustain the Commissioner in treating a portion of the percentage money—probably the major proportion—as ordinary income. Actually, the simplest, and probably the most nearly accurate, view of the facts in *Ferrer* was that the entire percentage payment represented a reward for Ferrer's services as an actor. Had Ferrer declined to take the lead in the movie, Huston most probably would have made no deal with him whatever. The fact that Ferrer also had some control over the story-property may have meant that he could ask somewhat more for his services than otherwise. Fundamentally, however, the entire receipt was compensation—or, at least, income from the taxpayer's trade or business—and quite probably all of it should have been lumped together with Ferrer's salary and found to be ordinary in the first instance.

17.04 Fragmentation and Imputed Interest. Up to this point, the issue of capital gain or ordinary income has been presented on an all-or-nothing basis. The futures contracts in *Corn Products* either were, or weren't, capital assets; the lease-cancellation payment in *Hort* either was, or wasn't, a "return of capital." By contrast, in the cases next discussed the property disposed of appears to possess elements that are mixed, to be neither wholly capital nor wholly ordinary. Under such circumstances, will the law require the asset to be fragmented into separate components for the purpose of characterizing the taxpayer's gain or loss, or will it insist on a finding that the property is either one thing or the other, but not both? This curious question is considered here in two contexts: first, the sale of an entire business—a "going concern"—whose assets include both capital and non-capital items; and second, the disposition of a security or other claim whose value includes an accrued or "imputed" interest factor. These two situations do not exhaust the fragmentation problem, however, and the same or a similar problem will be seen to arise again in later sections.

(a) Sale of an entire business. In *Williams v. McGowan,*[25] the taxpayer sold a hardware business which he owned and operated as a sole proprietor. The assets of the business included cash, inventory, accounts receivable, and fixtures and other depreciable property. The sale resulted in an overall net loss which the taxpayer reported as ordinary. The Commissioner sought to treat the loss as capital, however, on the ground that the hardware "business," viewed as an entity, was a capital asset. Speaking through Judge Learned Hand, the Second Circuit upheld the taxpayer. § 1221, Hand noted, specifically broke the elements of a business down into separate categories, such as stock-in-trade and depreciable assets. This, he reasoned, showed that Congress meant to "comminute" the business into fragments, and that it did not regard "the whole" as a capital asset. Since, apparently, the hardware business included ordinary assets only, the loss that resulted from the sale was

---

25. 152 F.2d 570 (2d Cir.1945).

held to be an ordinary loss. Dissenting, Judge Frank argued that it was artificial and unrealistic to carve up the transaction into distinct sales of separate properties. "Where a business is sold as a unit," he said, "the whole is greater than its parts. Businessmen so recognize; so, too, I think did Congress." In effect, therefore, while Hand viewed the separate classification of business assets as mandatory, whether those assets were sold piecemeal or as part of a sale of the entire concern, Frank regarded the "business" as distinguishable from its component parts and viewed the entirety as qualifying "property."

Who was right? Solely from the standpoint of capital gain policy, the majority's conclusion probably represents the better view (though, as shown below, it does lead to complications). If, as Frank insisted, the sale of a going business were treated as the sale of a single capital asset, the effect would be to extend capital gain to ordinary business income in many cases. Under the present Code and case-law, "business income" includes, among other things, profits or gains attributable to trade receivables and appreciated inventory. If Frank's "single-asset" view had prevailed, the statutory distinction between these kinds of assets and "true" investment property would be obliterated where the business was sold to a single buyer. But where more than a single purchaser was involved, or where the business was terminated through a series of transactions because no buyer could be found for all the property at once, presumably the separate-asset view espoused by Hand would prevail. Arguably, however, the difference between these latter situations and a one-shot sale of the business—the seller's interest being terminated in either event—ought not to lead to variable tax consequences. The holding in *Williams v. McGowan* prevents that result by requiring separate classification of the business assets regardless of the circumstances of disposition.

Having thus approved the outcome in *Williams,* it is necessary to add that the requirement of "comminution" tends to complicate the bargaining between the seller and the buyer of a business, because it usually means that they must agree not only on an overall purchase price for the company, but also on the specific allocation of that purchase price among the assets sold. This is important to the seller for the obvious reason that the allocation governs the amount of ordinary income he has to recognize on the sale; it is important to the buyer because it determines his basis for the assets acquired and hence his own potential for future ordinary income. To the extent the purchase price is allocated to non-capital assets—typically inventory—the seller's ordinary income is increased while the buyer's is reduced; to the extent allocated to depreciable assets, the seller may get some capital gain under § 1231, but also some ordinary income under §§ 1245 and 1250, while the buyer has a higher basis for computing depreciation; to the extent allocable to goodwill, the seller gets capital gain treatment and the buyer gets an asset whose cost (under new § 197) is amortizable over a 15–year term; finally, to the extent allocable to a non-depreciable asset such as land, the seller gets capital gain while the buyer is left with a cost that will not be recoverable until the asset itself is sold.[26] The interests of the two parties are thus in some respects adverse, a factor that may make agreement more difficult to reach. On the other hand, the need to agree upon an allocation protects the government from the danger that seller and buyer will take inconsistent positions, which, in a given case, might otherwise eliminate the ordinary income component on both sides.

(b) *Bond discount and imputed interest.* Suppose a corporate borrower issues a 5-year bond for $620. The bondholder is entitled to no interest payments during the 5-year term but on redemption at maturity the corporation agrees to pay the holder $1,000. As a formal matter, it can be argued that the $380 difference between the issue and the redemption price is "property appreciation" and should be taxed as capital gain, but, really, the argument is almost too weak to require refutation. The original issue discount of $380 represents compensation to the bondholder for the use of the borrowed funds and simply takes the place of annual interest payments. Recognizing this, § 1271—which otherwise treats gain or loss on sale or retirement of a bond as capital gain or loss— provides in effect that original issue discount shall be taxed to the bondholder as ordinary interest income. § 1272 requires, further, that the bondholder accrue such interest annually—rather than deferring it until maturity or sale—even though the holder may be an individual who is on the cash method of accounting. As respects the latter rule, the controlling analogy, I suppose, is to accrued interest on a savings account, which is taxed to the depositor each year whether withdrawn by him in cash or left to accumulate.

The same analogy should answer the question of *how much* interest is accruable by the bondholder annually. The implicit rate of return to the bondholder in our example is 10%, *i.e.,* $620 invested at a 10% constant rate of interest will grow to $1,000 at the end of 5 years. By accepting a discount bond instead of

---

26. The classification rules today differ somewhat from those that applied when *Williams* was decided. Goodwill would now be viewed as a capital asset, while, as indicated, depreciable property is governed by the special rules of § 1231, etc. (See 18.02). On the other hand, trade receivables are now excluded from capital asset status by § 1221(4).

insisting on annual interest payments, the bondholder—like a savings account depositor who leaves his annual interest in the account—is really increasing the principal amount of his loan from year to year. Thus, the original loan is $620. At 10%, interest for Year 1 is $62. Since the latter amount is left in the borrower's hands instead of being withdrawn, "principal" increases to $682 at the start of Year 2 and interest for that year is about $68. For years 3, 4 and 5 the accrued interest amounts would be $76, $83 and $91, respectively, with the total of all such annual accruals, plus the original issue price of $620, necessarily equalling the redemption price of $1,000.

Given the tax law's historical reluctance to grapple with the everyday miracle of compound interest, it may surprise some to learn that § 1272(a)(3)—added in 1982 at the urging of the Treasury—actually does require a "scientific" calculation of annual interest in connection with original issue discount bonds (*i.e.*, $62 in Year 1, $68 in Year 2, etc.). Prior to 1982, the relevant Code provision used a straight-line calculation, which, in our example, would produce level annual interest accruals of $76 ($380/5 years). Since the straight-line method inevitably *overstated* interest in the earlier years, the corrected method would appear to be more favorable to bondholders. For the same reason, however, it is *less* favorable to borrowers: the latter were previously permitted to compute their accrued interest expense on the same straight-line basis and thus take larger deductions in the earlier years than their true interest cost. But why, then, should the Treasury have sought the change? Wouldn't all this more or less balance out from the standpoint of the revenues? Hardly. Before 1982, original issue discount bonds were usually sold to tax-exempt entities, such as employee pension plans, or to lenders having unused loss carryovers or otherwise lacking in "tax appetite." Allowing the borrower to anticipate its interest deductions under the straight-line method was thus often harmless to the bondholder, who could, indeed, expect to receive a somewhat higher interest rate from the borrower as consideration for joining in the scheme. As has been seen (*e.g.*, 6.02(c)), any distortion in the timing of income and deductions can be converted into financial benefits for *both* parties to the relevant transaction, provided only that one of the parties is exempt or unprofitable, or confronts lower tax rates than the other.

Yet another legislative change should be mentioned. Prior to 1984, the ordinary treatment provided for by § 1272 applied only to discount in the *original* issue price of a bond. If discount developed because of later market fluctuations, redemption of the bond at par resulted in capital gain. Thus, suppose a bond originally issued for its par value of $100 dropped to $90 because of a rise in prevailing interest rates. An investor who bought the bond in the market for $90, and then simply held the bond until maturity and received $100 from the issuer, had a $10 capital gain. In effect, bond discount resulted in ordinary income only if the interest element was built into the issue price by the borrower.

Plainly, however, a distinction between market discount and original issue discount makes little sense in economic terms. Thus, the difference between the taxpayer's $90 purchase price (in the example just given) and the $100 he receives when the bond matures is "interest" as far as he is concerned. The taxpayer's aim is to pay $90 now for a promise to receive $100 later, and it doesn't matter to him (taxes aside) whether he buys the bond from another investor or from the bond-issuer directly.

The 1984 Act changes the treatment of market discount bonds and requires that investors report market discount as ordinary income when the bond is disposed of, whether through sale or redemption at maturity. Under § 1276(a), the reportable amount is limited to the gain realized on such disposition, so that no interest would be imputed if the bond mentioned in the preceding paragraph were finally sold for less than the investor's $90 purchase price. Original issue discount, by contrast, is accruable annually, presumably because the issuer itself will be amortizing the discount through annual interest deductions.

The Code sections just discussed—§§ 1271 *et seq.*—apply to bonds, debentures, notes and other conventional debt instruments. With respect to claims of a less formal character that are not covered by those sections—for example, a claim to a legacy or to unpaid fees or commissions—the courts have generally held that settlement or collection does not constitute a "sale or exchange." [27] As a result, if an investor purchases such a claim at a discount, any gain realized when the obligor makes payment will be treated as ordinary income. [28] The courts' theory in cases of this sort is that the taxpayer's claim is merely "extinguished" when it is satisfied by the obligor; no "exchange" occurs because the obligor himself acquires no property other than relief from the obligation. This application of the sale or exchange requirement is obviously rather wooden, but perhaps it here serves as recognition of the imputed interest element in the creditor's gain. As with discount bonds, such imputed interest can be identified as the difference between

27. *Fairbanks v. U.S.,* 306 U.S. 436 (1939).

28. *E.g., Pounds v. U.S.,* 372 F.2d 342 (5th Cir.1967) (settlement of a pur-chased commission claim held ordinary income).

the purchase price of the claim and the amount finally received from the obligor.

In an effort to avoid ordinary income in these circumstances, taxpayers have sometimes resorted to a sale of the purchased claim to a third party just prior to its collection. In *Jones v. Commissioner,*[29] the taxpayer purchased a remainder interest in a trust from the original remainderman. After the life-tenant's death but prior to actual distribution of the trust property, the taxpayer resold the remainder to another. Apparently, he feared that receipt of the trust property through distribution by the trustee would fail to qualify as a "sale or exchange." Conceding that the remainder (like any other "security") was a capital asset, the court held that despite the sale to a third party the taxpayer must recognize as ordinary income the implicit interest which had accrued on his investment. In effect, the accrued interest element was regarded as a non-capital component of the gain. The court therefore remanded the case to the trial court for the purpose of determining what portion of the total gain should be regarded as ordinary and what portion should be treated as capital.

The proceedings on remand are unreported, but perhaps the following would be illustrative. Assume that the trust in the *Jones* case owned property worth $100,000 when initially created; that the life-tenant had an actuarial life-expectancy of five years; and that Jones immediately purchased the remainder for $75,000. Viewing the remainder as analogous to a discount bond, the anticipated interest element is obviously $25,000 over the five-year period, or $5,000 a year on a straight-line basis. Suppose, however, that the life-tenant died after only *two* years, and suppose also that the trust property—say real estate—had risen in value by that time to $120,000. We could now identify three-elements of gain: (a) interest of $10,000 (*i.e.,* $5,000 × 2 years); (b) a mortality gain of $15,000; and (c) pure property appreciation of $20,000. Assuming the "sale or exchange" requirement was satisfied, the *Jones* decision apparently contemplates that (a) would be taxed as ordinary income, and (c) as capital gain. As to (b), the proper treatment is less clear. Since Jones was a casual investor and not an insurance company, however, the probability is that it, too, would be treated as capital gain.

17.05 Recurring Receipts. As noted in connection with the *Hort* case, the law distinguishes in a basic way between gain realized on a sale of appreciated property and periodic income such as dividends, interest and rents. The former, of course, is capital

---

29.   330 F.2d 302 (3d Cir.1964).

gain, the latter ordinary income. In *Hort,* the Court had to decide whether the sale of a carved-out income interest was "more like" a sale of appreciated property or "more like" the receipt of ordinary rent. The decision to treat the carved-out interest as ordinary was dictated, essentially, by a fear that recurring investment income would otherwise become convertible—pretty much on a wholesale basis—into low-taxed capital gain.

The cases discussed in this subsection—especially *Commissioner v. Brown* [30]—also involve the problem of differentiating between property appreciation and recurring income. Here, however, the issue concerns the *method* by which the purported sale has been effected, rather than the intrinsic nature of the asset disposed of. It is conceded that the property is a capital asset; what is questioned is whether the *transfer* qualifies as a sale. If, for example, the purported sale price is to be paid out in installments over an extended period of years, and if the payments themselves are contingent on the income to be derived from the property transferred, there may be legitimate doubt as to whether the transaction is a "sale" or merely a species of lease or profit-sharing arrangement. As a technical matter, capital treatment requires a "sale or exchange"; and in any event the philosophy of the capital gain preference assumes a completed disposition of the property in question. Accordingly, a finding that the transfer falls short of being a complete disposition normally means ordinary income to the transferor.

The discussion of *Brown,* which follows next, examines the "completed disposition" standard in the context of contingent-payment transactions. As will be seen, the Supreme Court has been liberal in characterizing such transactions as "sales". The *Carter* case, discussed thereafter, raises the further question of how the "fair market value" rule, established by the Court in *Burnet v. Logan* (14.03), relates to the treatment of the payments received. It turns out that "open" transactions—those in which a fair market value for the buyer's obligation *cannot* be ascertained—are treated more favorably than transactions that are deemed to be "closed". A brief consideration of the merits of this distinction concludes the section.

(a) Contingent payments. A transaction in which property is to be paid for out of income to be derived from the property itself obviously presents a borderline problem under the "sale or exchange" requirement. From a policy standpoint, the capital gain preference is intended, at least in part, to afford relief to taxpayers

---

30. 380 U.S. 563 (1965).

who are compelled to report in a single taxable year property appreciation which has accrued over an extended period of years. In addition, perhaps, the lower capital gain rate is designed to free taxpayers to shift investments in accordance with economic considerations by easing the impact of the taxable realization when appreciated property is sold. But if the property is transferred in exchange for future payments that will be spread out over a number of years, and if, in addition, those payments are contingent on the income-producing capacity of the property itself, then neither element of "policy" seems readily applicable. Assuming that the taxpayer's gain is deferred (whether through use of the installment method under § 453 or because of other applicable rules of realization) until the payments are received, the effect is to produce a kind of home-made averaging of income which renders doubtful the need for further relief through a reduction of the applicable rates. Further, as the taxpayer is to be paid out of future income from the property transferred, it seems doubtful whether a "shift" from one investment to another really can be said to have occurred.

These objections to permitting capital gain for deferred payment transactions—and especially for *contingent* deferred payment transactions—are not inconsiderable. But whatever their force, the fact is that neither Congress nor (for the most part) the courts have found them determinative. Thus, reporting gain on the installment basis under § 453 does not affect the seller's right to treat that gain as capital if the property sold is a capital asset. The installment method is *not* conditioned on a taxpayer's willingness to accept ordinary income from a transaction that would otherwise produce capital gain. The same is true where deferral of gain results from the taxpayer's use of the cash method of accounting or from the operation of the so-called fair market value rule. As with installment reporting under § 453, the justification for deferral— lack of ascertainable value, or the cash method of accounting— stands apart from the taxpayer's entitlement to capital gain.

Transactions in which the purchase price is payable out of income have been treated in the same way, on the whole, despite the obvious element of continued risk to the seller. Thus, after much litigation, the Commissioner finally agreed (and § 1235 now expressly provides) that the transfer of a patent in exchange for the transferee's promise to pay royalties based on production of the patented article was a sale that qualified for capital treatment, even though royalty payments were to continue over the entire useful life of the patent. Capital gain has also been approved where corporate stock was sold for amounts which were to be measured by the dividends payable on the shares over a stated period of years,[31] or even by the net profits of the business. It is, of course, well arguable that such transactions should be distinguished from those in which the buyer's obligation is independent of the income from the property transferred, with only the latter type being viewed as a sale or exchange. But, on the other hand, the difficulty of establishing a fixed price for patents, closely held businesses and other non-marketable assets is probably considerable in many cases—the property may lack a prior earnings record or be subject to other substantial uncertainties. Often, therefore, such property can only be sold on a contingent-payment basis. If such arrangements were automatically treated as non-sales, the effect would be to disqualify property of this character from capital gain treatment simply because of its inherent riskiness.

In *Commissioner v. Brown,* the taxpayer sold his stock in a lumber company to a charitable organization. The purchase price was $1,300,000, payable $5,000 down and the balance within 10 years out of the earnings of the lumber company. Following transfer of the stock to the charity, the assets of the company were leased back to an operating company managed and controlled by Brown himself. The operating company paid its profits over to the charity as deductible "rent", and the charity then paid the greater part of such rents to Brown as the purchase price of his stock. Once the entire purchase price was paid, the operating assets would belong to the charity. The figure of $1,300,000 was found to be a fair valuation for the lumber business.

Rejecting the Commissioner's contention that the transaction could not be a "sale" because the risks of the business remained with the seller, the Supreme Court held that the disposition of the taxpayer's stock was "complete," and that the amounts received were entitled to be treated as capital gain. The Court recognized that because the buyer was a tax-exempt charity no corporate tax would be owed on the earnings of the business. As a result, the purchase price could be paid out more rapidly than if the buyer were merely another taxable entity. In effect, as Justice Harlan pointed out in a concurring opinion, the charity had acquired the residual value of the lumber business by allowing the taxpayer to "use" its tax-exemption until the $1.3 million figure had been reached. In the Court's view, however, this factor did not alter the legal conclusion that property may be "sold" for tax purposes, even when the purchase price is payable out of the future earnings of the property itself.

31. *Estate of Marshall v. Comm'r,* 20 T.C. 979 (1953).

So-called bootstrap sales to charity, of the sort exemplified in *Brown,* were substantially curbed by Congress in the Tax Reform Act of 1969. § 514, which was added by the Act, provides, in effect, that unrelated income from debt-financed property shall be taxed to the charity as ordinary business income. This means that tax-exempt organizations are in no better a position than taxable entities when they seek to buy property out of its own future income. Since the income is now taxable to the charity, it can neither pay a higher price nor effect a quicker payout than other buyers. The Reform Act did not reverse the Court's determination that contingent-payment transactions will generally qualify as sales, however, and hence the status of such transactions continues to be controlled by *Brown.*

(b) *Open transactions.* As noted at 14.03, the Supreme Court in *Burnet v. Logan* held that contingent-payment transactions do not result in immediate recognition of gain to the transferor if the fair market value of the transferee's obligation is uncertain; and further, that gain is not to be recognized until the payments received exceed the transferor's basis for the property transferred. The *Brown* decision makes the additional point that such transactions will satisfy the "sale or exchange" requirement necessary for capital gain treatment, even when the property is to be paid for out of its own income.

These two sets of rules have produced a very favorable outcome when applied in combination. In *Commissioner v. Carter,*[32] the taxpayer was the sole stockholder of a corporation which was engaged in the oil brokerage business. The corporation was liquidated in 1942 and distributed to the taxpayer, together with other assets, certain brokerage contracts entitling it to commissions on future deliveries of oil. The value of the contracts was conceded to be unascertainable because the amount of the commissions to be received was contingent on various future events. Under Code § 331, the surrender of stock in a corporate liquidation is treated as a "sale or exchange" by the stockholder. Accordingly, the 1942 liquidation produced a capital gain because the value of the other assets distributed exceeded the taxpayer's basis for her stock.

In 1943, the taxpayer received $25,000 under the brokerage contracts. As to this later receipt, the Commissioner asserted that ordinary treatment was appropriate. The liquidation, he argued, had been completed in 1942; hence, the later payments could not be deemed to have been realized from the prior sale or exchange. Such later payments (in the Commissioner's view) were indepen-

---

32. 170 F.2d 911 (2d Cir.1948).

dent of the liquidation, and were therefore merely "commission income" taxable at ordinary rates.

The court of appeals held for the taxpayer, largely on the authority of *Burnet v. Logan.* The court reasoned that the "open" transaction rule of *Logan*—which applies where the property received lacks an ascertainable value—meant that the liquidation itself should be treated as an on-going and continuing event. The commission payments were thus attributable to the original "exchange", and hence qualified as capital gain. It would be "most unjust," the court said, to tax the commissions as ordinary, since, if the contracts *could* have been valued originally, that value would have been treated as realized from the liquidation. In effect, then, the taxpayer was entitled both to defer reporting her gain until the commission payments were actually received, and to report all such payments as gain from the "sale or exchange" of her shares, a capital asset.

Since the court in *Carter* stressed the comparison, we should ask just what the result would have been if the brokerage contracts *had* had an ascertainable value at the time of the liquidation. In *Waring v. Commissioner,*[33] the taxpayer, on the liquidation of his wholly-owned corporation, received a licensing agreement which entitled the corporation to receive royalties from a third party for the right to use the name "Waring" in connection with the sale of electric blenders. The taxpayer valued the contract at $300,000 and reported a capital gain on the excess of that amount over his stock basis. Upholding the Commissioner, the court found that the act of valuing the agreement *closed* the liquidation. Accordingly, royalties received by the taxpayer in subsequent years first were offset against his "tax-paid" basis for the licensing contract, that is, $300,000. After that, though, any further payments were taxable as ordinary income, because those further payments were not related to the prior sale or exchange.

In effect, then, in *Waring* the corporate liquidation produced (a) immediate recognition of capital gain, and (b) subsequent ordinary income for payments in excess of the value assigned to the licensing agreement. By contrast, in *Carter* the results were (a) no immediate recognition, and (b) subsequent capital gain.

These contrasting outcomes put more pressure than seems desirable on the initial question of ascertainable market value. Instead of letting such substantial tax differences turn on an accidental factor, it might be better (contrary to *Waring*) to permit contingent payment arrangements to produce capital gain whether

---

33.   412 F.2d 800 (3d Cir.1969).

or not the contract right or other claim is capable of being valued when received. The imputed interest rule of § 483 preserves some ordinary treatment in any case, and perhaps the only operative requirements that should apply to the remainder of the gain realized by the transferor are the capital asset and the completed disposition requirements. As respects the latter especially, it may be that the *Brown* decision goes too far in permitting contingent-payment transactions to qualify as sales or exchanges. This, however, appears to be a determination which bears a rational relationship to the capital gain preference, even if its present substance is debatable. By contrast, the distinction between "open" and "closed" transactions seems capricious and is essentially unrelated to any positive policy concept in the field.

SECTION 18.   SALES OF BUSINESS PROPERTY

The tax law in effect divides business assets into three categories. The first consists of so-called current assets, in particular inventory and accounts receivable, which are expressly excluded from the class of capital assets by § 1221(1) and § 1221(4). As indicated at 17.02, the inventory exclusion has been interpreted (in *Corn Products* as subsequently refined by *Arkansas Best*) to embrace commodities futures and other securities which, though not actually part of the taxpayer's stock-in-trade, are a surrogate for the taxpayer's basic raw materials or "an integral part of [its] inventory-purchase system." The second category consists of fixed assets—plant and equipment—which are likewise excluded from the class of capital assets by § 1221(2) but for which a special tax regime is established under § 1231 and related provisions. Finally, as our earlier discussion of *Williams v. McGowan* should suggest (17.04), a third category containing intangible property rights that do not come within the *Corn Products* rule (as refined), of which the most important member is business goodwill, must also be inferred. These residual rights become capital assets more or less by elimination. Since they are not excluded by specific provision or by the *Corn Products* rule, they must fall within the general language of § 1221, under which "capital asset" is defined to mean "property held (whether or not connected with [the taxpayer's] trade or business)". As far as business property is concerned, then, the only assets that qualify as "pure" capital assets are those few that belong to this last, residual category. Stock-in-trade and *Corn Products* property are both ordinary, while real or depreciable property is handled under the special rules mentioned above.

Having discussed "implied" categories of business property in the preceding Section, we concern ourselves in this Section solely

343

with the Code's express treatment of stock-in-trade and real or depreciable property used in business. From the standpoint of litigation and administrative controversy, § 1221(1), the stock-in-trade exclusion, has been by far the more troublesome of the two. The recurring question there has been whether the taxpayer's relationship to particular property is that of a "dealer"—one who is systematically engaged in buying and selling such property—or merely that of a casual "investor". Very probably, this tiresome characterization problem has been, and remains, one of the more actively litigated issues in the entire capital gain field. By contrast, relatively few interpretative questions have arisen under § 1221(2). Presumably, one has little difficulty in simply identifying property as "real or depreciable." On the other hand, from the standpoint of Code mechanics, the treatment of depreciable property such as buildings and equipment is far more detailed and extensive than that of stock-in-trade. Here, the question of policy has been how to integrate the capital treatment which § 1231 accords to gains from the sale of such assets with the annual allowance for depreciation under § 167, the latter being a deduction from ordinary income.

Section 18.01, next following, takes up the standards developed by the courts in distinguishing between "dealers" and "investors" for the purpose of § 1221(1). Section 18.02(a) summarizes the treatment of real or depreciable property under § 1231, and section 18.02(b) describes the so-called depreciation recapture rules, which appear in §§ 1245 and 1250.

18.01 Property Held for Sale to Customers. As indicated, § 1221(1) specifically excludes business merchandise from the capital asset definition. The cans on the grocer's shelf, the coal in the mine-owner's mine, the ships in the shipbuilder's yard, all are ordinary assets in the hands of a taxpayer whose business is to buy, dig, or produce those items for sale to customers. § 1221(1) uses no fewer than three statutory phrases to describe this kind of asset—"stock in trade," "inventory," and "property held by the taxpayer primarily for sale to customers in the ordinary course of his trade or business." However, since the last of the quoted phrases is the broadest and least technical of the three, it has largely swallowed up the first two and has been chiefly relied on by the Commissioner in his frequent efforts to draw borderline transactions into the ordinary income category.

The great majority of litigated cases under § 1221(1) have involved real estate, and perhaps one way to open up the subject is to ask just why this should be so. Why should land and buildings, more often than other kinds of property, appear to occupy an ambiguous status? Why shouldn't corporate securities (on the one

344

hand), or shirts and socks (on the other), have generated an equal volume of controversy?

As respects shirts and socks, at least, the answer is fairly clear. Those handy items, and indeed everything else in the category of consumption goods, are sold almost exclusively by professional dealers—*e.g.,* stores—for whom the status of the property as simple inventory is never questioned. Household durables—cars and washing machines—are sometimes sold by the consumer himself (more often traded-in), but the isolated and occasional nature of such transactions, as well as the prior household use, makes it clear that the requisite "business" context is lacking. Ambiguous cases do of course arise; nonprofessionals sometimes purchase unusual consumption items (stamps, antiques) for resale, and in such event they may be viewed as dealers if their activities are extensive. But on the whole, consumption goods which are dealt in by professionals are dealt in *only* by professionals, and the applicability of § 1221(1) is immediately clear.

What of corporate securities? Although stocks and bonds are typically held for investment, a very active stock-market speculator may engage in many transactions in the course of a year, trading hundreds of thousands or even millions of dollars worth of shares, and devoting all of his time and energy to that single activity. In common understanding, stock market speculation is his "business." Yet, apart from professional underwriters and securities dealers, persons who trade on the stock market, no matter how actively, can be perfectly confident that their gains and losses will be treated as capital. The reason is that the words "to customers," which were added to § 1221(1) in 1934 in order to prevent ordinary loss deductions in the declining market of that period, have also served to assure capital treatment for gains in the rising market of our era. In effect, individuals who buy and sell securities, usually through a broker, are not considered to be one another's "customers" within the meaning of the statute. As respects securities, therefore, the only condition that the taxpayer needs to meet to get preferential treatment is the holding-period requirement. If stocks or bonds are held for more than 1 year, any gain or loss is long-term gain or loss. No distinction is made between occasional investors and active traders, other than the statutory distinction between long- and short-term transactions.

The same construction has *not* been applied to real estate (or other property). Any person to whom land or buildings are sold is a "customer" of the seller, so that the question of ordinary or capital treatment depends on whether the property is held "primarily for sale", and on whether the taxpayer's conduct amounts to a "business." The reason why the "customers" requirement has been applied one way for securities and another way for other property may reside in the impersonal nature of the securities market. More probably, however, it is simply that Congress has been understood to have intended that language to be confined to the situation at which it was directed more than fifty years ago, namely, trading in securities.

The result is that those who "trade" actively in real estate are treated just like professional real estate dealers, while only "investors" in real estate qualify for capital gain. There is thus a need to distinguish between "traders" and "investors." By contrast, the category of "trader" is virtually irrelevant in the field of conventional merchandise because, as a practical matter, the only functioning category is that of "dealer." And it is irrelevant as respects securities because "traders" and "investors" are treated alike.

In determining whether real estate is held "primarily for sale ... in the ordinary course of ... business," the courts have emphasized the frequency and continuity of the taxpayer's dealings, the length of time the property was held, the presence or absence of development activities such as subdividing and installing utilities, the extent of the taxpayer's selling effort, and so on. The decided cases are too individual to usefully generalize about, and the "listing of factors" approach is probably the best that can be done by way of making relevant factual distinctions.

Many of the cases in this field involve gain which is traceable both to long-term property appreciation *and* to business activity. Thus, the taxpayer, having long ago acquired a substantial tract of land, now decides to dispose of the property. He finds, however, that the best, or perhaps the only, way of doing so is to subdivide the tract and sell off the units to individual buyers. A portion of the overall gain will then be attributable to historical appreciation and a portion to the "business" of subdivision and development. Neither full capital gain nor full ordinary income is correct in the circumstances, but the courts, lacking authority to fragment the taxpayer's gain, are compelled to opt for one or the other, with the preponderance of the "liquidation" cases coming out on the capital gain side.[34]

"Dual purpose" cases have raised similar problems. In *Malat v. Riddell*,[35] the taxpayer owned an interest in a parcel of land

34. *E.g., Curtis Co. v. Comm'r*, 232 F.2d 167 (3d Cir.1956): compare *Biedenharn Realty Co. v. U.S.*, 526 F.2d 409 (5th Cir.1976), finding ordinary income.

35. 383 U.S. 569 (1966).

which had been acquired either for the purpose of sale or for development as rental property, whichever should prove to be more profitable. Ultimately, because of problems relating to zoning and financing, the taxpayer gave up on the entire idea and sold his interest in the venture. Reversing the court of appeals, which had held the taxpayer's gain ordinary on the ground that "resale" had been a substantial reason for the original purchase, the Supreme Court held that the word "primarily" must be construed as "principally" or "of first importance," and remanded the case for further findings under that standard. On remand, the trial court found that the taxpayer was entitled to capital gain, because the "principal" purpose of the land venture had been to develop the property for rental, with resale being a second-best alternative. Since the taxpayer's gain, presumably, was traceable to property appreciation rather than development and sales activities, the final outcome seems not unreasonable in the circumstances.

If a taxpayer's real estate (or other property) is *not* regarded as stock-in-trade, its classification then depends on whether it is "used in the taxpayer's business"—for example, as a warehouse or factory building—or is merely held for investment. If the latter, the taxpayer's gain or loss is of course capital under the general language of § 1221. If the property is used in trade or business, on the other hand, it is specifically excluded from capital asset status by § 1221(2). This, however, means that the gain or loss will be governed by the special and, in a sense, even more favorable rules of § 1231, which are described in the subsection next following. As will be seen, § 1231 treats net gains from the sale of the property which it defines as capital gain (subject, in the case of real estate, to a rather mild depreciation-recapture requirement), while treating net loss as *ordinary* loss. Hence, a further (though considerably simpler) sub-classification of the property must be made even after the 1221(1) question has been resolved.

18.02 Fixed Assets: Real and Depreciable Property.

(a) § 1231. Land, buildings, and machinery—assets which accountants classify as "fixed"—are dealt with by the tax law in a curious, nonsymmetrical fashion. Under § 1231, gains and losses from the sale of real and depreciable property used in the taxpayer's business are swept into a special category. If recognized gains from the sale of such property exceed recognized losses for the taxable year, the gains and losses are all treated as long-term capital gains and losses. But if recognized losses exceed recognized gains, then the gains and losses are treated as ordinary. The effect, quite simply, is to treat net gain from dispositions of fixed

business assets as long-term capital gain, while treating net loss from such transactions as ordinary loss deductible from ordinary income.

Although the adoption of § 1231 was prompted by special wartime conditions which long ago ceased to be relevant, Congress chose to continue this peculiar capital gain-ordinary loss regime over the ensuing decades, and there has been little legislative interest in changing it. The explanation, in part at least, is that Congress has wished to encourage the replacement of, and to spur investment in, depreciable plant and equipment.

Apart from incentive effects, an argument can be made that nonsymmetrical treatment is actually correct as a matter of tax policy (depending, of course, on a willingness to accept capital-ordinary distinctions to begin with). Thus, on the gain side, it can be argued that sales of fixed assets, as opposed to stock-in-trade, are really extraordinary transactions which involve the disposition of a part of the business itself. They do not occur in the regular course of operations, and the gains they generate often represent appreciation that has accrued over an extended period of time. As respects losses, although symmetry would be expected normally, in the present context we find ourselves dealing with *depreciable* property, rather than corporate stock or the like. If the property were retained by the taxpayer for the remainder of its useful life, an ordinary loss would be allowed, in effect, through annual deductions for depreciation. The same would be true if the property were simply abandoned or scrapped without being sold at all. Since investment in depreciable property, thus, is recoverable through an offset against ordinary income, the result, arguably, should be no different when allowable depreciation is anticipated by the sale of the property at a loss. To be sure, this justification does not serve very well where land is concerned, because land is non-depreciable. However, the alleged difficulty of allocating the purchase price of real estate between land and buildings when both are sold together has evidently convinced Congress that it would be too burdensome to insist on separate capital loss treatment for the land component.

(b) The recapture principle. Since § 1231 permits capital treatment for gains from sales of *depreciable* property, the provision creates a special problem in respect to the depreciation allowance. The problem has been rendered acute by the adoption of accelerated depreciation rules. Thus, annual depreciation is a deduction from ordinary income, and the amount deducted is subtracted from the taxpayer's property basis. If the value of the property at a given date exceeds its adjusted basis—if, in effect, the depreciation

allowed for tax purposes has been greater than the actual decline in the property's value—then a sale of the property will produce a gain, and the gain under § 1231 will be capital. This means that the prior deductions from ordinary income will have been transmuted into capital gain through sale. While Congress *might* desire to sanction this highly advantageous combination of tax benefits as a way of encouraging investment in depreciable property, from the standpoint of tax policy it seems improper for taxpayers to receive capital treatment on the sale of business assets whose cost has been recovered out of ordinary income. Other instances of the same phenomenon—*e.g.,* the deduction of interest on funds borrowed to purchase growth stocks—have been noted previously.

To deal with this problem, the Code since 1962 has limited the ability of property-owners to combine ordinary depreciation deductions with capital gain by requiring the "recapture" of all or a portion of the depreciation when the property is sold. Under § 1245—which, roughly speaking, applies to depreciable property other than real estate—a taxpayer's gain on the sale of his property is taxed as ordinary income to the full extent of his prior depreciation deductions. In effect, a balancing inclusion is required to the extent that the proceeds of sale exceed the taxpayer's *adjusted* basis, but not in excess of his *original* basis for the property. To illustrate simply, if an asset purchased for $10,000 were depreciated to $6,000 and then sold for $9,000, the gain of $3,000 would be "recaptured" as ordinary income. If the same property were sold for $11,000, the first $4,000 of gain would again be ordinary under § 1245; the remaining gain of $1,000 would be capital gain under § 1231, subject to the netting rules of that provision.

§ 1250 (added in 1964) applies the recapture principle to real estate, but its effect is weaker than that of § 1245. Generally described (and omitting many details), § 1250 recaptures only the excess of depreciation actually taken over the depreciation that would have been allowed under the straight-line depreciation method. Recapture under § 1250 thus applies to the excess of accelerated over straight-line depreciation,[36] whereas § 1245 extends recapture to all depreciation previously allowed.

The difference in scope between the two provisions can be shown by returning to the depreciation illustration set forth at 6.08(d). There, the taxpayer purchased a depreciable asset for $4,000 which was expected to yield net income of $1,200 annually

36. Straight-line depreciation is required with respect to all real property acquired after 1986, so that recapture under § 1250 applies only to property placed in service before that date.

for a period of 5 years (salvage value was assumed to be zero). At a suitable discount rate, the schedule of present values of future returns was as follows:

Year:	1	2	3	4	5	Totals
Expected receipt	$1,200	$1,200	$1,200	$1,200	$1,200	$6,000
Present value	$1,045	$ 905	$ 790	$ 687	$ 573	$4,000

Assume that the taxpayer uses the straight-line method of depreciation, and hence takes an $800 deduction ($4,000 ÷ 5 years) in the first year. If there are no market changes of any kind (no inflation, no increase or decline in demand, etc.) the asset will have a resale value at the end of Year 1 of $3,427.* In effect, the year's operation will have cost the taxpayer $573 in true economic depreciation, although, as just stated, a deduction of $800 will have been allowed under the straight-line method. If, then, the taxpayer sells the asset at the start of Year 2 for $3,427, his basis will be $3,200 ($4,000 minus $800), and his gain will be $227.

If the asset in question is § 1245 property—*e.g.*, machinery or equipment—the $227 gain will be treated as ordinary income because it is less than the amount of the depreciation previously allowed. In effect, § 1245 recaptures the difference between straight-line and sinking-fund depreciation, a fairly rigorous result. By contrast, if the asset is assumed to be § 1250 property—an apartment building, say—the $227 gain is treated as capital gain. § 1250 extends only to the difference between accelerated and straight-line depreciation, and hence has a more limited reach.

Adding one last step, suppose demand for the taxpayer's product increases sharply during the first year and the asset is sold at the start of Year 2 for $4,027. In effect, there has been $600 ($4,027 minus the originally expected value of $3,427) of "pure" value appreciation. The taxpayer's gain is then $827 ($4,027 minus basis of $3,200). Once again, § 1245 would recapture the entire amount of the first year's depreciation—$800—even though only $227 is strictly traceable to over-rapid depreciation. The remaining $27 of gain would be given capital treatment under § 1231. § 1250, on the other hand, would allow the entire $827 gain to be treated as capital, because real-estate recapture (generally speaking) is limited to the amount of the prior depreciation that exceeds the straight-line allowance.

SECTION 19. PERSONAL SERVICES

There ought to be, and on the whole there is, less ambiguity about the status of personal service income under the capital gain

---

* That is, the sum of $1,045, $905, $790, and $687.

rules than about any other category of receipts. This follows from the fact that capital gain always requires a disposition of "property." Once claims for wages, salaries and fees are specifically excluded from the capital asset definition—a result apparently achieved by § 1221(4)—there is little in the way of "characterization," "motive," "relationship" or the like that is left to argue about. The status of other kinds of gains and losses varies to some extent from taxpayer to taxpayer: gain or loss from the sale of securities, for example, though usually capital gain or loss, can be ordinary if, under *Arkansas Best*, the securities are a substitute or surrogate for the taxpayer's stock-in-trade; real estate transactions may be either capital or ordinary depending on whether the taxpayer is a dealer or an investor; and so on. But personal service income is always ordinary, because personal services inevitably lack the essential characteristic of "property."

This, however, is not to say that interpretative problems have been wholly lacking. While the difference between personal service income and gain from the sale of property is normally clear, if our discussion at 8.02 is recalled it should not be difficult to foresee that line-drawing problems will arise with respect to the status of self-created property rights such as patents, copyrights and similar interests. Are these intangibles to be viewed as "property" because, like a share of stock, they are embodied in a legal certificate, have an extended useful life, sometimes entail an outlay of capital, and can be sold for a consideration by the original owner or his successors? Or are they to be regarded as personal service claims because they relate so closely to the expenditure of time and talent by their creators? Fortunately in one sense, the treatment of two major kinds of self-created intangibles is now largely resolved by specific Code provisions. As will be seen at 19.02, an abrupt distinction is made between patents and other kinds of intellectual property. While patents generally qualify as capital assets, copyrights and artistic creations are specifically excluded from the capital asset definition by § 1221(3).

The problem of services-or-property can be framed more generally. Since service income is ordinary while property gain is capital, there has been an incentive for highly-paid individuals to find devices by which personal rewards can be transmuted into property rights. The *Ferrer* case (17.03(c)) was an illustration of this: to a degree the taxpayer actually succeeded in converting his income from acting services into gain from the sale of a contract claim. While the capital gain component in *Ferrer* was small (and probably accidental), suppose that the same taxpayer had proceeded more directly by setting up a wholly-owned corporation whose "business" would be to "lease" its stockholder's services to movie producers for a fee.[37] Although the fee would be taxable as ordinary income to the corporation, Ferrer himself could forgo any direct salary payments and then subsequently sell the stock of the corporation to an accommodating buyer at a capital gain. In an era when ordinary tax rates for high-income individuals substantially exceeded the maximum corporate rate, a combination of the corporate income tax and the individual capital gain might well be less than the individual tax on ordinary service income received directly. The development of independent production companies in the movie and television field during the 1950's and 60's probably owed much of its inspiration to this petty calculus.

As indicated at 19.01, the property-service distinction has also been exploited—to a considerable degree with express Congressional approval—by yet another group of highly paid individuals, namely, corporate executives. Unable to escape the status of "employee," corporate executives have sought, where possible, to convert their salaries into property ownership through the medium of stock options and related devices. The treatment of employee stock options has a lengthy statutory and case-law history. Restored to favor by the 1981 Act, so-called incentive stock options now enjoy a preferred tax status (the preference had been eliminated in 1976), although of course repeal of the 60% capital gain deduction makes the preference somewhat less important.

19.01 Employee Stock Options. Suppose the taxpayer, a corporate executive, is granted an option by his employer to purchase 1,000 shares of the employer's stock at $5 a share. The option is exercisable at any time within the next three years, but it is not transferable to others and can only be exercised if the taxpayer is then still an employee of the company. In Year 1, when the option is granted, the stock is quoted at $6 a share, that is, $1 a share above the option price.

The taxpayer actually exercises the option in Year 2. By that time, however, the market value of the stock has jumped to $30, so that by exercising the option the taxpayer acquires property with a value of $30,000 for a cash investment of only $5,000. Now assume that he holds the stock itself for further appreciation, and then in Year 3 sells the entire 1,000 shares for $32,000. Plainly, the taxpayer has made an overall profit of $27,000—the difference between the $32,000 realized on selling the shares and his $5,000 cash investment. The question that arises, essentially, is whether

---

37. See *Comm'r v. Laughton,* 113 F.2d 103 (9th Cir.1940).

any portion of that gain should be viewed as ordinary compensation from his employment.

In *Commissioner v. LoBue*,[38] which involved a similar set of facts, the Supreme Court reversed a finding by the Tax Court that no portion of the gain was ordinary. The Tax Court had held that the purpose of the option grant was to give the taxpayer a "proprietary interest" in his employer and not to compensate him for his services. Observing that "the company was not giving away something for nothing," the Supreme Court found that it was simply "impossible" to view the stock option arrangement as anything but compensation. The measure of such compensation, moreover, was the difference between the option price and the market value of the shares at the time the option was exercised. This, said the Court, had been the uniform Treasury practice for decades.

Concurring in part and dissenting in part, Justice Harlan agreed with the Court majority that the Tax Court's "proprietary interest" exemption should be rejected. He argued, however, that the appropriate measure of ordinary compensation was the value of the options at the time they were granted rather than the spread between option price and stock value at the time of exercise. Whatever that earlier value may have been, said Harlan, it was *that* amount which represented the taxpayer's income from employment, and it was *then* that the taxpayer received ordinary compensation from his employer.

Using the figures in our initial illustration, the difference between the majority and the dissenting approach in *LoBue* is quite considerable, even though both agreed that the option was a compensatory device. Thus, the majority would find no income in Year 1 despite the fact that the value of the stock in the illustration then exceeded the option price by $1 a share. In Year 2, however, the majority would treat the difference between stock-value and option price—$25,000 in the illustration—as ordinary compensation. The employee would then become an investor with respect to the shares acquired, and would hold those shares at a basis of $30,000 (*i.e.*, $25,000 included in income plus the $5,000 purchase price). When the stock was sold in Year 3 for $32,000, the taxpayer would realize a further gain of $2,000. This, of course, would be taxed as a capital gain.

Under Harlan's approach, as stated, the option would be valued and taxed at the time it was granted in Year 1. Since the option was worth at least $1,000, that amount would be included as ordinary compensation for that year. No further income would

38.   351 U.S. 243 (1956).

result from the exercise of the option in Year 2, however, because that event would be regarded as a purchase rather than a realization. The taxpayer's basis for the shares acquired would then be $6,000—$1,000 included in income in Year 1 plus the $5,000 stock purchase price—and when the shares were finally sold for $32,000 in Year 3, a capital gain would be recognized of $26,000.

In effect, then, total income—$27,000—would be the same under either approach (indeed, it would be the same even if the Tax Court's view had been adopted). Under the majority, however, the greater part is ordinary and is realized in Year 2 when the option is exercised; under the dissent, there is some ordinary income in Year 1, but the greater part of the taxpayer's gain is taxed as capital gain in Year 3 when the stock is sold.

Is there a right or a wrong in all this? Ultimately, the conflict between majority and dissent appears to have turned on a question of fact, namely, whether the options granted to LoBue did, or didn't, have an ascertainable market value at the date of grant. The majority seemed to concede that if the options could have been valued in Year 1, then that value would indeed have been the measure of the taxpayer's ordinary compensation, with all further gain being capital. "But this," it said, "is not such a case. These . . . options were not transferable and LoBue's right to buy stock under them was contingent upon his remaining an employee of the company until they were exercised." Harlan, by contrast, would have found that when LoBue "received an unconditional option to buy stock at less than the market price, he received an asset of substantial and immediately realizable value, at least equal to the then-existing spread between the option price and the market price."

As usual, it is somewhat irritating to find substantial tax differences turning on the presence or absence of an ascertainable market value. In fact, however, the difficulty may be unavoidable. If (as the *LoBue* majority found) the option lacks an ascertainable value when granted, then, apparently, the only practical alternatives are (a) to accept the Tax Court's position that there is no compensation whatever, a difficult view to maintain when the transaction involves an employer and employee, or (b) to conclude that nothing of a taxable nature has occurred until the employee receives property that does have a measurable dollar value, but then to view *that* as a receipt of taxable compensation. Absent a fair market value for the options at the date of grant, there is, perhaps, no escape from the conclusion that exercise is the taxable event. And once again, since an employment relationship is involved, it is well-nigh "impossible" to regard the resulting income as anything but ordinary. On the other hand, the weakest feature of the majority opinion in *LoBue* is the unsupported finding that the options were in fact without an ascertainable value. The Court is far from persuasive on this point, and indeed the issue appears to have taken Justice Black somewhat by surprise.

Code § 83—which applies to stock options other than the "incentive" options covered by § 421—adopts as a "general rule" the position expressed by Justice Harlan in *LoBue*. The section provides that if an employee receives a nonforfeitable option which has an ascertainable fair market value at the date it is granted, that value (less any price paid for the option itself) constitutes ordinary income to the employee at that time. Hence, no further income will be recognized when the option is exercised. When the shares acquired are finally sold, the difference between the sale price and the taxpayer's stock basis will be taxable as capital gain. But if no value for the options can be ascertained at the date of grant, as would quite often be the case, then the tax results will be those approved by the majority in *LoBue*. While these results seem rather harsh, the alternative—complete escape from ordinary income—seems even less acceptable in the circumstances.

As noted above, the 1981 Act revived the preferential status of employee stock options where certain restrictive conditions are met. These conditions, set forth in § 422, include a requirement that the option price be at least equal to the market value of the underlying stock at the time the options are granted and that the stock itself be held for at least two years from the date of grant. If the statutory conditions are satisfied, then neither the grant nor the exercise of the option results in taxable income to the employee (in which event no business expense deduction is allowed to the employer). Gain will be recognized when—deferred until—the stock is sold. As in the Tax Court's version of *LoBue*, such gain will then be taxed as capital gain and the employee will have no ordinary compensation whatever.

19.02 Patents, Copyrights, and Self-Created Property. Regarded as a problem *de novo*, the proper treatment of patents and copyrights seems clear. If we take as a fixed premise the idea that personal service income is ordinary, then the income received by an inventor or an artist from the transfer of a patent or copyright fairly plainly belongs to the class of ordinary receipts. The principal element of value in either case derives from personal effort, and the mere fact that the patent or the copyright constitutes a legally protectable interest can hardly disguise the primary nature of the taxpayer's personal contribution. To be sure, patents (though not copyrights) may sometimes entail a commitment of

355

capital in the form of an outlay for materials and equipment. In consequence, it can be argued that "investment" also plays a role in the development of tangible innovations and, hence, that the capital and ordinary components should both be given recognition when the patent is disposed of. But a practical basis for making such a division would be exceedingly hard to formulate unless arbitrary rules of allocation were employed. Moreover, the same sort of problem exists elsewhere (indeed, everywhere) in the capital gain field; thus, investing in corporate shares involves both capital and an exercise of personal skill and judgment, yet no effort is made to "impute to the factors" where gain from the sale of stock is concerned. If, then, considerations of feasibility require an all-or-nothing determination in this as in other areas, one's intuition is that patents and copyrights should both be regarded as ordinary.

Congress, however, has viewed the matter from a different perspective and has reached a different conclusion. Since 1954, the Code, in § 1235, has awarded long-term capital gain to the amount received by a patent-owner on a transfer of "all substantial rights" to the patent, or of an undivided interest therein, even though payments are to be received periodically (*e.g.*, over the life of the patent) and are based on the use or sale of the patented article. No distinction, moreover, is drawn between professional inventors—chemists, engineers, etc.—and amateurs who putter around in their basements. The patent rules have thus been exceedingly generous. They were designed, however, not with an eye to tax policy as such, but, in the words of the Senate Committee, to "provide an incentive to inventors to contribute to the welfare of the Nation."

By contrast, poets and painters evidently require no special incentives—or else the work they do contributes little to the Nation's welfare—because § 1221(3) specifically excludes copyrights and artistic property from the capital asset definition. The exclusion, which was added in 1950, was intended to assure that all copyrights and similar property would be treated as noncapital, whether created by a professional or by an amateur. Prior judicial and administrative decisions—of which the best known involved a lump-sum sale of his war memoirs by General Eisenhower—had permitted amateur authors to report as capital gain the proceeds from the sale of their *first* published work (after which, presumably, they became professionals). § 1221(3) overcomes this interpretation and imposes ordinary treatment on amateur and professional authors (artists, etc.) alike.

Apart from patents and copyrights, the sale of a personal service business—say an accounting or a medical practice—may also generate a question of services-or-property. The consideration paid for a professional practice might be allocable partly to the seller's covenant not to compete—that is, his agreement to refrain from practicing his profession for a given number of years or in a defined area—and partly to the goodwill of the business. Goodwill, in this context, would apparently refer to the seller's reputation and following among his clients, customers or patients. Payments for non-compete agreements, generally, are viewed as ordinary. If an advance bonus for services to be performed in the future results in ordinary income, then a payment to refrain from such performance should be treated similarly. As to professional goodwill, however, while this "asset" could easily be regarded as a personal attribute of the seller akin to the use of his name, the courts have held that if the seller's practice is actually transferable to another practitioner for a consideration, then the thing transferred must have an independent existence which entitles it to be regarded as "property." Hence, evidently, payments allocated to professional goodwill will qualify for capital gain.

In *Miller v. Commissioner*,[39] the widow of the famed orchestra leader received a payment from Universal Pictures in connection with the making of "The Glen Miller Story." The amount paid, more than $400,000, was in consideration for the taxpayer's granting to the company an "exclusive right" to produce a motion picture "based upon the life ... of Glen Miller." Rejecting her claim to capital gain, the court of appeals found that Mrs. Miller had no "capitalizable" property interest in the reputation of her deceased husband. Although the $400,000 plainly had been paid for something—presumably, the possibility that Mrs. Miller did have a protectable interest had seemed plausible to Universal—the court found no supporting authority in state law for the proposition that a decedent's heirs may inherit a right to his public image. Accordingly, the Commissioner was upheld in treating the payment as ordinary income.

Weakly reasoned in its reliance on state property concepts, Judge Kaufman's opinion also seems a little rough on Mrs. Miller. It is true, as the court noted, that if Miller himself had sold his "story" to the movies during his lifetime, the proceeds of such sale would have been ordinary. Since Miller was in the entertainment business, payment for an "appearance," whether in person or by proxy, would clearly be a return to personal effort. His widow, however, was in quite a different status. She, in effect, had acquired by inheritance (or at least Universal thought so) an "enterprise" called "Glen Miller." While it could be argued that a

39. 299 F.2d 706 (2d Cir.1962).

sale of movie-rights alone was a kind of carving-out (there might also have been book rights, rights to the Glen Miller "sound," etc. that went with the name), it seems likely that the only economic interest of any real value that remained after Miller's death was the right to do a movie of his life.   The fact that this interest was ill-defined or uncertain under state law seems irrelevant in view of the transaction that actually took place between the parties.   What should have counted, one supposes, was the circumstance that the thing conveyed—call it an inchoate right or contingent *chose* in action, if you like—had been acquired by inheritance rather than through the taxpayer's personal efforts.   No element of services pertained as far as Mrs. Miller was concerned, and hence her claim to capital gain treatment was really fairly strong.

AFTERWORD

The aim of this book is essentially reductionist. The income tax course has a reputation for difficulty, but the fact is that the technical problems which it presents are relatively few in number, and it may be reassuring to the student to perceive that this is so.

Thus, most of the cases discussed in Parts A, D and E—"Income", "Accounting", and "Gains and Losses"—involve nothing more than the timing of gross income and deductions. Where income is concerned, this is usually presented as a problem of realization. Has the income or gain been realized in the current year, or can it be deferred to a later period? Often, the reason that realization becomes a problem at all is that the receipt at issue is in "kind" rather than in cash. The courts are then caught between a desire to avoid the messy task of valuation and a reluctance to allow the taxpayer to effectively defer his tax obligations by accepting income in the form of property or other non-cash benefits. Resolution of the conflict may depend on how burdensome the task of valuation seems to be, as compared with how serious will be the escape from tax if it is not undertaken. Where deduction is concerned, the timing question, usually, is simply how to schedule the recovery of asset-cost. Unlike realization, cost-recovery rules are normally fixed by express statutory provisions, as in the case of depreciation methods. The discussion of the tax-shelter phenomenon at 13.02 suggests that Congress' outlook has been somewhat ambivalent—a wish to encourage investment and expansion, but a concern with the resulting tax-avoidance, the two together creating an inconsistent pattern of incentives and deterrents.

Part B—"Deductions"—is dominated by the need to divide taxpayers' lives between personal pursuits and business. Though inescapable, the distinction is necessarily an artificial one in human terms. Rules of an arbitrary character emerge, but in the end there are not very many of them and they tend to be concentrated on the single issue of personal-or-business. The main question is plain enough at all events, even if the answers given in individual cases are sometimes unsatisfactory or even silly.

Part C—"Attribution"—stems from a combination of two factors: the separate taxability of the individual members of the family, and the progressive nature of the rate structure. Judicial opinions in this area are frequently extravagant, occasionally preposterous. I have tried to suggest, however, that the courts' reasoning need not be taken very seriously in most instances, and

359

that the student will do better to simply stress the *results* of the decided cases. Fortunately, much of the governing law has been codified in the grantor trust sections of the Code and elsewhere.

Finally, Part F—"Capital Gains"—essentially entails an effort to distinguish between investment appreciation, on the one hand, and ordinary income from personal services, business, or property-ownership on the other. This remains an area of uncertainty because the statute itself, particularly the definitional section, is so primitive and sketchy. To say this is not to reduce the difficulties; but recognizing that the deficiency is largely one of draftsmanship may help to dispel any notion that there are great and abiding mysteries about the meaning of "capital asset" before which one must stand in awe. In reality, there exists a narrow range of interpretative problems that are relatively easily summarized. These problems reflect the circumstance that the job of statutory classification has been somewhat neglected by the legislature or, perhaps, has simply not been viewed as one of high priority.

Often, and to the surprise of many students, the income tax course turns out to be among the best and most successful in the entire law-school curriculum. The reason for this is that the questions raised in the course are reasonably specific, and there are right answers as opposed to wrong ones. Courses of broader scope, by contrast, often suffer from a certain undergraduate malaise. Approached as a set of technical constructs (and apart from the weight of statutory detail), the tax course is relatively easy to teach and understand. My effort has been to assist in that direction by making the technical issues easier still.

———————

NOTE: WHAT IS THE TRUE VALUE
OF A TAX PREFERENCE? *

Brief reference has been made at various points to so-called tax preferences—the exemption for municipal bond interest, for example, or the exclusion of imputed rents from owner-occupied residences, or the phenomenon of accelerated depreciation. Quite obviously, such preferences have the effect of permitting taxpayers who own a "preferred" asset to receive income free of tax. Not wanting to complicate matters in the main text, I have made little effort to show in detail how these preferences relate to a progressive rate structure but have simply left the reader to infer that the value of a dollar of tax-exempt income is equal to $1 times the taxpayer's marginal tax rate. While this is true as far as it goes, it probably doesn't go far enough. Tax preferences exist in a dynamic market, which means that they, like other valuable goods, are the object of competitive bidding. An asset—say a municipal bond— that yields tax-*exempt* dollars is bound to be worth more to investors than an asset—say an ordinary corporate bond—that yields the same number of *taxable* dollars. Because in the final analysis investors are interested in *after*-tax income, they will certainly be willing to pay more for a tax-exempt income-stream than a taxable one, everything else being equal.

The vital question is, how *much* more? Paying a premium for a tax advantage obviously reduces the value of the advantage to the payor. The higher the cost of an exempt asset as compared with the cost of an equivalent taxable asset, the *less* the value of the exemption to the buyer. Indeed, if the premium were high enough, the value of the exemption would dwindle to the vanishing point.[1] Once again, therefore, the important question is: how *much* of a premium do investors have to pay when they buy an asset that enjoys a tax-preference?

Perhaps this issue is best approached by trying to answer a simpler question first. Let's assume that we have a progressive tax

---

* This Note—which is intended to be explanatory and illustrative—explains and illustrates by reference to the pre-1986 rate schedule rather than the current rates for two reasons. First, computations are simpler—50% is a handier number than 39.6%; second, the outcomes and comparisons are more dramatic if the rate-structure is steeply progressive. The implication, of course, is that the "true value" of a tax-preference would indeed tend towards zero if we had a flat-tax system and gave up the idea of progression altogether.

1. *See* Bittker, *Tax Shelters and Tax Capitalization—or, Does the Early Bird Get a Free Lunch?*, 38 Nat'l.Tax J. 416 (1975).

system and that the rates themselves (as was true before the 1986 Act) rise from a minimum of zero (on amounts covered by the standard deduction) to a maximum of 50%. Under these circumstances, will individual taxpayers all pay the same amount for an asset that produces ordinary taxable income—a corporate bond, for example—irrespective of their particular bracket rates? Or will high-bracket taxpayers pay more, or less, for the bond than low-bracket taxpayers? If the income tax were proportionate—say a flat 25% rate for everyone—we would feel pretty confident that the after-tax value of an income-stream would be the same for all investors, and hence that everybody would pay the same price for the bond just mentioned. But what happens to asset prices when a progressive tax system is introduced, with some investors paying tax at one rate and some at another?

The answer is: nothing. Assuming that financing costs (interest paid to a bank or other lender for funds borrowed to purchase the bond) are deductible, the value of a bond that yields taxable income is the same to a 50% taxpayer as it is to a 20% taxpayer. Going further, the value of the bond to all investors under a progressive tax system is the same as it would be under a proportionate tax system—indeed, it is the same under a progressive (or proportionate) tax system as it would be if there were no income tax at all. The reason, briefly, is that if financing costs are deductible, the reduction in income caused by an income tax (at *whatever* rate) is offset by a precisely proportional reduction in the after-tax rate at which the income-stream is capitalized.[2] It follows that a 50% taxpayer, a 20% taxpayer, and a 0% taxpayer (such as a charity) will all place the same value on any particular investment.

An illustration may help to make the point. Suppose that a fully taxable corporate bond is expected to yield $100 a year in perpetuity. Assume that, apart from any tax considerations, the expected income-stream would be capitalized at a rate of 12%. Under the usual formula for determining the present value of a

---

2. Samuelson, op.cit. supra, p. 149. Thus, in valuing an investment, if the income-stream is reduced by tax, then the capitalization rate must also be applied on an after-tax basis. "Capitalization rate" is just another name for the rate of interest at which an investor can borrow to finance the purchase of the asset he wants to own. Since interest on a loan is normally deductible, the applicable capitalization rate equals the interest rate *after* allowing for the deduction. As shown in the arithmetical illustration below, if the interest rate *before* tax is 12% and the investor is in the 50% bracket, the interest rate *after* tax, and hence the capitalization rate, is 50% of 12%, or 6%.

It doesn't matter whether the investor actually has to borrow to buy the asset. If he raises the money he needs by selling an asset he already owns, then, in effect, he gives up one after-tax income-stream to buy another. He is simply "borrowing" from himself.

perpetuity (see Appendix *infra*), the value of the bond would be $100/.12 = $833. Will the bond have a different value to a 50%, a 20% or a 0% taxpayer?

	After-tax Earnings	After-tax Capitalization Rate	Present Value
50% taxpayer:	$100(1–t) = $50 where t = 50%	.12(1–t) = .06	$\frac{\$50}{.06}$ = $833
20% taxpayer:	$100(1–t) = $80 where t = 20%	.12(1–t) = .096	$\frac{\$80}{.096}$ = $833
0% taxpayer:	$100(1–t) = $100 where t = 0%	.12(1–t) = .12	$\frac{\$100}{.12}$ = $833

Surprise! The progressive income tax has no effect whatever on the price that investors in different tax-brackets will pay for the same capital asset. The bond is worth $833 to everybody.

But now suppose that Congress, for reasons of national policy, decides that it would like to encourage investors to put more money than they otherwise would into a certain type of investment, say bonds issued by low-income housing developers. In effect, Congress wants more of the nation's savings devoted to investments of this particular sort, because it believes that low-income housing deserves a boost. Accordingly, Congress amends the Internal Revenue Code to provide that half of the annual income from such bonds shall be exempt from tax. *Now* what happens to investors in different brackets and to the value of the asset? The twofold answer is (a) that the value of low-income housing bonds will rise substantially, and (b) that 50% taxpayers will pay more for such bonds than will taxpayers at any lower bracket-level. Indeed, if the market works perfectly, it should be the case that 50% taxpayers will acquire *all* the low-income housing bonds that are issued by developers. To illustrate—

	After-tax Earnings	After-tax Capitalization Rate	Present Value
50% taxpayer:	$50(1–t) + $50 = $75 where t = 50%	.12(1–t) = .06	$\frac{\$75}{.06}$ = $1,250
20% taxpayer:	$50(1–t) + $50 = $90 where t = 20%	.12(1–t) = .096	$\frac{\$90}{.096}$ = $938
0% taxpayer:	$50(1–t) + $50 = $100 where t = 0%	.12(1–t) = .12	$\frac{\$100}{.12}$ = $833

So, whereas a fully taxable bond has the same value to all taxpayers no matter what their tax bracket, a tax-exempt bond is worth more to high-bracket taxpayers than to those in lower brackets. And since the exemption has its greatest value for taxpayers in the very highest bracket, it should follow that the newly issued housing bonds will be taken over *entirely* by the members of that class. In the illustration above, the 50-percenters are willing to pay as much as $1,250 for the bonds. No lower-bracket investor would find it advantageous to match that price, and hence the 50% group will presumably buy all the housing bonds that are available.

In view of these effects, does the enactment of the partial tax-exemption impair tax equity? Are similarly situated taxpayers being treated alike, or is there now an element of undue favoritism in the system? The answer is that *if* everything worked out as neatly as shown above, the system would contain no favoritism whatever. From the standpoint of "horizontal equity," the proper test is whether after-tax returns are the same for taxpayers who are in the same tax bracket and who make an identical dollar investment, one in an exempt asset, the other in a taxable asset. In the case above, an investment of $1,250 in the *exempt* bond yields $75 a year after tax for a 50% taxpayer. The same dollar investment in an equivalent *taxable* bond by another 50% taxpayer yields 12% of $1,250 = $150 before tax, and 50% of $150 = $75 after tax. Hence, two taxpayers in the same tax bracket come out the same whichever bond they buy. Once again, the non-exempt bond yields $150 pre-tax, while the exempt bond yields only $100. But the non-exempt investor pays a tax of $75 while the exempt investor pays only $25. The buyer of the taxable bond carries out Congress' will by paying $75 in tax; the buyer of the exempt bond carries out the same Congressional will by paying $25 in tax and $50 ($150–$100) in sacrificed yield, also a total of $75. After tax (whether actual or implicit), each investor winds up with the same $75.

What about "vertical equity"? Is the prior relationship between high- and low-bracket taxpayers maintained, or is there some loss in progressivity because of the bond exemption? Again, *if* everything works out as neatly as described above, the progressivity of the rate structure will be unaffected. Thus, a 20% taxpayer who invests $1,250 in a taxable bond yielding $150 will pay a tax of $30 (*i.e.,* 20% of $150). As already shown, a 50% taxpayer who invests the same amount in an exempt bond pays a "tax" (actual and implicit) of $75. The ratio $30/$75 is the same as the ratio 20%/50%, so that the vertical relationship between high- and low-bracket taxpayers is preserved despite the tax exemption.

Finally, what about "efficiency"? Is Congress achieving the goal it had in view when it enacted the preference? Are low-income housing developers receiving *all* the dollars that the Treasury is giving up? The answer is yes. To be sure, $417 ($1,250–$833) of resources are being drawn into low-income housing investment that would not go there if the legislated preference were absent; in effect, $1,250 is being "forced" into the exempt bonds whereas normal market operations would allocate only $833. But this is the *intended* result; it is a product of legislative design. Congress *means* to interfere with the market in precisely the degree indicated.

The rather striking conclusion that can be drawn from this discussion is that, under ideal conditions, tax preferences—exemptions, or partial exemptions, of income derived from designated investments—are both efficient (given the legislative aim) *and* equitable. Thus, the enactment of a partial exemption for low-income housing bonds means that those bonds will be issued at a higher price than taxable bonds of equivalent yield. Moreover, all such bonds should pass into the hands of 50%-bracket taxpayers, because the partial exemption has the greatest value to them and they will (or should) outbid all investors at lower bracket levels. As a result, the beneficiary of the exemption, indeed the *only* beneficiary, should be the housing developer who issues the bonds, because the higher issue price of $1,250 will precisely offset the benefit of the tax-exemption to the bond-purchaser. This is as it should be, of course, because it is housing developers (and nobody else) who are *supposed* to benefit under the Congressional scheme.

Unfortunately for all this heady analysis, in the real world it appears that tax preferences are *not* fully capitalized. It is a familiar observation, for example, that state and local bonds (the interest on which is exempt from tax under § 103) are frequently purchased by individuals and corporations paying tax at *less* than the topmost rate. Put differently, the yield on exempt municipal bonds is customarily higher (*i.e.,* closer to that of fully taxable corporate bonds) than it would be if all such bonds were bought up by top-bracket taxpayers who paid a price equal to the full value of the exemption to *them*. Apparently, the volume of municipal bonds is too large—the credit needs of state and local governments are simply too great—for all such securities to be absorbed by taxpayers in the highest bracket. In addition, Code § 265(2) specifically disallows deductions for interest on amounts borrowed to purchase municipal bonds (see 6.05), which means that top-bracket taxpayers are limited to financing such purchases out of their own resources and cannot use borrowed money for that purpose. For these and other reasons, municipal bonds have to be priced so as to appeal to taxpayers in lower brackets as well. In effect, the issue price of the bonds has to be low enough to produce a yield attractive to taxpayers who fall *below* the topmost tax bracket. At the same time, of course, such bonds can and will be purchased by taxpayers who *are* at the highest bracket level.

Although this state of affairs may sound more democratic, the ironic fact is that the sale of municipal bonds to taxpayers below the 50% bracket renders the preference afforded by such bonds both inequitable *and* inefficient. This can be confirmed by returning to our numerical illustration. If, for example, the low-income housing bonds (half the interest on which is exempt from tax) have to be sold to 40% taxpayers, then the issue price of those bonds cannot be more than $1,110:

	After-tax Earnings	After-tax Capitalization Rate	Present Value
40% taxpayer:	$50(1–t) + $50 = $80 where t = 40%	.12(1–t) = .072	$\frac{\$80}{.072} = \$1,110$

But recall that 50%-bracket taxpayers would be willing to pay as much as $1,250 for these same bonds. Since the bonds have to be issued at $1,110 in order to clear the market, however, it is pretty plain that 50% taxpayers are going to get an undeserved break. Instead of having to invest $1,250 to obtain a net yield of $75, they need invest only $1,110 and can use their saving of $140 for other things, including additional investment. Hence, 50% taxpayers who purchase the bonds for $1,110 now get a *real* tax benefit, of which the present value is $140. In addition, and relatedly, the cost to the federal government of enacting the tax subsidy for housing bonds is now greater than the benefit that is actually realized by housing developers. Thus, the cost to the government (meaning the rest of us) includes the tax benefit realized by taxpayers *above* the 40% level, *e.g.*, the $140 just mentioned. But this amount never reaches the housing developers for whose particular benefit (we presume) the tax preference was enacted. The preference scheme buys less in the way of low-income housing than it costs, and it is therefore inefficient even in its own terms.

Our initial question—"What is the true value of a tax preference?"—can now be answered. If the market for tax-exempt assets worked perfectly—if *all* tax-preferred income-streams wound up in the hands of the highest-bracket taxpayers—tax preferences on the whole would be valueless to their holders and harmless to the rest of us. The preferences would operate efficiently in achieving particular legislative goals, in the sense that all the benefits would go to the intended beneficiaries; and they would leave intact the horizontal and vertical relationships that one regards as equitable.

Apparently, however, the market for tax preferences does not work perfectly; all exempt assets do *not* come to rest in the hands of top-bracket taxpayers. As a result, there is some loss of tax equity as among taxpayers, and likewise some inefficiency from the government's standpoint. How much of each is difficult to say.

APPENDIX: PRESENT VALUE

This book has used the concept of "present value" and "discounting to present value" at many points. The following excerpt (reprinted with permission) explains the concept and supplies the relevant Tables:

ALCHIAN AND ALLEN, UNIVERSITY ECONOMICS
205–209 (2d ed. 1967).

The *more distant* the deferred service (or income, or goods), the *lower* its present price. A dollar deferred two years is worth less today than a dollar deferred one year, if the rate of interest is positive. At an interest rate of 6 percent, the current price of $1 deferred a year is 94 cents—the amount that will grow at 6 percent in one year to $1. This is given by the formula

$$p_1 = \frac{A}{(1 + r)} = \frac{\$1.00}{(1 + .06)} = \$.943.$$

To get the present price for $1 deferred *two* years, simply repeat the above operation. If $1 deferred one year from now is now worth 94 cents, then deferring the dollar an additional year again reduces its present value by the same proportion. For two years, this is .943 × .943 = .890. A dollar due in two years is worth 89 cents today.

This same relationship can be expressed by noting that at 6 percent per year 89 cents will grow in one year to 94 cents, and then in the second year the 94 cents will grow to exactly $1. This can be expressed in form

$$p_2 (1 + r) (1 + r) = A.$$

where p_2 represents the amount now that will grow at the 6 percent annual rate of interest to $1, the amount A, at the end of the two-year period. Solving for p_2, we get

$$p_2 = \frac{A}{(1 + r)(1 + r)} = \frac{A}{(1 + r)_2} = \frac{\$1.00}{(1.06)_2} = \$.890.$$

Two years' discounting is measured by the factor $1/(1 \$ .06)^2 = .890$; three years of discounting is obtained by multiplying the future amount due in three years by $1/(1.06)^3 = .839$. The present value of $1 deferred t years from today is obtained by use of the factor $1/(1.06)^t$. Multiplying the amount due at the end of t years by this present-value factor gives the present value (or present price, or discounted value) of the deferred amount, A, due in t

368

years. A set of these present-value factors is given in Table 13–1 for various rates of interest and years of deferment. The present-value factor decreases as t is larger: the farther into the future the amount due is deferred, the lower is its *present* value.

TABLE 13–1

Present Value of $1: What a Dollar at End of Specified Future Year Is Worth Today

Year	3%	4%	5%	6%	7%	8%	10%	12%	15%	20%	Year
1	.971	.962	.952	.943	.935	.926	.909	.893	.870	.833	1
2	.943	.925	.907	.890	.873	.857	.826	.797	.756	.694	2
3	.915	.890	.864	.839	.816	.794	.751	.711	.658	.578	3
4	.889	.855	.823	.792	.763	.735	.683	.636	.572	.482	4
5	.863	.823	.784	.747	.713	.681	.620	.567	.497	.402	5
6	.838	.790	.746	.705	.666	.630	.564	.507	.432	.335	6
7	.813	.760	.711	.665	.623	.583	.513	.452	.376	.279	7
8	.789	.731	.677	.627	.582	.540	.466	.404	.326	.233	8
9	.766	.703	.645	.591	.544	.500	.424	.360	.284	.194	9
10	.744	.676	.614	.558	.508	.463	.385	.322	.247	.162	10
11	.722	.650	.585	.526	.475	.429	.350	.287	.215	.134	11
12	.701	.625	.557	.497	.444	.397	.318	.257	.187	.112	12
13	.681	.601	.530	.468	.415	.368	.289	.229	.162	.0935	13
14	.661	.577	.505	.442	.388	.340	.263	.204	.141	.0779	14
15	.642	.555	.481	.417	.362	.315	.239	.183	.122	.0649	15
16	.623	.534	.458	.393	.339	.292	.217	.163	.107	.0541	16
17	.605	.513	.436	.371	.317	.270	.197	.146	.093	.0451	17
18	.587	.494	.416	.350	.296	.250	.179	.130	.0808	.0376	18
19	.570	.475	.396	.330	.277	.232	.163	.116	.0703	.0313	19
20	.554	.456	.377	.311	.258	.215	.148	.104	.0611	.0261	20
25	.478	.375	.295	.232	.184	.146	.0923	.0588	.0304	.0105	25
30	.412	.308	.231	.174	.131	.0994	.0573	.0334	.0151	.00421	30
40	.307	.208	.142	.0972	.067	.0460	.0221	.0107	.00373	.000680	40
50	.228	.141	.087	.0543	.034	.0213	.00852	.00346	.000922	.000109	50

Each column lists how much a dollar received at the end of various years in the future is worth today. For example, at 6 percent a dollar to be received ten years hence is equivalent in value to $.558 now. In other words, $.558 invested now at 6 percent, with interest compounded annually, would grow to $1.00 in ten years. Note that $1.00 to be received at the end of fifty years is, at 6 percent, worth today just about a nickel. And at 10 percent it is worth only about .8 of one cent, which is to say that 8 mills (.8 of a cent) invested now would grow, at 10 percent interest compounded annually, to $1.00 in fifty years. Similarly $1,000 in fifty years is worth today $8.52, and $10,000 is worth today $85—all at 10 percent rate of growth.... Why not make that investment? Formula for entry in table is $p = A/(1 + r)^t$.

FUTURE AMOUNTS CORRESPONDING TO GIVEN PRESENT VALUES

Instead of deriving present values of future amounts, we can derive for any annual rate of interest the future amount that will be exchangeable for any present value. How much will $1 paid now purchase if the future amount is due in one year, or in two years, or in three years? At 15 percent per year, $1 will be worth $1.15 in one year. And at 15 percent for the next year, that $1.15 will in turn grow to $1.32. Hence, $1 today is the present price or value of $1.32 in two years. In terms of our formula, this can be expressed

369

$$p_2 (1 + r)(1 + r) = A.$$
$$\$1 (1.15)(1.15) = \$1 (1.32) = \$1.32.$$

If the future amount is deferred three years, the term (1.15) enters three times, and if deferred t years, it enters t times. For three years, the quantity (1.15) is multiplied together three times, denoted $(1.15)^3$, and equals 1.52. Therefore, in three years \$1 will grow to \$1.52. In general, the formula is

$$p_t (1 + r)^t = A$$

for any present payment, p_t, that is paid for an amount A available t years later. The multiplicative factor $(1 + r)^t$ is called the *future-value* (or *amount*) *factor*. Values of this future-amount factor for different combinations of t and r are given in Table 13–2.

TABLE 13–2

Compound Amount of \$1: Amount to Which \$1 Now Will Grow by End of Specified Year at Compounded Interest

Year	3%	4%	5%	6%	7%	8%	10%	12%	15%	20%	Year
1	1.03	1.04	1.05	1.06	1.07	1.08	1.10	1.12	1.15	1.20	1
2	1.06	1.08	1.10	1.12	1.14	1.17	1.21	1.25	1.32	1.44	2
3	1.09	1.12	1.16	1.19	1.23	1.26	1.33	1.40	1.52	1.73	3
4	1.13	1.17	1.22	1.26	1.31	1.36	1.46	1.57	1.74	2.07	4
5	1.16	1.22	1.28	1.34	1.40	1.47	1.61	1.76	2.01	2.49	5
6	1.19	1.27	1.34	1.41	1.50	1.59	1.77	1.97	2.31	2.99	6
7	1.23	1.32	1.41	1.50	1.61	1.71	1.94	2.21	2.66	3.58	7
8	1.27	1.37	1.48	1.59	1.72	1.85	2.14	2.48	3.05	4.30	8
9	1.30	1.42	1.55	1.68	1.84	2.00	2.35	2.77	3.52	5.16	9
10	1.34	1.48	1.63	1.79	1.97	2.16	2.59	3.11	4.05	6.19	10
11	1.38	1.54	1.71	1.89	2.10	2.33	2.85	3.48	4.66	7.43	11
12	1.43	1.60	1.80	2.01	2.25	2.52	3.13	3.90	5.30	8.92	12
13	1.47	1.67	1.89	2.13	2.41	2.72	3.45	4.36	6.10	10.7	13
14	1.51	1.73	1.98	2.26	2.58	2.94	3.79	4.89	7.00	12.8	14
15	1.56	1.80	2.08	2.39	2.76	3.17	4.17	5.47	8.13	15.4	15
16	1.60	1.87	2.18	2.54	2.95	3.43	4.59	6.13	9.40	18.5	16
17	1.65	1.95	2.29	2.69	3.16	3.70	5.05	6.87	10.6	22.2	17
18	1.70	2.03	2.41	2.85	3.38	4.00	5.55	7.70	12.5	26.6	18
19	1.75	2.11	2.53	3.02	3.62	4.32	6.11	8.61	14.0	31.9	19
20	1.81	2.19	2.65	3.20	3.87	4.66	6.72	9.65	16.1	38.3	20
25	2.09	2.67	3.39	4.29	5.43	6.85	10.8	17.0	32.9	95.4	25
30	2.43	3.24	4.32	5.74	7.61	10.0	17.4	30.0	66.2	237	30
40	3.26	4.80	7.04	10.3	15.0	21.7	45.3	93.1	267.0	1470	40
50	4.38	7.11	11.5	18.4	29.5	46.9	117	289	1080	9100	50

This table shows to what amounts \$1.00 invested now will grow at the end of various years, at different rates of growth compounded annually. For example, \$1.00 invested now will grow in thirty years to \$5.74 at 6 percent. In other words, 5.74 due thirty years hence is worth now exactly 1.00 at a 6 percent rate of interest per year. ... The entries in this table are the reciprocals of the entries in Table 13–1; that is, they are the entries of Table 13–1 divided into 1. ... Formula for entries in table is $A = 1(1 + i)^t$.

For example, at 6 percent in five years, the future-amount factor is 1.34, which means that a present payment of \$1 will buy, or grow to, the future amount \$1.34 at the end of five years. Notice that the entries in Table 13–2 are simply the reciprocals of the entries in Table 13–1.

PRESENT CAPITAL VALUE FOR SERIES
OF FUTURE AMOUNTS

If there is a sequence of amounts due at future times, we can find a present value for this series of amounts. Just as we add up the costs of individual items in a market basket of groceries, we add up the present values of each of the future amounts due. That sum is the present value of the whole series of amounts due at various future dates.

This series might be compared with an oil well that each year on December 31 spurts out one gallon of oil that sells for $1. To simplify the problem, let's first suppose that the series of dollars (spurts of oil) continues for only two years. If the interest rate is 6 percent, the present value of $1 deferred one year is 94 cents (see Table 13–1, column of .06 rate of interest for one year); and the present value of $1 due in two years is 89.0 cents (see the same table, same column, but now read the entry for year 2). The sum of the present capital values of both amounts due, the one in one year and the other in two years, is the sum of 94.3 cents and 89.0 cents, which is $1.83. To say that the rate of interest is 6 percent per year is equivalent to saying that you can exchange in the market $1.83 today for the right to receive $1 in one year *and* another dollar in two years.

Suppose the sequence is to last three years, with three $1 receipts. The aggregate present value is augmented by the present value of the dollar due in the third year. At a 6 percent rate of interest, this extra dollar has a present value of 83.9 cents (see Table 13–1). Therefore, the present value of the three-year series is $2.67 (given in Table 13–3). We have noted that this present value of a series of amounts due is called the *capital value* of the future receipts. Capital value is the current *price* of the rights to the stream (series) of receipts.

Some technical jargon will be convenient for subsequent analyses. The sequence of future amounts due is called an *annuity,* a word that suggests *annual* amounts. A two-year sequence is a two-year annuity. The term "annuity" denotes the series of annual amounts for a specified number of years. A person who has purchased the right to a stream of future annuities or amounts due—for example, his pension benefits—is sometimes called an *annuitant.*

APPENDIX

TABLE 13–3

Present Value of Annuity of $1, Received at End of Each Year

Year	3%	4%	5%	6%	7%	8%	10%	12%	15%	20%	Year
1	0.971	0.960	0.952	0.943	0.935	0.926	0.909	0.890	0.870	0.833	1
2	1.91	1.89	1.86	1.83	1.81	1.78	1.73	1.69	1.63	1.53	2
3	2.83	2.78	2.72	2.67	2.62	2.58	2.48	2.40	2.28	2.11	3
4	3.72	3.63	3.55	3.46	3.39	3.31	3.16	3.04	2.86	2.59	4
5	4.58	4.45	4.33	4.21	4.10	3.99	3.79	3.60	3.35	2.99	5
6	5.42	5.24	5.08	4.91	4.77	4.62	4.35	4.11	3.78	3.33	6
7	6.23	6.00	5.79	5.58	5.39	5.21	4.86	4.56	4.16	3.60	7
8	7.02	6.73	6.46	6.20	5.97	5.75	5.33	4.97	4.49	3.84	8
9	7.79	7.44	7.11	6.80	6.52	6.25	5.75	5.33	4.78	4.03	9
10	8.53	8.11	7.72	7.36	7.02	6.71	6.14	5.65	5.02	4.19	10
11	9.25	8.76	8.31	7.88	7.50	7.14	6.49	5.94	5.23	4.33	11
12	9.95	9.39	8.86	8.38	7.94	7.54	6.81	6.19	5.41	4.44	12
13	10.6	9.99	9.39	8.85	8.36	7.90	7.10	6.42	5.65	4.53	13
14	11.3	10.6	9.90	9.29	8.75	8.24	7.36	6.63	5.76	4.61	14
15	11.9	11.1	10.4	9.71	9.11	8.56	7.60	6.81	5.87	4.68	15
16	12.6	11.6	10.8	10.1	9.45	8.85	7.82	6.97	5.96	4.73	16
17	13.2	12.2	11.3	10.4	9.76	9.12	8.02	7.12	6.03	4.77	17
18	13.8	12.7	11.7	10.8	10.1	9.37	8.20	7.25	6.10	4.81	18
19	14.3	13.1	12.1	11.1	10.3	9.60	8.36	7.37	6.17	4.84	19
20	14.9	13.6	12.5	11.4	10.6	9.82	8.51	7.47	6.23	4.87	20
25	17.4	15.6	14.1	12.8	11.7	10.7	9.08	7.84	6.46	4.95	25
30	19.6	17.3	15.4	13.8	12.4	11.3	9.43	8.06	6.57	4.98	30
40	23.1	19.8	17.2	15.0	13.3	11.9	9.78	8.24	6.64	5.00	40
50	25.7	21.5	18.3	15.8	13.8	12.2	9.91	8.30	6.66	5.00	50

An annuity is a sequence of annual amounts received at the end of each year. This table shows with each entry how much it takes today to buy an annuity of $1 a year at the rates of interest indicated. For example, an annuity of $1 a year for twenty years at 6 percent interest could be purchased today with $11.40. This amount would, if invested at 6 percent, be sufficient to yield some interest which, along with some depletion of the principal in each year, would enable a payout of exactly 1 a year for twenty years, at which time the fund would be completely depleted. And $1,000 a year for twenty years would, at 6 percent compounded annually, cost today $11,400, which is obviously 1,000 times as much as for an annuity of just $1. Formula for entry is $p = [1 - (1 + i)^{-t}]/i$.

How about a four-year annuity? The fourth year's $1 has a present value of 79.2 cents, which, when added to the present value of a three-year annuity of $1 a year, gives $3.46. A five-year annuity would have a present value of $4.21, because the dollar received at the end of the fifth year is now worth 74.7 cents. Proceed to the end of ten years, and you will find that the present capital value of a ten-year annuity of $1 each year is $7.36.

If we extended the series to twenty years (still with $1 at the end of each year) at 6 percent per year, the present capital value would increase to $11.40. Notice that the *present* value of the *last half* of that series (the ten amounts due in the eleventh through the twentieth years) is only $4.04 (= 11.40 – 7.36). At a 6 percent interest rate, $4.04 *today* will buy you $1 a year for ten years, beginning at the end of the eleventh year from now.

Table 13–1 gives the present value of each separate future payment in the annuity. For convenience, Table 13–3 gives the present value of annuities of various lengths, where the payment *at*

372

the end of each year is $1. Looking at that table under the 6 percent interest rate, you will find that the present capital values for the *sum* of the discounted amounts due in the preceding examples are the entries in the rows for one, two, three, four, five, ten, and twenty years. Look at the entry for two years at 6 percent. It is the sum of .943 and .890, based on the data of Table 13–1. For an annuity lasting fifty years, the entry is 15.8—which means that a fifty-year annuity of $1 per year, with the first payment coming at the end of one year, has a present capital value of only $15.80 (at 6 percent).

Even an annuity that lasted forever (called a *perpetuity*), or for as long as you and your heirs desire, would have a finite capital value—namely, $16.67.

A second thought will remove the mystery from the fact that an infinitely long series of $1 amounts due yearly has a finite (limited) price today. To get a perpetual series of payments of $1 every year, all one has to do is keep $16.67 on deposit in a bank, if he can get 6 percent per year. Every year the interest payment of $1 can be taken out, and this can be done forever. In effect you pay $16.67 today to purchase an infinitely long sequence. But you can also see that the first fifty years of receipts (a fifty-year annuity) has a present value of $15.80. Hence, the remaining infinitely long series of $1 receipts, beginning fifty years from now, is worth today only about 87 cents. Distant events have small present values!

———————

*

TABLE OF CASES

References are to Pages

375

*

INDEX

References are to Paragraphs

---

†